Studies in Public Budgeting

Series editor
Yilin Hou

More information about this series at http://www.springer.com/series/13526

Thomas P. Lauth

Public Budgeting in Georgia

Institutions, Process, Politics and Policy

Thomas P. Lauth
School of Public and International Affairs
University of Georgia
Athens, GA, USA

Studies in Public Budgeting
ISBN 978-3-030-76022-9   ISBN 978-3-030-76023-6 (eBook)
https://doi.org/10.1007/978-3-030-76023-6

© The Editor(s) (if applicable) and The Author(s), under exclusive license to Springer Nature Switzerland AG 2021
This work is subject to copyright. All rights are reserved by the Publisher, whether the whole or part of the material is concerned, specifically the rights of translation, reprinting, reuse of illustrations, recitation, broadcasting, reproduction on microfilms or in any other physical way, and transmission or information storage and retrieval, electronic adaptation, computer software, or by similar or dissimilar methodology now known or hereafter developed.
The use of general descriptive names, registered names, trademarks, service marks, etc. in this publication does not imply, even in the absence of a specific statement, that such names are exempt from the relevant protective laws and regulations and therefore free for general use.
The publisher, the authors, and the editors are safe to assume that the advice and information in this book are believed to be true and accurate at the date of publication. Neither the publisher nor the authors or the editors give a warranty, expressed or implied, with respect to the material contained herein or for any errors or omissions that may have been made. The publisher remains neutral with regard to jurisdictional claims in published maps and institutional affiliations.

This Springer imprint is published by the registered company Springer Nature Switzerland AG
The registered company address is: Gewerbestrasse 11, 6330 Cham, Switzerland

*For Tom, Bob, John and Dave
and for their mother,
Jeannie*

Series Editor's Preface

Though the earliest rudimentary budget and budgeting practices can be traced to ancient civilizations, modern government budget and public budgeting developed more recently in human history. From the perspective of high politics, *The Bill of Rights* (1689, Britain) made it possible, for the first time, for a legislative body to exert control over the outlays of a monarch, adopt a tax system, and pass tax laws. Without explicit legislative approval, the King could neither tax nor spend. It took another century, until 1789, to translate that political possibility of legislative control over the purse into administrative reality. That was the beginning of the official budget document. Several more decades passed before it became an annual routine for the finance minister to propose government revenues and expenditures for approval by the legislature. A treasury accounting department, responsible to the legislature, was established to supervise this process and ensure that government outlays were made in accordance with appropriations.

Therefore, when the Founding Fathers of the United States created the new republic in the 1780s, they had no system on which to model budgetary affairs. As a result, they left the fundamental laws taciturn on these issues. The Congress dominated fiscal affairs, with no formal role for the President. In this fashion, the nation muddled along until the early twentieth century, when the US economy was already humming to the top of the world but its fiscal house was in disarray. Roaring industrialization and rising urbanization demanded more and better public programs. In response, the US government assumed increasing responsibilities and exercised unprecedented regulation of the economy, but with inadequate efforts at systematically rationalizing its activities.

Public intellectuals keenly realized that tax reforms alone were far from sufficient. Responsible fiscal governance also necessitated expert review of appropriation proposals and enhanced executive authority in budgetary affairs. While seeking inspiration, European budget practices caught their attention. In 1912, President Taft's Commission on Economy and Efficiency formally recommended to Congress *The Need for a National Budget*. These efforts produced the Executive Budget of modern government and the public budgeting procedures for accountable and responsible governance.

This new tool of democratic governance was immediately put to the test – first in large municipalities, then in the states. The leading progressivists believed that government could be run like big corporations – if private companies can do something well, there is no reason the government cannot. Economy and efficiency were the lodestar. The Public Budgeting Movement culminated at the federal level with the enactment of the *Budget and Accounting Act* of 1921, which was signed into law by President Warren Harding on June 10 of the same year. In December, the country's first federal Executive Budget, for fiscal year 1923, was transmitted to Congress for approval. Thus began a new era.

A century has passed since the enactment of the *Budget and Accounting Act*. A centennial is an occasion for celebration; but more importantly, it is a time to reflect on the budgetary successes and failures that have occurred. Overall, the country's budget system worked well for decades, at least until the late 1960s. Though it is presumptuous to credit the budget system with all the successes of the prior four decades, it is fair to say that the system helped guarantee smooth and effective governance. On the other hand, the vicissitudes of budgetary missteps since the 1970s highlight increasing urgency for a comprehensive reexamination of the design, especially the rules and mechanisms of the existing budget system.

In a figurative sense, "reinventing" the tool for democratic governance and efficient administration is a continuous process. At any single point in time, a budget and its formulating process may look static, with seemingly chaotic threads. However, under an evolutionary lens, patterns will emerge. Each generation of practitioners and researchers is uniquely situated to continue "reinventing" these vital governance tools. The formation of budget and budgeting will remain in an evolutionary mode. Our task is to discern the latent long-run patterns, to extract rules from the patterns, and to formulate principles that will guide future administrations toward better outcomes. This *Studies in Public Budgeting* series is designed to serve this purpose.

We identified and invited expert policymakers and distinguished scholars to contribute the volumes in this series. Each author has paid decades of devoted attention to the practice or study of budgeting; each volume in the series contributes a unique perspective on the core issues.

As the series editor, I express heartfelt thanks to Springer International for its dedication and support in this Herculean effort.

Syracuse, NY, USA Yilin Hou
February 2021

Series Editor's Endorsement

This volume is a lucid exposition of detailed and careful analysis of public budgeting in a representative state in the US federal system. The book is carefully designed and meticulously executed. The book is the culmination of the author's half a century keen observation and objective examination that is based on a seamless combination of academic insight and practitioner perspectives. It is a refreshing course for both academics and practitioners.

Yilin Hou, Syracuse University

Acknowledgements

My first experience with Georgia state budgeting came in the summer of 1975 when, after accepting a faculty appointment at Georgia State University, I received a letter that began by noting that I probably had been reading in the newspaper about the recession-induced budget difficulties the state was facing which would necessitate revoking faculty salary increases that had been agreed to for the 1975–76 academic year. I was not yet living in Georgia and had *not* been reading about the state's financial difficulties, but from that time on, I began paying close attention to such matters. To my relief, the letter went on to say that I need not be concerned because as a new employee, my agreed upon salary would be honored.

My knowledge of the Georgia budget process is mostly the result of conversations I have had over the years with elected officials and professional budgeters. Several of them were students in my classes at Georgia State University, 1975–1981, and The University of Georgia, 1981–2013. I learned more from them about Georgia budgeting than they learned from me.

Thank you to Jim McIntyre, Clark Stevens, Hank Huckaby, Tim Burgess, Bill Tomlinson, Shelley Nickel, Tim Connell, Trey Childress, David Tanner, Teresa MacCartney, Winford Poitevint, Pete Hackney, Robert Hobbs, John Brown, Hank Thomassen, Steve Wrigley, Steve Anthony, Carolyn Bourdeaux, Valerie Hepburn, Mary Salmon Walker, Rob Watts, Dan Ebersol, Jim Lyle, Steve Rieck, Wes Clarke, David Lee, Rick Dunn, and Danny Kanso. Their insights were invaluable and their generosity was unbounded. Special thanks to Hank, Steve, David, Teresa and Danny who read and made constructive comments on several of my manuscripts over the years.

Thank you to Governors Carl Sanders, Lester Maddox, Jimmy Carter, George Busbee, Joe Frank Harris, Zell Miller and Roy Barnes for talking with me about their use of the line-item veto and to Governor Nathan Deal for talking with me about his efforts to rebuild the state's Revenue Shortfall Reserve. Special thanks to Zell Miller for reading a couple of my manuscripts. I treasure his comment, "Enjoyed very much reading both of these. It's good work and I have nothing to add or correct."

Thank you to Paul Broun, Sr., Don Johnson, Terry Coleman, George Hooks, Ben Harbin, Terry England, Jack Hill, Earl Ehrhart, Mark Burkhalter and David Shafer for talking with me about the legislative side of budgeting. They trusted me with information, confident that I would not misuse it. Special thanks to Terry England who read a couple of my manuscripts in recent years and made constructive comments.

Terry England, Hank Huckaby, Danny Kanso and Yilin Hou read a complete draft of this manuscript and made valuable suggestions for its improvement. Their efforts and expertise have made it a better book. I thank them for their generosity and friendship.

Thank you to Augustus Bacon Turnbull, III. Gus Turnbull's *Politics in the Budgetary Process: The Case of Georgia* (1967) was his Ph.D. dissertation at the University of Virginia. It has served as the foundation for all future research on Georgia budgeting. He served as an aide to Governor Carl Sanders.

Thank you to James Salzer, reporter for the *Atlanta Journal-Constitution*, whose beat includes Georgia budgeting and financial news. I have met him only once and then briefly, but I have been an avid reader of his articles for many years. His reporting has been a valuable source of information on contemporary events and an indispensable source for establishing and confirming historical accuracy.

If errors of fact or interpretation remain despite the counsel of others, I alone am responsible.

Thank you to Jere W. Morehead, President of the University of Georgia, and Matthew R. Auer, Dean of the University's School of Public and International Affairs, for extending to me the courtesy of a place to work on campus during my retirement years. Thank you to Sarah Causey, Georgia State Documents Librarian at the University of Georgia Library, for her expertise and rapid responses in providing documents that I was not able to find on my own.

Thank you to the Springer team: Yilin Hou, Series Editor, who encouraged me to write this book; Lorraine Klimowich, Senior Editor–Economics and Political Science, who believed in the book and recommended its publication; and Maria David, Project Coordinator and Lakshmanan Radha, Project Manager, who guided me through the production process.

Throughout my career and for most of my life, Jeannie McGregor Lauth has been my partner and best friend. She read the first draft of every chapter of this book, trying mightily to ensure that I adhered to the rules of grammar, punctuation and syntax that we both learned many years ago at St. Philip Grade School in Pittsburgh, PA. Of course, she bears no responsibility for my occasional failure to implement her recommendations. I am grateful for her love, support and encouragement. Her friendship made sheltering in place fun, as the book was being completed.

Athens, Georgia
December, 2020

Contents

1	**Introduction to Budgeting in Georgia**.	1
	What Else Is a Budget?.	1
	A Statement of the Relationship Between Proposed Expenditures and Anticipated Revenues	2
	A Record of Past Performance and a Plan for Future Actions	2
	An Instrument for Legislative Control of the Executive Branch, as Well as a Device Through Which a Chief Executive Attempts to Direct and Control Agencies Within the Executive Branch	3
	A Technique for Allocating Scarce Resources Among Competing Governmental Agencies and Programs.	3
	At the National Level, a Method for Regulating Aggregate Economic Demand Through Taxing and Spending Decisions, While in the States, a Method for Using Taxing and Spending Decisions to Promote Economic Growth and Income Redistribution.	4
	A Mechanism for Accountability in the Management of Public Funds .	5
	The State of Georgia	6
2	**Fiscal Conservatism and Fiscal Conservatives**.	9
	Fiscal Conservatism in Georgia	9
	Governors as Fiscal Conservatives	11
	Richard B. Russell, Jr. (1931–1933).	12
	Eugene Talmadge (1933–1937 and 1941–1943).	13
	Eurith D. Rivers (1937–1941).	16
	Ellis Arnall (1943–1947).	17
	Melvin E. Thompson (1947–1948).	18
	Herman Talmadge (1948–1955)	20
	Marvin Griffin (1955–1959).	21
	S. Ernest Vandiver, Jr. (1959–1963)	23
	Carl E. Sanders (1963–1967)	25
	Lester Maddox (1967–1971).	27
	Jimmy Carter (1971–1975).	29

	George D. Busbee (1975–1983)	31
	Joe Frank Harris (1983–1991)	33
	Zell B. Miller (1991–1999)	34
	Roy E. Barnes (1999–2003)	35
	Sonny Perdue (2003–2011)	36
	Nathan Deal (2011–2019)	38
	Summary	40
	Conclusion	41
3	**Patterns and Trends in Georgia Revenue**	**43**
	Revenue Patterns and Trends	44
	Income Taxes	46
	Sales Tax	49
	Sales Taxes on Internet Sales	54
	Motor Fuel Tax	55
	Cigarette Tax	58
	Property Tax	59
	Motor Vehicle Tax	60
	Bond Proceeds	61
	Lottery Proceeds	64
	Tobacco Settlement Agreement	64
	Hospital and Nursing Home Provider Fees	65
	Tax Expenditures	66
	Federal Grants and Other Funds	69
	Revenue Sources in Retrospect	72
	Tax Reform	74
	The Budget and the Economy: 1990–2019	75
4	**Patterns and Trends in Georgia Spending**	**83**
	Public Education	83
	Higher Education	87
	Health and Human Services	92
	Corrections	97
	Transportation	100
	State Spending Over 50 Years	101
	State Grants to Local Governments	105
	A Low Spending State	106
5	**The Executive Budget in Georgia**	**109**
	The Budget Idea	109
	The Executive Budget in Georgia	111
	Conclusion	118
6	**The Annual Budget Process**	**119**
	The Budget Process in the Constitution	119
	The Budget Cycle	120
	Georgia Fiscal Year 2020 Budget Cycle	123

	Midyear Appropriations Amendment	126
	Dimensions of the Midyear Appropriations Amendment	128
	Legislator and Agency Expectations	132
	Appropriations Committee Staff	134
	Fiscal Affairs Subcommittees	134
	Budget Reduction Behavior	135
	Georgia and Federal Budget Processes: A Comparison	138
	Conclusion	143
7	**From Line-Item to Performance Budgeting**	**145**
	Line-Item Budgeting	146
	Zero-Base Budgeting	147
	Performance Evaluation Measures	151
	Budget Redirection	152
	Results-Based Budgeting	153
	Prioritized Program Budgeting	155
	Zero-Base Budgeting Redux	158
	Conclusion	162
8	**The Line-Item Veto in Executive-Legislative Relations**	**163**
	Introduction	163
	The Line-Item Veto in Georgia	164
	Carl Sanders (1963–1967)	172
	Lester Maddox (1967–1971)	172
	Jimmy Carter (1971–1975)	172
	George Busbee (1975–1983)	174
	Joe Frank Harris (1983–1991)	175
	Zell Miller (1991–1999)	177
	Roy Barnes (1999–2003)	178
	Political Party Transition	179
	Sonny Perdue (2003–2011)	180
	Governor Perdue's First Term in Retrospect	183
	Governor Perdue's Second Term in Retrospect	189
	Nathan Deal (2011–2019)	189
	Governors Perdue and Deal	192
	Frequency of Use of the Line-item Veto	195
	Conclusion	195
9	**Budget Priorities and Achievements of Georgia Governors, 1963–2019**	**197**
	Carl E. Sanders	197
	Lester G. Maddox	201
	Jimmy Carter	202
	George D. Busbee	203
	Joe Frank Harris	205
	Zell B. Miller	205

	Roy E. Barnes	207
	George E. "Sonny" Perdue	209
	Nathan Deal	210
	The Nine Governors	213
10	**Milestones and Comparative Perspective**	**217**
	Milestones	218
	Income Tax and Sales and Use Tax	218
	The Budget Act of 1962	218
	General Obligation Debt Authority	219
	Executive Branch Reorganization, 1972 and Zero-Base Budgeting, 1973	220
	Revenue Shortfall Reserve	221
	Lottery for Education	222
	Criminal Justice Reform	222
	Program Budget Format	223
	Great Recession	223
	Department of Behavioral Health and Developmental Disabilities (DBHDD)	224
	Medicaid Expansion	224
	Motor Fuel Excise Tax	226
	The COVID-19 Recession	226
	Milestones Impact	227
	Georgia in Comparative Perspective	228
	Process and Politics	228
	Low Taxes and Low Spending	229

Articles on Public Budgeting in Georgia by the Author 233

Index 235

About the Author

Thomas P. Lauth is Dean *Emeritus* of the School of Public and International Affairs and Professor *Emeritus* of Public Administration and Policy at the University of Georgia. He is the author or co-author of many articles and book chapters on Georgia state budgeting, and co-editor of *Governors, Legislatures, and Budgets: Diversity Across the American States* (1991) and *Budgeting in the States: Institutions, Processes and Politics* (2006). He is a recipient of the *Aaron B. Wildavsky Award for Lifetime Scholarly Achievement in Public Budgeting* and is a fellow of the National Academy of Public Administration. He earned a B.A. in government from the University of Notre Dame, and a Ph.D. in political science from the Maxwell School of Citizenship and Public Affairs, Syracuse University.

Chapter 1
Introduction to Budgeting in Georgia

This book is about budgets and budgeting in the state of Georgia. Almost everyone knows that a budget is a plan for spending limited amounts of money. In old French, a *bougette* is a small pouch in which things are kept and carried.[1] In early times, the things kept and carried often were coins and currency; in later times, according to Jesse Burkhead, they frequently were financial documents. Over time, the contents and the pouch became synonymous, thus a *bougette* became a spending plan.[2]

What Else Is a Budget?

In addition to being a spending plan, usually in the form of a written document, a public budget serves several other functions. First, it is a statement of the relationship between anticipated revenues and proposed expenditures. Second, it is a record of past performance and a plan for future actions. Third, it is an instrument for legislative control of the executive branch, as well as a device through which a chief executive attempts to direct and control agencies within the executive branch. Fourth, it is a technique for allocating scarce resources among competing governmental agencies and programs. Fifth, at the national level, it is a method for regulating aggregate economic demand through taxing and spending decisions, while in the states it may be a method for using taxing and spending decisions to promote economic growth and income distribution or redistribution. Sixth, it is a mechanism

---

[1] *Webster's New World Dictionary of the American Language*. Cleveland and New York: The World Publishing Company, 1956. p. 190.

[2] Jesse Burkhead, *Government Budgeting*. New York: John Wiley and Sons, Inc. 1956. p. 2.

© The Author(s), under exclusive license to Springer Nature Switzerland AG 2021
T. P. Lauth, *Public Budgeting in Georgia*, Studies in Public Budgeting,
https://doi.org/10.1007/978-3-030-76023-6_1

for accountability in the management of public funds. In short, it is both an administrative activity and a political process.[3]

A Statement of the Relationship Between Proposed Expenditures and Anticipated Revenues

In Georgia, proposed expenditures and anticipated revenues are required to be in balance with each other. Unlike the federal government budget, the state budget may not have a planned deficit. Specifically, the General Assembly may not appropriate funds for a fiscal year which, in aggregate, exceed the total of anticipated revenue collections for that year, plus any surplus in the state treasury from unexpended funds of the previous fiscal year.[4] The governor is responsible for preparing the fiscal year revenue estimate. In practice, the revenue estimate is produced by a professional economist who is a contract employee of the Governor's Office, but the official estimate is a policy decision of the governor. The surplus amount is the total of lapsed or unspent agency funds from the previous fiscal year.[5] If during the fiscal year actual revenue collections fall short of the revenue estimate upon which appropriations were based, the governor is authorized to require state agencies to reduce their spending, and also to withhold a percentage of subsequent agency allotments so as to maintain spending within actual revenues.[6]

A Record of Past Performance and a Plan for Future Actions

The format of the Georgia *Governor's Budget Report* arrays for each budget agency actual expenditures for two previous years, the budgeted amount for the current year, the agency's request and the Governor's recommendation for the upcoming fiscal year.[7] This budget format makes it possible for members of the General Assembly, the news media, other government agencies and the general public to compare proposed agency spending with actual spending in the recent past. Increases or decreases in agency budget totals may be observed and, perhaps more importantly, changes in spending for individual programs within agencies for the current and upcoming fiscal year may be observed as plans for future actions.

---

[3]This paragraph is significantly influenced by the consideration of these subjects in Aaron Wildavsky, *Budgeting: A Comparative Theory of Budgetary Processes*. Boston: Little, Brown and Company, 1975. pp. 1–8.

[4]*Constitution of the State of Georgia*, 1997, Section IX, Paragraph IV (b). Official Code of Georgia Annotated, 45-12-76.

[5]Official Code of Georgia Annotated (O.C.G.A.), 45-12-75 (2) and 45-12-89.

[6]Official Code of Georgia Annotated (O.C.G.A.), 45-12-86.

[7]Official Code of Georgia Annotated (O.C.G.A.), 45-12-75 (3) and (5).

An Instrument for Legislative Control of the Executive Branch, as Well as a Device Through Which a Chief Executive Attempts to Direct and Control Agencies Within the Executive Branch

In Georgia, legislative control of the executive branch is manifest in the constitutional requirement that no money may be spent without an appropriation made by the General Assembly,[8] and that the governor is required to submit to the General Assembly within five days after it convenes in regular session each year a budget message, a budget report and a draft appropriations bill.[9]

Chief executive direction and control are manifest in the legal requirements that each state agency must submit to the Governor's Office of Planning and Budget[10] estimates of its financial requirements for the next fiscal year and that the governor, acting through the Office of Planning and Budget, must review those agency estimates and revise them if deemed advisable, before submitting a budget report to the General Assembly.[11] Agencies are usually advocates for spending and central budgeters are expected to represent the governor's policy priorities.

A Technique for Allocating Scarce Resources Among Competing Governmental Agencies and Programs

Financial resources for government budgets are almost always scarce. If they were not, budgeting probably would not be necessary. Decisions about the acceptable level of taxation, of course, set parameters for the level of available revenue and the level of government spending. Within those parameters, scarcity also occurs when the budget requests made by state agencies, individually or in aggregate, are greater than the resources available to satisfy those requests. This may occur when there is a revenue shortfall, or even in good financial times when the spending expectations of agencies, or programs within agencies, are not well aligned with the spending priorities of the governor or legislative leaders. In such cases, agency or program budget reductions and reallocations may occur, resulting in agency and program winners and losers.

Scarcity may also occur for reasons beyond the control of the government, such as the Great Recession in 2008 and 2009 or the COVID-19 recession in 2020. Georgia's balanced budget provision dictated that as available resources declined,

---

[8] *Constitution of the State of Georgia*, 1997, Section IX, Paragraph I.
[9] *Constitution of the State of Georgia*, 1997, Section IX, Paragraph II (a). Official Code of Georgia Annotated, 45-12-74 and 75 (7).
[10] Official Code of Georgia Annotated (O.C.G.A.), 45-12-72.
[11] Official Code of Georgia Annotated, (O.C.G.A.), 45-12-78 and 79.

commensurate spending cuts were required to maintain the state's budget in balance. The governor was authorized by statute to withhold a percentage of agency allotment requests so as to maintain state spending within the level of actual revenues.[12] Whatever the reasons for scarcity, the budget is a technique for deciding which spending requests will be satisfied and which ones will not be satisfied.

At the National Level, a Method for Regulating Aggregate Economic Demand Through Taxing and Spending Decisions, While in the States, a Method for Using Taxing and Spending Decisions to Promote Economic Growth and Income Redistribution

Taxation aims to raise revenue and spending aims to purchase goods and services. However, taxing and spending may also be used as instruments of national fiscal policy to counter trends in the business cycle and achieve economic stabilization. For example, the Employment Act of 1946[13] charges the federal government with promoting full employment, production and purchasing power, and the Full Employment and Balanced Growth Act of 1978[14] commits the government to a policy of full employment, balanced growth, a balanced budget and price stability. More recent examples of using taxing and spending decisions to influence the economy were the Emergency Economic Stabilization Act of 2008[15] and the American Recovery and Reinvestment Act of 2009.[16] The former, following the subprime mortgage crisis, authorized the U.S. Treasury to purchase troubled assets such as mortgage-backed securities and to infuse cash into banks and other financial institutions. This legislation was commonly known as a government "bailout" of the troubled financial system. The latter, in response to the Great Recession, sought to provide temporary relief programs for those most affected by the recession, to protect jobs and create new ones, and stimulate the economy through investments in infrastructure and other public services. The Coronavirus Aid, Relief and Economic Security (CARES) Act of 2020[17] was an economic stimulus response to the COVID-19 pandemic. It included one-time cash payments to individuals, increased unemployment benefits, a paycheck protection program in the form of forgivable loans to small businesses and grants to state and local governments. The CARES Act, at $2.2 trillion, was the largest economic stimulus package in U.S. history.

---

[12] Official Code of Georgia Annotated (O.C.G.A.), 45-12-86.
[13] Pub. L. 79-304.
[14] Pub. L. 95-523.
[15] Pub. L. 110-343.
[16] Pub. L. 111-5.
[17] Pub. L. 116-136.

States are not inflation and recession fighters in the same way the federal government can be; they are much less effective in macroeconomic fiscal policy. Their economies are largely driven by how the national economy is performing. States may, however, use taxing and spending decisions to promote economic growth. For example, they may provide tax benefits to economic entities to encourage them to enter the state economy with the expected long-term benefit of an increased volume of economic activity that is then revenue producing through corporate income and consumer sales taxation. The Georgia Department of Economic Development promotes tax credits on its website: "Tax credits give Georgia businesses the opportunity to minimize or even eliminate state corporate income tax. They apply to all qualifying companies … rooted in Georgia or new to the state. Typically, tax credits apply to 50% of a company's annual state corporate income tax liability." Examples of using taxing and spending decisions as economic incentives include tax credits to the film industry beginning in 2008 to bring film production to Georgia and the decision in 2005 not to collect a tax on the sale of jet fuel purchased by Delta Airlines, an international carrier with its corporate headquarters and transportation hub in Atlanta.

States may also use tax and expenditure decisions in ways that affect income distribution, claiming resources from some by way of taxation and providing benefits to others by way of expenditures. For example, the Medicaid program established in Georgia in 1966 provides healthcare benefits to low-income individuals, children and individuals with disabilities, funded in part from the state's general revenue base.[18]

A Mechanism for Accountability in the Management of Public Funds

Allotment, transfer control and post-audit are the three most important techniques for achieving financial accountability in the management of public funds. Performance evaluation is a technique for assessing program accomplishments.

In Georgia, the Office of Planning and Budget exercises centralized control over expenditures after the budget has been approved by the General Assembly and signed into law by the governor through its *allotment* process. Executive branch agencies are required to submit a monthly work program and plan of expenditures for budget office approval, which regulates spending on a monthly basis and ensures that agency spending is for the purpose for which it was appropriated.[19] The General Assembly exercises control over agency spending during the execution phase of the budgetary process through its control of the *transfer* process. The General

---

[18] Medicaid is a state-federal program which in addition to state funding also receives federal matching grants.

[19] Official Code of Georgia Annotated (O.C.G.A.), 45-12-82 and 83.

Assembly's Fiscal Affairs Subcommittee has the authority to approve or disapprove agency requests to transfer funds from one line-item to another and from one program to another. In the 2005 fiscal year (FY 2005), the state's budget process transitioned from a line-item/object-of-expenditure format to a program format. Control is also achieved when the Department of Audits and Accounts[20] performs end-of-year *audits* of agency and program spending compliance. The state Auditor issues on or before December 31st of a given year a final report on state agency spending of appropriated funds for the fiscal year that ended on June 30th of that year.

Performance evaluation is intended to link program mission and objectives with program accomplishments, so as to provide adequate funding to support mission and objectives but also to provide funding based upon performance. Among the several duties of the Office of Planning and Budget is to "Develop and implement a program budgeting system that relates funding to achievement of established goals and objectives, measures agency performance against attainment of planned outcomes, and provides for program evaluation for policy and funding determinations."[21] Since the adoption of program budgeting in 2005, the *Governor's Budget Report* has included a variety of performance indicators for agencies and their programs.

Budgets are financial documents. Budget*ing* is about resource allocation, financial management and fiscal accountability, as well as political preferences and public policies. The following chapters further explore these topics by examining the state's culture of fiscal conservatism in Chapter 2, trends and patterns of the state's taxing and spending decisions in Chapters 3 and 4, the emergence of the executive budget in Georgia and the annual budget process itself in Chapters 5 and 6, the emergence of program budgeting in the state process in Chapter 7, executive-legislative interactions as illustrated by use of the line-item veto in Chapter 8, the policy priorities of nine governors in Chapter 9 and significant milestones in Georgia budgeting in Chapter 10.

The State of Georgia

The State of Georgia, through its annual budget, provides funding for a variety of services delivered to its citizens located across the state from its highest elevation at Brasstown Bald in the north Georgia mountains to Tybee Island Lighthouse on the south-Georgia seacoast. Georgia citizens are located in large numbers in the Atlanta metropolitan area, in Augusta and Savannah on the east coast, in Columbus on the western border, in Macon in middle Georgia, and in the rural communities of middle- and south-Georgia.

Georgia is located in the southeastern United States, bounded by North Carolina and Tennessee to the north, Florida to the south, South Carolina and the Atlantic

---

[20] Official Code of Georgia Annotated (O.C.G.A.), 50-6-1.
[21] Official Code of Georgia Annotated (O.C.G.A.), 45-12-73 (2).

Ocean to the east and Alabama to the west. It is the largest state by area located east of the Mississippi River, and has a growing and increasingly diverse state population. Georgia's population increased between 1990 and 2019 by 62.8% from 6,512,602 to 10,601,148, increasing every year at an average annual rate of 1.7%.[22] Population growth means more taxpayers, but also more citizens to serve and more students to educate. From 1990 to 2006, Georgia's per capita personal income was between 90% and 95% of U.S. per capita personal income.[23] After 2007, the state's per capita personal income was between 84% and 89% of U.S. per capita personal income,[24] suggesting that Georgians may have been hit somewhat harder by the Great Recession than residents of other states. Georgia's per capita personal income was 85.1% of U.S. per capita personal income in 2019, ranking 38th among all states.[25] In 2019, the state's poverty rate was 14.3%, higher than the U.S. poverty rate of 11.8%.[26] In 2012, at the end of the Great Recession, it had been 19%.

Georgia is becoming a more diverse state. In 1960, its population was 71.4% white, 28.5% black and 0.1% other. In 1990, it was 71.0% white, 27.0% black and 2.1% other.[27] In 2018, it was 58.3% white, 31.6% black and 10.2% other.[28] Hispanics may self-identify as white, but if considered as a separate category from non-Hispanic whites, Hispanics constituted 9.7% of the Georgia population in 2018.[29] Asians are the fastest growing group in the other category.

The Georgia economy is robust and diverse, ranging from agriculture in middle- and south-Georgia, especially peanuts, pecans, and poultry; vestiges of the textile industry mostly in north-Georgia; transportation, especially shipping at the port of Savannah and commercial and passenger traffic at Hartsfield-Jackson International airport in Atlanta; as well as finance, insurance, real estate, medicine, technology and tourism centered, but not exclusively, in Atlanta. Atlanta has professional teams in baseball, basketball, football and soccer, and was host to the Olympic Games in 1996. Georgia also is the home of several military installations, thanks not only to its climate but also to the efforts of several influential and long-serving members of U.S. Congress from Georgia.[30]

---

[22] U.S. Department of Commerce, Census Bureau, Population Division, Intercensal Estimates of the Resident Population for the United States, Regions, States and Puerto Rico, 2019.

[23] U.S. Department of Commerce, Bureau of Economic Analysis, Regional Data, Personal Income, 2019.

[24] Percentages calculated by the author.

[25] U.S. Department of Commerce, Bureau of Economic Analysis, Table 1. Personal Income, Population, and Per Capita Personal Income, by State and Region, 2018–2019, March 2020.

[26] U.S. Census Bureau, QuickFacts, Georgia, July 1, 2019.

[27] U.S. Department of Commerce, Census Bureau, Table 25. Georgia – Race and Hispanic Origin: 1790 to 1990. September 13, 2002.

[28] U.S. Department of Commerce, Census Bureau, American Community Survey, July 1, 2018.

[29] U.S Department of Commerce, Census Bureau, American Community Survey, Hispanic or Latino Origin by Race – Georgia, 2018.

[30] From 1951 to 1965, U.S. Senator Richard B. Russell was Chairman of the Senate Committee on Armed Services and U.S. Representative Carl Vinson was Chairman of the House Armed Services

Georgia is a politically conservative state, once consistently Democratic, then reliably Republican and now somewhat more competitive. It voted four times for Franklin D. Roosevelt (1932, 1936, 1940 and 1944), a Democrat and neighbor in Warm Springs, Georgia; for Harry S Truman (1948), a Southern Democrat; twice for Adlai E. Stevenson (1952 and 1956), a Democrat; for John F. Kennedy (1960), a Democrat; but beginning in 1964 voted for Republicans such as Barry M. Goldwater (1964) and Richard M. Nixon (1972), as well as southern neighbor George C. Wallace (1968), of the American Independent Party. It voted twice for former Georgia Governor Jimmy Carter (1976 and 1980), before voting for Republicans Ronald Reagan (1984) and George H. W. Bush (1988). It narrowly cast its vote once for Democrat and southern neighbor Bill Clinton (1992) but did not vote for him a second time when it voted for Robert J. Dole (1996), a Republican. After that time, it voted for Republicans George W. Bush (2000 and 2004), John S. McCain (2008), Mitt Romney (2012) and Donald J. Trump (2016), before narrowly voting for Democrat Joe Biden (2020).

The Georgia governorship and both chambers of the General Assembly were controlled by Democrats from the end of Reconstruction until 2002. In that year, the governorship and the state Senate were won by Republicans, and in 2004 the House of Representatives was won by Republicans. The governorship and both chambers of the General Assembly have been Republican since that time. However, Democrats are not without influence in the General Assembly and the 2018 gubernatorial election was highly competitive.[31] Charles Bullock argues that in the South, in states like Georgia that have strong economies and attract an increasingly diverse population, the Democratic party is becoming stronger.[32]

Committee; except for 1953 and 1954 when they were Ranking Members. U.S. Senator Sam Nunn was Chair of the Senate Committee from 1987 to 1995.

[31] Using the top-of-the-ticket vote for president and governor as an indicator, the Republican percentage of the two-party vote, after increasing between 2000 and 2006, decreased through 2018, and fell just below a plurality of the two-party vote in 2020.

[32] Charles S. Bullock, III, "Growth Versus Stagnation and a New Realignment," in Charles S. Bullock, III, and Mark J. Rozell, eds., *The New Politics of the Old South: An Introduction to Southern Politics*. Seventh Edition. Lanham, Maryland: Rowman & Littlefield Publishers, Inc., 2021. Chapter 2.

Chapter 2
Fiscal Conservatism and Fiscal Conservatives

Fiscal conservatism is a political and economic philosophy favoring low taxation, low government spending and low government debt. Originally known as *classical liberalism*, this philosophy came to be known as *conservatism*[1] during the 1930s in order to distinguish itself from the emerging interventionist, regulatory, welfare state policies then becoming known as *liberalism*.[2]

Fiscal Conservatism in Georgia

In fiscal matters, Georgia is a conservative state where policy makers favor balanced budgets, low taxes, limited debt and limited government spending. On the revenue side, policy makers resist tax increases and rely sparingly on bond revenue (borrowing) to pay for government spending. In FY 2018, Georgia ranked 50th in state revenues per capita, 42nd in state tax collections per capita, and 47th in state debt per capita.[3] On the expenditure side, policy makers prefer private spending over public spending and within public sector spending prefer economic

---

[1] Friedrich A. Hayek, *The Constitution of Liberty*. Chicago, Illinois: University of Chicago Press, 1960. Barry Goldwater, *The Conscience of a Conservative*. Shepherdsville, Kentucky: Victor Publishing Company, Inc., 1960.

[2] John Maynard Keynes, *The General Theory of Employment, Interest and Money*. London: Macmillian and Co., 1936. Arthur M. Schlesinger, Jr., *The Crisis of the Old Order:1919–1933*. Boston: Houghton Mifflin Company, 1957. Arthur M. Schlesinger, Jr., *The Coming of the New Deal: 1933–35*. Boston: Houghton Mifflin Company, 1959. Arthur M. Schlesinger, Jr., *The Politics of Upheaval: 1935–36*. Boston: Houghton Mifflin Company, 1960.

[3] Tax Foundation, Washington, DC, 2018. www.taxfoundation.org/taxdata/

development and infrastructure projects over transfer payments. In FY 2007 Georgia ranked 43rd in state spending per capita.[4]

Fiscal conservatism in Georgia state government is manifest in at least six ways.[5] First, the state has a constitutional balanced budget requirement. This means that the state cannot incur a deficit or borrow to obtain operating funds. The General Assembly is prohibited from appropriating funds in excess of an amount equal to the sum of anticipated revenue collections and any surplus remaining in the state treasury at the beginning of the fiscal year.[6]

Second, the state has low debt limits and low use of debt. State debt (for capital projects) is limited to 10% of the net revenue receipts in the fiscal year immediately preceding the year in which debt is incurred.[7] In most recent years, the state's debt has been 5–6%, well below the constitutional limit.

Third, the state requires reserves. The Revenue Shortfall Reserve, established in 1976 in response to a severe revenue shortfall in the previous year, is Georgia's "rainy day" fund. All surplus funds at the end of a fiscal year are added to the Revenue Shortfall Reserve, which may not exceed 15% of the previous year's net revenue collections. The General Assembly may appropriate up to 1% of the reserve fund for funding K-12 education needs. The governor may release for appropriation an amount that is in excess of 4% of the reserve, but an amount not less than 4% must be retained in the reserve fund to cover any deficit in the amount by which total annual expenditures exceed net annual revenues. The purpose of the rainy day fund is to enable the state to absorb decreases in revenue collections due to an economic recession without having to reduce the adopted budget.[8]

Fourth, the state has relatively low taxes, a graduated individual income tax with a top rate of 5.75% and a sales tax of 4%. The top income tax rate was 6% from 1937 until 2018. The sales tax rate was enacted at 3% in 1951 and increased to 4% in 1989. Of the 41 states with an individual income tax, eight have flat rates, ranging from 3 to 5%, and 33 have graduated rates with the top rate ranging from 3 to 13% but with most states having top rates between 4 and 8%. Of the 45 states with a sales tax, Georgia is one of 11 states with a rate of approximately 4%; 33 states have rates between 5 and 7%.

Fifth, the governor has the sole authority to set the state's revenue estimate.[9] The state economist[10] calculates a range of likely revenue yields under various assumptions, but as noted in Chapter 1, the selection of a specific figure that becomes the official state revenue estimate is a policy decision of the governor. This revenue-setting prerogative is the keystone of the governor's budget power. Revenue esti-

---

[4] Tax Foundation, Washington, DC, 2009. www.taxfoundation.org/taxdata/
[5] Thanks to Henry M. Huckaby for helping me frame this topic.
[6] Constitution of the State of Georgia, 1983, Article III, Section IX, Paragraph IV[b].
[7] Constitution of the State of Georgia, 1983, Article VII, Section IV, Paragraph II[b].
[8] Official Code of Georgia Annotated, 45-12-93.
[9] Official Code of Georgia Annotated, 4-12-75 (2).
[10] The state economist is a contract employee of the Georgia Office of Planning and Budget.

mates usually have been conservative, leading in most years to an underestimation of actual revenue collections.[11] An advantage of conservative revenue estimates is that they reduce the risk of revenue shortfalls. An "incorrect" estimate that underestimates the actual revenue yield is also politically preferable to one that overestimates collections. Of course, if revenue estimates are too conservative, there is insufficient new revenue projected to permit the funding of gubernatorial and legislative initiatives. Nevertheless, the traditional practice in Georgia of underestimating revenue collections has contributed to a surplus in most years, which has been directed to the Revenue Shortfall Reserve.[12]

Sixth, conservative financial management practices in combination with a relatively robust economy, have consistently earned for the state AAA bond ratings. A long-time chairman of the Senate Appropriations Committee frequently spoke of the connection between conservative financial practices and the state's ability to achieve AAA bond ratings.[13]

The balanced budget requirement, reserve requirement, low debt limit and low use of debt, low tax rates, conservative revenue estimating practices, and financial management practices that earn AAA bond ratings, taken as a whole, are manifestations of the culture of fiscal conservatism in Georgia government.[14]

Governors as Fiscal Conservatives

The roots of fiscal conservatism run deep in Georgia history. William Anderson writes, "Georgia was in the early 1900s very much agricultural, and very much cotton, and this meant few governmental services: little road construction, little manufacturing, unsophisticated approaches to finance and economics, and isolated people."[15] Numan Bartley characterized two eras in Georgia, one in which the fundamental purpose of government was to protect the state from outside intervention, and a later one in which the role of state government was to promote economic growth.[16]

---

[11] The years 1991, 1992, 2002, 2003, 2008, 2009, 2010 and 2020 are the notable exceptions.

[12] Thomas P. Lauth, "Budgeting During a Recession Phase of the Business Cycle: The Georgia Experience," *Public Budgeting & Finance*, Vol. 23 (Summer 2003): 31.

[13] George Hooks, Biennial Institute for Georgia Legislators, University of Georgia, Athens, Georgia, December 1994, December 1996, December 1998, December 2000, and December 2002.

[14] This section on fiscal conservatism is adapted from my chapter on Georgia in Edward J. Clynch and Thomas P. Lauth, eds., *Budgeting in the States: Institutions, Processes, and Politics*. Westport, Connecticut: Praeger Publishers, 2006. pp. 33–35.

[15] William Anderson, *The Wild Man from Sugar Creek: The Political Career of Eugene Talmadge*. Baton Rouge, LA: Louisiana State University Press, 1975. p. 20

[16] Numan V. Bartley, "Georgia Governors in an Age of Change," in Harold P. Henderson and Gary L. Roberts, eds. *Georgia Governors in an Age of Change: From Ellis Arnall to George Busbee*. Athens, GA: The University of Georgia Press, 1988. p. 293.

Fiscal conservatism often is evident in the actions and statements of governors. Eighteen governors have served since 1931, the year in which the Budget Act of that year established the governor as director of the budget, and 2019. A sampling of the actions and statements of those governors will serve to illustrate the persistence of fiscal conservatism in the state, albeit with some variations.

Richard B. Russell, Jr. (1931–1933)

Richard Russell was elected governor of Georgia on November 4, 1930. In effect, he had been elected on October 1, 1930 when he won the Democratic primary. He had no opposition in the November general election. He was sworn in on June 27, 1931. (During his administration the date of the governor's inauguration was changed to January following election rather than June.) Immediately prior to being elected governor, Russell was Speaker of the House of Representatives from 1927 to 1931, having served as a member of the House since 1921. In his first annual meeting with the House and Senate, he pledged his cooperation and recognition of the legislature as a separate and distinct branch of government.[17] The 1931 General Assembly was the only one during Russell's brief governorship. He served only 18 months before being elected to the U.S. Senate.

Russell became governor during the Great Depression. Georgia's farmers were struggling and unemployment was high. Tax revenue was declining and the state was unable to meet its financial obligations.[18] In his inaugural address, Russell stated that there would be unpaid appropriations by the end of 1931, but he promised to balance the state's expenditures and income, by practicing strict economy, reorganizing state departments and agencies and reducing the cost of government. Claiming that education and highways were the "twin paths to progress," he said that spending for these purposes was an investment for the future.[19]

State government reorganization was a centerpiece of Russell's gubernatorial platform; he saw it as a way to address the states depression-induced debt. The Reorganization Act of 1931 consolidated more than 100 departments, boards and commissions into 14 state agencies, and eliminated the boards of trustees that governed individual institutions of the university system, replacing them with the University System of Georgia Board of Regents as the single governing body over all state colleges and universities.[20] The practice of tax collection by individual

---

[17] Gilbert C. Fite, *Richard B. Russell, Jr., Senator from Georgia.* Chapel Hill, NC: The University of North Carolina Press 1991. p. 83.

[18] Gilbert C. Fite, *Richard B. Russell, Jr., Senator from Georgia.* Chapel Hill, NC: The University of North Carolina Press 1991. pp. 79–80.

[19] Gilbert C. Fite, *Richard B. Russell, Jr., Senator from Georgia.* Chapel Hill, NC: The University of North Carolina Press 1991. pp. 79–80.

[20] The Allen Commission on Simplification and Coordination, established by Governor Lamartine G. Hardman (1927–31) provided a foundation for Governor Russell's reorganization.

agencies was to be ended and a centralized state tax commission was established.[21] The Budget Act of 1931 established a budget bureau and named the governor as director. Russell's biographer, Gilbert C. Fite writes:

> Under the new system, the departments of government submitted their requests to the budget bureau, controlled by the governor, which would recommend an overall budget to the legislature. The General Assembly could not amend the budget if it created a deficit. To balance outgo with income, Russell squeezed the state agencies and saved some funds through reorganization. With utmost economy, he was able to pay the Confederate veteran's pensions ..., keep all schools open, and maintain a highway building program. At the end of his eighteen months as governor, the state had not only met its current requirements but had paid about $2.8 million on the old unpaid appropriations. No previous governor had ever exerted such tight control of the state budget.[22]

Eugene Talmadge (1933–1937 and 1941–1943)

The political scientist V.O. Key, Jr. wrote about Eugene Talmadge (1884–1946), who was elected three times as commissioner of agriculture and four times as governor, in the following way: "He was a practical man, in favor of a balanced budget, a low tax rate, and not much pubic regulation of private enterprise."[23] Further, "Talmadge generally favored restricted state services and a limited use of governmental powers. These attitudes and his low-tax beliefs found him favor with the highest economic forces in the state."[24] Historian Numan Bartley describes Eugene Talmadge as the spokesman for dirt farmers and the common folk who during his three terms as governor, strongly opposed the New Deal, rejecting such federal programs as old age assistance and aid to dependent children, minimum wages, agriculture price supports and highway construction funds.[25] He was, according to Bartley, the "champion of the outs".[26] Historian Harold Henderson writes, "Talmadge's view of negative government contrasted sharply with President Roosevelt's positive state philosophy. He opposed an old-age pension because he believed it would make people dependent upon the government."[27] According to Henderson, "Talmadge espoused a political philosophy of low taxes and few

---

[21] Gilbert C. Fite, *Richard B. Russell, Jr., Senator from Georgia*. Chapel Hill, NC: The University of North Carolina Press 1991. p. 88.

[22] Gilbert C. Fite, *Richard B. Russell, Jr., Senator from Georgia*. Chapel Hill, NC: The University of North Carolina Press, 1991. pp. 89–90.

[23] V.O. Key, Jr., *Southern Politics in State and Nation*. New York: Vintage Books, 1949. p.116

[24] V.O. Key, Jr., *Southern Politics in State and Nation*. New York: Vintage Books, 1949. p.128

[25] Numan V. Bartley, *The Creation of Modern Georgia*. Second Edition. Athens, GA: The University of Georgia Press, 1990. pp. 173–76.

[26] Numan V. Bartley, *The Creation of Modern Georgia*. Second Edition. Athens, GA: The University of Georgia Press, 1990. p. 173.

[27] Harold Paulk Henderson, *The Politics of Change in Georgia: A Political Biography of Elis Arnall*. Athens, GA: The University of Georgia Press, 1991. p. 12.

government services. He extolled the virtues of thrift, hard work and rural living. Unfortunately for Georgians, Talmadge's concept of negative government offered few solutions to the plight of his fellow citizens other than cutting taxes, reducing government services, lowering the price of automobile tags and reorganizing the highway department."[28] Talmadge biographer William Anderson writes,

> First, Gene's conservative philosophy was that a government should take a bare minimum of tax money from its citizens, because it had no need or right to be so involved in their lives that it needed much money to operate. And second, he felt he knew what a big government with money could do to the minds of the people. … Gene knew that if the starving farmer were given food and money as a handout, there would necessarily be controls, and a dependency on government as thinker and doer would emerge. The southern farmer, would therefore, remain in subjugation, only this time to the government instead of to the local bank or the Wall Street boys. It would be a psychological indebtedness far worse than the region's traditional financial indebtedness.[29]

Anderson reports Talmadge's governmental philosophy as, "The only way I know a government can help the people is to stay out of business, and be a fair referee between the people, and let its citizens do the business, and then just take as little toll out of their property as you can for government."[30] Talmadge opposed the sales tax, fearing that the increase in revenue would lead to an increase in the size of state government.[31] According to Anderson,

> The business community generally supported Talmadge because he said that government should leave them alone. They particularly approved of his hatred of taxes. In an era of prosperity, this might have been fine, but in the depressed thirties Talmadge's hands-off approach simply let the people wither and die alone. If the business men supplied the money, the poorer farmer class supplied the core vote that gave Talmadge his power.[32]

Eugene Talmadge was not only a fiscal conservative, he also was according to Howard, Fleischman and Engstrom, almost dictatorial as governor, calling out the state militia to enforce his executive orders when other branches of government opposed his policies.[33] A financial crisis in 1936, while somewhat amusing today, illustrates the state of financial management and constitutional government in Georgia at that time. The following sequence of events were reported by William

---

[28] Harold Paulk Henderson, *The Politics of Change in Georgia: A Political Biography of Elis Arnall*. Athens, GA: The University of Georgia Press, 1991. p. 6.

[29] William Anderson, *The Wild Man from Sugar Creek: The Political Career of Eugene Talmadge*. Baton Rouge, LA: Louisiana State University Press, 1975. p. 66.

[30] William Anderson, *The Wild Man from Sugar Creek: The Political Career of Eugene Talmadge*. Baton Rouge, LA: Louisiana State University Press, 1975. p. 115.

[31] Harold Paulk Henderson, *The Politics of Change in Georgia: A Political Biography of Elis Arnall*. Athens, GA: The University of Georgia Press, 1991. p. 9.

[32] William Anderson, *The Wild Man from Sugar Creek: The Political Career of Eugene Talmadge*. Baton Rouge, LA: Louisiana State University Press, 1975. pp. 237–238.

[33] Robert M. Howard, Arnold Fleischman and Richard Engstrom, *Politics in Georgia*, Third Edition. Athens, GA: The University of Georgia Press, 2017. p. 36.

Anderson.[34] The 1935 session of the General Assembly ended without an enacted appropriations bill, although funding for the remainder of 1935 had been appropriated in the 1933 biennial legislative session. Sometime in 1936 the state's money was expected to run out. Governor Talmadge, unwilling for political reasons to call the General Assembly into special session to fix the problem, proposed to handle the situation by having the state treasurer and comptroller issue checks on unappropriated money, based upon written requests from state agencies and warrants issued by the governor. However, the state constitution provision stating, "No money shall be drawn from the Treasury except by appropriation made by law," seemed to prohibit such an approach. Talmadge contended that any monies appropriated in 1933, but still remaining in the state treasury and not allotted to departmental budgets, had therefore not lapsed, and could be spent without the need for current legislative appropriation. He believed that such funds, in addition to tax revenues directly collected by various departments would be sufficient to run the government. He further stated that the appropriation for 1936 was the same as the appropriation for 1935, that previously appropriated amounts were appropriated indefinitely, and had not been repealed or replaced. The state treasurer opposed this interpretation of the constitution and the governor's executive action. He argued that unspent appropriations were void and that only appropriations by the 1935 General Assembly would have been valid for the 1936–37 biennium. The treasurer then removed the state's collateral bonds and cash reserve from the vaults and deposited them in the Federal Reserve Bank of Atlanta, presumably out of reach of the governor. Governor Talmadge then announced the removal of both the state treasurer and comptroller, constitutionally elected officials, from office and when they refuse to physically relinquish their posts, he had them physically removed by the State Adjutant General. The state's clearing house banks refused to honor a state check for $100,000 until there had been a judicial determination of the crisis. The situation evoked outrage as reflected in newspapers across the state, while Governor Talmadge blamed the New Deal. A state Superior Court ruled that neither the state treasurer (nor the replacement treasurer Governor Talmadge had appointed after removing the elected treasurer) could sign checks for money that had not been appropriated. However, the state Supreme Court upheld the governor's removal of the state treasurer and state comptroller and the appointment of a new treasurer, subject to review of the General Assembly. The state's collateral bonds were then returned and its checks were cashed. Governor Talmadge won this encounter, but constitutional government in Georgia may not have fared so well.

---

[34] William Anderson, *The Wild Man from Sugar Creek: The Political Career of Eugene Talmadge*. Baton Rouge, LA: Louisiana State University Press, 1975. pp. 141–152.

Eurith D. Rivers (1937–1941)

Zell Miller wrote in 1958: "E. D. (Ed) Rivers was one of the most progressive governors that Georgia ever had."[35] Major laws enacted during his administration include: a free school book program, a minimum 7 months school term, an expanded public health program, the highway patrol system, and the social security program of welfare for the aged, dependent, and blind.

Rivers ran for governor five times and was twice elected, in 1936 and 1938. He was Speaker of the House of Representatives during the first two Eugene Talmadge terms. In 1935, he broke with Talmadge over the New Deal program, which Talmadge opposed and Rivers favored. Miller characterizes the views of Rivers as "liberal," and those of Talmadge as "conservative, in fact, reactionary."[36]

Rivers advocated tax reform to enable Georgia to afford participation in New Deal programs, but was unsuccessful. His participation in such programs during an era of low state revenue resulted in substantial state debt at the end of his administration. As Speaker of the House of Representatives in 1935, Rivers led the House to pass legislation, including a proposed constitutional amendment that, if approved by the voters, would authorize the levying of a tax for the payment of old age pensions. Governor Talmadge vetoed the bill on the grounds that the taxes would be too heavy and the pension wrong in principle.[37] In retaliation, the House of Representatives refused to pass an appropriations bill before adjournment, hoping to force Talmadge to call a special session of the legislature where they could make another attempt to pass social security legislation.[38] Talmadge refused to call such a session and said he would use the appropriations bill from the previous year. As noted earlier, when the Secretary of the Treasury and the Comptroller General declared this action illegal, Talmadge ordered the state militia to remove both officials. Miller writes, "Talmadge was virtually the dictator of Georgia at this time."[39]

Governor Rivers sought to implement the New Deal in Georgia as a solution to the state's economic problems.[40] In this connection, the beginning of the state's fiscal year was changed in 1937 from January 1 to July 1 to coordinate with that of the federal government, which at that time began on July 1. However, Georgia's economy generated insufficient revenue for the state to take advantage of federal

---

[35] Zell Bryan Miller, *The Administration of E. D. Rivers as Governor of Georgia*. Master of Arts Thesis, The University of Georgia, 1958. p. iv.

[36] Zell Bryan Miller, *The Administration of E. D. Rivers as Governor of Georgia*. Master of Arts Thesis, The University of Georgia, 1958. p. 11.

[37] Zell Bryan Miller, *The Administration of E. D. Rivers as Governor of Georgia*. Master of Arts Thesis, The University of Georgia, 1958. p. 13.

[38] Zell Bryan Miller, *The Administration of E. D. Rivers as Governor of Georgia*. Master of Arts Thesis, The University of Georgia, 1958. p. 14.

[39] Zell Bryan Miller, *The Administration of E. D. Rivers as Governor of Georgia*. Master of Arts Thesis, The University of Georgia, 1958. p. 16.

[40] Numan V. Bartley, *The Creation of Modern Georgia*. Second Edition. Athens, GA: The University of Georgia Press, 1990. p. 190.

matching funds for New Deal programs such as public works. Rivers proposed new taxations, such as a 1% gross income tax, a 3% retail sales tax, or luxury taxes, in that order of preference.[41] All were defeated by the legislature that said new taxes were not needed and that the governor should instead further economize. Economizing resulted in cutting services and terminating state employees. He transferred funds from the Highway Department to fund education and borrowed from banks to restore the transferred funds, which incurred significant state debt obligations.[42]

The Rivers administration ended January 14, 1941. He did not run in 1942, deferring to Ellis Arnall. He ran again in 1946, but lost to Gene Talmadge.

Ellis Arnall (1943–1947)

Ellis Arnall served as Georgia's governor from 1943 to 1947, the first twentieth century governor to serve a 4-year term.[43] A constitutional amendment sponsored by Eugene Talmadge changed the governor's term to 4 years, effective in 1943. Historian and Arnall biographer Harold Henderson notes that, "Arnall considered himself a liberal on the question of providing governmental services, but deemed himself a conservative in fiscal policy…"[44] Upon entering office, Arnall inherited a substantial state debt and a revenue system that was inadequate to provide the existing level of state services. Georgia lacked a general sales tax and relied upon the motor fuel tax as its major source of income.[45] Arnall pledged in his gubernatorial campaign not to raise taxes,[46] but even if he had not, he opposed the general sales tax in principle because of its regressive nature.[47] He believed the state debt should be paid off and diverted state revenue into sinking funds to pay off state obligations,

---

[41] Governor E. D. Rivers message to the General Assembly, February 8, 1939. Reprinted in *The Atlanta Constitution*, February 9, 1939: 10

[42] Zell Bryan Miller, *The Administration of E. D. Rivers as Governor of Georgia*. Master of Arts Thesis, The University of Georgia, 1958. p. 97.

[43] The Reconstruction Constitution of 1868 lengthened the term of Georgia governors from 2 to 4 years. The Constitution of 1877 returned the term to 2 years. Rufus Bullock (1868–71) was the first governor elected under the new provision, but resigned before completing a full 4-year term. James Milton Smith (1872–77) served a full 4-year term.

[44] Harold Paulk Henderson, *The Politics of Change in Georgia; A Political Biography of Ellis Arnall*. Athens, GA; The University of Georgia Press, 1991. p. 98.

[45] Harold Paulk Henderson, *The Politics of Change in Georgia; A Political Biography of Ellis Arnall*. Athens, GA; The University of Georgia Press, 1991. p. 52.

[46] Harold Paulk Henderson, *The Politics of Change in Georgia; A Political Biography of Ellis Arnall*. Athens, GA; The University of Georgia Press, 1991. p. 97.

[47] Harold Paulk Henderson, *The Politics of Change in Georgia; A Political Biography of Ellis Arnall*. Athens, GA; The University of Georgia Press, 1991. p. 99.

and, according to Harold Henderson, considered removal of the debt burden to be one of the major accomplishments of his administration.[48]

In Arnall's administration the greatest increase in state spending was for education. Henderson reports that, "By fiscal year 1946 the state's appropriation for the public schools had increased 41%, and the university system appropriation had increased 131% over the last fiscal year of the Talmadge administration."[49] Arnall obtained legislative approval for a Teachers Retirement System in 1943,[50] although the state's financial situation did not permit funding it until 1945. He also recommended removal from the governor the power to suspend the state treasurer and state comptroller-general, and recommended transfer of the power to appoint the state auditor from the governor to the legislature.[51] The legislature approved both recommendations.

Henderson writes that Arnall supported state's rights, but unlike Talmadge he had a more positive view of government and recognized the state's responsibility to provide needed services to its citizens.[52] Further, Henderson writes, "He was a segregationist, but also advocated progress for black citizens."[53] Arnall sought the governorship again in 1966, coming first in the Democratic primary but losing the primary run-off with Lester Maddox, and running a distant third as a write-in candidate in the general election.

Melvin E. Thompson (1947–1948)

M. E. Thompson served as governor from 1947 until 1948. He was elected lieutenant governor in 1946 and became governor when Eugene Talmadge, who was elected governor in 1946, died December 21, 1946, before taking the oath of office. Immediately following Talmadge's death, controversy ensued regarding the correct provision of the Georgia Constitution that determined who would then be governor. One provision (Article V, Section I, Paragraph I) held that the incumbent governor would hold office "until his successor shall be chosen and qualified." A second provision (Article V, Section 1, Paragraph VII) held that "in case of the death,

---

[48] Harold Paulk Henderson, *The Politics of Change in Georgia; A Political Biography of Ellis Arnall.* Athens, GA; The University of Georgia Press, 1991. pp. 98–99.

[49] Harold Paulk Henderson, *The Politics of Change in Georgia; A Political Biography of Ellis Arnall.* Athens, GA; The University of Georgia Press, 1991. p.100.

[50] Numan V. Bartley, *The Creation of Modern Georgia.* Second Edition. Athens, GA: The University of Georgia Press, 1990. p. 194.

[51] Harold Paulk Henderson, *The Politics of Change in Georgia; A Political Biography of Ellis Arnall.* Athens, GA; The University of Georgia Press, 1991. p. 54.

[52] Harold Paulk Henderson, *The Politics of Change in Georgia; A Political Biography of Ellis Arnall.* Athens, GA; The University of Georgia Press, 1991. p. 124.

[53] Harold Paulk Henderson, *The Politics of Change in Georgia; A Political Biography of Ellis Arnall.* Athens, GA; The University of Georgia Press, 1991. p. 151.

resignation or disability of the Governor, the Lieutenant Governor shall exercise the executive power." A third provision (Article V, Section I, Paragraph IV) held that if following the general election, "no person shall have [a] majority, then from the two persons having the highest number of votes ... the General Assembly shall immediately elect a Governor." Uncertainty over which constitutional provision should be followed, and the presence of competing claimants, led to the infamous three-governors controversy.[54] In March 1947, following 2 months of controversy, the Georgia Supreme Court upheld Thompson's claim to the governorship.[55] However, the political ill-will resulting from the controversy made it nearly impossible for Governor Thompson to obtain cooperation from the General Assembly. In its 1947 session, the General Assembly failed to pass an appropriations bill and under the law at that time the appropriations act from the previous year remained in force. Thompson was able to achieve some of his program objectives because, even without a new and higher appropriation state revenue collections exceeded expectations, providing additional funding for education including teacher pay increases, roads and bridges and other government functions.[56] Herman Talmadge defeated M. E. Thompson in the 1948 general election and served the remaining 2 years of the term to which Eugene Talmadge had been elected in 1946. M. E. Thompson served less than 2 years as governor. He had served as executive secretary to Governor Ellis Arnall, a Southern progressive, and Arnall appointed him state revenue commissioner. He once described himself as one of Ellis Arnall's disciples,[57] even though Arnall did not support him for lieutenant governor in 1946 because of a prior commitment. Had the circumstances of his coming to the governor's office been different, he might have governed in fiscal matters more in the progressive-conservative tradition of Ellis Arnall than the conservative tradition of Eugene Talmadge, but that at best is speculation.

---

[54] Charles S. Bullock, III, Scott E. Buchanan and Ronald Keith Gaddie, *The Three Governors Controversy: Skullduggery, Machinations, and the Decline of Georgia's Progressive Politics*. Athens, GA: The University of Georgia Press, 2015, and Harold P. Henderson, "M. E. Thompson and the Politics of Succession," in Harold P. Henderson and Gary L. Roberts, eds. *Georgia Governors in an Age of Change: From Ellis Arnall to George Busbee*. Athens, GA: The University of Georgia Press, 1988. pp. 49–65.

[55] *Thompson v. Talmadge*, 201 GA 867, 871–907 (1947).

[56] Harold P. Henderson, "M.E. Thompson and the Politics of Succession," in Harold P. Henderson and Gary L. Roberts, eds. *Georgia Governors in an Age of Change: From Ellis Arnall to George Busbee*. Athens, GA: The University of Georgia Press, 1988. p. 63.

[57] Gene-Gabriel Moore, "M.E. Thompson Recollections," in Harold P. Henderson and Gary L. Roberts, eds. *Georgia Governors in an Age of Change: From Ellis Arnall to George Busbee*. Athens, GA: The University of Georgia Press, 1988. p. 67.

Herman Talmadge (1948–1955)

Herman Talmadge (1913–2002) was also a fiscal conservative, but somewhat less so than his father. Historian Harold Paulk Henderson has written, "Departing from his father's Jefferson philosophy of government, Talmadge favored a major expansion of state services. He realized that the state's existing revenue sources ... could not provide sufficient revenue to fund the major expansion of state services he advocated."[58] As a political pragmatist, Talmage opposed efforts in the 1950 session of the General Assembly to increase state taxes, won reelection as governor in 1950, and in the 1951 legislative session supported the enactment of a 3% state sales tax which gave Georgia the necessary revenue to finance the expansion of state services,[59] including the Minimum Foundation Program for education.[60] In 1952, he secured a constitutional amendment to earmark all motor fuel and auto tag tax revenues for the building and maintaining of state roadways.[61] He also secured a constitutional amendment to develop and use state authorities to enable the state to circumvent the constitutional prohibition against spending more revenue than it collected. Such authorities were used to sell bonds to fund capital projects such as schools, highways and state buildings.[62] Political Scientist Roger N. Pajari writes that Talmadge was successful in promoting the modernization of Georgia's economy.[63] His economic development initiatives included the expansion of Georgia's Port Authority, creation of the State Forestry Commission and, with the help of the motor fuel tax, the building of state highways and bridges.[64] According to Pajari, Talmadge dominated the General Assembly, its leadership and committee system, especially over the spending of state funds realized through the new sales tax.[65]

---

[58] Harold Paulk Henderson, *Ernest Vandiver: Governor of Georgia*. Athens, GA: The University of Georgia Press, 2000. p. 24

[59] Harold Paulk Henderson, Ernest Vandiver: Governor of Georgia. Athens, GA: The University of Georgia Press, 2000. p. 25

[60] Numan V. Bartley, *The Creation of Modern Georgia*. Second Edition. Athens, GA: The University of Georgia Press, 1990. p. 206.

[61] Roger N. Pajari, "Herman E. Talmadge and the Politics of Power," in Harold P. Henderson and Gary L. Roberts, *Georgia Governors in an Age of Change: From Ellis Arnall to George Busbee*. Athens, GA: The University of Georgia Press, 1988. p. 82.

[62] Roger N. Pajari, "Herman E. Talmadge and the Politics of Power," in Harold P. Henderson and Gary L. Roberts, *Georgia Governors in an Age of Change: From Ellis Arnall to George Busbee*. Athens, GA: The University of Georgia Press, 1988. p. 82.

[63] Roger N. Pajari, "Herman E. Talmadge and the Politics of Power," in Harold P. Henderson and Gary L. Roberts, *Georgia Governors in an Age of Change: From Ellis Arnall to George Busbee*. Athens, GA: The University of Georgia Press, 1988. p. 76.

[64] Roger N. Pajari, "Herman E. Talmadge and the Politics of Power," in Harold P. Henderson and Gary L. Roberts, *Georgia Governors in an Age of Change: From Ellis Arnall to George Busbee*. Athens, GA: The University of Georgia Press, 1988. p. 82.

[65] Roger N. Pajari, "Herman E. Talmadge and the Politics of Power," in Harold P. Henderson and Gary L. Roberts, *Georgia Governors in an Age of Change: From Ellis Arnall to George Busbee*. Athens, GA: The University of Georgia Press, 1988. p. 85.

Further, he concludes that Talmadge's economic modernization initiatives appealed to the conservative, urban business vote, while his stand on race appealed to the segregationist rural Georgia counties.[66]

Marvin Griffin (1955–1959)

As fiscal conservatives, Georgia governors tend to favor low taxes, limited spending and a restricted level of government activities. Indeed, Marvin Griffin, as a fiscal conservative, promised during his 1954 gubernatorial campaign not to increase state taxes. However, upon taking office Griffin was faced with insufficient revenues to meet state budget commitments and the need to cut department and program spending in order to balance the budget. He recommended that the 1955 General Assembly create a task force to look into the budget situation. The legislature responded by establishing the State Program Study Committee, which in May 1955 issued a report recommending tax increases. On June 2, 1955 Governor Griffin called for an extraordinary (special) session of the General Assembly to consider the recommendations of the State Program Study Commission, and on June 6th addressed the opening of the special session.

In summarizing the State Program Study Commission report,[67] Governor Griffin pointed out that the state had a need for additional revenue. The sales tax and business tax were providing insufficient revenue to meet the needs of a government with a growing population and the attendant demands for services. The state was spending over half of its budget for education, and over 90% of its budget on four departments, education, highways, health and welfare.

The state of education was depicted as: inadequate teacher salaries, teacher retention problems, unaffordable higher education tuition, deferred maintenance and inability to afford needed new construction at both the local government level and in the university system, and insufficient support for transportation at the local level. He said the state had the lowest per student public school spending in the country, that the state was unable to meet its funding formula requirements and that accreditation for some units of the university system was in jeopardy.

The state's highway system was suffering from inadequate maintenance and insufficient new construction, and the state was not able to take advantage of federal highway matching funds. The state was not able to extend health services to rural areas, and there was inadequate support for the training of health care professionals at the state medical school. The state was providing inadequate staff and services to

---

[66] Roger N. Pajari, "Herman E. Talmadge and the Politics of Power," in Harold P. Henderson and Gary L. Roberts, *Georgia Governors in an Age of Change: From Ellis Arnall to George Busbee*. Athens, GA: The University of Georgia Press, 1988. p. 78.

[67] Governor Marvin Griffin's address to the General Assemble at the opening of the Extraordinary Session, June 6, 1955. Text reprinted in the *Atlanta Constitution*, June 7, 1955: 12.

the patient population at state facilities, and was not able to provide matching funds to take advantage of federal programs.

The amount needed to address these financial shortcomings was estimated to be $65,000,000. Governor Griffin recommended the following package of tax increases:

- Cigarette tax increase from 3 cents to 5 cents per package. Estimate: $5,000,000
- State warehouse charge on alcoholic beverage from $1 to $2.25 per gallon. Estimate: $4,000,000
- Tax on beer raised to 4 cents per can or bottle. Estimate: $3,800,000
- Sliding fee for motor vehicle license fees from $5 to $15. Estimate: $6,000,000
- ½ cent per gallon fee increase to the motor fuel tax. Estimate: $5,000,000
- $1 per year for drivers' licenses. Estimate: $1,000,000
- Make transient trucks subject to Georgia's motor fuel tax.
- Increase the insurance premium tax from 2% to 2 ½% on foreign companies, and increase the rate from ¼ of 1% to ¾ of 1% for domestic companies, Estimate: $1,500,000
- Extend sales tax to certain services. Estimate: $20,500,000
- Eliminate federal income tax payments as deductions. Estimate: $18,000,000
- Retain corporate tax rate at 5 ½%.
- Maintain the 6% budget reduction for all state agencies imposed by predecessor.

Critics of the tax plan claimed that Governor Griffin had broken his promise and contended that the state should cut spending rather than raise taxes.[68]

The General Assembly approved $40,000,000 in new taxes. They enacted tax increases on wine and beer, small loans, cigarettes, automobile tags, gasoline, insurance premiums and a fee on driver's licenses and transient truck fuel. By executive order, the liquor warehouse fee was increased. The idea of extending the sales tax to services was not approved. The tax on insurance premiums was increased, but at a rate lower than the governor recommended.[69]

- Gasoline: increased tax from 6 to 6 ½ cents a gallon
- Cigarettes: increased tax from 3 to 5 cents per package
- Beer: increased tax from 2 to 4 cents a can
- Wine: increased tax on foreign wines by 100%
- Motor Vehicle Tags: established a sliding scale to double auto tags and increase truck tags by 10%.
- Income: disallow deduction of federal tax payments by corporations and individuals. Increased individual exemptions by $500, with $100 for each dependent.
- Insurance: increased premium tax ¼ of 1%

---

[68] See Scott E. Buchanan, *"Some People Who Ate My Barbecue Didn't Vote for Me," The Life of Georgia Governor Marvin Griffin*, Nashville, TN: Vanderbilt University Press, 2011. pp. 132–144.
[69] Albert Riley, "Griffin Told Where to Spend Fund," and M. L. St. John, "Income Tax Passes After Floor Fight," *Atlanta Constitution*, June 18, 1955: 1 and 3.

- Small loans: levied 3% fee on small loan charges
- Driver's Licenses: levied $1 annual charge (from previous $1 for life)
- Transient Trucks: levied a fee on fuel
- Liquor warehouse fee enacted by executive order

Although these were not tax increases in the high yield income or sales taxes, they were significant increases enacted to address the problem of growing demand for state services exceeding the growth in revenue available to provide them.

S. Ernest Vandiver, Jr. (1959–1963)

Ernest Vandiver was elected governor in 1958 and took office in January 1959. His biographer Harold Paulk Henderson writes, "Certainly Vandiver qualified as a fiscal conservative." Henderson cites several Vandiver contemporaries attesting to his fiscal conservatism, referring to him as "thrifty," "frugal" and "tight," treating state money just like he would his own.[70]

Describing legislative-executive relations at the onset of the Vandiver administration, Henderson writes, "At the time of the Vandiver administration, legislative independence did not exist, and a governor exercised tremendous influence over the legislature, which included selecting its leadership."[71] Describing the budget process, Henderson cites the leading scholar on the Georgia budget process of that era, "Augustus B. Turnbull, III concluded in his study of the state's budget process that 'the years from 1931 to 1961 showed a rather steady decline in the degree of legislative control over the budget.'"[72] Henderson cites Governor Vandiver himself, "Vandiver described the existing process as one in which 'the state auditor, working with the governor during that era, prepared an executive budget, who presented it to the legislature for adoption, and usually within a 30–45 minute period it was passed just as the governor had presented it.'"[73] He also cites the Speaker of the House of Representatives George T. Smith, "The appropriations laws at that time were written in such a way that unless you enacted a new appropriations bill every 2 years, you continued to travel on the old appropriations bill, and you did not have to account for how the money was spent except for the amount that was included in the last appropriation bill. Well, the income of the state was increasing. So all that

---

[70] Harold Paulk Henderson, *Ernest Vandiver: Governor of Georgia*. Athens, GA: The University of Georgia Press, 2000. pp. 229–230.

[71] Harold Paulk Henderson, *Ernest Vandiver: Governor of Georgia*. Athens, GA: The University of Georgia Press, 2000. p 94.

[72] Harold Paulk Henderson, *Ernest Vandiver: Governor of Georgia*. Athens, GA: The University of Georgia Press, 2000. p. 143.

[73] Harold Paulk Henderson, *Ernest Vandiver: Governor of Georgia*. Athens, GA: The University of Georgia Press, 2000. p. 143.

money over and above that set out in the last appropriation bill, the Governor could spend it as he pleased, as long as it was legal."[74]

Governor Vandiver promised during the 1958 election to restore the budgetary powers of the General Assembly. He got the General Assembly in 1960 to propose a constitutional amendment that would, in the governor's words, "restore the legislature to its rightful responsibility of appropriating money."[75] The voters approved the amendment in the general election in 1960 and, as a result, the governor submitted a new appropriation bill to the 1961 legislative session– the first since 1956.[76]

In his 1962 State of the State Address, Governor Vandiver, based upon recommendations from the 1961 House-Senate Budget Study Committee, recommended a constitutional amendment to: require biennial appropriations bills, limit appropriations to no more than state revenues and any surplus, cap debt obligations of state authorities to no more than 15% of the total budget, and create a system of budgetary control. He also called for the establishment of a modern Budget Bureau, an office to restore responsibility and accountability to the budgetary process.[77] The governor's budget reform legislation unanimously passed the legislature. It created a budget bureau with the governor designated as the ex officio director of the budget, and created an administrative head of the agency, the state budget director, appointed by the governor. The law limited state general appropriations acts to two fiscal years.

The legislature proposed two constitutional amendments. The first proposed amendment divided the legislative session in odd-numbered years into (1) a 12-day period in which the budget would be presented, (2) a recess until the second week in February to give the legislature's fiscal committees time to analyze the budget requests of the chief executive, and (3) a period of no more than 33 additional days, during which time action would be taken on the budget. The second proposed amendment required the governor to submit general appropriations bills to the legislature every odd-numbered year. The legislature unanimously proposed both amendments, which were approved by the voters in the 1962 general election.[78]

As discussed in greater detail in Chapter 5, these legislative actions and constitutional amendments became the basis of today's executive budget system in Georgia.

---

[74] Harold Paulk Henderson, *Ernest Vandiver: Governor of Georgia*. Athens, GA: The University of Georgia Press, 2000. pp. 143–144.

[75] Harold Paulk Henderson, *Ernest Vandiver: Governor of Georgia*. Athens, GA: The University of Georgia Press, 2000. p. 144.

[76] Harold Paulk Henderson, *Ernest Vandiver: Governor of Georgia*. Athens, GA: The University of Georgia Press, 2000. p. 144.

[77] Harold Paulk Henderson, *Ernest Vandiver: Governor of Georgia*. Athens, GA: The University of Georgia Press, 2000. p. 154.

[78] Harold Paulk Henderson, *Ernest Vandiver: Governor of Georgia*. Athens, GA: The University of Georgia Press, 2000. pp. 154–155.

Carl E. Sanders (1963–1967)

Carl Sanders was elected to the Georgia House of Representatives in 1954, to the state Senate in 1956 and was elected governor in 1962. As governor, he was a fiscal conservative who promoted education, pursued industrial development and initiated the modernization of state government. His biographer, James F. Cook, notes that in his inaugural address of 1963 Sanders stated, "Change in government can be dangerous," but "change to achieve efficiency, economy and better government is wise and justified."[79] Governor Sanders' spending and taxing proposals were focused on state support for education. The first Sanders budget recommendation to the General Assembly in 1963 allocated 56% of the total budget to education. His 1964 legislative program proposed several tax increases to raise additional revenue for education, a three cents tax on cigarettes, a 50 cents per gallon tax increase on spirits, elimination of the vendors' commission on collection of the retail sales tax, a 1% increase in the corporate income tax, and an increase in the tax on beer of 12 cents a case. Cook notes that "The legislature is always reluctant to increase taxes, but Sanders convinced the members that additional revenue was essential. His proposals were adopted with only minor changes."[80] His proposed spending for fiscal years 1966 and 1967 also focused heavily on education.[81] During his 4 years, he increased public school teacher salaries and university system faculty salaries, and provided funding for public school building and university system construction.

Governor Sanders established the Governor's Commission for Efficiency and Improvement in Government known as the Bowdoin Commission after its chairman William R. Bowdoin, reflecting his interest in the modernization of Georgia government. The state merit system, the Department Agriculture, the Department of Education, the Highway Department and the prison and mental health systems were the foci of the Commission's efforts to improve the operations of state government.[82]

Although Sanders increased the sin taxes on alcoholic beverages and cigarettes, true to his fiscal conservatism he did not propose increases in the high yield individual income or sales taxes. He did not need to; the economy was good to him during his administration. Between 1963 and 1966, state revenue collections increased by 38.6%, at an average annual rate of 11.5%.[83] Sanders left office at the

---

[79] James F. Cook, *Carl Sanders: Spokesman of the New South*. Macon, GA: Mercer University Press, 1993. p. 124.

[80] James F. Cook, *Carl Sanders: Spokesman of the New South*. Macon, GA: Mercer University Press, 1993. p. 169.

[81] James F. Cook, *Carl Sanders: Spokesman of the New South*. Macon, GA: Mercer University Press, 1993. p. 220.

[82] James F. Cook, "Carl Sanders and the Politics of the Future," in Harold P. Henderson and Gary L. Roberts, eds. *Georgia Governors in an Age of Change: From Ellis Arnall to George Busbee*. Athens, GA: The University of Georgia Press, 1988. pp. 174–176.

[83] From $422,532,658 in FY 1963 to $585,583,839 in FY 1966. *Georgia Department of Revenue, 2000 Statistical Report*. p. 6.

end of 1966 with a surplus in the state treasury. Cook quotes Governor Sanders as attributing it to "sound fiscal responsibility, economy and efficiency in government."[84]

Regarding his role as governor in the state budgetary process, Carl Sanders in a 1988 reflection wrote:[85]

> Naturally, I am inclined to view that state government operates much more effectively with a strong governor system, rather than with a system in which the legislature achieves something close to operational responsibility through the budget process and various overview committees. States in the South which have historically been recognized as having less aggressive, less progressive state governments, such as Mississippi and South Carolina, have for decades had a system in which the legislature essentially determines the budget and the governor is only a participant in that process rather than the clear leader of the process.
>
> I fully understand the concept of separation of powers and the concept of checks and balances. But the kind (sic) of matters that state governments have to address on a year-to-year basis are the kinds of practical things that there will always be strong differences of opinions about exactly how to accomplish. Therefore, there is the danger that rather than aggressive leadership we will get constant compromise on how to administer education, how to operate the prison system, how to run the health care system, and other practical aspects of state government.
>
> I am very proud of the overall record of my administration, and I have complete admiration for the people who served in the General Assembly during those years. But there is no doubt in my mind that if it had not been possible for my administration to be operated under what is normally referred to as a "strong governor system," then my agenda would have been less than half as long and our accomplishments would have been cut in half.

Governor Sanders served during a unique window of opportunity between 1963 and 1967. The Budget Act of 1962[86] that enhanced the powers of the governor was fully operational, but the 1966 election that delayed selection of the governor and enabled the legislature to choose its own leaders, had not yet occurred. Biographer Cook writes, "Sander was the last governor to totally dominate the General Assembly. He determined the budget, set the legislative agenda, picked the speaker of the House and chose committee chairmen."[87]

---

[84] James F. Cook, *Carl Sanders: Spokesman of the New South*. Macon, GA: Mercer University Press, 1993. p. 261.

[85] Carl E. Sanders, "A Time for Progress," in Harold P. Henderson and Gary L. Roberts, eds. *Georgia Governors in an Age of Change: From Ellis Arnall to George Busbee*. Athens, GA: The University of Georgia Press, 1988. pp. 189–190.

[86] Georgia Laws, 1962: 17–37. Approved February 12, 1962.

[87] James F. Cook, "Carl Sanders and the Politics of the Future," in Harold P. Henderson and Gary L. Roberts, eds. *Georgia Governors in an Age of Change: From Ellis Arnall to George Busbee*. Athens, GA: The University of Georgia Press, 1988. p. 184.

Lester Maddox (1967–1971)

Lester Maddox was elected governor in 1966. He ran unsuccessfully for mayor of Atlanta twice, in 1957 against incumbent William B. Hartsfield and in 1961 against Ivan Allen, Jr. He ran unsuccessfully for lieutenant governor against Peter Zack Geer in 1962. Maddox was a segregationist and demagogue. Following the 1964 Civil Rights Act, Maddox's Pickrick restaurant was tested. After confrontations with civil rights activists and court orders regarding his refusal of service, Maddox closed the Pickrick.[88]

Maddox won the 1966 Democratic primary, coming second to Ellis Arnall in the voting (Jimmy Carter came third) but because neither candidate received a majority there was a primary run-off which Maddox won. He came second to Republican Howard "Bo" Callaway in the general election but because neither candidate received a majority of the vote (Ellis Arnall received write-in votes) the election was decided by the Georgia General Assembly, which elected Maddox governor in January 1967. The U.S. Supreme Court in December 1966 overturned a three-judge federal court decision and upheld the Georgia Constitution provision that provided for election of a governor by a vote of the General Assembly in the event that none of the candidates received a majority of the popular votes.[89] Justice Hugo Black for the majority held there was nothing in the U.S. Constitution prohibiting the process defined in the Georgia Constitution. The Georgia Supreme Court also upheld the Georgia Constitution provision. In his inaugural address, Governor Maddox asked the General Assembly to propose a constitutional amendment to be presented to the voters in the 1968 general election requiring a run-off election for governor between the top two candidates in the event no candidate received a majority in the general election.

In addition to pledging "honesty and morality" in government, "prudent expenditure of all public funds," and the expectation that every state employee will "give his or her best at all times," Governor Maddox, consistent with his fiscal conservative principles, pledged "efficiency, sound economy and good business practices" in all state activities. Because there was not a governor-elect until the day before Maddox took office, Governor Carl Sanders had prepared the biennial budget. It was thought to be somewhat inflated with requests Sanders would not have to fund.[90] Maddox's first budget reduced the total budget and redirected spending toward his priorities, with increases for education, law enforcement, welfare and corrections.[91] In his Budget Message on January 13, 1967, Governor Maddox stated:

---

[88] Bob Short, *Everything is Pickrick: The Life of Lester Maddox*. Macon, GA: Mercer University Press, 1999. p. 64.
[89] *Fortson v. Morris*, 385 U.S. 231 (1966), reversed 262 F. Supp. 93 (1966).
[90] Bob Short, *Everything is Pickrick: The Life of Lester Maddox*. Macon, GA: Mercer University Press, 1999. p. 103.
[91] Bob Short, *Everything is Pickrick: The Life of Lester Maddox*. Macon, GA: Mercer University Press, 1999. p. 104.

> For four years now, the State of Georgia has had in operation a modern budget system. It has worked well. The success in administration of several budgets serves as proof that Georgia's new budget law are (sic) fulfilling a need long felt in this state. ... We are fortunate, indeed, that our new budget machinery assures a smooth transition from the old administration to the new. This allows a continuity of sound fiscal policy as Georgia approaches the challenges of the future.[92]

He then said that the revenue estimates for the remainder of fiscal year 1967 and for fiscal years 1968 and 1969, made by the Sanders administration in the fall of 1966, were too optimistic in view of current national and state economic conditions, and encouraged the General Assembly to enact appropriations that were not beyond reasonable revenue expectations, but not too little which would result in the curtailment of needed state services.[93]

Governor Maddox's spending priorities as identified in his inaugural address were for improvements in public and higher education, a salary increase for public elementary and secondary education teachers as well as university system academic and non-academic personnel, funding for state participation in the then-new Medicaid program, improvement in mental health facilities, modernization of state prisons, state highway construction, improvement and maintenance, and assistance to local governments. He stated that these spending increases could be financed without the need for new taxes, based upon revenue growth and attention to efficiency in the administration of state government. According to Maddox biographer, Bob Short, his inaugural address and first budget message generally surprised his critics and pleased his supporters.[94] It was a mix of progressive policies and conservative financial management. Maddox also sought to curtail the practice of spending "surplus" funds, that is revenue collected in excess of estimates, on new initiatives that had recurring costs that then strained future budgets. He advocated fiscal restraint by focusing "surplus" spending on one-time projects that had fewer recurring costs.[95]

Maddox also reformed the Department of Industry and Trade and revitalized it for the purpose of attracting financially viable industry and commerce into the state.[96] In his 1969 State of the State, Maddox characterized himself, "As one who prides himself upon being a fiscal conservative and a hardheaded businessman ..."

Lester Maddox was elected lieutenant governor in 1970, the year in which Jimmy Carter was elected governor. Maddox and Carter feuded throughout 1971–75.[97]

---

[92] Lester Maddox, State of the State and Budget Message, January 13, 1967.

[93] Bob Short, *Everything is Pickrick: The Life of Lester Maddox*. Macon, GA: Mercer University Press, 1999. pp. 214–215.

[94] Bob Short, *Everything is Pickrick: The Life of Lester Maddox*. Macon, GA: Mercer University Press, 1999. pp. 102–104.

[95] Lester Maddox, State of the State Address, January 14, 1969.

[96] Bob Short, *Everything is Pickrick: The Life of Lester Maddox*. Macon, GA: Mercer University Press, 1999. pp. 118–119.

[97] Bob Short, *Everything is Pickrick: The Life of Lester Maddox*. Macon, GA: Mercer University Press, 1999. pp. 125–137.

Maddox again ran for governor in 1974 against George Busbee and Bert Lance. He reminded voters of his accomplishments as governor in prison reform, pardon and parole reform, corruption control and competitive bidding practices. Maddox came first in the popular voting and Busbee came second, but because neither candidate received a majority, a run-off was held, which Busbee won. Busbee reminded voters of the Maddox-Carter feud and criticized Maddox's inattention to his job as lieutenant governor. Maddox was the American Independent Party candidate for President of the United States in 1976, running against Jimmy Carter. He entered the race after George Wallace withdrew due to his health condition.[98] Maddox campaigned against the federal government, specifically against the Great Society and racial integration. Maddox also ran for governor in 1990 against Zell Miller, Andrew Young, Lauren McDonald and Roy Barnes. He came fifth.

Jimmy Carter (1971–1975)

Jimmy Carter was elected governor in 1970, defeating former governor Carl Sanders in the Democratic primary and easily defeating the Republican candidate. He was a candidate for governor in 1966, coming third in the Democratic primary behind former governor Ellis Arnall and the eventual winner Lester Maddox. He was elected to the Georgia Senate in 1962 and served two terms in that body.

The signature initiatives of the Carter administration were government reorganization and zero-base budgeting. Carter biographer Gary Fink described his government reorganization plan as the first comprehensive government reorganization in Georgia since Richard Russell's administration in the early 1930s. He also described it as the "most significant accomplishment of his governorship."[99] Governor Carter's reorganization plan restructured state government, 65 budgeted departments were reduced to 22 departments, and numerous unbudgeted commissions, agencies and boards were eliminated, with their functions being transferred to one of the 22 departments.[100]

Political Scientist Betty Glad reports that Governor Carter announced zero-base budgeting in his 1972 State of the State address and viewed it as part of his reorganization initiative. She writes that in the first budget cycle there were 1100 decision packages, an unwieldy number; that beyond the first budget cycle it began to focus mostly on funding changes, that is the increments; that agency heads gamed the ranking process; that the "cut-off line" shifting upward or downward to

---

[98] Bob Short, *Everything is Pickrick: The Life of Lester Maddox*. Macon, GA: Mercer University Press, 1999. p. 178.

[99] Gary M. Fink, "Jimmy Carter and the Politics of Transition," in Harold P. Henderson and Gary L. Roberts, eds., *Georgia Governors in an Age of Change*. Athens, GA; The University of Georgia Press, 1988. p. 238.

[100] Bob Short, *Everything is Pickrick: The Life of Lester Maddox*. Macon, GA: Mercer University Press, 1999. p. 131.

accommodate less or more packages did not work; that it increased administrative costs, that is time, effort and paper; and that there was no indication that it led to a reallocation of resources. She concludes that it was an attractive management concept promising rationality and efficiency, but that it did not work in practice. However, she notes that Carter did get some political benefit for seeming to rationalize the state's administrative process.[101] On this topic, Gary M. Fink wrote, "While in reality zero-base budgeting was something of a gimmick that was never fully implemented, it did lead to periodic reexamination of budget priorities."[102] Jimmy Carter said the principle of zero-base budgeting was, "… each time a budgeting process came up, to make sure that we not only considered new additions to the budget but also assessed the need for expenditures that had been approved in previous years."[103] Thomas P. Lauth wrote in 1978, "Evidence obtained through interviews with Georgia budget officials indicates that zero-base budgeting procedures have had only a marginal impact on the traditional practices of budget preparation. However, despite the persistence of incremental budgeting practices, ZBB has been able to function as a management approach to budgeting which requires more extensive program information and greater justification for funding requests."[104] A more extensive description of zero-base budgeting is provided in Chapter 7.

Gary Fink described Carter as a fiscal conservative, a social liberal and a racial moderate.[105] Responding to a question about his 1970 gubernatorial campaign and the Atlanta newspapers, Carter said, "I was a South Georgian and I was looked upon as a fiscal conservative, and the Atlanta newspapers quite erroneously, because they didn't know anything about me or my background here in Plains, decided that I was also a racial conservative."[106]

Numan Bartley summarized Carter's governorship in the following way:

> Carter's tenure as governor confirmed the triumph of a[n] ideology that stressed economic expansion, businesslike administration, and free market individualism. His administration endeavored to replace political "pork barrel" bargaining with centralized and expert decision making, to promote continued industrial expansion, and to find a new social stability

---

[101] Betty Glad, *Jimmy Carter: in Search of the Great White House*. New York: W.W. Norton & Company, 1980. pp. 197–80

[102] Gary M. Fink, "Jimmy Carter and the Politics of Transition," in Harold P. Henderson and Gary L. Roberts, eds., *Georgia Governors in an Age of Change*. Athens, GA; The University of Georgia Press, 1988. p. 241.

[103] Gary L. Roberts, "Jimmy Carter: Years of Challenge, Years of Change," in Harold P. Henderson and Gary L. Roberts, eds., *Georgia Governors in an Age of Change*. Athens, GA; The University of Georgia Press, 1988. p. 251.

[104] Thomas P. Lauth, "Zero-Base Budgeting in Georgia State Government: Myth and Reality," *Public Administration Review*, Vol. 38 (September/October 1978). pp. 420–430 at p. 420.

[105] Gary M. Fink, "Jimmy Carter and the Politics of Transition," in Harold P. Henderson and Gary L. Roberts, eds., *Georgia Governors in an Age of Change*. Athens, GA; The University of Georgia Press, 1988. p. 244

[106] Gary L. Roberts, "Jimmy Carter: Years of Challenge, Years of Change," in Harold P. Henderson and Gary L. Roberts, eds., *Georgia Governors in an Age of Change*. Athens, GA; The University of Georgia Press, 1988. p. 253.

in the wake of the civil rights movement. Carter was unusually conservative on fiscal issues, often innovative on other matters, and virtually always attentive to administrative procedure. Reorganization and other governmental reforms generally made state decision making more centralized and efficient.[107]

Writing about Carter's cooperative relationship with the Georgia General Assembly, Betty Glad notes that he used the governor's "emergency fund" ($2 million) to make grants to his friends in the legislature to obtain their support on legislative matters.[108] Writing about Carter's conflictive relationship, Glad notes that in the 1974 session of the General Assembly, that body line-itemized the FY 1975 appropriations bill in retaliation for the state Department of Human Resources moving blocks of funds for disputed and controversial policy purposes. Carter used the line-item veto.[109] Thomas P. Lauth and Catherine C. Reese write, "The new line-item budget was an attempt to protect legislative intent. Governor Carter had opposed this move on the part of the legislature as 'an encroachment into executive prerogatives,' at one time threatening a lawsuit to prevent the action and later threatening to veto the entire appropriations act. In the end, he vetoed a combined total of 18 items in the FY 1974 Amended General Appropriations Act and FY 1975 General Appropriations Act." Continuing they write, "The General Assembly's effort to restructure the appropriations bill in order to assert legislative intent was met by Governor Carter's resurrection of the line-item veto to protect executive prerogative and reduce pork barrel spending."[110]

George D. Busbee (1975–1983)

George Busbee was elected governor in 1974 and served from 1975 to 1983. He was the first governor to serve two consecutive 4-year terms. A 1976 constitutional amendment made this possible.[111] Before being elected governor, he served 18 years in the General Assembly, and was the Democratic majority leader for 8 years. Although Busbee was a long-serving and very experienced legislator, executive-legislative conflict over the budget was part of his first administration.

---

[107] Numan V. Bartley, *The Creation of Modern Georgia*. Second Edition. Athens, GA: The University of Georgia Press, 1990. p. 231.

[108] Betty Glad, *Jimmy Carter: in Search of the Great White House*. New York: W.W. Norton & Company, 1980. pp. 192–93.

[109] Betty Glad, *Jimmy Carter: in Search of the Great White House*. New York: W.W. Norton & Company, 1980. p. 195.

[110] Thomas P. Lauth and Catherine C. Reese, "The Line-Item Veto in Georgia: Fiscal Restraint or Inter-Branch Politics?" *Public Budgeting & Finance*, Vol. 26, No. 2 (Summer 2006). pp. 1–19 at pp.12–13.

[111] On November 2, 1976, Georgia voters approved gubernatorial succession to a 4-year term, by a vote of 772,441 (64.5%), Yes and 425,208 (35.5%), No. "Amendment Votes Certified," *Atlanta Constitution*, November 13, 1976: 4-A.

His highest policy priority was education, specifically kindergarten. His second priority was achieving economic growth through attracting international business to Georgia. Other priorities were such infrastructure programs as completion of the interstate highway program in Georgia and an expansion of Georgia port facilities.[112] During his 8 years in office, Busbee faced a national recession and then high rates of inflation.

In June 1975, faced with declining state revenues Busbee called a special session of the General Assembly. In order to reduce what he perceived to be an impending budget deficit, he proposed to eliminate a tax relief bill which the House of Representatives leadership considered its best accomplishment in the 1975 regular session of the General Assembly. He also proposed deferring pay raises for teachers and state employee until January 1, 1976, and deferring funding for the kindergarten program passed in the 1975 session until 1976. A subsequent court decision required the state to pay University System of Georgia (USG) faculty retroactively because they had signed contracts.[113] The court decision did not require retroactive pay to primary and secondary school teachers.

Governor Busbee also encountered financial problems with the state's Medicaid program. According to Busbee, "When I took office, Medicaid was an administrative nightmare, with claims being paid on an average of 4 months after being filed. Providers were overpaid, underpaid, paid for the same service more than once, and paid for services that were not rendered."[114] In order to address these fiscal problems, Busbee recommended and the General Assembly in 1977 established a Department of Medical Assistance as a single state agency to administer the Medicaid program,[115] separating that program from the comprehensive Department of Human Resources and requiring the Medicaid program to become financially self-sustaining rather than being able to rely upon a larger parent department to financially sustain it.

In the 1979 session of the General Assembly, the Georgia Senate passed an appropriations bill that was $25 million higher than the version the House of Representatives had passed, and perhaps more importantly, higher than the governor's revenue estimate. However, an opinion by the state Attorney General held that the Senate could not raise the revenue estimate; setting the revenue estimate was an executive power, not a legislative power. Because the state's balanced budget requirement limits appropriations to the amount of the governor's revenue estimate, the House-Senate Conference Committee faced the unenviable task of not only

---

[112] George D. Busbee, "Building a New Economic Order," in Harold P. Henderson and Gary L. Roberts, eds., *Georgia Governors in an Age of Change*. Athens, GA: The University of Georgia Press, 1988. pp. 279–285.

[113] *Busbee et al. v. Georgia Conference, American Association of University Professors* et al., 235 Ga. 752 (1975). 221 S.E.2d 437.

[114] George D. Busbee, "Building a New Economic Order," in Harold P. Henderson and Gary L. Roberts, eds., *Georgia Governors in an Age of Change*. Athens, GA: The University of Georgia Press, 1988. p. 282.

[115] Georgia Laws, 1977: 384–396. HB 502 was approved March 1, 1977.

reaching compromises on individual items that differed in the House and Senate versions of the appropriations bill, but also finding a way to reduce the Senate version by $25 million.[116]

George Busbee was a fiscal conservative, believing in the balanced budget and pledging in both of his election campaigns not to raise taxes. In a year-end interview with the *Atlanta Constitution* in 1978 he is quoted as saying, "... our people want some assurances that the growth of government is going to be held in check and that stopping government waste and inefficiency is a real priority and not rhetoric." "Our people are working in greater numbers than ever before and are making more money than ever before, but they've had it with high taxes, inflation and runaway government spending." "We have done our part on the state level by holding the line on taxes at a time when 36 states responded to a recession by raising taxes."[117]

Joe Frank Harris (1983–1991)

Joe Frank Harris was elected governor in 1982, after serving 18 years in the Georgia House of Representatives, including 8 years as Chair of the House Appropriations Committee. The top two priorities of Governor Harris's administration were education and economic development. He believed that quality education produced a well-prepared work force which in turn was essential for economic development. He emphasized the importance of education in attracting outside investors to Georgia.[118] His main achievement in education was the Quality Basic Education Act in 1985.[119] In his biography, Governor Harris wrote:[120]

> I have a basic philosophy in fiscal management, something I learned while growing up and working to make a living: You can't borrow yourself out of debt, and you can't spend money you don't have. A business or a government can't do this either. My philosophy is that if you were not able to buy something, then you work until you get yourself into a position where you can afford it. You simply do without in the interval. I think we're seeing that business and government organizations are successful because someone is taking a lead in that kind of management.

---

[116] Beau Cutts, "Tax Relief Funds May be Released," *Atlanta Constitution*, March 23, 1979: 1-A and 31-A.

[117] David Morrison, "Governor: 'Can't Rest on Laurels'," *Atlanta Constitution*, January 1, 1979: 1 and 21.

[118] Joe Frank Harris, "Visions for a Better Georgia," in Harold P. Henderson and Gary L. Roberts, eds., *Georgia Governors in an Age of Change: From Ellis Arnall to George Busbee*. Athens, GA: The University of Georgia Press, 1988. p. 300.

[119] Debbie Newby, "Harris Signs Education Bill: Vows to Pursue Quality," *Atlanta Journal*, April 16, 1985: B1.

[120] Joe Frank Harris, *Joe Frank Harris, Personal Reflections on a Public Life*. Macon, Georgia: Mercer University Press, 1998. p. 121.

After I got elected to the General Assembly and got familiar with the state budgetary process, I realized more than ever that the funds you borrow are, in a sense, spending today for our children and grandchildren to repay tomorrow. When the government issues bonds for the funds that they are borrowing, the interest paid on that money sometimes actually costs more than the principal you are spending.

Another of our financial rules was not to spend money on projects that would not remain. For example, if you borrowed money for twenty years, the capital outlay or asset should still be there twenty years later or you should have some equity or value remaining.

Another principal that I tried to operate with was anytime you could reduce your debt and utilize additional or extra revenue to buy back or pay-off old bonds, there would be an additional savings beyond being fiscally responsible.

We've also fully replenished our revenue shortfall reserve— the state's rainy-day fund. The shortfall reserve is a vital element in preparing for the future of Georgia.

Clearly, Joe Frank Harris was a fiscal conservative. His approach to incurring debt stands in contrast with the more aggressive use of debt by his successor, Governor Zell Miller.

Zell B. Miller (1991–1999)

Zell B. Miller was elected governor in 1990, defeating Republican state senator Johnny Isakson, and served from 1991 through 1998. Prior to becoming governor, Miller was elected to the Georgia Senate in 1960 where he served two terms. He served as executive secretary for Governor Lester Maddox and later served for 2 years as a member of the State Board of Pardons and Parole. In 1974 he was elected Lieutenant Governor, a position he held for 16 years; reelected state-wide three times. In 1980 he lost in the Democratic U.S. Senate primary to incumbent Senator Herman Talmadge.

Zell Miller was a fiscal conservative, but is perhaps better described as a "progressive-conservative." In 2003, after completing his two terms as governor (1991–1999), he wrote:

> I know from personal experience that you can be a Democrat and have a solid Democratic agenda while cutting taxes and holding the line on spending. When I was governor of Georgia, we cut taxes by almost a billion dollars, reduced spending, and cut personnel by 5,000 positions. That was why I was able to raise the salaries of university professors and public-school teachers to the highest in the South and get a lottery passed by the voters in my Bible Belt state. Then we provided pre-kindergarten education for every four-year old in the state; technical training for every high school graduate; and the HOPE Scholarship, which gives every Georgia student who has a B average, and maintains it, a tuition-free college education— every one! But if people in my state hadn't trusted the government with their money— if we hadn't simultaneously cut taxes and controlled spending— these progressive education measures would have been taken apart, labeled as 'big spending' by a Democrat governor.[121]

---

[121] Zell Miller, *A National Party No More: The Conscience of a Conservative Democrat*. Atlanta, GA: Stroud & Hall Publishers, 2003. pp. 16–17.

As anticipated, when I took office in January 1991, Georgia and the nation were in a recession. State revenues had slipped below the level of appropriations, and the reserves were completely empty. Even so, I refused to raise taxes to bring the budget into balance.[122]

When I finally completed all the procedures for my first budget, I ended up cutting state expenditures by a total of $944 million, raising hunting and fishing and driver's license fees for the first time in decades, and abolishing about 5,000 state jobs over a period of three years. But it was this disciplined approach to state finances that enabled the Miller Administration to achieve its goals while simultaneously reducing taxes by $833 million through three tax cuts— two income tax cuts and, at last, the removal of the state sales tax from groceries.[123]

Beginning with Governor Miller, the *Governor's Budget Report* to the General Assembly has included a transmittal letter that highlights the governor's spending priorities and occasionally also underscores his approach to financial management. As can be seen in excerpts from the FY 1999 *Governor's Budget Report,* Governor Miller highlighted sound financial and business practices and tax reductions.[124]

In presenting to you the eighth and last budget of my Administration I am continuing to follow the same sound financial and business practices that I began with in 1990.

One of the records of which I am most proud is the one involving money we did not spend, deciding to return it to our citizens in the form of tax reductions.

During Governor Miller's administration, personal and dependent exemptions on the state income tax were increased, and the state's 3% sales tax on groceries was eliminated. In order to achieve his goals of increased funding for education, a merit-based scholarship program and a pre-kindergarten program, he instituted a lottery for new funding. His budget process reform known as Budget Redirection (discussed in Chapter 7) facilitated 6% pay raises for teachers for four straight years and funding for expansion of state prison facilities.

Roy E. Barnes (1999–2003)

Roy E. Barnes was elected governor in 1998 and served from 1999 through 2002. Prior to becoming governor, he was elected in 1974 to the Georgia Senate where he served for 16 years. Following an unsuccessful run for governor in 1990 against Zell Miller, he was elected to the Georgia House of Representatives where he served from 1992 to1998. Educational reform was one of Governor Barnes top priorities. Aimed at raising academic standards, the reform sought to reduce pupil-teacher ratios, improve student performance, improve teacher training and development and

---

[122] Zell Miller, *A National Party No More: The Conscience of a Conservative Democrat.* Atlanta, GA: Stroud & Hall Publishers, 2003. p. 44.

[123] Zell Miller, *A National Party No More: The Conscience of a Conservative Democrat.* Atlanta, GA: Stroud & Hall Publishers, 2003. pp. 47–48.

[124] *Governor's Budget Report*, Fiscal Year 1999.

achieve accountability based upon criterion referenced testing. Although his education reform proposals were well intentioned, he encountered opposition from teachers which contributed to his defeat in 2002 after one term in office. His successful effort to remove the Confederate battle flag from the Georgia state flag also contributed to his defeat.[125]

Governor Barnes initiated a grant plan for local property tax relief, Homeowners Tax Relief Grant,[126] which if implemented over an 8-year period would have increased the state homestead exemption from $2,000 to a projected $20,000.

Like a couple of his predecessors, Governor Barnes had to deal with the effects of a national recession. Governor Barnes used state budget reductions in FY 2002 and FY 2003 to ensure fund availability for his FY 2003 proposals for teacher salary increases and continued state funding of local government property tax cuts, while keeping the state budget in balance.[127]

In the *Governor's Budget Report* for all 4 years, FY 2000, FY 2001, FY 2002 and FY 2003, Governor Barnes characterizes his revenue estimate each year as "conservative."[128]

Sonny Perdue (2003–2011)

George E. "Sonny" Perdue was elected governor in 2002 and served from 2003 through 2010. Prior to becoming governor, he was elected in 1990 to the Georgia Senate where he served for 11 years, 8 years as a Democrat before changing parties and serving three more years as a Republican. He was Democratic majority leader, 1995–96, and president pro tempore, 1997–98. In 2002 he defeated incumbent Democrat Governor Roy Barnes and in 2006 he was reelected defeating Democratic Lieutenant Governor Mark Taylor. The following excerpts from Governor Perdue's budget reports to the General Assembly clearly demonstrate his fiscally conservative revenue, spending and saving policies.

Introduction to *Governor's Budget Report, FY 2004:*

> As he came into office in January 2003 the state was facing declining revenues. Governor Perdue ordered reduced spending by state agencies, used a portion of the state's rainy day fund and recommended a modest tax increase on tobacco products. He concluded his budget message to the General Assembly, "… we are stewards elected by the people, not mere appropriators tasked with spending other people's money."[129]

---

[125] James C. Cobb, *The South and America Since World War II*. New York: Oxford University Press, 2011. p. 267.

[126] Georgia Laws, 1999: 273–276. HB 553 was approved April 15, 1999.

[127] Thomas P. Lauth, "Budgeting During a Recession Phase of the Business Cycle: The Georgia Experience," *Public Budgeting & Finance*, Vol. 23 (Summer 2003): 26–38.

[128] *Governor's Budget Report*, Fiscal Year 2000, Fiscal Year 2001, Fiscal Year 2002 and Fiscal Year 2003.

[129] *Governor's Budget Report*, Fiscal Year 2004.

Introduction to *Governor's Budget Report, FY 2005:*

> We have come through a year of an economic downturn across America that has impacted Georgia and reduced our state revenues. In the face of these conditions we are managing the state with strong conservative fiscal policy and restraint on our spending. I am glad to report that we are one of only seven states that has maintained a Triple "A" bonding rating by all three major bond rating companies. This has been accomplished by our responsible cutting of expenditures in FY 2004 and by requiring our state agencies to reduce their FY 2005 budget requests by a significant 7.5%.[130]

Introduction to *Governor's Budget Report, FY 2007:*

> By continuing with a conservative revenue forecast and spending policy, I expect to continue to build our reserves in the future.[131]

Introduction to *Governor's Budget Report, FY 2008:*

> Government has a responsibility to control the public purse as carefully as any family would control their household budget.[132]

Introduction to *Governor's Budget Report, FY 2009:*

> My revenue estimates for the Amended FY 2008 and FY 2009 budgets are based on prudent revenue projections. My Amended FY 2008 and FY 2009 budgets fund initiatives that give Georgians the opportunity to fulfill their potential, while illustrating prudence and discipline through limited growth in state government.[133]

Introduction to *Governor's Budget Report, FY 2010:*

> The economic challenges facing this state and the nation have a real impact on state resources. Just as Georgia's families have seen the effects of the economy on their budgets, Georgia state government must face the challenge of doing more with less as well.
>
> Throughout my administration, my budget recommendations have been based on a conservative fiscal policy. The result is a leaner state government that lives within its means ...
>
> At the start of my first term in 2003, I entered office under difficult financial conditions. That experience reinforced my belief that just as a family needs to save for a rainy day, so does the state. Putting a little aside in good times means that you have cushion to get you through the bumps that will inevitably come ahead. I worked with the General Assembly to rebuild our Revenue Shortfall Reserve... We used some of the reserve to balance the FY 20008 budget at year's end, and I am recommending a judicious use of a portion of the reserve account to help us balance the FY 2009 and FY 2010 budgets.
>
> As economic conditions began to weaken early in 2008, I began a series of proactive steps to deal with the expected weakness in state revenue by revising revenue projections downward ... instructing agencies to curtail discretionary spending, and withholding state funds by 6% to state agencies.
>
> To maintain a strong infrastructure in education, transportation, economic development and other state services, my bond package is targeted to those areas that will endure the long-term prosperity of this state. It takes advantage of our AAA bond rating and the lower constructions costs we are seeing because of the national recession.[134]

---

[130] *Governor's Budget Report*, Fiscal Year 2005.
[131] *Governor's Budget Report*, Fiscal Year 2007.
[132] *Governor's Budget Report*, Fiscal Year 2008.
[133] *Governor's Budget Report*, Fiscal Year 2009.
[134] *Governor's Budget Report*, Fiscal Year 2010.

Introduction to *Governor's Budget Report, FY 2011:*

> Georgia has a long history of prudent and conservative fiscal management. Our AAA bond rating has been protected allowing us to fund capital projects in such areas as education, transportation and economic development at significant budget savings. Our policies of spending restraint during healthy economic times have now become our best asset. The Revenue Shortfall Reserve, built ... with the help of the General Assembly before the current recession, has been instrumental in protecting critical state services for the last two years. Throughout this economic decline we continue to be vigilant, adjusting our spending as the realities of the recession affect our tax revenues.[135]

Nathan Deal (2011–2019)

Nathan Deal was elected governor in 2010, defeating former Secretary of State Karen Handel in the Republican primary and former Governor Roy Barnes in the general election. Before becoming governor, he was elected in 1980 to the Georgia Senate as a Democrat and in 1990 was elected president pro tempore of the Senate. He was elected to the U.S. House of Representatives as a Democrat in 1992, but switched to the Republican Party in 1995, and continued to serve in the House of Representatives until 2010. Among Deal's gubernatorial priorities was criminal justice reform, which focused on accountability courts intended to address the underlying cause of criminal activity (such as drug abuse) rather than just punishing behavior. The success of this program is credited with fewer imprisonments of lower risk offenders, thereby reducing the need for state spending on prison facilities.

Selected excerpts from Governor Deal's annual budget message to the General Assembly record his fiscally conservative revenue, spending and saving policies.

Introduction to *Governor's Budget Report, FY 2012:*

> Economic conditions have stabilized over the last year and continued improvement is expected in calendar 2011. However, revenue growth will continue to be modest compared to that of prior economic recovery periods. My budget recommendations are based upon a prudent and conservative analysis of current conditions. While we hope for a stronger uptick in the economy, it cannot be assured. Also the last two years of budget shortfalls have left our reserves very low. Unlike the federal government, Georgia must have a budget that balances expenses and revenues. If revenues decline, our only recourse would be a further cut in budgets.[136]

Introduction to *Governor's Budget Report, FY 2013:*

> After several difficult years for both Georgia and its citizens, we are now seeing slow but steady progress in the state's economic and fiscal condition, and we are guardedly optimistic. Our long history of conservative fiscal management has served us well. Georgia remains

---

[135] *Governor's Budget Report*, Fiscal Year 2011.
[136] *Governor's Budget Report*, Fiscal Year 2012.

one of only eight states with a Triple-A bond rating by all three rating agencies. We have grown our rainy day fund ... and for the past two years, I have balanced budgets without any new tax increases.[137]

Introduction to *Governor's Budget Report, FY 2014:*

Our state continues to make steady progress as we emerge from the economic difficulties of the last several fiscal years. Solid fiscal stewardship and steady economic growth allowed us to finish Fiscal Year 2012 in a strong position, growing the rainy day fund for the third straight year ... and maintaining the prestigious triple-A bond rating with all three rating agencies. Though we have faced unprecedented economic challenges in recent years, we have met these challenges through sound, conservative fiscal management, by living within our means and maintaining a balanced budget that prioritizes the most critical needs of Georgia's citizens and makes strategic investments in our state's future.[138]

Introduction to *Governor's Budget Report, FY 2015:*

Georgia ended Fiscal Year 2013 in a strong fiscal position. Revenue growth exceeded projections resulting in the addition of more than $339 million to the rainy day fund and bringing its balance to more than $717 million, a five-fold increase (518%) over the last three years. Our rapid rebuilding of the Revenue Shortfall Reserve is the result of conservative fiscal management and living within our means during lean economic years. A robust rainy day fund is an important tool in maintaining our triple-A bond rating with all three rating agencies. Both a healthy reserve and highest quality bond rating are essential in building a business climate that shows Georgia is a reliable and economically strong state in which to invest.[139]

Introduction to *Governor's Budget Report, FY 2017:*

... our prudent budget practices have allowed us to continue building our Rainy Day Fund to its current level of over $1.4 billion. While this number may seem large, we dipped into these reserves for roughly the same amount during the last recession, yet population and demand have increased since then. Insistence on a healthy reserve helps Georgia maintain its AAA bond rating from all three credit-rating agencies—Moody's, S&P and Fitch. Georgia is one of only nine states that has met that standard.[140]

Introduction to *Governor's Budget Report, FY 2018:*

Our budget instructions to agencies this year again asked them to keep their budget requests to Georgia's Office of Planning and Budget equal to the appropriations they received last year, with some exceptions for workload increases. We must be fully ready to absorb whatever the fickle winds of economics blow our way. Through prudent budgeting practices, we have grown our Rainy Day Fund to over $2 billion, and I want to commend the General Assembly for its support in this matter. Reserves are often easy targets in years of prosperity, but they are desirable stores of grain during years of proverbial famine. Furthermore, credit rating agencies have cited our healthy reserve levels as a key reason for Georgia retaining its coveted AAA rating, which saves millions in taxpayer dollars.[141]

---

[137] *Governor's Budget Report*, Fiscal Year 2013.
[138] *Governor's Budget Report*, Fiscal Year 2014.
[139] *Governor's Budget Report*, Fiscal Year 2015.
[140] *Governor's Budget Report*, Fiscal Year 2017.
[141] *Governor's Budget Report*, Fiscal Year 2018.

Introduction to *Governor's Budget Report, FY 2019:*

> Over the last seven years, I have remained optimistic in the strength of Georgia's economic growth, but conservative in the revenue estimates used for the budget. This has helped ensure that taxpayers were not faced with draconian cuts in services mid-year if revenues did not grow as planned, and it has helped rebuild our Revenue Shortfall Reserve. A rainy day fund that held just $116 million at the end of 2010, holds $2.3 billion today. The rapid replenishment of our reserve has been recognized by all three credit rating agencies and has helped Georgia maintain its triple A credit rating, saving our taxpayers millions.
>
> The FY 2019 budget also includes an additional $361.7 million for the Teachers Retirement System to fully fund the actuarially determined employer contribution to keep our pension system on sound footing and ensure the state can meet its future obligations to those who have dedicated their careers to serving the education needs of our children
>
> Seven years ago, Georgia like other states, was faced with an economic crisis unlike any seen since the Great Depression. While other states raised taxes or increased debts to address the crisis, Georgia made difficult decisions and sound investments to position ourselves to be stronger than ever after the crisis had passed.[142]

Summary

Fiscal conservatism in Georgia means balanced budgets, low taxes, limited debt, limited government spending and maintaining reserves. Governors and other policy makers have resisted major tax increases unless they were thought to be absolutely necessary to address unmet service needs, as in 1951 when Governor Herman Talmadge proposed a 3% state sales tax or in 1989 when Governor Joe Frank Harris agreed to increase it to 4%, or even when Governors Griffin and Perdue proposed tax increases on cigarettes. However, during the depths of the Great Recession, Governor Sonny Perdue chose to impose substantial spending cuts across state government rather than increasing income or sales taxes to counter declining state revenues.

Conversely, following recovery from recessions, Governor Zell Miller in 1996 championed elimination of the 4% sales tax on food purchased for at-home consumption, to reduce the regressive effect of that tax. Governor Perdue in 2010 signed a bill that eliminated taxes on retirement income for senior citizens, to encourage retirees to come to Georgia, and signed legislation to gradually eliminate the state's property tax. Governor Nathan Deal in 2018 signed a bill emerging from the General Assembly to reduce the state corporate and highest individual income tax rate from 6% to 5.75% beginning in 2019.

Georgia governors are proud of the state's low debt limit, 10% of the net revenue receipts from the previous fiscal year, and of their low use of debt, routinely between 5 and 6%, as they preserve the state's AAA bond rating. They also place a high

---

[142] *Governor's Budget Report*, Fiscal Year 2019.

priority on directing "surplus" funds to the state's Revenue Shortfall Reserve, or rainy day fund. This is made possible by not over-spending during good financial times and the practice of conservative revenue estimates, which in combination, feed the rainy day fund.

Conclusion

The Budget Act of 1931 established a budget bureau and named the governor as director. However, it was not until the Budget Act of 1962 that Georgia had a modern-era executive budget system. Georgia governors between 1931 and 1962 were all fiscally conservative, but some such as E. D. Rivers and Ellis Arnall were social progressives. All governors were segregationists. Since 1962, all governors have been fiscally conservative but some such as Carl Sanders, Jimmy Carter, Zell Miller, Roy Barnes and Nathan Deal, in differing degrees, were also social progressives. Beginning with Jimmy Carter in 1971, Georgia governors were no longer segregationists.

Fiscal conservatism is both a financial management philosophy and a political philosophy. As a financial management philosophy, conservative revenue, spending and saving policies are thought to demonstrate prudence and discipline in the handling of public resources. As a political philosophy, those policies also express a preference for the size and role of the state, manifest in limited spending for such public benefits as education, health care, offender rehabilitation, or infrastructure. In Georgia state government, fiscal conservatism is both a financial management philosophy and a political philosophy.

Chapter 3
Patterns and Trends in Georgia Revenue

Government budgets provide insights into the attitudes, motives and values of a state's people and their representatives, revealing the manner in which they tax themselves and the purposes for which they spend public money. This chapter and the one that follows examine the revenue and expenditure patterns of Georgia state government during the past six decades, focusing on the six decennial midpoints of 1965, 1975, 1985, 1995, 2005 and 2015. The decade of the 1960s is an appropriate starting point for this examination because the Budget Act of 1962[1] established the foundation of the modern executive budget system in Georgia. The executive budget system will be addressed in Chapter 5.

Georgia raises revenue through a combination of the individual income tax, corporate income tax, sales and use tax, motor fuel tax, and several miscellaneous taxes on such things as alcoholic beverages, tobacco products and motor vehicles, as well as from agency fees and sales, such as fees for entry into state parks, license fees for such activities as hunting and fishing and driving motor vehicles, and hospital and nursing home provider fees.[2] Revenue is also obtained from lottery proceeds, bond proceeds and tobacco settlement funds. Lottery proceeds were initially earmarked for specific education functions such as pre-kindergarten programs, the HOPE[3] scholarship program, and capital outlays for education technology, but more recently are limited to the HOPE scholarship program and pre-kindergarten programs. Bond proceeds fund a variety of capital projects. Tobacco settlement funds are payments by the large tobacco companies to most of the state governments to help states cover health care costs related to tobacco use.

---

[1] Georgia Laws, 1962: 17–37. Official Code of Georgia Annotated (O.C.G.A), Title 45, Chapter 12.

[2] Hospital and Nursing Home Provider Fees are used to fund Medicaid, PeachCare-for-Kids and nursing homes that serve the medically indigent. They also are used to obtain federal funds for these programs.

[3] Helping Outstanding Pupils Educationally (HOPE).

Revenue Patterns and Trends

Georgia revenue increased between FY 1965 and FY 2015 from $523,598,667 to $21,555,644,411. Revenue collected in 2015 was approximately 41 times the amount collected in 1965, increasing at an average annual rate of 7.7%.[4] During this 50-year period, the individual income tax grew at an average annual rate of 10.5%.[5] During the same period, the sales and use tax grew at an average annual rate of 6.7%,[6] the corporate income tax grew at an average annual rate of 6.3% and the motor fuel tax grew at an average annual rate of 4.6%, all slightly below the state average. These growth patterns and trends can also be seen in Table 3.1 and Figure 3.1 which show the individual income tax at 12% of total state revenue in FY 1965 and at 45% of state revenue in FY 2015. Sales and use tax revenue declined from 40% of total state revenue in 1965 to 25% in 2015, with very little growth between FY 2005 and FY 2015, partially the result of the Great Recession between FY 2008 and FY 2010. Corporate income tax revenue declined slightly from 9% to 5% between FY 1965 and FY 2015. The motor fuel tax declined from 20% in FY 1965 to 5% in 2015, but following a redesign of the tax in 2015 would increase as a percentage of total tax collections. Throughout the six decennials, the sales and use tax and the individual income tax remained the dominant sources of state revenue, although they reversed the first-place position. The individual income tax surpassed the sales and use tax as the state's largest revenue source in FY 1983.[7] The individual income tax grew throughout the 50-year period as a source of state revenue as population and per capita personal income increased. The sales and use tax, while increasing during the period, declined as a relative share of state revenue as untaxed services and untaxed internet sales became a larger share of economic transactions in the state.

From FY 2000 to FY 2020, the combined total of income tax and sales and use tax collections in Georgia as a share of total tax collections was on average 81.2%. David Sjoquist has reported that among all states that have both income and sales taxes, the percentage of tax revenue from the total of these two taxes in 2010 ranged from a low of 31.9% to a high of 80.2%, with Georgia being the highest.[8]

---

[4] The real average annual growth rate controlling for inflation (June CPI-U, 1982–84 = 100) was 3.5%.

[5] The real average annual growth rate controlling for inflation (June CPI-U, 1982–84 = 100) was 6.2%.

[6] The real average annual growth rate controlling for inflation (June CPI-U, 1982–84 = 100) was 2.5%.

[7] State of Georgia, Department of Revenue, *Annual Statistical Report*, FY 1983. p. 1.

[8] David L. Sjoquist, "State Tax Structures: Past Trends and Future Possibilities," in Marilyn Marks Rubin and Katherine G. Willoughby, eds., *Sustaining the States: The Fiscal Viability of American State Governments*. Boca Raton, FL: CRC Press, 2015. p. 58.

Table 3.1 Georgia State revenue FY 1965 – FY 2015 by revenue source

	FY 1965	FY 1975	FY 1985	FY 1995	FY 2005	FY 2015
Individual Income Tax	$64,281,852	$360,068,147	$1,718,317,033	$3,834,269,241	$7,276,607,819	$9,678,524,026
Corporate Income Tax	$48,125,256	$133,200,547	$417,135,396	$676,635,748	$729,640,400	$1,000,536,425
Sales Tax	$207,564,075	$563,661,307	$1,527,882,705	$3,506,939,197	$5,215,447,136	$5,390,353,066
Motor Fuel Tax	$106,625,856	$228,158,926	$385,768,023	$521,853,591	$850,940,019	$1,025,819,044
Other Taxes	$74,144,033	$238,500,733	$396,173,109	$718,354,856	$1,127,915,480	$2,013,626,917
Fees and Sales	$22,857,595	$53,219,099	$162,537,147	$367,605,842	$613,445,813	$1,325,883,555
Total Taxes and Fees	$523,598,667	$1,576,808,759	$4,607,813,413	$9,625,658,475	$15,813,996,667	$20,434,743,033
Lottery Proceeds				$514,881,260	$813,490,096	$982,460,046
Tobacco Settlement Funds					$159,362,266	$138,441,332
Total Revenue	$523,598,667	$1,576,808,759	$4,607,813,413	$10,140,539,735	$16,786,849,029	$21,555,644,411

Source: Governor's Budget Report, FY 1965, FY 1977, FY 1987, FY 1997, FY 2007 and FY 2017

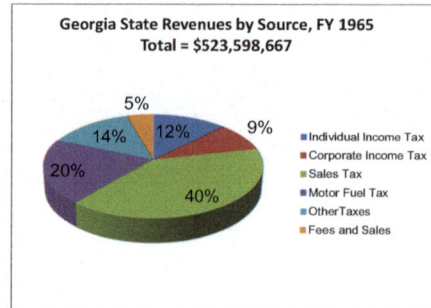
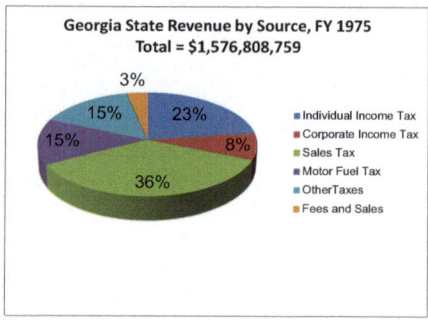
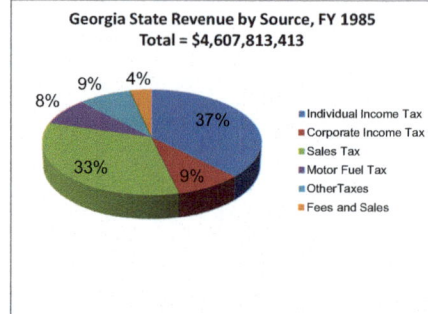
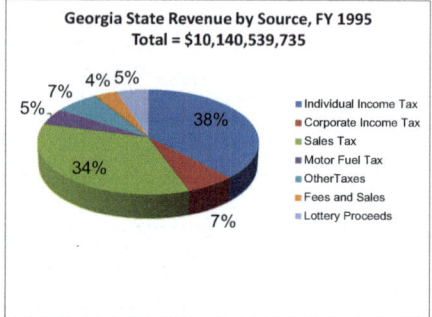
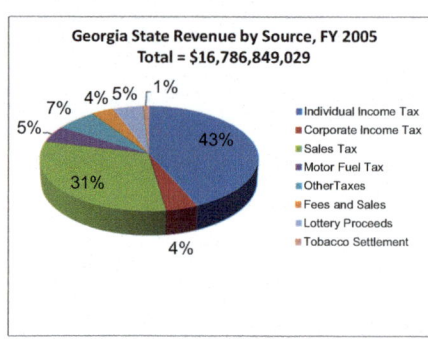
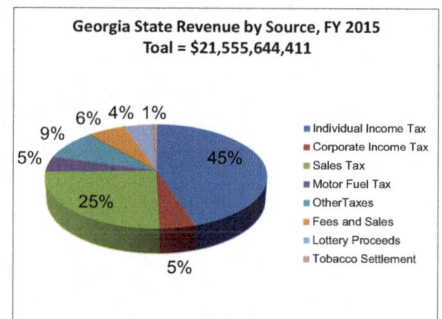

Fig. 3.1 Georgia State revenue by source, FY 1965 – FY 2015

Income Taxes

The corporate and individual income taxes were adopted in 1929, in the administration of Governor Lamartine G. Hardman (1927–31). Georgia was among the early states to adopt the income tax. Governor Hardman entered office facing a state deficit and debt, which resulted from the General Assembly appropriating in excess of available revenues. He appointed a citizens' tax commission to advise him on the matter and subsequently proposed a state income tax that he signed into law on August 22, 1929, effective October 1, 1929.[9] The state tax commissioner R.C. Norman wrote:

---

[9] Acts and Resolutions of the General Assembly of the State of Georgia, 1929: 92–99. Approved August 22, 1929. "Boykin Income Tax Measure Signed into Law by Gov. Hardman; Becomes

This tax is the most effective method of reaching large salaries and income from stocks, bonds and other investments, and reaches a class of taxpayers who are able to pay but paid little if anything under the old system.

The modern state must supply services if it keeps pace with progress. The state is called upon today to render services that were not dreamed of a generation ago. We must have paved roads, modern schools, care for our unfortunates, look after the health of our people, pay pensions and do very many things to promote the progress, welfare and happiness of our citizens.[10]

He estimated that between $4,000,000 and $6,000,000 would be collected in the initial year of the new law and that the state would be able to satisfy its debts by the end of 1931.[11] Individuals and corporations were to pay one-third of the income tax amount owed to the federal government, net of allowable exemptions.

Litigation ensued challenging the constitutionality of the income tax law on the grounds that it was double taxation and that it would be dependent upon increases or decreases in the federal income tax law. The double taxation contention was that with the state property tax as a first tax, a tax on income derived from property amounted to a second tax on that property. The Georgia Supreme Court unanimously upheld the constitutionality of the income tax law.[12] The Court held that a tax on income is not a tax on property within the meaning of the Georgia Constitution, and that the new tax law did not vest in the U.S. Congress the legislative power of the state of Georgia.[13]

In 1931, a separate income tax rate structure for Georgia was established, ranging from 1% to 4% on income increments of $5,000 and 5% on all income over $20,000. In 1937, an income tax bracket structure was established that remained in place with minor modifications until 2018. The initial rate was 1% for the first $1,999 of net income, increasing by 1% with every $2,000 until reaching $10,000. Incomes over $10,000 were taxed at 6%. Exemptions for single persons were reduced from $1,500 to $1,000 and for married persons from $3,500 to $2,500.[14]

The top individual income tax rate remained at 6% until 2019, when it was reduced to 5.75%.[15] Individuals reach the top bracket with incomes over $7,000 and

---

Effective October 1," *Atlanta Constitution*, August 23, 1929: 3.

[10] R. C. Norman, "New Law Will Pay All Debt of the State by End of 1931, Thinks Tax Commissioner (R.C.) Norman," *Atlanta Constitution*, November 11, 1929: 4.

[11] "New Law Will Pay All Debt of the State by End of 1931, Thinks Tax Commissioner (R.C.) Norman," *Atlanta Constitution*, November 11, 1929: 4; "Steps Are Taken to Enjoin Boykin Law Next Week," *Atlanta Constitution*, November 16, 1929: 1; "$4,000,000 Revenue Is Seen Under Georgia Income Tax," *Atlanta Constitution*, November 23, 1929: 9.

[12] *Marie C. Featherstone v. R.C. Norman, State Tax Commissioner*, 170 Ga. 370, 153 S.E. 58, April 16, 1930.

[13] Harold Stephens, "Boykin Tax Upheld by Supreme Court," *Atlanta Constitution*, April 17, 1930:1.

[14] Acts and Resolutions of the General Assembly of the State of Georgia, 1937: 109–148. Approved March 30, 1937. "Rivers' Inauguration is Planned Tuesday," *Atlanta Constitution*, January 6, 1937: 2.

[15] Georgia Laws, 2018: 8–18. HB 918 was approved March 2, 2018.

couples filing jointly reach it with combined incomes over $10,000. The legislation that reduced the top income tax rate to 5.75% also includes a provision that would further reduce the rate to 5.5% if the General Assembly passes and the governor signs a joint resolution for this purpose on or after January 13, 2020.[16] It was assumed that this would happen in 2020, but when the COVID-19 pandemic interrupted the 2020 legislative session and significantly reduced revenue collections, it did not happen. In 2020, e*xemptions* are $7,400 for a taxpayer and spouse filing jointly, $3,700 for each spouse filing separately, $2,700 for single filers, and $3,000 for each dependent. The s*tandard deductions* are $5,400 for a single filer, $3,550 for a married taxpayer filing a separate return and $7,100 for married persons filing a joint return.[17] There is an e*xclusion* of $35,000 of retirement income for taxpayers 62–64 years of age and of $65,000 of retirement income for taxpayers over age 65. The retirement income exclusion was gradually increased from 2002 through 2012,[18] when the present rate was established. In 2010, the General Assembly extended the phased in retirement income exclusion for taxpayers 65 years of age or older to $100,000 for 2013, $150,000 for 2014, $200,000 for 2015 and an unlimited amount for 2016 and thereafter.[19] However, in 2012 the legislature reversed itself and eliminated further exclusions beyond the 2012 amount of $65,000.[20] In November 2014, the voters of Georgia through referendum approved a constitutional amendment establishing a permanent ceiling on the individual income tax at the 6% rate.[21]

Georgia taxable income		
Tax rate	Single filer	Married filing jointly
1%	$0–$750	0–$1,000
2%	$751–$2,250	$1,001–$3,000
3%	$2,251–$3,750	$3,001–$5,000
4%	$3,751–$5,250	$5,001–$7,000
5%	$5,251–$7,000	$7,001–$10,000
5.75%	$7,001 +	$10,000 +

---

[16] Georgia Laws, 2018: 8–18, at 17. HB 918 was approved March 2, 2018.
[17] Georgia Laws, 2021: ____. HB 593, "The Tax Relief Act of 2021," was approved March 22, 2021.
[18] Georgia Laws, 2002: 1149–1151. HB 136 was approved May 15, 2002.
[19] Georgia Laws, 2010: 9–84 at 81–83. HB 1055 was approved May 12, 2010.
[20] Georgia Laws, 2012: 257–302 at 273–275. HB 386 was approved April 19, 2012.
[21] Georgia Laws, 2014: 888–889. SR 415 was approved April 22, 2014. The ballot question was whether or not the Constitution of the State of Georgia should be amended to prohibit an increase in the maximum marginal income tax rate in effect on January 1, 2015. On November 4, 2014, the "Yes" vote was 1,855,380 (73.9%) and the "No" vote was 655,917 (26.1%). Proponents argued that it would promote job growth by guaranteeing a low-income tax rate. Opponents argued that it would limit revenue options for future decision makers, and that it was unnecessary because no one was proposing a tax increase.

Forty-one states have individual income taxes that tax wages and salary income, two states (New Hampshire and Tennessee) have income taxes that tax only dividends and investment income, and seven states do not have the income tax.[22] Nine states have a single tax rate and 32 have graduated rates. The highest top marginal rate is 13.3% in California and the lowest top marginal rates are 2.9% in North Dakota and a 3.07% fixed rate in Pennsylvania.

The corporate income tax has been a less important revenue source for Georgia than has the individual income tax. The corporate income tax rate was set at one-third of the federal income tax rate from 1929 to 1931. Thereafter, the rate changed periodically. It was 4% from 1931–1937, 5.5% from 1937–1949, 7.5% in 1949 and 1950, 5.5% from 1951–1955, 4% from 1955–1964, 5% from 1965–1969, 6% from 1969–2018 and 5.75% beginning in 2019.[23] As seen above, the corporate income tax was a declining share of total tax revenue from 1965 (9.2%) to 2015 (4.6%). It was 5.2% in 2020. Throughout this time period the corporate income tax was either the third or fourth largest revenue producer, similar in size and periodically alternating places with the motor fuel tax.

Forty-four states have a corporate income tax, four states have a gross receipts tax (Nevada, Ohio, Texas and Washington), and two states do not have either a corporate income tax or a gross receipts tax (South Dakota and Wyoming). Thirty states, including Georgia, have single-rate systems and 14 states have graduated-rate systems. Rates for the corporate income tax range from 2.5% in North Carolina to a top rate of 12% in Iowa.[24]

Sales Tax

The sales and use tax was adopted in 1951,[25] in the administration of Governor Herman Talmadge (1948–1955). Georgia was among the later states to adopt the sales tax. Governor Talmadge had promised in the 1948 election campaign that there would be no new taxes unless they were submitted to the people for their approval in a state-wide election. However, upon taking office he quickly realized that the demands for improved schools, increased old-age pensions and accelerated road building could not be achieved without more revenue. Initially, Talmadge proposed increasing existing taxes on gasoline, cigarettes, liquor, wine, beer and corporate income.[26] However, the numbers did not work and still more revenue was needed. He then promoted the idea that when the people indicated their approval for

---

[22] States not having an income tax are Alaska, Florida, Nevada, South Dakota, Texas, Washington and Wyoming.
[23] State of Georgia, Department of Revenue, *FY 2019 Statistical Report*, p. 20
[24] Tax Foundation, "State Corporate Income Tax Rates and Brackets for 2020," January 28, 2020.
[25] Georgia Laws, 1951: 360–387. HB 2 was approved February 20, 1951.
[26] Roy Harris, "Harris Says Sales Tax Certain," *Atlanta Constitution*, January 11, 1950: 4.

expanded services by electing him, they in effect approved the necessary tax increase. The *Atlanta Constitution* in an editorial wrote, "The people did not vote specifically for a sales tax, but they did vote for expanded state services, knowing that the sales tax was the only method by which sufficient revenue could be raised."[27]

Governor Talmadge recommended and the 1951 General Assembly passed an appropriations bill that nearly doubled that of the previous year, $207,000,000 compared with $108,000,000, funded by a 3% consumer retail sales tax. The new tax was expected to raise $100 million annually. Reflecting the strength of the state's rural interests, the new sales tax exempted fertilizer, feed, seed and insecticides purchased by farmers. It also did not apply to personal services.[28] The appropriations bill provided funding for the state's Minimum Foundation Program for Education. The legislature also passed revisions to the income tax law, increasing exemptions for dependents, allowing deductions for medical expenses and providing deductions for capital gains/losses.[29] The "emergency" tax increases of the previous year were rolled back. More than 100 so-called "nuisance" taxes including fees on drivers, and hunting and fishing licenses were repealed.[30]

The *Atlanta Constitution* editorialized on January 9, 1951, "Nothing else could bring in the 75–90 million dollars in additional revenue which Georgia must raise if we are to have acceptable schools and highways."[31] A day later the paper wrote, "We have supported the sales tax, and still support it because it is the only way to get the money Georgia needs."[32] Still later, the *Atlanta Constitution* wrote[33]:

> There were two chief objectives before the Assembly.
> Foremost was that of the schools. Georgia simply had to advance education. There was no other course.
> It was this fact which led us to endorse a sales tax and to urge its passage, so long as coupled with it was tax revision in general. We did this despite the fact that we do not like a sales tax. But, it was something which had to be done for Georgia. It was like taking a bad-tasting dose of medicine which nevertheless will help the patient.
> There was another major need. The roads of Georgia must be improved and new roads built. Too much of rural Georgia is in the mud. (The sales tax, incidentally, did right by the farmer in exempting his seeds, fertilizers and insecticides.)
> There were other needs in Georgia, but these two are paramount.

---

[27] Editorial, "The People and the Sales Tax," *Atlanta Constitution*, March 30, 1951: 20, and Editorial, "The People Will Keep Watching," *Atlanta Constitution*, April 3, 1951: 12.

[28] M. L. St. John, "3 Pct. Sales Tax Passed, Assembly Ends Session," *Atlanta Constitution*, February 17, 1951: 1.

[29] Dupont Wright, "Far-Reaching Legislation Passed by '51 Assembly," *Atlanta Constitution*, February 17, 1951: 5.

[30] M. L. St. John, "House Passes Tax of 3 Pct., 139–29," *Atlanta Constitution*, January 25, 1951: 1.

[31] Jack Tarver, "Don't Sidetrack Tax Revision," *Atlanta Constitution*, January 9, 1951: 10.

[32] Editorial, "A Sound Program," *Atlanta Constitution*, January 10, 1951: 10

[33] Editorial, "A Cooperative Victory for Georgia," *Atlanta Constitution*, February 19, 1951: 8.

The sales and use tax almost immediately became the state's largest revenue source at 41% of revenues in FY 1951–52, ahead of the gasoline tax at 22% and the income tax at 16%.[34]

The sales and use tax was increased from 3% to 4% in 1989,[35] during the administration of Governor Joe Frank Harris (1983–1991). In January 1989, Governor Harris's $7.1 billion budget recommendation to the General Assembly for FY 1990 proposed a 6 cent per gallon increase in the state's motor fuel tax for the purpose of road and highway construction. Increasing the motor fuel tax from 7½ cents per gallon to 13½ cents per gallon was estimated to produce approximately $261 million a year.[36] The state constitution required that the new revenue be allocated to the Department of Transportation beginning with the 1991 fiscal year, but could be used for general state government purposes in the 1990 fiscal year.[37] Such an increase would be the first major tax increase since 1971, when the motor fuel tax was increased by 1 cent per gallon from 6½ cents to 7½ cents per gallon,[38] after being increased by ½ cent per gallon to 6½ cents per gallon in 1955.[39] The state motor fuel tax was enacted in 1921 and was the state's top revenue producer until 1951, when the state's new sales tax became the leading source of state revenue.[40]

The Speaker of the House of Representatives, Thomas B. Murphy, announced his opposition to the motor fuel tax increase. His objection was reported to be that earmarking additional funds to the Department of Transportation would make it more unresponsive to the General Assembly.[41] In late January, the House Ways and Means Committee voted against the motor fuel tax proposal. Subsequently, an alternate proposal was introduced that would increase the state sales tax by 1%, from 3% to 4%, producing an estimated $700 million per year. At that time, motor fuel con-

---

[34] *Statistical Report of the Department of Revenue of the State of Georgia for the Fiscal Years 1950–51 and 1951–52.* p. 10

[35] Georgia Laws, 1989: 62–74. HB 474 was approved March 9, 1989.

[36] *Governor's Budget Report, Fiscal Year 1990.* p. 11.

[37] A. L. May, "House Likely to Kill 6¢ Gas Tax Hike," *Atlanta Journal-Constitution*, January 8, 1989: A-1.

[38] In 1971, Governor Jimmy Carter supported a recommendation by Director of the Highway Department, Bert Lance, to increase the state motor fuel tax by 2 cents per gallon, from 6½ cents to 8½ cents. Such an increase was estimated to produce $50 million to be used for road building. "Carter Backs Gas Tax Rise to Build Roads," *Atlanta Constitution*, January 5, 1971: 6-A. In the 1971 session, the House Ways and Means Committee unanimously recommended passage of a 2 cent per gallon increase, but the full House and the Senate passed a 1 cent increase, raising the rate to 7½ cents per gallon. "Carter Signs Budget," *Atlanta Constitution*, March 20, 1971: 11-A.

[39] The 6½ cents per gallon motor fuel tax rate had been established in 1955, when it was increased from 6 cents per gallon during a special session of the General Assembly called by Governor Marvin Griffin to consider a variety of possible tax and fee increases. The ½ cent per gallon increase was estimated to have produced $5 million additional revenue. "New U.S. Fuel Tax Expected to Cost Georgians ten Million," *Atlanta Constitution*, June 29, 1956: 33-A

[40] Georgia Department of Revenue, 2000 *Annual Statistical Report.* p. iii.

[41] David Beasley and Brian O'Shea, "House Sets Stage for Sales Tax Hike on Roads Program," *Atlanta Constitution*, February 1, 1989: A-7.

sumers, in addition to paying the 7½ cents per gallon motor fuel tax, also paid a 3% tax (second motor fuel tax) on the purchase.

According to newspaper reports at the time, leaders of the House of Representatives favored the sales tax increase because, in addition to generating more revenue, it would decrease the need for future tax increases. Governor Harris continued to favor the motor fuel tax increase because the proposed sales tax increase would generate more revenue than was needed to fund state programs. The leadership of the Department of Transportation preferred the earmarked motor fuel tax, but indicated that it was amenable to the sales tax increase if the General Assembly would agree to designate a set amount of the new revenue for road and highway construction. Some legislators objected to increasing the sales tax because it is regressive, with a burden inversely related to the ability to pay.[42] The House of Representatives passed the sales tax increase in early February. Although the 3% tax on motor fuel sales (second motor fuel tax) was earmarked for the Department of Transportation and transportation projects, the fourth cent was designated for the general state treasury.[43] Lieutenant Governor Zell B. Miller proposed a Senate version of the state sales tax increase that would exempt food for home consumption from the tax, intended to reduce regressivity, but would not exempt food from any local sales taxes. The House version had considered but rejected a food exemption. The Senate version was estimated to produce approximately $335 million per year.[44] The Republican minority rejected both the proposed motor fuel tax increase and the proposed sales tax increase, preferring instead across-the-board spending reductions, and perhaps small sin tax increases on cigarettes and alcoholic beverages.[45] Complicating the policy making process in the 1989 legislative session was the impending 1990 gubernatorial election in which several of the legislative decision makers were positioning themselves as likely gubernatorial candidates, for example, House Appropriations Committee Chairman Lauren "Bubba" McDonald, Lieutenant Governor Zell Miller, the governor's Senate floor leader Roy Barnes and the House minority leader, Representative Johnny Isakson. Governor Harris was nearing the end of his second term and was not eligible to again succeed himself. Reflecting political differences among policy makers, the House Ways and Means Committee Chairman, Terry Coleman was quoted by the *Atlanta Constitution* as saying, the food exemption "worries me because it has the appearance of the old, liberal-left leanings that we in Georgia fight annually."[46] In rebuttal, Lieutenant

---

[42] David Beasley and Brian O'Shea, "House Sets Stage for Sales Tax Hike on Roads Program," *Atlanta Constitution*, February 1, 1989, A-7; David Beasley and Brian O'Shea, "1-Cent Hike in Sales Tax is Proposed," *Atlanta Journal*, February 2, 1989, A-1.

[43] David Beasley and Brian O'Shea, "House Oks 1-Cent Hike in Sales Tax," *Atlanta Constitution*, February 8, 1989, A-1.

[44] Brian O'Shea, "Miller: No Sales Tax Hike on Grocery Items," *Atlanta Constitution*, February 9, 1989: B-1.

[45] A. L. May and Brian O'Shea, "Proliferation of Tax Plans May Cause Jam," *Atlanta Constitution*, February 10, 1989: A-1.

[46] Brian O'Shea, "Sales Tax Heats Up Budget Talk," *Atlanta Constitution*, February 21, 1989: B-1.

Governor Miller was quoted also by the *Atlanta Constitution* as saying, "It's not something left-wing, revolutionary or liberal." "For the proponent of the single biggest tax increase in the history of the state of Georgia to call someone, who wants to cut that increase in half, a 'liberal" is really ludicrous."[47] The key personalities in this controversy were Lieutenant Governor Zell Miller, a political moderate and House Speaker Tom Murphy, a conservative. Speaker Murphy favored the sales tax increase over a motor fuel tax increase because the latter would increase Department of Transportation discretion over anticipated new revenue. Lieutenant Governor Miller also favored the sales increase, but only with a food exemption to mitigate its regressive impact.[48]

In early March, House and Senate leaders compromised on a 1 cent sales tax increase that exempted selected foods. The compromise had two aspects. First, the tax would not apply to fresh foods such as meat, milk, bread, fruit and vegetables, but it would apply to processed, canned and frozen foods.[49] Second, the exemption would be delayed until September 1, 1990 which gave the state the full revenue from the tax increase during the 1990 fiscal year (July 1, 1989 – June 30, 1990).

Because Governor Harris's proposed budget was predicated on a motor fuel tax increase that would have produced an estimated $261 million in new revenue and the compromise sales tax increase was estimated to produce $687 in new revenue, the General Assembly adjourned temporarily to decide how to spend the new revenues in the next fiscal year.[50] In the end, the bulk of the new revenue was allocated to state employee pay raises, prison construction, education programs and roads and highways. Reflecting the last-minute nature of the decision making, the $7.5 billion appropriation for the 1990 fiscal year contained several "unspecified" allocations to departments.

The state's 1989 budget process was an atypical one. The regular order is for the governor to propose a spending plan and for the House of Representatives and the Senate, in turn, to make relatively minor changes in the governor's recommendation. However, by enacting a last-minute tax increase that resulted in a substantial amount of new revenue, the General Assembly, for this year at least, significantly increased its role in state spending decisions.

---

[47] Brian O'Shea, "Sales Tax Heats Up Budget Talk," *Atlanta Constitution*, February 21, 1989: B-1.

[48] Lieutenant Governor Zell Miller provides a candid account of his legislative fights with Speaker Tom Murphy in his book: Zell Miller, *A National Party No More: The Conscience of a Conservative Democrat*. Atlanta, GA: Stroud & Hall, 2003. pp. 45–46.

[49] Georgia Laws, 1989: 62–74 at 64. During the administration of Governor Zell Miller, in an effort to improve vertical equity, i.e., reduce regressivity, the sales tax was removed from food almost entirely over a three-year period beginning, October 1, 1996. During FY 1997 the sales tax was reduced from 4% to 2%; it was reduced by an additional 1% in each of the following two years. Georgia Laws, 1996: 1–4. HB 265 was approved January 11, 1996.

[50] Brian O'Shea and M. L. May, "One Cent Increase in Sales Tax Approved by General Assembly: Governor Harris's Compromise Ends Deadlock," *Atlanta Constitution*, March 9, 1989, 1A and 14A, and Brian O'Shea, "One Cent Increase in Sales Tax Approved by General Assembly: Some Foods to be Exempt by Fall 1990," *Atlanta Constitution*, March 9, 1989: 1A and 13A.

A 4% state sales tax, however, is not the entire sales tax levy on Georgia tax payers. If a local option sales tax (LOST) of 1%, a special purpose local option sales tax (SPLOST) of 1% and special local option sales taxes for such purposes as education and/or transportation (E-SPLOST and/or T-SPLOST) of 1% are added on, the combined state and local sales tax may range from 5% to 8%. There are a number of exemptions in the application of the state's sales tax, including on the sale of food for at home consumption,[51] on energy used in manufacturing[52] and on the sale of Girl Scout cookies.[53]

Forty-five states have a sales tax and most of them also have local government sales taxes.[54] The top state rate is 7.25% in California. The lowest non-zero rates are 2.9% in Colorado and 4% in Georgia and four other states.

Sales Taxes on Internet Sales

Since the beginning of the twenty-first century, an increasing number of sales are online transactions rather than face-to-face exchanges. This transition in the way business is conducted has been facilitated by advancements in electronic communications. The transition to internet buying and selling, although convenient for merchants and consumers, is problematic in two ways. It gives an unfair economic advantage to internet merchants over so-called brick and mortar merchants because state governments find it more difficult to collect the sales tax from internet merchants than from brick and mortar merchants. It also results in foregone revenue for state governments from one of the two most important revenue sources that are used to finance state services.

For many years, application of the sales tax to online sales was made difficult by the U.S. Supreme Court's holdings that a state may not require a business that has no physical presence in the state to collect its sales tax.[55] However, in 2018 the Supreme Court held in *South Dakota v. Wayfair, Inc.* that the physical presence rule was unsound and incorrect and overruled the cases holding it.[56] The Court noted that, "The physical presence rule has long been criticized as giving out-of-state sellers an advantage. Each year, it becomes further removed from economic reality and results in significant revenue losses to the States." Further, the Court opined, the physical presence rule "… is a judicially created tax shelter for businesses that limit their physical presence in a State but sell their goods and services to the State's

---

[51] Georgia Laws, 1996: 1–4. HB 265 approved January 11, 1996.
[52] Georgia Laws, 2012: 257–302. HB 386 approved, April 19, 2012.
[53] Georgia Laws, 1996: 1643–1647. HB 1399 approved April 25, 1996.
[54] The states without the sales tax are Alaska, Delaware, Montana, New Hampshire and Oregon.
[55] *National Bella Hess, Inc. v. Department of Revenue of Illinois*, 386 U.S. 753 (1967) and *Quill Corporation v. North Dakota*, 504 U.S. 298 (1992).
[56] *South Dakota v. Wayfair, Inc.*, 585 U.S. ____, 138 S. Ct. 2080, 201 L. Ed 2d 404 (2018).

consumers, something that has become easier and more prevalent as technology has advanced." And yet further, "By giving some online retailers an arbitrary advantage over their competitors who collect state sales taxes, ... physical presence rule has limited State's ability to seek long-term prosperity and has prevented market participants from competing on an even playing field." In short, the Supreme Court held that states may require out-of-state sellers to collect and remit sales tax. The Court also emphasized the importance of a state's tax laws not placing a burden on interstate commerce. This decision paved the way for Georgia and other states to devise policies to collect their sales tax on online sales.

In its 2018 Session, just months before the Supreme Court decision in the South Dakota case, the Georgia General Assembly enacted a law, effective January 1, 2019, requiring online retailers with at least $250,000 in gross revenue per year from retail sales or 200 separate sales a year in Georgia to collect and remit to the state sales taxes on purchases, or to send "tax due" notices to customers who spend at least $500 per year on their sites.[57] Under the second option, customers were obligated to pay the taxes to the Georgia Department of Revenue. However, as in other states, customer compliance was likely to be low.

However, taking into account the Court's holding in the South Dakota case, the General Assembly in its 2020 Session, enacted a new law that reduced the sales threshold for establishing a state presence from $250,000 to $100,000, and eliminated the option of having customers remit taxes due on internet purchases to the Department of Revenue. The new law makes "marketplace facilitators" liable for collecting from the purchaser the full amount of taxes levied on retail sales and remitting those taxes to the Department of Revenue.[58] A marketplace facilitator is an entity operating a website that facilitates retail sales on behalf of a marketplace seller. It is expected that this law will enable the state to capture sales tax revenue that was owed, but until the 2018 Supreme Court decision was legally beyond its reach.

Motor Fuel Tax

The motor fuel tax was first levied in Georgia in 1921 as a tax of 1 cent per gallon on distributors of motor fuel.[59] In 1923, the motor fuel tax was increased to 3 cents per gallon and a fund was created for highway and bridge construction under the supervision of the State Highway Department.[60] In 1925, it was increased from 3 to 3½ cents, with the additional one-half cent to be appropriated to the State Road

---

[57] Georgia Laws, 2018: 259–261. HB 61 was approved May 3, 2018. Official Code of Georgia Annotated (O.C.G.A.) 48-8-2.
[58] Georgia Laws, 2020: 1–4. HB 276 was approved January 30, 2020, effective April 1, 2020.
[59] Georgia Laws, 1921: 83–85. Approved August 10, 1921.
[60] Georgia Laws, 1923: 41–44. Approved August 14, 1923.

Fund for construction of state roads.[61] In 1927, it was increased to 4 cents per gallon, with 2½ cents designated for state roads, 1 cent designated for grants to counties and ½ cent designated for public schools.[62] In 1929, it was increased again to 6 cents per gallon, with 4 cents designated for state roads, 1 cent designated for counties and 1 cent for public schools.[63] In 1937, the Motor Fuel Tax Law retained the 6 cents per gallon tax rate and stipulated that the proceeds be distributed: 4 cents per gallon to the State Highway Department for use in construction on the state highway system, 1 cent per gallon distributed to counties to be used *exclusively* for construction and maintenance of roads, and 1 cent per gallon distributed to the public schools of the state.[64]

The 1945 *Constitution of the State of Georgia* prohibited the practice of allocating taxes to particular objects. However, in 1952 the *Constitution* was amended earmarking motor fuel tax revenue for highway purposes.[65] The Constitution specifies that "all money derived from motor fuel taxes received by the state in each of the immediately preceding fiscal years" is to be appropriated for the purpose of "providing and maintaining an adequate system of public roads and bridges" in the state.[66] This provision did not preclude the General Assembly from appropriating additional funds for transportation purposes.

In 1949, the Motor Fuel Tax was increased from 6 cents per gallon to 7 cents per gallon.[67] In 1951, it was reduced from 7 cents to 6 cents per gallon.[68] In 1955, it was increased to 6½ cents per gallon.[69] In 1966, it was maintained at 6½ cents per gallon when the Motor Fuel Tax Law was amended to exclude the tax from sales between distributors and purchases of motor fuel for non-highway use.[70] In 1971, it was increased to 7½ cents per gallon.[71] In 1979, the state added a "second motor fuel tax" of 3%,[72] with the expectation that additional appropriations for transportation would then no longer be necessary. In 1989, when the state's sales and use tax was increased from 3% to 4%, the sale of motor fuel was exempt from the first 3% of the sales and use tax (the second motor fuel tax remained in force), but the sale of motor fuel was subject to the fourth percent. However, that additional 1% was not a motor

---

[61] Georgia Laws, 1925: 65. Approved August 26, 1925.

[62] Georgia Laws, 1927: 104–108. Approved August 24, 1927.

[63] Georgia Laws, 1929: 99–103. Approved August 19, 1929.

[64] Georgia Laws, 1937: 167–207 at 180. Approved March 18, 1937.

[65] Georgia Laws, 1951: 849–852. Sen. Res. 5 approved February 21, 1951. On November 4, 1952, Amendment No. 2, was approved by the voters 330,327 (62%) – 205,668 (38%).

[66] *Constitution of the State of Georgia*: Article III, Section IX, Paragraph VI (b).

[67] Georgia Laws, 1949 Extraordinary Session: 19–21. HB 4 was approved July 30, 1949.

[68] Georgia Laws, 1951: 446–448. HB 41was approved February 21, 1951.

[69] Georgia Laws, 1955 Extraordinary Session: 52–55. HB 7 was approved on June 14, 1955.

[70] Georgia Laws, 1966: 61–68. HB 302 was approved February 28, 1966.

[71] Georgia Laws 1971: 81–83. HB 112 was approved March 12, 1971.

[72] Georgia Laws, 1979: 1274–1277. HB 663 was approved April 17, 1979.

fuel tax earmarked for transportation[73] but revenue available for general state purposes. In 2003, the second motor fuel tax was modified with the State Revenue Commissioner authorized to determine the per gallon tax based upon 4% of the average state-wide price for motor fuel.[74] Over the years, the motor fuel tax has evolved from an occupation tax on distributors of motor fuel, to a tax on users of the state's roads with tax proceeds dedicated for road construction and maintenance.

Today, the motor fuel tax is an excise tax of 26 cents per gallon which is constitutionally earmarked[75] for the construction and maintenance of the state's roads and bridges. Prior to July 1, 2015 the motor fuel tax was 7½ cents per gallon plus a 4% tax on total fuel sales, 3% of which went to the transportation fund (the second motor fuel tax) and 1% of which went to the state general fund. Now all of the motor fuel tax goes to the Department of Transportation.

The motor fuel excise tax[76] was probably the largest tax increase since the initial income and sales taxes. The combined 7½ cent per gallon excise tax, plus the 4% sales tax was estimated to be approximately 21½ cents per gallon.[77] The new excise tax of 26 cents per gallon was an increase. Tax increases are not easily enacted in fiscally conservative Georgia. However, there was a perception among policy makers that many state roads were in poor condition and many bridges were operationally inadequate and structurally deficient, and that improved roads, highways and bridges were necessary to facilitate commerce in the state. Designing the revision as entirely an excise tax per gallon rather than a sales tax was intended to increase revenue predictability because volume of consumption tends to fluctuate less than the price of fuel. Designing it as a tax on fuel consumption dedicated entirely to road and highway improvement was intended to make it more politically acceptable. The local economic benefits of construction projects also made the tax increase palatable for many legislators.[78] In order to capture revenue from out-of-state users of the state's highways, a hotel/motel tax of $5 per room was also part of the transportation package.

---

[73] Georgia Laws, 1989: 62–73 at 65. HB 474 approved March 9, 1989.
[74] Georgia Laws, 2003: 355–358 at 357. HB 504 approved May 9, 2003.
[75] *Constitution of the State of Georgia,* Article III, Section IX, Paragraph VI (b).
[76] Georgia Laws, 2015: 236–264. HB 170, "Transportation Funding Act of 2015," Approved May 4, 2015.
[77] Conversation with Terry England, Chair, Appropriations Committee, House of Representatives, August 13, 2018.
[78] Conversation with Terry England, Chair, Appropriations Committee, House of Representatives, August 13, 2018.

Cigarette Tax

The cigarette tax began in 1923 as a tax on persons, firms or corporations engaged in the retail sale of cigarettes and cigars. It was a tax of "ten per centum" of the sale price at retail of each package of cigarettes and each cigar sold by such dealers. The funds collected were earmarked for the Board of Health for buildings and equipment for the State Tuberculous Sanatorium.[79] It became 5 cents per package in 1955, 8 cents per package in 1964 and 12 cents per package in 1971.[80]

The cigarette tax was increased in the 2003 Session of the General Assembly from 12 cents per package to 37 cents per package, an increase of 208%. It was raised in anticipation of a revenue shortfall in the FY 2004 budget. The state was struggling to find ways to deal with a revenue shortfall in the FY 2003 budget. A sluggish economy had constricted state revenue collections, and reductions in state agency spending were not enough to produce a balanced budget. James Salzer reported that a tax increase, even one on a "sin" tax, was not what state legislators wanted to vote for in advance of the 2004 election. Indeed, many Republican legislators had recently pledged not to increase taxes.[81] Further, conservative legislators saw the revenue shortfall as an opportunity to reduce the size of government through even greater spending reductions and had little interest in a tax increase.[82]

Governor Sonny Perdue early in the 2003 General Assembly session proposed raising the cigarette tax from 12 cents to 58 cents per package, an increase of 383%, estimating that such an increase would raise $348 million. That proposal was defeated in the House of Representatives, with a majority of both Democrats and Republicans voting against it.[83] Democrats held a majority in the House of Representatives, but according to Salzer, they were not willing to vote for a tax increase unless Governor Perdue persuaded his fellow Republicans to also vote for it going into the 2004 election year. Near the end of the legislature's 40-day session, various proposals for a tax increase smaller than the governor's original proposal were considered, but all were rejected as either too high for merchants operating near the border of neighboring states with lower rates,[84] or unacceptable in principle for legislators who preferred more spending reductions to any tax increase. Faced with the threat of a special legislative session to balance the budget, the General Assembly passed a bill increasing the cigarette tax from 12 cents to 37 cents per

---

[79] Acts and Laws of the General Assembly of the State of Georgia, 1923: 39–41 and Extraordinary Session, 1923: 69–71.

[80] Georgia Department of Revenue, *Annual Statistical Report*, 2000. pp. iii–iv.

[81] James Salzer, "Tobacco Tax Bill Closer to a Vote," *Atlanta Journal-Constitution*, March 19, 2003: B1.

[82] James Salzer, "Tax Hike May Turn on GOP Holdouts," *Atlanta Journal-Constitution*, April 14, 2003: B1.

[83] James Salzer, "Perdue's Tobacco Tax Hike Defeated," *Atlanta Journal-Constitution*, March 27, 2003: A1.

[84] James Salzer, "Legislators Dig In on Tax; Budget, Special Session Hinge on Tobacco Debate," *Atlanta Journal-Constitution*, April 24, 2003: C4.

package, estimated to raise $180 million which was more than enough to cover the projected revenue deficiency for FY 2004. To make the tax increase more palatable for the governor and conservatives in the legislature, the bill also included a provision increasing the amount of retirement income seniors could exclude from taxes,[85] that is, a tax cut.[86] The legislation was also promoted as an action to discourage teenage smoking with a corresponding long-term reduction in health care costs.

Revenue from the cigarette tax increased from $112 million in 2003 to $229 million in 2004, an increase of 104%. The average annual increase in the ten-year period preceding the rate change had been only 2.9%, although cigarette tax revenue for 2003 had increased by 31% over 2002, suggesting greater sales in anticipation of the new tax rate.

The Georgia cigarette tax rate (for a package of 20) ranks 48th among the states,[87] suggesting that another increase in this tax might be possible without much political repercussion. However, a proposal during the 2020 legislative session to increase the cigarette tax from 37 cents per package to $1.35 per package, to mitigate spending reductions with increased revenue, failed to be enacted. The highest state cigarette tax rate is $4.35 in Connecticut and the lowest rate is $0.17 in Missouri; the national average is $1.01.

Property Tax

The property tax was once the principal source of state revenue. It was an *ad valorem* levy on the market value of real property. David Sjoquist reported that at the end of the nineteenth century it constituted almost three-quarters of state revenue.[88] The *ad valorem* tax rate was set at 5 mills in 1904 by constitutional amendment.[89] It was levied at the rate of 5 mills from 1904 until 1952 when the rate was reduced to .25 mills.[90] The Income Tax Acts of 1929 and 1931 had directed the state Revenue

---

[85] The exclusion amount was increased from $15,000 to $35,000 phased in over three years.

[86] Georgia Laws, 2003: 665–706 at 690. HB 43 was approved June 6, 2003. James Salzer, "Tobacco Deal Reached; Legislators Warn Hike Might Not Pass Muster," *Atlanta Journal-Constitution*, April 24, 2003: C4.

[87] Tax Foundation, *Facts & Figures*, January 1, 2019.

[88] David L. Sjoquist, "A Brief History of the Property Tax in Georgia," Atlanta, Georgia: Fiscal Research Center, Andrew Young School of Policy Studies, Georgia State University (2008). p. 7.

[89] Georgia Laws, 1903: 21–22. Approved August 17, 1903.The *Constitution of the State of Georgia*, Article 7, Section 1, was amended by voters on October 5, 1904 by a vote of 31,637 (70%) for ratification and 13,643 (30%) against ratification. *The Atlanta Constitution*, October 12, 1904. p. 3.

[90] Georgia Laws, 1952: 469–472. SR 22, "Property Tax – Proposed Amendment to the Constitution," was adopted January 29, 1952. The Amendment was approved by voters on November 4, 1952: 304,299 (76%) – 97,912 (24%). *Constitution of the State of Georgia*, Article VIII, Section I, Paragraph II (a): The annual levy of state ad valorem taxes on tangible property for all purposes, except for defending the state in an emergency, shall not exceed one-fourth mill on each dollar of the assessed value of the property.

Commissioner to reduce the *ad valorem* tax rate commensurate with new revenue from the income tax.[91] Following the passage of the Sales and Use Tax Act in 1951 it was set at .25 mills, where it remained for more than a half century. Beginning in tax year 2011, the state-level property tax was phased out over a five-year period, reducing by .05 mills each year, until it was eliminated effective January 1, 2016.[92] By the twenty-first century the property tax had become a minor source of state revenue, well below the individual and corporate income taxes, the sales and use tax, and the motor fuel tax in its contribution to total state tax revenue. In the years immediately preceding the phase out, it was less than .5% of total state tax revenue. The property tax remains a primary source of revenue for county and municipal governments and local school districts. State law stipulates millage limits; local governing bodies choose the millage rate.

Motor Vehicle Tax

Consistent with Georgia's history of taxing real property at market value, the state has long had an *ad valorem* motor vehicle tax, for which the revenue is received primarily by local governments. Before March 1, 2013, new vehicle purchases were subject to a county sales tax[93] and the state *ad valorem* tax was due each year thereafter, payable within 30 days of the vehicle registrant's preceding birthday. For this reason, the state *ad valorem* tax on motor vehicles was dubbed the "birthday tax." The amount of the tax is based on the current value of the vehicle. This system still applies for vehicles purchased prior to March 1, 2013.

The 2012 General Assembly replaced the annual *ad valorem* tax and purchase sales tax with a one-time state and local title ad valorem tax (TAVT) at a rate of slightly below 7% of the fair market value of the motor vehicle, to be paid at the time of application for a certificate of title. The rate began at 6.5% in 2013, was adjusted to 7% by 2015 and was lowered to 6.6% for 2020. It may periodically be further adjusted, but it can never be more than 9%. TAVT proceeds are divided between the state and local governments. The tax applies not only to purchases of new vehicles from dealers but also to the purchase of used vehicles from individuals, collectable at the point of titling the vehicle. The ability to tax private sales is

---

[91] Georgia Laws, 1929: 92–99. "Income Taxes," approved August 22, 1929; Georgia Laws, 1931 Extra Session: 24–60, "Income Tax Act of 1931," approved March 31, 1931.

[92] Georgia Laws, 2010: 9–84, at 80. HB1055 was approved May 12, 2010. Georgia Department of Revenue, *Property Tax Administration 2017 Annual Report*, February 14, 2018. p. 17.

The tax was 0.25 mills in 2011, 0.20 mills in 2012, 0.15 mills in 2013, 0.10 mills in 2014, 0.05 mills in 2015 and 0.00 mills in 2016.

[93] The sales tax varies by county, but is most likely between 5% and 8%.

thought to have partially offset the loss of sales tax revenue.[94] The annual motor vehicle registration fee (tag fee), currently $20, continues as under the prior system.

Bond Proceeds

Before 1972, the State of Georgia was prohibited by its Constitution from incurring debt. During the 1950s and 1960s this constitutional limitation was circumvented by the creation of public corporations, usually called authorities, with the power to issue bonds to obtain funds for the construction of public facilities, which were then leased to state government agencies. Rental payments by state agencies, under lease contracts, were used to retire the authority's bonds. When the bonds were fully retired, the facility became the property of state government. Rental payments appeared in the budget as, "authority lease rental".[95] In 1972, the state Constitution was amended to authorize the state to incur general obligation debt and to guarantee revenue bonds, effective January 1, 1973.[96]

General obligation (GO) bonds are sold to investors to raise revenue to fund capital projects,[97] and are backed by the full faith, credit and taxing power of the state.[98] Revenue bonds can only be issued for specific purposes as outlined in the state Constitution, and are retired from the earnings of a public enterprise.[99]

A bond issued by the State of Georgia is a promise to individual investors or financial institutions to pay the bond's face amount (principal) at a specific time (maturity) and to make agreed upon interest payments at periodic intervals until the loan is retired. The State is the borrower and investors or institutions are the lenders. Periodic payments of the loan principal and interest are called *debt service*. Debt service appears in the *Governor's Budget Report* and in the appropriations act as "General Obligation Debt Sinking Fund." The debt sinking fund is debt service on bonds authorized in current year appropriations as well as on bonds authorized in prior year appropriations. For example, in the FY 2019 Appropriation Act the total

---

[94] Jaime Sarrio, "New Car Tax a Boon for Area; Additional Revenue Exceeds Expectations," *Atlanta Journal-Constitution*, August 20, 2013: A1.

[95] In 1953, this arrangement was upheld by the Georgia Supreme Court in *McLucas v. State Bridge Building Authority*, 210 Ga. 1 (1953), 77 S.E.2d 531. Merritt B. Pound and Albert B. Saye, *Handbook on the Constitutions of the United States and Georgia*. Tenth Edition, Athens, GA: The University of Georgia Press, 1984. pp. 63–64.

[96] Georgia Laws, 1972: 1523–1533. The November 7, 1972 vote on the proposed constitutional amendment to permit the state to issue general obligation bonds was Yes – 476,435 (66.9%) and No – 235,038 (33.1%). Bob Fort, "The Final Returns Are In," *Atlanta Constitution*, November 17, 1972: 16. The constitutionality of the new method of financing the state's capital outlay needs was upheld by the Georgia Supreme Court in *Sears v. State of Georgia*, 232 Ga. 547 (1974), 208 S.E.2d 93.

[97] *Constitution of the State of Georgia*, Section IV, Paragraph I (c).

[98] *Constitution of the State of Georgia*, Section IV, Paragraph VI

[99] *Constitution of the State of Georgia*, Section IV, Paragraph I (f).

state funds GO Debt Sinking Fund appropriation was $1,267,392,608, of which $121,390,402 was for debt service on new GO bonds and $1,146,002,206 was for debt service on previously authorized bonds.

The state's debt service limit is 10% of prior year net Treasury receipts.[100] Prior to the ratification of a new state Constitution in 1983, the maximum percentage permitted by the Constitution was 15%. Even though the constitutional limit is 10%, the state Debt Management Plan has since FY 2006 utilized a debt limit cap of 7%.[101] Table 3.2 shows that in practice the state incurs debt well below the constitutional limit, generally in the range of 5–6% of prior year Treasury receipts. The state's debt management plan "serves as a guide to the State in ensuring the availability of funding for necessary capital projects to meet the State's future needs while maintaining the balance between the State's need for capital and the ability and willingness of the State to repay additional debt."[102] In addition to tracking debt service as a percent of state net revenues, the debt management plan tracks several other debt ratios as measures of debt burden, such as debt per capita, debt as a percent of total income of the state's population, debt as a percent of the state gross domestic product, and debt as a percent of the full valuation of all taxable property.[103] The Georgia State Financing and Investment Commission (GSFIC), established in 1973,[104] is responsible for issuing general obligation bonds authorized by the General Assembly, for receiving the proceeds of bond sales, for investing those proceeds, and for disbursing them for designated capital outlay projects.[105]

Borrowing for capital construction projects is generally sound fiscal policy if the anticipated usable life of the project exceeds the length of time of the debt obligation because it enables such projects to be purchased when needed, spreads the cost over the useful life of the project, distributes the project cost across present and future users through their current taxes, and it prevents very large projects from distorting the annual budget by crowding out other necessary spending.

The State of Georgia enjoys AAA bond ratings from all three rating firms,[106] which means it is considered a credit worthy borrower whose bonds pose low risk for lenders and that it is able to borrow at the most favorable interest rates. Such a determination is based upon a variety of factors such as the economic condition of the state, the stability of state government institutions, the financial condition of state government as indicated by its revenue, spending and debt records, and probably the existing level of state debt.

---

[100] *Constitution of the State of Georgia*, Section IV, Paragraph II (b)

[101] State of Georgia, *Debt Management Plan, Fiscal Year 2019 – Fiscal Year 2023.* p. 18.

[102] State of Georgia, *Debt Management Plan, Fiscal Year 2019 – Fiscal Year 2023.* p. 27.

[103] State of Georgia, *Debt Management Plan, Fiscal Year 2019 – Fiscal Year 2023.* p. 21.

[104] Georgia Laws, 1973: 750–778. SB 358, "The Georgia State Financing and Investment Commission Act," was approved April 13, 1973.

[105] *Constitution of the State of Georgia*, Section IV, Paragraph VII (a)

[106] Moody's, Standard and Poor's and Fitch.

Bond Proceeds

Table 3.2 Debt service as percentage of prior year net treasury receipts

Fiscal year	Annual debt service	Net treasury receipts	Percentage
1984	$217,914,572	$3,572,370,034	6.1%
1985	$272,720,948	$4,010,602,173	6.8%
1986	$313,331,312	$4,607,813,413	6.8%
1987	$321,327,170	$5,020,737,038	6.4%
1988	$374,071,409	$5,421,324,773	6.9%
1989	$376,504,953	$5,890,910,203	6.4%
1990	$369,685,654	$6,467,686,421	5.7%
1991	$387,732,035	$7,196,336,132	5.4%
1992	$392,743,216	$7,295,236,287	5.4%
1993	$431,894,693	$7,452,615,507	5.8%
1994	$491,857,523	$8,346,367,907	5.9%
1995	$504,930,220	$9,409,526,943	5.4%
1996	$568,226,855	$10,303,573,061	5.5%
1997	$588,641,451	$11,166,835,592	5.3%
1998	$606,591,877	$11,905,829,999	5.1%
1999	$702,079,328	$12,478,602,944	5.6%
2000	$700,994,815	$13,539,916,503	5.2%
2001	$730,856,404	$14,959,980,702	4.9%
2002	$877,399,865	$15,768,578,047	5.6%
2003	$885,771,950	$15,126,479,334	5.9%
2004	$931,047,735	$14,737,541,220	6.3%
2005	$1,020,462,428	$15,530,262,707	6.6%
2006	$1,109,553,454	$16,789,925,631	6.6%
2007	$1,183,981,964	$18,343,186,033	6.5%
2008	$1,173,214,321	$19,895,976,560	5.9%
2009	$1,307,062,392	$19,799,131,881	6.6%
2010	$1,278,325,792	$17,832,362,806	7.2%
2011	$1,314,870,945	$16,251,240,187	8.1%
2012	$1,228,532,294	$17,546,374,291	7.0%
2013	$1,219,674,733	$18,316,792,805	6.7%
2014	$1,231,358,905	$19,539,691,059	6.3%
2015	$1,282,438,777	$20,256,765,495	6.3%
2016	$1,293,491,829	$21,557,498,539	6.0%
2017	$1,289,557,703	$23,476,964,893	5.5%
2018	$1,360,383,742	$24,519,402,190	5.5%
2019	$1,309,352,179	$25,649,499,261	5.1%
2020	$1,332,638,909	$26,973,017,172	4.9%

Source: Governor's Budget Report, FY 1999, FY 2009 and FY 2020

Lottery Proceeds

Lottery proceeds are another source of state revenue. Approximately three-quarters of the states operate some form of lottery. Georgia was the 36th state to adopt a lottery. Lotteries seldom generate a large proportion of total state revenue, but they are attractive to both citizens and government officials because they generate revenue without imposing new or increased taxes. However, if lotteries are regarded as a tax rather than a voluntary payment, they are regressive in that they place a greater relative burden on low-income players than on high-income players. Some states put lottery revenue in the general fund but many direct it to specific purposes such as education.

The Georgia lottery began in 1993 and lottery proceeds were part of the state budget in FY 1994. The lottery was part of Zell B. Miller's platform in the 1990 gubernatorial campaign; it was proposed in the 1991 and 1992 Sessions of the General Assembly, subject to voter approval,[107] and voters approved a constitutional amendment in November 1992 to establish the lottery.[108] Georgia lottery proceeds were initially earmarked for education programs in three areas: voluntary pre-kindergarten for four-year-olds, HOPE scholarships[109] and student loans, and capital improvements for education, especially the development and maintenance of instructional technology. After FY 2002, lottery proceeds were appropriated only for pre-K and HOPE. The lottery for education is discussed in Chapter 4.

Between FY 1994 and FY 2019, a total of $19.4 billion was appropriated to the Lottery for Education Account. Annual appropriations to the account, on average, have been 4.2% of total state appropriations.

Tobacco Settlement Agreement

Another Georgia revenue source is the Tobacco Master Settlement Agreement. In 1998 the attorneys general of 46 states, including Georgia, settled their lawsuit against the four largest U.S. tobacco companies for recovery of their tobacco-related health care costs. The tobacco companies agreed to annual payments to the states to compensate them for a portion of the medical costs related to caring for persons with smoking-related illnesses. The tobacco companies also agreed to cease certain tobacco marketing activities, especially those targeting youth. Annual payments to states began in 2000. Tobacco settlement funds are a relatively small portion of the state's total treasury receipts each year, an average of slightly less than 1% per year

---

[107] Georgia Laws, 1992: 3173–3211. HB 1541, "State Lottery – Tickets; Exemption from Sales and Use Taxes; Enacting Legislation," was approved May 7, 1992.

[108] The lottery was approved on November 4, 1992, with 1,131,168 (52%) in favor and 1,031,675 (48%) opposed.

[109] HOPE is the acronym for Helping Outstanding Pupils Educationally.

over the 20-year period. Georgia, unlike some states, budgets the entire amount of settlement funds for direct health care and cancer treatment and prevention expenditures.[110] In FY 2020, $136,008,335 (91%) was allocated to direct health care and $14,151,643 (09%) was allocated to cancer treatment and prevention.[111]

Hospital and Nursing Home Provider Fees

The Hospital Provider Fee is used to fund Medicaid and PeachCare-for-Kids. Hospitals, other than state-owned hospitals, are assessed a 1.45% fee on their net patient revenue. Payments are made to the Indigent Care Trust Fund. Most of the revenue from the fee is used to fund Medicaid services, but some of the revenue is used to match federal funds for Medicaid, thereby increasing the state's total payments to hospitals serving Medicaid patients. The Medicaid matching ratio is approximately one-third state dollars and two-thirds federal dollars. In effect, the combined state-federal payments to hospitals, so-called reimbursements rates, offset what the hospitals pay through the provider fee. This funding procedure also enables the state to not have to redirect funds from other purposes in order to make the federal funding match. In general, hospitals that serve more Medicaid patients receive more funding from the reimbursement rate than they pay in the provider fee, and hospitals that serve fewer Medicaid patients receive less funding from the rate than they pay in the fee. The "Provider Payment Agreement Act" establishing this program was approved in 2010 and was renewed in 2013, 2017 and 2019.[112]

The state also imposes a fee on nursing homes that is used to obtain federal financial participation in the state's medical assistance payments to nursing homes that serve the medically indigent.[113] Nursing home fees for this purpose are based upon patient days in the facility, are paid quarterly and are deposited in the Indigent Care Trust Fund. The General Assembly is authorized to appropriate as state funds to the Department of Community Health all the moneys contributed to the trust fund, including interest earned, to be used to match federal indigent care funds.

The Hospital Provider Fee now raises more than $300 million per year and the Nursing Home Provider Fee raises more than $150 million per year. In the ten years that the Hospital Provider Fee has been collected, it has amounted to about 1.25%

---

[110] Valerie A. Hepburn, "The Master Settlement Agreement and State Budgeting Choices: Does 'Found Money' Change Budgeting Behavior?" Doctoral Dissertation, The University of Georgia, 2006.

[111] *Governor's Budget Report, Amended Fiscal 2019 and Fiscal 2020.* p. 36.

[112] Georgia Laws, 2010: 9–84 at 77–80. HB 1055 was approved May 12, 2010. Georgia Laws, 2013: 1–4. SB 24 was approved February 13, 2013. Georgia Laws, 2017: 1. SB 70 was approved February 13, 2017. Georgia Laws, 2019: 183–192. HB 321 was approved April 15, 2019, and is in force through June 30, 2025. Official Code of Georgia Annotated (O.C.G.A.) 31-8-179.

[113] Georgia Laws, 2003: 435–438. HB 526 was approved May 31, 2003. Official Code of Georgia Annotated (O.C.G.A.) 31-8-6.

of total General Fund revenue collections. In the 17 years that the Nursing Home Provider Fee has been collected, it has amounted to .75% of total General Fund revenue collections. Although these revenue amounts are not large, they generate twice as much in federal matching funds based upon the two-thirds to one-third funding formula. They also make it unnecessary for the state to take funds away from other purposes in order to make the federal match.

Tax Expenditures

Tax expenditures are foregone revenue collections that result from tax *deduction*, tax *exemption* or tax *credit* policies. They are intended to achieve a variety of policy objectives such as the promotion of economic development or the provision of tax relief for low or fixed-income individuals. Significant income tax *deductions* in Georgia are the standard deduction for individual tax filers, married couples filing jointly and dependents, and itemized deductions for state and local tax payments and home mortgage interest payments. Social Security income and retirement income for senior citizens (up to $65,000) are income tax *exemptions*.

Tax *credits* are provisions in the state tax code that provide for a reduction in a taxpayer's liability that would otherwise be due. Unlike tax exemptions or deductions, tax credits reduce tax liability by the total amount of the credit, dollar for dollar. Tax credits are used by the state to encourage certain kinds of activities such as economic development, employment, education, housing development or environmental protection. When tax credits are used to satisfy tax liabilities, state tax collections are reduced. The expectation of tax credits is that their benefit to the state will be greater than the foregone revenue. A positive benefit-cost relationship may or may not be achieved, but it frequently is unknown and sometimes is a matter of dispute. The most comprehensive study of tax credits in Georgia is by Sherman A. Cooper and Laura Wheeler in 2015.[114] Cooper and Wheeler identified 40 tax credits and categorized them by the credit rate, sunset date, administrative control, limitations on use of the credit and interactions with other credits. They also provided information on the amount of the credit utilized during the period 2009–2013. The study reports that some credits have a sunset date, other do not; some are transferable (they may be sold), others are not; some are limited to a maximum percent of taxpayer liability, some are not limited; some may carry forward to future years while others must be used in the year in which they were earned. Some tax credits are relatively small in scope and cost, but others are large and at times controversial, such as the credit for film production in the state.

In 2020, the Georgia Department of Audits and Accounts issued two reports asserting that the film tax credit, Georgia's largest tax credit, granted credits to film

---

[114] Sherman A. Cooper and Laura Wheeler, *Georgia Tax Credits: Details of the Business and Personal Credits Allowed Against Georgia's Corporate and Individual Income Tax*. Atlanta, Georgia: Georgia State University, Andrew Young School, Fiscal Research Center (2015).

production companies in excess of what they actually earned.[115] The film tax credit provides an income tax credit to production companies that spend at least $500,000 on qualified productions. The base credit rate is 20% with an additional 10% for the promotion of Georgia. More than $3 billion in credits were generated from 2013–2017, according to the audit. The credits are transferable and most credits are sold by production companies to other taxpayers who have greater tax liability in Georgia. The Department of Audits and Accounts stated, "While Georgia's film tax credit has increased the production of movies, television, and interactive entertainment in the state, the information available to decision makers regarding the credit's impact has been incomplete and inaccurate. The economic impact and jobs attributable to the credit have been overstated, even before considering the cost of the credit."[116] The report was critical of the Georgia Department of Revenue and the Department of Economic Development for overestimating the film industry's economic impact in Georgia and for awarding tax credits higher than actually earned. In 2020, the General Assembly passed legislation requiring film companies operating in Georgia to be audited by the Georgia Department of Revenue or a third-party auditor designated by the department. The legislation also imposed greater restrictions on the ability of film companies to transfer or sell their unused tax credits to other entities also having a tax liability in Georgia.[117] While tax credits are presumed to be cost beneficial, the extent of the benefit sometimes is uncertain.

The Georgia Budget & Policy Institute estimated that the state's tax expenditure policies – deductions, exemptions and credits – have amounted to approximately $8 billion annually in foregone revenue in recent years, approximately two-thirds of which is attributable to exemptions from the state sales tax for the purchase of groceries, prescription drugs and products used in manufacturing.[118]

The recent history of Delta Air Lines' tax exemption on the purchase of jet fuel provides an interesting case study of the interaction of politics and tax expenditure policy. Delta, with its hub in Atlanta, is a major contributor to the Georgia economy. The airline transports millions of passengers each year into and out of the Hartsfield-Jackson International Airport, or at least did prior to the COVID-19 pandemic. It facilitates national and international commerce in the state, employs numerous Georgians and paid taxes to the state and local governments on the jet fuel it purchased in Atlanta and Savannah. In recognition of Delta's economic value to the state, the General Assembly in 2005 placed a $15 million limit on the amount the

---

[115] Georgia Department of Audits and Accounts, Performance Audit Division, Report No. 18-03A, "Administration of the Georgia Film Tax Credit," January 2020. Georgia Department of Audits and Accounts, Performance Audit Division, Report No. 18-03B, "Impact of the Georgia Film Tax Credit," January 2020.

[116] Georgia Department of Audits and Accounts, Performance Audit Division, Report No. 18-03B, "Impact of the Georgia Film Tax Credit," January 2020. p. 1.

[117] Georgia Laws, 2020: ____. HB 1037 was approved June 26, 2020, signed August 4, 2020, to become effective January 1, 2021.

[118] Wesley Tharp, "Tax Facts: Georgia Gives Up Billions through the Tax Code," Georgia Budget & Policy Institute, Atlanta, Georgia, January 2015.

airline had to pay in state sales tax and local sales tax.[119] That amount was less than what Delta had paid in the previous year, and jet fuel purchases in each of the next two years were expected to exceed that amount. The tax exemption was periodically renewed for ten years until it was repealed in 2015.[120] In the 2018 legislative session, a bill was under consideration to lower personal and corporate income tax rates, double the standard deductions amounts, and restore the sales tax exemption on jet fuel. However, in February 2018, Delta announced that it was ending its policy of discounted fares for National Rifle Association (NRA) members. At that time, the school shooting in Parkland, Florida and the attendant debate over gun control were in the news.[121] Several Republican officials and candidates for office expressed the opinion that the provision benefitting Delta should be removed from the bill.[122] Lieutenant Governor Casey Cagle, the presiding officer of the state Senate and a candidate for his party's 2018 gubernatorial nomination, announced that he would not support the jet fuel tax exemption unless Delta reversed its policy regarding NRA discount fares. Delta did not recant. The provision to exempt jet fuel was removed from the tax bill that was passed.[123] The editorial board of the *Atlanta-Journal Constitution* expressed the opinion that maintaining a business environment conducive to economic growth should prevail over "baldly partisan politics."[124] In June 2018, the Department of Revenue instructed state vendors to stop collecting the local sales tax on jet fuel as of July 1.[125] On July 30, 2018, Governor Nathan Deal issued an executive order suspending indefinitely collection of the state sales tax on jet fuel, effective August 1, 2018.[126] The General Assembly ratified the governor's executive order in a special session that had been convened to provide funds for Hurricane Michael clean-up and repairs.[127] As of now, Delta enjoys the jet fuel tax exemption and continues to contribute to the Georgia economy.

---

[119] Georgia Laws, 2005: 725–728. HB 341 was approved May 3, 2005.

[120] Georgia Laws, 2015: 48–49. HB 319 was approved April 15, 2015.

[121] Kelly Yamanouchi, "Delta Ending Discount Rates for NRA Members, *Atlanta Journal-Constitution*, February 25, 2018: B8.

[122] Tamara Hallerman and Greg Bluestein, "Gun Debate Fallout: Delta NRA Spat Puts Politicians in Strange Positions, Democrats and GOP Switch Normal Roles During Controversy," *Atlanta Journal-Constitution*, March 4, 2018: A17.

[123] Georgia Laws, 2018: 8–18. HB 918 was approved March 2, 2018.

[124] Andre Jackson, "Gold Dome Punishment of Delta Air Lines: The Editorial Board Opinion," *Atlanta Journal-Constitution*, March 4, 2018: A22.

[125] Department of Revenue, Policy Bulletin SUT-2018-03, June 1, 2018.

[126] Executive Order 07.30.18.01, July 30, 2018. The executive order was effective only until the next meeting of the General Assembly when it must have been ratified, modified or terminated.

[127] Georgia Laws, 2018 Extraordinary Session: ES7-ES15. HB 5EX was approved November 17, 2018.

Federal Grants and Other Funds

It is customary in media and other accounts to describe the Georgia budget as the amount of state revenue appropriated for a fiscal year. However, that amount is only a portion of the total state budget. For example, in FY 2019, the state budget was $26,226,914,974. However, the total FY 2019 budget was $51,032,179,073.[128] State funds were only 51.4% of the total budget.[129] The difference between total funds and state funds is comprised of "Federal Funds," "Other Funds," and "Intra-State Transfers." For FY 2019, Federal Funds and Grants, amounted to $14,039,743,958, and Federal Recovery Funds amounted to $36,134,183. The combination of traditional federal funds and the post-recession federal recovery funds amounted to 27.6% of the total Georgia budget. As seen in Table 3.3, throughout the six decennials, federal funding was between 25% and 29% of total Georgia revenue.

Many state agency budgets include little or no federal funds. However, several agencies receive a considerable amount of federal funding for their programs, often requiring state matching funds. All federal funds received by the state are continually appropriated in the exact amounts and for the purposes authorized and directed by the federal government in making the grant.[130] The Department of Community Health received the largest amount of federal funding at $7,768,765,416 which represented 50.7% of its budget. The Department of Community Health administers health care programs for low-income individuals through the Medical Assistance Program[131] and provides health care to low-income children through the PeachCare-for-Kids program. The Department of Labor received a smaller amount of federal funding, $104,179,469, but that amount was 81.3% of the department's budget. The Department of Labor administers the unemployment insurance program that collects taxes from employers and distributes benefits to eligible claimants, and provides job search assistance to unemployed Georgians. Several other departments received amounts of federal funding that represented more than one-half of their total budgets. The Department of Defense received federal funding, 77.6% of its total, for the training and support of Army and Air National Guard units. The Department of Community Affairs received federal funding, 66.1% of its total, for grant and loan programs to promote economic development among local governments and private entities. Its federal funding was intended to improve the supply of affordable housing for low/moderate income individuals through housing rehabilitation and constructions programs, as well as through housing tax credits and low interest loans. The Department Public Health received federal funding, 57.5% of its

---

[128] Georgia Laws, 2018: Appendix. HB 684 approved May 2, 2018.

[129] The *Atlanta Journal-Constitution*, May 3, 2018: A1, reported, "Deal on Wednesday signed a historic $26.2 billion budget …" but did not mention that the total budget was $51 billion.

[130] Official Code of Georgia Annotated (O.C.G.A.) 45-12-91, and *Constitution of the State of Georgia*, Article III, Section IX, Paragraph II (b).

[131] State and federal dollars fund Medicaid with federal dollars traditionally paying for approximately 67% of health care costs each year.

Table 3.3 State, federal and other funds as percent of total Georgia budget, FY 1965 – FY 2015

	FY 1965	FY 1975	FY 1985	FY 1995	FY 2005	FY 2015
State Appropriations	$471,286,947	$1,716,498,693	$4,302,000,000	$9,775,460,431	$16,125,208,162	$20,836,744,620
Federal Funds	$216,160,124	$777,075,524	$1,807,921,079	$4,520,929,548	$7,664,493,918	$12,184,984,411
Other Funds	$49,602,337	$212,807,554	$977,623,328	$2,550,193,891	$4,972,921,466	$9,353,167,188
Total Appropriations	$737,049,408	$2,706,381,771	$7,087,544,407	$16,846,583,870	$28,762,623,546	$42,374,896,219
State Percent of Total	63.9%	63.4%	60.7%	58.0%	56.1%	49.2%
Federal Percent of Total	29.3%	28.7%	25.5%	26.8%	26.6%	28.8%
Other Percent of Total	6.7%	7.9%	13.8%	15.1%	17.3%	22.1%

Source: Governor's Budget Report, FY 1965, FY 1975, FY 1985, FY 1995, FY 2005, and FY 2015

total, for a variety of preventive health services, and for maternal and child health services including health and nutritional services for infants. The Department of Human Services, 57.4% federal funds, is the state agency administering the Temporary Assistance for Needy Families (TANF) program. With the help of federal funding, it also provides home energy assistance for low-income individuals, after school care with the aim of preventing child abuse and neglect, health and other support programs for older Georgians with the aim of enabling them to live in their homes and communities, and disability assistance programs through the Vocational Rehabilitation program. The Department of Early Care and Learning, 47.5% federal funds, administers the federal Child Care and Development Block Grant, and operates programs to train child care providers and to provide meals for children in day care settings. The Department of Transportation, 44.3% federal funds, is responsible for federal highway planning and construction programs in Georgia.

According to a study published by the Rockefeller Institute of Government,[132] Georgia is one of 42 states that has a positive balance of payments with the federal government, meaning it receives more from Washington in grants-in-aid than its citizens pay to the federal government in personal income and employment taxes. For federal fiscal year 2018, Georgia ranked 15th among the states with a federal expenditure of $1.23 per $1 of receipts from Georgia. It ranked 30th among the states in per capita federal expenditures per dollar of receipts from Georgia.

In addition to federal grants-in-aid, Georgia receives funds from other non-tax sources.

Other Funds for FY 2019 were $6,562,704,363 or 12.9% of the total budget. This category is comprised of several fund sources, but the two largest by far are "agency funds," that is, funds collected by state agencies and retained to be spent on agency programs, $3,589,962,795, and "research funds" earned almost entirely by units of the University System of Georgia, $2,334,323,592. The total budget of the Board of Regents of the University System of Georgia for FY 2019 was $7,818,298,952. State funds were $2,428,245,232 or 31.1% of the total budget. The largest portion of the Board of Regents budget came from Other Funds, $5,390,053,720 or 68.9% of the total. Within the Other Funds category, "agency funds", funds collected by University System institutions from tuition and fees and retained to be spent on institutional programs were $3,054,451,434 or 56.7%, and "research funds," including grants and contracts from such federal entities as NSF, NIH, CDC, and others, were $2,334,323,592 or 43.3% of the total.[133]

These other fund sources increased over the six decennials from 7% in FY 1965 to more than 20% in FY 2015 as university tuition payments, health insurance payments, and Medicaid service payments increased. As a result, state appropriations

---

[132] Laura Schultz and Michelle Cummings, "Giving or Getting? New York's Balance of Payments with the Federal Government: 2020 Report," Albany, New York: Rockefeller Institute of Government, State University of New York, January 2020. pp. 13–14.

[133] The *total* Board of Regents budget in FY 2019 was 15.3% of the *total* Georgia budget and the Board of Regents *state funds* budgets was 9.3% of the Georgia *state funds* budget.

as a proportion of total appropriations decreased steadily from 64% in FY 1965 to slightly less than 50% in 2015, as seen in Table 3.3.

A final revenue category, Intra-State Government Transfers, was $4,166,681,595 or 8.1% of the FY 2019 budget. The largest item by far in this category is Health Insurance Payments, $3,672,579,618. The Department of Community Health through its State Health Benefit Plan (SHBP) Division manages the health insurance coverage for state employees, school system employees, retirees and their dependents. Intra-Government Transfers represented 25.8% of the department's FY 2019 budget. Two other agencies by the nature of their functions typically have had a large portion of their annual budgets funded through Intra-State Transfers. The State Accounting Office, 73.0% in FY 2019, and the Department of Administrative Service, 79.9%, are authorized to assess other state agencies for the cost of the administrative and financial services they provide.

Georgia state agencies are instructed to spend federal and other funds first before using state funds, which permits unused state funds to be transferred into the Revenue Shortfall Reserve at the end of the fiscal year.[134]

Revenue Sources in Retrospect

The dominant forms of taxation in Georgia have been the individual income tax and the sales and use tax, at 45% and 25% respectively of total state taxes in 2015. Revenue from the individual income tax grew the most dramatically over the six decennials. The sales and use tax also grew substantially until 2005, after which the rate of growth leveled off between 2005 and 2015. Even as these two revenue sources became the state's dominant sources, the motor fuel tax remained a significant source of revenue. Beginning in 1995, lottery proceeds became an important new source of revenue for the state. Table 3.4, "History of Georgia State Tax Rates" shows rates for the property tax, motor fuel tax, cigarette tax, individual income tax, corporate income tax, sales and use tax and motor vehicle tax, the year in which the tax was enacted and the years when the rate was changed.

Georgia's revenue collection policy tends to be conservative.[135] As noted in Chapter 2, Georgia in 2018 ranked 42nd among all states in tax collections per capita and 50th in state revenue per capita.[136] Georgia ranked 24th in individual income tax collections per capita, 36th in corporate income tax collections per capita and 43rd in general sales tax collections per capita. Georgia also ranked 47th in state debt per capita. Low rankings among all of the states on income and sales tax

---

[134] Terry England, Chair, House Appropriations Committee. Message on December 9, 2019.

[135] Thomas P. Lauth, "Georgia: Shared Power and Fiscal Conservatism," in Edward J. Clynch and Thomas P. Lauth, eds., *Budgeting in the States: Institutions, Processes and Politics*. Westport, Connecticut: Praeger Publishers, 2006. pp. 33–35.

[136] Tax Foundation, *Facts & Figures*, January 1, 2019.

Revenue Sources in Retrospect

Table 3.4 History of Georgia State tax rates

Date	Property tax	Motor fuel tax	Cigarette tax	Individual income tax	Corporate income tax	Sales and use tax	Motor vehicle tax
1904	5 mills						
1921	↓	1¢/gal.					
1923	↓	3¢/gal.	10% of sale				
1925	↓	3½¢/gal.	↓				
1927	↓	4¢/gal.	↓				
1929	↓	6¢/gal.	↓	1/3 federal amount	1/3 federal amount		
1931	↓	↓	↓	1–4%	4%		
1937	↓	↓	↓	1–6%	5.5%		
1949	↓	7¢/gal.	↓	↓	7.5%		
1951	↓	6¢/gal.	↓	↓	5.5%	3%	
1952	.25 mills	↓	↓	↓	↓	↓	
1955	↓	6½¢/gal.	5¢/package	↓	4%	↓	
1964	↓	↓	8¢/package	↓	5%	↓	
1969	↓	↓	↓	↓	6%	↓	
1971	↓	7½¢/gal.	12¢/package	↓	↓	↓	
1979	↓	7½¢/gal. + 3% 2nd MFT	↓	↓	↓	↓	
1989	↓	↓	↓	↓	↓	4%	
2003	↓	↓	37¢/package	↓	↓	↓	
2012	.20 mills	↓	↓	↓	↓	↓	
2013	.15 mills	↓	↓	↓	↓	↓	
2014	.10 mills	↓	↓	↓	↓	↓	6.5%
2015	.05 mills	↓	↓	↓	↓	↓	6.75%
2016	0 mills	26¢/gal.[a]	↓	↓	↓	↓	7.0%
2017		26.3¢/gal.	↓	↓	↓	↓	↓
2018		26.8¢/gal.	↓	↓	↓	↓	↓
2019		27.5¢/gal.	↓	1–5.75%	5.75%	↓	↓
2020		27.9¢/gal.	↓	↓	↓	↓	↓
							6.6%

[a]Motor Fuel Tax adjusted each year based upon the Consumer Price Index (CPI). The adjustment will no longer be used after July 1, 2022
Date: Years in which a change occurred in one of the tax rates

collections and state debt is consistent with the state's culture of fiscal conservatism and limited government. These rankings also suggest lower state capacity for spending on public and higher education, health care, infrastructure and other public benefits as will be seen in the next chapter.

Tax Reform

There have been various proposals in recent years to reform the basic structure of the Georgia tax system. Reform advocates often express a preference for shifting the tax burden from wealth to consumption. There have been proposals to reduce the top individual income tax rate, to replace the current graduated income tax brackets with a single rate and even to eliminate the income tax entirely. Other reform proposals would restore the sales tax to the purchase of food for at home consumption, extend the sales tax to the transaction of certain services, and to apply the sales tax to internet transactions.

Specifically, the 2010 Special Council on Tax Reform and Fairness[137] recommended reduction of the then-current 6% individual income tax top rate to 4%, elimination of the exemption on senior citizen unearned income, elimination of a variety of economic development tax credits and sales tax exemptions, elimination of the sales tax exemption on food for at home consumption, imposition of a sales tax on selected personal and household services (such as shoe repair, haircuts, veterinary services and vehicle services), taxation of e-commerce transactions, increasing the cigarette tax to an average of taxes charged in adjacent states, and a change to the motor fuel tax.[138]

The House of Representatives in March 2020, just before the General Assembly Session was suspended due to the COVID-19 pandemic, passed a bill to reduce the top individual income tax from 5.75% to a flat rate of 5.375%, eliminating the graduated rate system. However, following the resumption of the Session in June 2020 with reports on hand of plummeting revenue collections in April and May, the bill was not enacted by the Senate.

Eliminating or even further reducing the individual income tax rate probably is not a good idea, arguments notwithstanding that Georgia's neighbors Florida and Tennessee do not have an income tax. The individual income tax and sales tax, Georgia's two high-yield taxes, have different positive and negative features with regard to adequacy and fairness. In combination they tend to mitigate the negative effects of each other. The state tax system needs to produce adequate revenue to support the state's level of activities and services as determined by the governor and the General Assembly, in order to maintain a constitutionally-required balanced budget. If the income tax rate were to be significantly reduced, much less eliminated, revenue from that source would decline or disappear and a far greater proportion of state revenue would need to be raised by the sales tax. Even though the General Assembly's action in 2020 to make "marketplace facilitators"liable for collecting the retail sales tax from purchasers using the internet will likely increase the sales tax yield, a reduced income tax rate or no income tax at all, would surely require an increased sales tax rate. However, because the sales tax in a regressive tax, with the burden of the tax inversely related to the ability to pay, whereas the

---

[137] Georgia Laws, 2010: 729–731. HB 1405 approved June 1, 2010.
[138] Special Council on Tax Reform and Fairness for Georgia Recommendations, January 7, 2011.

income tax is a progressive tax, the unfairness of the tax system would be exacerbated. Further, having both an individual income tax and a sales tax spreads the burden of revenue raising among a broader range of taxpayers.

In 2006, a tax and expenditure limitation (TEL) proposal argued that the annual revenue estimate should not be the sole determinant of the state's budget. Instead, the budget should be determined by annual population growth and any change in the rate of inflation.[139] This TEL proposal was not enacted. There also are periodic proposals to increase the state's cigarette tax, usually presented as not only a source of additional revenue but also a public health measure. The 2010 Special Council on Tax Reform and Fairness for Georgia recommended increasing the cigarette tax to 68 cents a pack, an increase of 31 cents. This recommendation was not enacted and in 2020 the state's tobacco tax remains at 37 cents per pack.

The Budget and the Economy: 1990–2019

Georgia's balanced budget requirement entails the principle that spending must be aligned with available revenue. Robust revenue collections permit new or enhanced spending; revenue shortfalls require budget cuts and spending reductions. Fiscal conservatives believe that revenue increases should come from economic growth rather than from new or increased taxes. Therefore, the state's capacity to fund necessary and desired spending is inextricably connected to the health of its economy. The following tables on employment (Table 3.5), personal income (Table 3.6) and gross domestic product (Table 3.7) provide an indication of the health of the Georgia economy between 1990 and 2019.

Between 1990 and 1999, Georgia employment grew at the average annual rate of 2.8% per year, compared with the national average annual rate of 1.3% per year. Georgia employment grew more rapidly than U.S. employment in almost every year of this period, and Georgia employment as a share of U.S. employment, increased steadily from 2.6% in 1990 to 3.0% in 1999.[140] The Georgia unemployment rate was also below the national rate each year between 1990 and 1999.[141] During the same period, Georgia per capita personal income grew at the average annual rate of 4.8% per year, while the U.S. per capita personal income grew at the average annual rate of 4.3% per year. Georgia per capita personal income as a percent of U.S. per capita personal income grew steadily from 90.9% in 1990 to 95.1 in 1999.[142] Between 1990 and 1999, Georgia gross total domestic product (GDP) in current dollars grew at the average annual rate of 8.3%, while the U.S. GDP grew at the average annual

---

[139] Final Report of the Senate Limited Taxation Study Committee, Senate Research Office, 2006.

[140] U.S. Department of Labor, Bureau of Labor Statistics, Employment Status of the Civilian Noninstitutional Population, 1949 to date.

[141] U.S. Department of Labor, Bureau of Labor Statistics, Local Area Unemployment Statistics: Georgia.

[142] U.S. Department of Commerce, Bureau of Economic Analysis, Regional Data, Personal Income.

Table 3.5 Georgia and U.S. Employment and Unemployment Rates, 1990–2019

Year	U.S. Employment	Annual percent change	Georgia employment	Annual percent change	Georgia percent of U.S.	U.S. unemployment rate	Georgia unemployment rate
1990	118,793,000		3,112,143		2.6%	5.6	5.5
1991	117,718,000	−0.9%	3,110,038	−0.1%	2.6%	6.8	5.0
1992	118,492,000	0.7%	3,169,497	1.9%	2.7%	7.5	7.2
1993	120,259,000	1.5%	3,279,881	3.5%	2.7%	6.9	5.9
1994	124,900,000	3.9%	3,405,726	3.8%	2.7%	6.1	5.1
1995	124,900,000	0.0%	3,502,330	2.8%	2.8%	5.6	5.1
1996	126,708,000	1.4%	3,648,382	4.2%	2.9%	5.4	4.6
1997	129,558,000	2.2%	3,788,057	3.8%	2.9%	4.9	4.5
1998	131,463,000	1.5%	3,901,829	3.0%	3.0%	4.5	4.3
1999	133,488,000	1.5%	3,996,286	2.4%	3.0%	4.2	3.9
Avg. annual change		1.3%		2.8%			
Change 1990–1999		12.4%		28.4%			
2000	136,891,000		4,070,215		3.0%	4.0	3.7
2001	136,933,000	0.0%	4,082,040	0.3%	3.0%	4.7	3.9
2002	136,485,000	−0.3%	4,119,610	0.9%	3.0%	5.8	4.9
2003	137,736,000	0.9%	4,180,971	1.5%	3.0%	6.0	4.8
2004	139,252,000	1.1%	4,238,673	1.4%	3.0%	5.5	4.8
2005	149,320,000	7.2%	4,354,877	2.7%	2.9%	5.1	5.3
2006	144,427,000	−3.3%	4,491,570	3.1%	3.1%	4.6	4.8
2007	146,047,000	1.1%	4,594,816	2.3%	3.1%	4.6	4.5
2008	145,362,000	−0.5%	4,655,861	1.3%	3.2%	5.8	6.1
2009	139,877,000	−3.8%	4,306,977	−7.5%	3.1%	9.3	10.2
Avg. annual change		0.2%		0.6%			
Change 2000–2009		2.2%		5.8%			
2010	139,064,000		4,193,763		3.0%	9.6	10.3
2011	139,869,000	0.6%	4,262,111	1.6%	3.0%	8.9	10.4
2012	146,469,000	4.7%	4,351,369	2.1%	3.0%	8.1	9.1
2013	143,929,000	−1.7%	4,369,634	0.4%	3.0%	7.4	8.2
2014	146,305,000	1.7%	4,399,189	0.7%	3.0%	6.2	7.2
2015	148,834,000	1.7%	4,487,958	2.0%	3.0%	5.3	5.9
2016	151,436,000	1.7%	4,665,829	4.0%	3.1%	4.9	5.3
2017	153,337,000	1.3%	4,837,031	3.7%	3.2%	4.4	4.6
2018	155,761,000	1.6%	4,905,874	1.4%	3.1%	3.9	3.8

(continued)

Table 3.5 (continued)

Year	U.S. Employment	Annual percent change	Georgia employment	Annual percent change	Georgia percent of U.S.	U.S. unemployment rate	Georgia unemployment rate
2019	157,538,000	1.1%	4,917,038	0.2%	3.1%	3.7	3.6
Avg. annual change		1.4%		1.8%			
Change 2010–2019		13.3%		17.2%			

Source: U.S. Department of Labor, Bureau of Labor Statistics, Employment Status of the Civilian Noninstitutional Population, 1949 to date, and Local Area Unemployment Statistics-Georgia

rate of 5.5%. Georgia GDP as a percent of U.S. GDP increased from 2.4% in 1990 to 3.0% in 1999.[143] In short, a relatively strong state economy contributed to the state's revenue growth during the 1990s.

The Georgia economy in the decade of the 2000s was somewhat weaker than it had been in the previous decade. Between 2000 and 2009, Georgia employment grew at the average annual rate of 0.6% per year, compared with the national average annual rate of 0.2% per year. Georgia employment grew more rapidly than U.S. employment in most years of this period, but not by much, and Georgia employment as a share of U.S. employment, only increased from 3.0% in 2000 to 3.1% in 2009. The Georgia unemployment rate was below the national rate in only six of ten years between 2000 and 2009. During the same period, Georgia per capita personal income grew at the average annual rate of only 1.9% per year, while the U.S. per capita personal income grew at the average annual rate of 2.8% per year. Georgia per capita personal income as a percent of U.S. per capita personal income declined from 94.1% in 2000 to 86.7% in 2009. Between 2000 and 2009, Georgia gross total domestic product (GDP) in current dollars grew at the average annual rate of 3.2%, while the U.S. GDP grew at the average annual rate of 3.9%. Georgia GDP as a percent of U.S. GDP decreased from 3.0% in 2000 to 2.8% in 2009.[144] The impact of the Great Recession in 2008 and 2009 was reflected in somewhat slower growth in the state's economy.

The Georgia economy in the most recent decade was stronger than the previous one, showing signs of steady recovery following the Great Recession. Between 2010 and 2019, Georgia employment grew at the average annual rate of 1.8% per

---

[143] U.S. Department of Commerce, Bureau of Economic Analysis, Regional Data.
[144] U.S. Department of Commerce, Bureau of Economic Analysis, Regional Data.

Table 3.6 Georgia and U.S. Per Capita Personal Income, 1990–2019

Year	U.S.	Annual Percent change	Georgia	Annual Percent change	Georgia % U.S.
1990	$19,621		$17,835		90.9%
1991	$20,030	2.1%	$18,322	2.7%	91.5%
1992	$21,090	5.3%	$19,360	5.7%	91.8%
1993	$21,733	3.0%	$20,087	3.8%	92.4%
1994	$22,575	3.9%	$21,090	5.0%	93.4%
1995	$23,607	4.6%	$22,235	5.4%	94.2%
1996	$24,771	4.9%	$23,475	5.6%	94.8%
1997	$25,993	4.9%	$24,404	4.0%	93.9%
1998	$27,557	6.0%	$26,159	7.2%	94.9%
1999	$28,675	4.1%	$27,275	4.3%	95.1%
Avg. annual change		4.3%		4.8%	
Change 1990–1999		46.1%		52.9%	
2000	30,657		28,861		94.1%
2001	31,589	3.0%	29,751	3.1%	94.2%
2002	31,832	0.8%	30,111	1.2%	94.6%
2003	32,681	2.7%	30,803	2.3%	94.3%
2004	34,251	4.8%	31,960	3.8%	93.3%
2005	35,849	4.7%	33,331	4.3%	93.0%
2005	38,114	6.3%	34,687	4.1%	91.0%
2007	39,844	4.5%	35,523	2.4%	89.2%
2008	40,904	2.7%	35,175	−1.0%	86.0%
2009	39,284	−4.0%	34,042	−3.2%	86.7%
Avg. annual change		2.8%		1.9%	
Change 2000–2009		28.1%		18.0%	
2010	40,546	3.2%	34,522	1.4%	85.1%
2011	42,735	5.4%	36,580	6.0%	85.6%
2012	44,599	4.4%	37,254	1.8%	83.5%
2013	44,851	0.6%	37,549	0.8%	83.7%
2014	47,058	4.9%	39,795	6.0%	84.6%
2015	48,978	4.1%	41,681	4.7%	85.1%
2016	49,870	1.8%	42,693	2.4%	85.6%
2017	51,885	4.0%	44,536	4.3%	85.8%
2018	54,446	4.9%	46,482	4.4%	85.4%
2019	56,633	4.0%	48,199	3.7%	85.1%
Avg. annual change		3.8%		3.8%	
Change 2010–2019		39.7%		39.6%	

Source: U.S. Department of Commerce, Bureau of Economic Analysis, Regional Data, Personal Income

Table 3.7 U.S. and Georgia GDP, All Industries, 1999–2019

Year	U.S. GDP (millions)	Annual Percent change	GA GDP (millions)	Annual Percent change	GA % U.S.
1990	$5,963,144.0		$140,646.1		2.4%
1991	$6,158,129.0	3.3%	$147,759.8	5.1%	2.4%
1992	$6,520,327.0	5.9%	$160,061.8	8.3%	2.5%
1993	$6,858,559.0	5.2%	$171,658.9	7.2%	2.5%
1994	$7,287,236.0	6.3%	$187,995.6	9.5%	2.6%
1995	$7,639,749.0	4.8%	$203,397.1	8.2%	2.7%
1996	$8,073,122.0	5.7%	$219,989.0	8.2%	2.7%
1997	$8,577,556.0	6.2%	$245,596.2	11.6%	2.9%
1998	$9,062,817.0	5.7%	$264,804.9	7.8%	2.9%
1999	$9,630,663.0	6.3%	$288,994.3	9.1%	3.0%
Avg. annual change		5.5%		8.3%	
Change 1990–1999		61.5%		105.5%	
2000	10,252,347.0		307,611.6		3.0%
2001	10,581,822.0	3.2%	318,753.0	3.6%	3.0%
2002	10,936,418.0	3.4%	326,929.6	2.6%	3.0%
2003	11,458,246.0	4.8%	340,410.6	4.1%	3.0%
2004	12,213,730.0	6.6%	364,255.2	7.0%	3.0%
2005	13,036,637.0	6.7%	386,785.0	6.2%	3.0%
2006	13,814,609.0	6.0%	402,144.6	4.0%	2.9%
2007	14,451,860.0	4.6%	415,131.9	3.2%	2.9%
2008	14,712,845.0	1.8%	412,911.9	−0.5%	2.8%
2009	14,448,932.0	−1.8%	407,024.5	−1.4%	2.8%
Avg. annual change		3.9%		3.2%	
Change 2000–2009		40.9%		32.3%	
2010	14,992,052.0		416,883.8		2.8%
2011	15,542,582.0	3.7%	429,547.0	3.0%	2.8%
2012	16,197,007.0	4.2%	444,132.2	3.4%	2.7%
2013	16,784,851.0	3.6%	460,585.1	3.7%	2.7%
2014	17,527,258.0	4.4%	485,816.7	5.5%	2.8%
2015	18,224,780.0	4.0%	513,565.6	5.7%	2.8%
2016	18,715,040.0	2.7%	539,525.1	5.1%	2.9%
2017	19,519,424.0	4.3%	566,473.6	5.0%	2.9%
2018	20,580,223.0	5.4%	592,153.4	4.5%	2.9%
2019	21,427,690.0	4.1%	616,333.3	4.1%	2.9%
Avg. annual change		4.0%		4.4%	
Change 2010–2019		42.9%		47.8%	

Source: U.S. Department of Commerce, Bureau of Economic Analysis, Regional Data. Federal Reserve of St. Louis, Economic Research, Gross Domestic Product

year, compared with the national average annual rate of 1.4% per year. Georgia employment grew more rapidly than U.S. employment in half the years of this period, but again not by much, and Georgia employment as a share of U.S. employment, only increased from 3.0% in 2010 to 3.1% in 2019. The Georgia unemployment rate was slightly above the national rate in nine of ten years between 2010 and 2019. During the same period, Georgia per capita personal income and U.S. per capita personal income grew at the same average annual rate of 3.8%. Georgia per capita personal income as a percent of U.S. per capita personal income remained steady at 85.1% in 2010, 2015 and 2019. Between 2010 and 2019, Georgia gross total domestic product (GDP) in current dollars grew at the average annual rate of 4.4%, while the U.S. GDP grew at the average annual rate of 4.0%. Georgia GDP as a percent of U.S. GDP remained steady from 2.8% in 2010 and 2.9% in 2018.[145] The state economy was stronger in 2010–2019 than in 2000–2009, although not quite as strong as in 1990–1999.

Compared with the U.S. economy, the Georgia economy was relatively strong during the three decades, 1990–2019, and that strength was reflected in stable revenue conditions for state government. Annual revenue growth is presented in Table 3.8. Between FY 1990 and FY 1999, revenue grew at an average annual rate of 6.6%,[146] despite relatively low growth in FY 1991 and FY 1992. Between FY 2000 and FY 2009, revenue grew at an average annual rate of 2.0% hampered by negative growth in FY 2002 and FY 2003 and the Great Recession in FY 2008 and FY 2009.[147] The first indication of a fiscal downturn came in FY 2008 when revenue collections were 0.7% less than the previous year and continued when revenue collections for FY 2009 and FY 2010 were 10.5% and 9.1% less than in the previous fiscal years. Recovery began in FY 2011 with revenue collections increasing year-over-year by 7.8% and continued through the end of the decade with revenue collection between FY 2010 and FY 2019 growing at an average annual rate of 5.9%.

By 2019, Georgia's economy had recovered from the Great Recession and was continuing to grow, albeit at a somewhat slower pace than in the immediate post-recession years, but no recession was in sight.[148] According to economic forecasts from both Georgia State University and the University of Georgia, population growth, higher defense spending, building construction and headquarters expansion of many Fortune 1000 companies were contributing to Georgia's economic growth.[149] Revenue collections for the first three quarters of FY 2020 (July through March)

---

[145] U.S. Department of Commerce, Bureau of Economic Analysis, Regional Data.

[146] Calculated in Excel by the formula:
(ending year amount/beginning year amount)^(1/(number of years − 1))-1.

[147] The National Bureau of Economic Research (NBER) reported that the recession began in December 2007 and ended in June 2009.

[148] Kenneth Heaghney, Georgia Fiscal Research Center, Georgia State University, "Testimony before Georgia House and Senate Appropriations Committees," January 22, 2019. James Salzer, "Solid Economy Forecast Boosts Budget Hopes; Georgia State Economist Says Growth May Be Slow, but Outlook 'Positive'," *Atlanta-Journal Constitution*, January 23, 2019: A1.

[149] Selig Center for Economic Growth, Terry College of Business, The University of Georgia, "Georgia Economic Outlook," December 6, 2018.

Table 3.8 Georgia Revenue Collections, FY 1990 – FY 2020

Fiscal Year	Net Revenue	% Growth
1990	$6,802,402,000	
1991	$6,861,631,000	0.9%
1992	$6,992,517,000	1.9%
1993	$7,826,861,000	11.9%
1994	$8,444,864,000	7.9%
1995	$9,115,243,000	7.9%
1996	$9,928,508,000	8.9%
1997	$10,543,106,000	6.2%
1998	$11,090,777,000	5.2%
1999	$12,068,478,000	8.8%
2000	$13,041,655,000	8.1%
2001	$13,934,126,000	6.8%
2002	$13,044,947,000	−6.4%
2003	$12,709,799,000	−2.6%
2004	$13,670,638,000	7.6%
2005	$14,709,913,000	7.6%
2006	$16,341,090,000	11.1%
2007	$17,567,795,000	7.5%
2008	$17,449,859,000	−0.7%
2009	$15,619,041,000	−10.5%
2010	$14,198,824,000	−9.1%
2011	$15,310,413,000	7.8%
2012	$16,052,536,000	4.8%
2013	$17,003,992,000	5.9%
2014	$17,883,284,000	5.2%
2015	$19,028,524,000	6.4%
2016	$20,814,604,000	9.4%
2017	$21,745,105,000	4.5%
2018	$22,706,424,000	4.4%
2019	$23,793,052,000	4.8%
2020	$22,748,258,000	−4.4%

Source: Georgia Department of Revenue, Annual Statistical Reports, FY 1991–2019

were slightly ahead of FY 2019 collection, 2.1% year-over-year. However, following the onset of the COVID-19 recession, revenue collections plummeted in April (−35.9%), May (−10.1%) and June (−8.8%), and FY 2020 ended with revenue collections 4.4% less than FY 2019 collections. Fiscal Year 2020 was one of only six fiscal years between 1990 and 2020, indeed between 1960 and 2020, in which revenue collections were less in current dollars compared with the previous fiscal year.[150]

---

[150] FY 2002, FY 2003, FY 2008, FY 2009 and FY 2010 were the other years. Controlling for the effects of inflation (CPI: 1982–84 = 100), FY 1975, FY 1980, FY 1991 and FY 1992 were also years in which revenue collections were less in constant dollars compared with the previous fiscal year.

Chapter 4
Patterns and Trends in Georgia Spending

During the past half century, a relatively small number of state agencies, five or six out a total of nearly 40, have accounted for between 75 and 85% of the state's spending. For the most part, they have been the same agencies, the Department of Education which establishes state-wide education standards and provides state funding to local school systems, the University System of Georgia Board of Regents which governs the state's network of 26 higher education institutions, the Department of Transportation which built and maintains the state's highway and bridge system, the Department of Corrections which operates the state's prison and offender rehabilitation system, and the Department of Human Resources which during most of this period functioned as an umbrella agency for the state's several health and welfare functions. Beginning in the 1980s, the General Obligation Debt Sinking Fund was added to the budget as a line-item and by the 2000s it had become one of the major items of state spending.

Public Education

Public education is the dominant function of state government based upon the proportion of the state budget devoted to it. State appropriations to the Department of Education increased over the past six decades from $239,866,325 in FY1965 to $7,944,481,675 in FY 2015, 49.1% of state appropriations in FY 1965 and 38.1% in FY 2015. As seen in Fig. 4.1, after decreasing from 49.1% of state appropriations in FY 1965 to 35.1% in FY 1975, as the Department of Human Resources and the University System of Georgia Board of Regents increased their shares of the budget in those years, the Department of Education stabilized its share of the state budget at 36% to 38% between FY 1985 and FY 2015. It has consistently been the largest purpose of state spending, constituting more than one-third of the state budget in each of the six decennials.

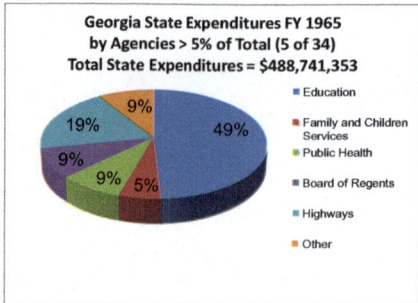
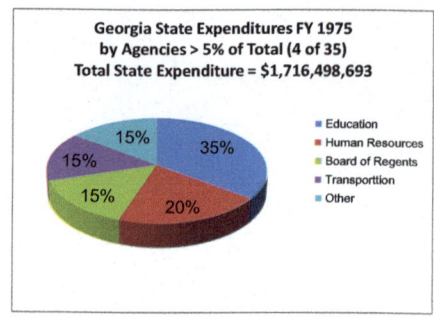
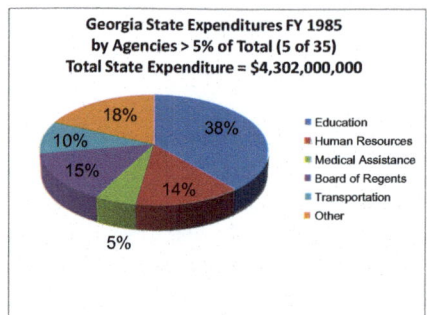
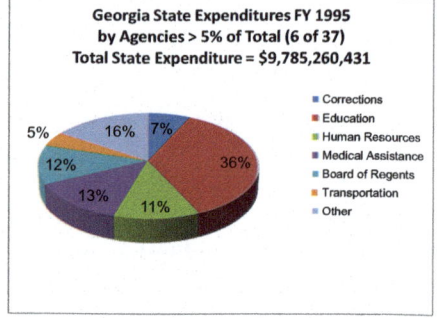
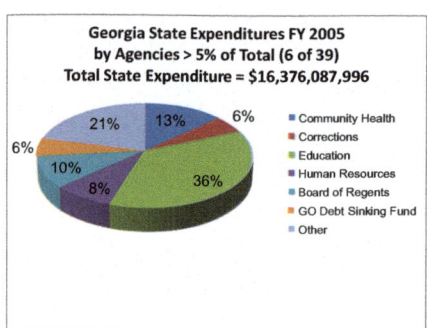
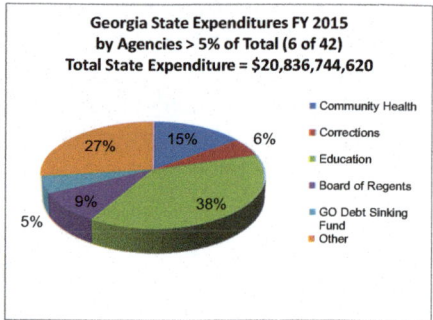

Fig. 4.1 Georgia state expenditures by agencies, FY 1965 – FY 2015

Public education is an obligation of the State of Georgia, free to citizens prior to the college or postsecondary level, supported by taxation.[1] It is delivered through local school systems within curriculum standards and teacher training guidelines established by the state Department of Education. The State Board of Education establishes policies that the Georgia Department of Education administers under the direction of the State Superintendent of Schools, an elected official. Public education is funded through a combination of state-level resources derived from the individual income tax, corporate income tax and sales tax, distributed by formula to

---

[1] *Constitution of the State of Georgia*, Article VIII, Section I, Paragraph 1.

local school systems, and local-level resources derived mostly from the ad valorem tax on real and personal property.

Although public education had been a state responsibility since the eighteenth century, it was not until the mid-nineteenth century that Georgia made much of an effort to have a comprehensive state school system for white children.[2] Significant educational improvement began in 1949, during the administration of Governor Herman Talmadge, with the enactment of the Minimum Foundation Program of Education (MFPE),[3] which extended the school year to 9 months, provided funding for adding a twelfth grade in all school systems, increased teacher salaries, and made funding available for pupil transportation. The General Assembly funded the MFPE beginning in 1951, facilitated by the enactment of the state sales tax in the same year. In 1951, the General Assembly also established the State School Building Authority[4] to lease state-built buildings to local school boards, which accelerated the state's conversion from small or one-room schools to modern consolidated school buildings. Georgia's public schools were segregated through the 1950s and resistance to the U.S. Supreme Court's desegregation decisions[5] continued into the 1960s. Although Georgia has made steady progress in funding for public education since that period, it still lags behind the per pupil expenditure levels of many other states.

In 1974, during the administration of Governor Jimmy Carter, the Georgia General Assembly enacted the Adequate Program for Education in Georgia (APEG),[6] intended to further improve public elementary and secondary education in the state. Governor Carter advocated a reform that ensured that all school districts would receive the same amount of state financial support regardless of the financial capacity of the district. Under APEG, each local school district was required to generate an amount of local effort in direct proportion to the ratio of its property wealth to that of the state as a whole.[7] Carter also advocated greater support for vocational education.

The Quality Basic Education (QBE) program was enacted by the General Assembly in 1985,[8] during the administration of Governor Joe Frank Harris. It was a major advancement in the way the state funds public schools and remains today the principal framework for funding public education in Georgia. It increased the level of state and local government financial support, required significant local financial effort, while at the same time taking into account the different resource capacities of local school systems. QBE established a formula to determine the cost

---

[2] Denise S. Mewborn, "Public Education (PreK-12)," *The New Georgia Encyclopedia*. Athens, GA: The University of Georgia Press, 1996.
[3] Georgia Laws, 1949: 1406–1422. HB 140 was approved February 25, 1945.
[4] Georgia Laws, 1951: 241–261. HB 1 was approved February 19, 1951.
[5] *Brown v. Board of Education of Topeka*, 347 U.S. 48 (1954); 349 U.S. 294 (1955).
[6] Georgia Laws, 1974: 1045–1100. SB 672 was approved March 26, 1974.
[7] Calvin L. Brown, "The Adequate Program for Education in Georgia," *Journal of Education Finance*, Vol. 4 (Spring 1978): 402–411 at 403–404.
[8] Georgia Laws, 1985: 1657–1784. SB 82 was approved April 16, 1985. Georgia Laws, 1987: 1169–1299. SB 179 was approved April 16, 1987.

per student of various programs provided by school districts, such as grade level instruction and special category programs.[9] In addition to state formula funding, local school systems are expected to contribute a local share based on revenue generated by five mills of property taxes on their system's tax digest.[10] Providing local share funding is a condition of participating in the QBE program. Local school systems ranking below the statewide average of per pupil tax wealth are eligible for additional financial assistance through a Quality Basic Education Equalization grant.[11] School districts may levy more than five mills and many do, up to a maximum levy of 20 mills.[12] In some years, the state has been unable or unwilling to fully fund the QBE formula. However, the QBE program was fully funded in FY 2019 and FY 2020,[13] before being reduced by $950 million in FY 2021 as the state was responding to the COVID-19 recession.

In 1993, Georgia enacted a pre-kindergarten program funded with lottery-for-education proceeds. The lottery was part of Governor Zell Miller's platform in the 1990 gubernatorial campaign, and voters approved a constitutional amendment in November 1992 to establish the lottery.[14] Georgia lottery proceeds were initially earmarked for education programs in three areas: voluntary pre-kindergarten for 4-year-old children, HOPE scholarships and student loans, and capital improvements for education, especially the development and maintenance of instructional technology. After FY 2002, lottery proceeds were appropriated only for pre-K and HOPE.

The Georgia Department of Early Care and Learning was established in 2004 with the mission of providing child care and educational services for children from birth through age four.[15] Among other things, it administers the lottery funded pre-K program and licenses and regulates child care centers. The new agency was the successor to the Office of School Readiness, which had been established in 1996. Although a relatively small agency, approximately 1.5% of the state budget in 2019, it is an integral part of the state's education system.

In addition to state funding for public education, many Georgia school systems are also eligible for federal funding under Title I of the Elementary and Secondary Education Act.[16] Title I of the Act provides financial assistance to schools and school districts with a high percentage of students from low-income families. The purpose of the funding is to support supplemental instruction for underachieving students.

---

[9] Official Code of Georgia Annotated (O.C.G.A.), 20-2-161.
[10] Official Code of Georgia Annotated (O.C.G.A.), 20-2-164.
[11] Official Code of Georgia Annotated (O.C.G.A.), 20-2-165.
[12] A tax rate of one mill represents a tax liability of one dollar per $1,000 of assessed value.
[13] In FY 2020, QBE formula spending amounted to approximately 90.0% of the Department of Education total budget.
[14] Georgia Laws, 1992: 3173–3211. HB 1541, "State Lottery – Tickets; Exemption from Sales and Use Taxes; Enacting Legislation," was approved May 7, 1992. The lottery was approved on November 4, 1992, with 1,131,168 (52%) in favor and 1,031,675 (48%) opposed.
[15] Georgia Laws, 2004: 645–681. S.B. 456 was approved May 12, 2004.
[16] Pub.L. 89–10, 1965.

Despite these education spending achievements, Georgia still lags behind the per pupil expenditure levels of other states. In the latest U.S. Census Bureau ranking (2017) of per pupil public elementary and secondary school revenue and spending,[17] Georgia is 36th in total revenue (from federal, state and local sources) devoted to education, 37th in revenue from state sources devoted to education, 30th in spending for teacher salaries and 30th in spending for employee benefits. Georgia with $11,758 in total revenue per pupil devoted to education is below the national average of $14,273, but ahead of the average of 10 other states in the southern region ($11,210).

Higher Education

Public higher education in Georgia is provided through universities governed by the University System of Georgia Board of Regents and funded through a combination of state appropriations, student tuition and fees, as well as institution-generated research grants and donor gifts. State appropriations to the University System of Georgia Board of Regents increased over the past six decades from $43,950,000 in FY1965 to $1,939,087,764 in FY 2015. However, after increasing from 9.0% of state appropriations in FY 1965 to 15.1% of appropriations in FY 1975, it decreased steadily as a share of total state appropriations from 14.6% in FY 1985 to 12.1% in FY 1995, 10.1% in FY 2005 and 9.3% in FY 2015. Institutions of the University System of Georgia have come to rely to a greater extent on their own funding sources, such as student tuition and fees, external grants to support faculty research and philanthropic gifts from alumni, friends and foundations.

As can be seen in Table 4.1, following the Great Recession, state appropriations became a declining share and student tuition became an increasing share of the Board of Regents budget. State appropriations as a share of, appropriations + tuition + fees, declined from 62.2% in FY 2007 to 50.1% in FY 2020. State appropriations increased between FY 2008 and FY 2020 by 38.7% and student tuition increased by 106.2%. A special institutional fee that was initiated in FY 2013 as a short-term revenue measure continued to generate approximately $200 million annually and has been approximately 5% of budget share during its years of existence.

The purpose of the HOPE Scholarship program, funded through the lottery-for-education initiative, was to increase participation and completion rates in higher education for Georgia students. Initially, it was available to all high school students with a family income below $66,000 and a 3.0 grade point average (GPA) in a college preparatory curriculum or a 3.2 GPA in high school curricula.[18] In the second year of the program, the HOPE Scholarship was available to all high school students

---

[17] 2017 Census of Governments: Finance – Survey of School System Finances. Tables 11 and 12.
[18] *Budget Report Fiscal Year, 1994.* p. 24.

Table 4.1 State appropriations and tuition as shares of resident instruction budget, FY 2007 – FY 2020

Year	State appropriations	Tuition	Special institutional fee	Federal-State stimulus	Percent change appropriations	Percent change tuition	Appropriations share
2007	$1,656,017,384	$1,005,462,318					62.2%
2008	$1,802,917,461	$906,447,547			8.9%	−9.8%	66.5%
2009	$1,971,696,830	$990,799,579			9.4%	9.3%	66.6%
2010	$1,794,043,592	$1,110,789,246			−9.0%	12.1%	61.8%
2011	$1,698,668,785	$1,348,991,332		$23,186,142	−5.3%	21.4%	55.7%
2012	$1,553,681,395	$1,493,995,961			−8.5%	10.7%	51.0%
2013	$1,631,690,795	$1,613,666,155	$201,047,577		5.0%	8.0%	47.3%
2014	$1,676,074,685	$1,677,551,095	$204,669,283		2.7%	4.0%	47.1%
2015	$1,729,907,930	$1,765,103,181	$206,960,404		3.2%	5.2%	46.7%
2016	$1,795,857,875	$1,888,812,577	$209,492,820		3.8%	7.0%	46.1%
2017	$1,897,455,350	$1,934,433,196	$213,165,139		5.7%	2.4%	46.9%
2018	$2,047,001,762	$2,002,496,950	$212,403,630		7.9%	3.5%	48.0%
2019	$2,153,266,402	$2,015,938,502	$215,580,726		5.2%	0.7%	49.1%
2020	$2,296,261,553	$2,073,258,377	$216,586,138		6.6%	2.8%	50.1%
2007–20					38.7%	106.2%	

Source: Annual Budget Reports, University System of Georgia, June 20, 2019

with a family income below $100,000.[19] In the years thereafter the family income threshold was eliminated. HOPE Scholarship grants were established as the difference between the amount paid by Pell or other federal grants and the tuition and fees at any Georgia public college an eligible student actually attended. The HOPE program is administered by the Georgia Student Finance Commission and scholarship grants are made directly to higher education institutions on behalf of the student.

Today, the HOPE Scholarship is an enormously popular and highly successful program. However, there was initial skepticism about it and in some instances, outright opposition. Many church leaders opposed the lottery, arguing that gambling is an unwholesome activity, that a lottery would encourage compulsive gamblers and that lottery players would be disproportionately the poor who can ill-afford such an expense. Others expressed concern that the availability of lottery proceeds would lead to a reduced level of general state funding for education. The *Atlanta Constitution* urged voters not to vote for the constitutional amendment that would establish the lottery for education.[20] It was supported by higher education leaders.[21]

The state lottery-for-education law requires that, "net proceeds of lottery games ... shall be used to support improvements and enhancements for educational purposes and that such net proceeds shall be used to supplement, *not supplant*, existing resources for educational purposes and programs."[22] In an effort to ensure that state general funds for education would not be cut and replaced by lottery proceeds, the state constitution was amended and the following language was added:

> ... Net proceeds after payment of ... operating expenses shall be separately accounted for and shall be specifically identified by the Governor in his annual budget presented to the General Assembly as a separate budget category entitled "Lottery Proceeds" and the Governor shall make specific recommendations as to educational programs and educational purposes to which said net proceeds shall be appropriated. In the General Appropriations Act adopted by the General Assembly, the General Assembly shall appropriate all net proceeds of the lottery or lotteries by such separate budget category to educational programs and educational purposes as specified by the General Assembly.[23]

Further, lottery reserves were required.[24]

---

[19] *Budget Report Fiscal Year, 1995.* p. 28.

[20] Cynthia Tucker, "No on the Lottery," *Atlanta Constitution*, October 20, 1992: A-18.

[21] Charles Walston and Robert Vickers, "Tuition Plan Controversial from the Start: Educators Praise It, but Foes Contend Miller is Trying to 'Buy' Votes," *Atlanta Constitution*, September 24, 1992: E-1.

[22] Official Code of Georgia Annotated (O.C.G.A.), 50-27-1.

[23] *Constitution of the State of Georgia*, Article I, Section II, Paragraph VIII (c).

[24] The lottery laws require two reserves that are funded as a percentage of lottery collections and are intended to avoid disruption in lottery-funded programs should lottery proceeds fall short of annual appropriations. The original law required an amount to be set aside each year equal to 10% of the prior year's total lottery proceeds. If net funds in the Lottery for Education Account are not sufficient to meet appropriations, funds are to be drawn from the reserve to make up the shortage. The lottery law was amended in 1994 to require a second reserve called the Scholarship Shortfall Reserve Subaccount. The scholarship reserve law requires a reserve equal to 50% of the amount of

Georgia has resisted the temptation to replace general purpose funding for education with lottery proceeds and shift general purpose funds to other state government functions for several reasons. First, the Constitution and statute require transparency in addition to earmarking. When fungibility is detectible, it is made more difficult. Second, the personal commitment of Governor Zell Miller, the chief advocate of the lottery-for-education initiative, ensured that during his administration lottery proceeds were used "to supplement, not supplant, existing resources for educational purposes and programs." Third, the policy architecture of the lottery-for-education program made fungibility unlikely because lottery proceeds were pledged for the initiation of three new programs, pre-kindergarten, HOPE scholarships and student loans, and instructional technology improvements. The policy architecture created expectations of spending for specific new programs, not simply promises of more spending for education in general. Fourth, a relatively strong state economy during the early years of the lottery made substitution unnecessary. The strength of state general revenues enabled Georgia decision makers, for the most part, to resist the temptation of fungibility and to appropriate lottery funds as additions to, rather than substitutions for, state general education funds.[25]

The lottery-for-education program encountered some bumps in the road in later years. By 2003, the number of HOPE scholars was increasing faster than the rate of growth in lottery revenues. Tuition at state colleges and universities was also increasing and, in combination with increasing student numbers, threatened the financial sustainability of the lottery-for-education program.[26] At that time, in addition to covering full tuition and fees, the HOPE scholarship also provided a book allowance. Further, it was discovered that there was not a standardized method across the state for determining a "B" average; some districts required an average of 82 to receive a B and other districts considered 80 as a B.[27] This distinction mattered because the Georgia Student Finance Commission was awarding scholarships to students with a "B" average. A number of adjustments to the HOPE scholarship program were proposed and considered during the 2004 Session of the General Assembly, including: standardize the "B" average requirement, reinstate the family income limit, eliminate the book allowance, require a minimum SAT score in addition to a B average,[28] and freeze tuition and fees for several years at their then-current level. The General Assembly approved a bill creating a uniform requirement of B = 3.0 based upon a 4.0 scale, with the expectation that it would reduce the

---

scholarship proceeds disbursed during the preceding year. Georgia Laws, 1994: 1662–1663. SB 711 was approved April 19, 1994.

[25] Thomas P. Lauth and Mark D. Robbins, "The Georgia Lottery and State Appropriations for Education: Substitution or Additional Funding?" *Public Budgeting & Finance*, Vol. 22, No. 3 (Fall 2002): 89–100 at 99.

[26] James Salzer, "HOPE Faces Funds Crunch," *Atlanta Journal-Constitution*, July 31, 2003: B1.

[27] Nancy Badertscher, "HOPE Looking to Survive," *Atlanta Journal-Constitution*, August 22, 2003: A1.

[28] James Salzer and Andrea Jones, "HOPE Panel Readies Report," *Atlanta Journal-Constitution*, December 16, 2003: D1

number of eligible scholarship recipients, and gradually phased out book and fee payments.[29]

In 2011, the lottery-for-education program again encountered financial difficulty, with enrollment in the state's colleges and universities and increases in tuition costs outpacing the growth rate of lottery revenue. Governor Nathan Deal recommended and the General Assembly approved another program revision aimed at keeping it financially viable.[30] At that time, students with a 3.0 GPA or better received a HOPE scholarship that covered all of their tuition and provided some funding for books and fees. Under the revised plan, approximately 10% of HOPE recipients would receive full tuition grants and would be known as Zell Miller Scholars. Included in this category were high school valedictorians, salutatorians and students graduating with a 3.7 GPA or better and a 1200 SAT or 26 ACT score. In order to retain full-tuition status, such students would be required to maintain a 3.3 GPA college/university average. Students with a 3.0 GPA or better would continue to receive HOPE grants, but the amount of the grant would be determined by lottery revenues rather than tuition rates. For the initial year of the revised program, the grants were equal to 90% of the 2010–11 academic year tuition rates.[31] Funding for books and fees was eliminated. During the 2014 gubernatorial election campaign, Governor Zell Miller was featured in a campaign advertisement giving Governor Deal credit for saving HOPE. The *Atlanta Journal-Constitution's* PolitiFact Georgia rated Miller's claims "mostly true."[32]

In FY 1994, appropriations to the lottery-for-education program were almost equally divided among pre-kindergarten, HOPE scholarship and capital outlays. In the early years, appropriations for the HOPE scholarship gradually increased as a percentage of the total lottery for education program. After FY 2002, appropriations for capital outlays were discontinued. As can be seen in Table 4.2, appropriations for the HOPE scholarship continued to increase as a percentage of the total, increasing from 48% in FY 2002 to 61% in FY 2003 and continuing to increase as a share of the total to almost 70% in FY 2019. Lottery appropriations as a percentage of state appropriations have on average been 4.2%.

When University System of Georgia Board of Regents spending is combined with that of the Department of Education, the Student Finance Commission and the Technical College System of Georgia,[33] the amount of spending for all education programs exceeds one-half of the state budget, totaling 52.3% in 2015.

---

[29] Georgia Laws, 2004: 922–936. HB 1325, "HOPE Scholarship; Comprehensive Revision," was approved May 17, 2004.

[30] Georgia Laws, 2011: 1–18. HB 326, "HOPE Scholarship and Grants; Comprehensive Revision," was approved March 15, 2011.

[31] For FY 2020, the HOPE Award as a percentage of tuition was at or slightly above 90% for most of the 27 University System of Georgia institutions. The exceptions were Augusta University-Health Sciences (86.6%), Georgia Institute of Technology (74.9%), Georgia State University (85.8%) and The University of Georgia (78.5%). Georgia Student Finance Commission, 2020.

[32] Nancy Badertscher and April Hunt, "Scholarship Claim on Target," *Atlanta Journal-Constitution*, October 31, 2014: B-1.

[33] Formerly known as the Department of Technical and Adult Education.

Table 4.2 HOPE as percent of total lottery for education appropriations, FY 1994 – FY 2019

Fiscal year	State appropriations	Lottery funds	Pre-K	HOPE	Capital/training	HOPE percent of lottery	Lottery percent of state
1994	$8,958,192,764	$125,000,000	$40,000,000	$39,710,010	$45,289,990	31.8%	1.4%
1995	$9,785,260,431	$240,173,298	$80,000,000	$87,948,601	$88,288,601	36.6%	2.5%
1996	$10,700,856,569	$420,556,569	$157,646,245	$120,281,000	$142,629,324	28.6%	3.9%
1997	$11,341,527,653	$546,198,773	$199,677,427	$164,474,361	$182,046,985	30.1%	4.8%
1998	$11,781,453,880	$510,000,000	$208,545,359	$175,439,127	$126,015,514	34.4%	4.3%
1999	$12,528,603,880	$530,000,000	$217,828,959	$221,147,965	$91,023,076	41.7%	4.2%
2000	$13,291,103,880	$543,000,000	$224,779,234	$235,533,326	$82,687,440	43.4%	4.1%
2001	$14,471,828,880	$530,000,000	$232,645,928	$227,382,697	$69,971,375	42.9%	3.7%
2002	$15,454,610,013	$550,000,000	$237,868,003	$264,942,647	$47,189,350	48.2%	3.6%
2003	$16,105,985,466	$625,000,000	$245,186,797	$379,813,203		60.8%	3.9%
2004	$16,174,683,712	$691,795,656	$250,490,013	$441,305,643		63.8%	4.3%
2005	$16,376,321,131	$645,000,000	$270,909,450	$374,090,550		58.0%	3.9%
2006	$17,415,249,819	$811,629,758	$290,081,308	$521,548,450		64.3%	4.7%
2007	$18,654,564,058	$841,554,506	$301,953,447	$539,601,059		64.1%	4.5%
2008	$20,230,620,936	$841,554,506	$324,857,346	$516,697,160		61.4%	4.2%
2009	$21,180,140,103	$882,255,743	$337,018,148	$545,237,595		61.8%	4.2%
2010	$18,569,866,489	$938,089,332	$349,596,285	$588,493,047		62.7%	5.1%
2011	$17,890,512,513	$1,127,652,261	$349,596,285	$778,055,976		69.0%	6.3%
2012	$18,299,477,557	$832,402,256	$335,294,298	$497,107,958		59.7%	4.5%
2013	$19,342,059,819	$904,439,791	$298,602,245	$605,837,546		67.0%	4.7%
2014	$19,920,261,481	$910,819,213	$312,173,660	$598,645,583		65.7%	4.6%
2015	$20,836,744,620	$947,948,052	$314,300,032	$633,648,020		66.8%	4.5%
2016	$21,828,789,407	$977,772,176	$321,295,348	$656,476,828		67.1%	4.5%
2017	$23,739,409,078	$1,073,563,561	$357,858,688	$715,704,873		66.7%	4.5%
2018	$24,997,351,235	$1,130,965,151	$364,845,613	$766,119,538		67.7%	4.5%
2019	$26,226,914,974	$1,201,496,219	$367,284,433	$834,211,786		69.4%	4.6%

Health and Human Services

The Department of Human Resources (DHR)[34] was created in 1972, as part of Governor Jimmy Carter's state government reorganization plan and reflecting a national trend toward comprehensive human services agencies. It incorporated the functions of such existing agencies as the Department of Family and Children Services, the Board of Children and Youth, the Commission on Aging and the Division of Vocational Rehabilitation.[35] Comprehensive social service agencies were at that time thought to achieve organizational economies of scale, the integration of social services, and one-stop-shopping for social service customers. DHR existed for 37 years until 2009 when it was reorganized into several departments. A free-standing Department of Community Health had been established in 1999 to operate the state's Medicaid and PeachCare-for-Kids programs. In 2009, a stand-alone Department of Behavioral Health and Developmental Disabilities was established and DHR was restructured. A separate Department of Public Health was reestablished in 2011.

In 1999, during the administration of Governor Roy Barnes, the General Assembly established the Department of Community Health (DCH).[36] The new department, in addition to having responsibility for the state's Medicaid program, was given responsibility for handling health insurance acquisition for state employees, retirees and their dependents. Consolidating the purchase of health insurance for Medicaid eligible Georgians and state employees was one of the underlying reasons for establishing the department, according to Governor Barnes and the chair of the House Appropriations Committee subcommittee on Health.[37] At the time, the combination of Medicaid enrollees and state employees was approximately two million persons—formidable buying power in the health insurance market. The Department of Community Health has three major divisions. The Medicaid division purchases health care on behalf of persons who are aged, blind, disabled, or low income. The division is also responsible for the PeachCare-for-Kids program which provides medical and dental coverage for children whose parents' income is too high to qualify for Medicaid, but who cannot afford private health insurance. The State Health Benefit Plan manages health insurance coverage for state employees, school system employees, retirees, and their dependents. The Healthcare Facility Regulation division inspects, monitors, licenses, registers, and certifies a variety of health and long-term care programs to ensure that facilities operate at acceptable levels of care and in compliance with the regulations governing them. Also attached

---

[34] In some states, such a department was called a Department of Human Services, to distinguish it from a human resources (personnel) unit.

[35] Georgia Laws, 1972: 1–64. HB 1424 and SB 449 were approved April 6, 1972.

[36] Georgia Laws, 1999: 296–317. SB 241 was approved April 19, 1999.

[37] Charles Walston, "Buying Power Seen in Health Agency Bill" *Atlanta Journal-Constitution,* March 18, 1999: D3. Andy Miller, "Community Health Supposed to Save by Buying in Bulk," *Atlanta Journal-Constitution,* March 21, 1999: D-6.

to the department are the Georgia Board of Dentistry which is responsible for the regulation of dentists and dental hygienists and the Georgia Board of Pharmacy which is responsible for the regulation of pharmacists and pharmacies.

In 2009, during the administration of Governor Sonny Perdue, the General Assembly established the Department of Behavioral Health and Developmental Disabilities (DBHDD).[38] The department provides treatment and support services to people with mental illnesses and addictive diseases, and support to people with developmental disabilities, through three divisions of Mental Health, Addictive Diseases and Developmental Disabilities. The impetus for the new department was concern about patient treatment in the mental health division of the Department of Human Resources. In 2009, Georgia entered into an agreement with the U.S. Department of Justice regarding this matter. While the state did not admit to violating patients' constitutional rights by compromising their safety, it agreed to a 5-year plan of improvements in state psychiatric hospitals.[39]

> The Settlement Agreement signed October 19, 2010 between the United States of America and the State of Georgia requires funding for community services directed towards developmental disabilities and mental health consumers of the Department of Behavioral Health and Developmental Disabilities (DBHDD). The agreement also calls for DBHDD to partner with other state agencies such as the Department of Community Health and the Department of Community Affairs in order to support the needs of its consumers.[40]

The settlement agreement established targets from FY 2011 to FY 2015 for developmental disabilities, mental health and quality management, with state compliance with the targets established in the agreement to be verified by an independent reviewer.

The 2009 reorganization of the Department of Human Resources (DHR), in addition to establishing the new Department of Behavioral Health and Developmental Disabilities, maintained the free-standing Department of Community Health that had been established in 2009 and reconstituted DHR as the Department of Human Services (DHS). The new DHS has four divisions. The Division of Aging Services provides a variety of services to promote the health, independence and protection of elderly Georgians. The Division of Family and Children Services provides child welfare and economic assistance services. The Division of Child Support Services helps children by enforcing parental obligation to pay financial support. The Division of Residential Child Care inspects and monitors a variety of child care programs to ensure that they operate at acceptable levels and in accord with state rules and regulations. It also has two attached agencies, the Council on Aging and the Department of Vocational Rehabilitation.

In the 2009 reorganization, the Division of Public Health was transferred from the Department of Human Resources to the Department of Community Health (DCH). In 2011, the Division of Public Health and the Office of Health Improvement

---

[38] Georgia Laws, 2009: 453–610. HB 228 was approved May 4, 2009.
[39] Alan Judd and Andy Miller, "State, Feds Agree to Plan to Fix Mental Care," *Atlanta Journal-Constitution*, January 16, 2009: A-1.
[40] *Governor's Budget Report*, FY 2011 through FY 2015.

from DCH were transferred to a newly created Department of Public Health (DPH).[41] The intent of establishing a separate department was to "… allow the state's public health challenges to get the attention they deserve."[42] DPH has three major functions: to diagnose, investigate, and monitor any diseases, injuries, and health conditions that may have an adverse effect upon Georgia's communities and people; to ensure the health and safety of Georgia's citizens by providing health protective services, including emergency preparedness; and to establish and implement sound public health policy.[43]

DHR was 19.8% of the state budget in FY 1975, 13.8% of the budget in FY 1985, 11.5% in FY 1995, declining to 8.4% in FY 2005 after the Department of Community Health (DCH) had been established in 1999 and 2.5% in FY 2015 after the Department of Behavioral Health and Development Disabilities (DBHDD) was established in 2009. Even though DHR declined as a share of the state budget, spending for health and human services increased.

The four health and social service agencies established in 1999, 2009 and 2011 together constituted 21.6% of the state budget in FY 2019: Behavioral Health and Development Disabilities, 4.4%, Community Health, 13.1%, Human Services 3.0% and Public Health 1.1%. They have grown at different rates during the period 2010–2020: Behavioral Health and Developmental Disabilities by 76.2% at an average annual rate of 5.8%, Community Health by 31.4% at an average annual rate of 2.8%, Human Services by −45.4% at an average annual rate of −5.9%, and Public Health by 39.4% at an average annual rate of 4.2%. During this same period, the state budget increased by 48.3% at an average annual rate of 4.0%.

In FY 2019, funds from the federal government supported a significant portion of health and human services spending in Georgia. While it was only 11.2% of the Department of Behavioral Health and Developmental Disabilities budget, it was 69.6% of the Department of Community Health budget, 58.5% of the Department of Human Services budget, and 58.9% of the Department of Public Health budget.

Sometimes a spending decision is not about spending, but about not spending. Such was the case in 2014 when the General Assembly enacted and Governor Nathan Deal signed legislation requiring the legislature's approval before the state could expand its Medicaid program under provisions of the Patient Protection and Accordable Care Act.[44] Prior to this action, Medicaid expansion could have been an executive decision. However, Governor Deal said the state could not afford to expand Medicaid services to potential new enrollees. In his State of the State Address, he said, "Had we elected to expand Medicaid, it would have required us to include approximately $209 million in this upcoming year's budget alone to cover the added cost."[45]

---

[41] Georgia Laws, 2011: 705–752. HB 214 was approved May 13, 2011.

[42] Carrie Teegardin "Deal Makes Public Health a State Cabinet Post; Youth Obesity Targeted," *Atlanta Journal-Constitution*, April 14, 2011: B1.

[43] *Governor's Budget Report FY 2019*. p. 220.

[44] Pub. L. 111–148 (2010).

[45] Nathan Deal, State of State the Address, January 13, 2016.

The Affordable Care Act enabled states to expand their Medicaid programs to cover uninsured adults at or below 138% of the federal poverty level. The federal government would pay 100% of expanded coverage for the first 3 years (2014, 2015 and 2016) and 90% of the cost thereafter. As originally enacted, the Affordable Care Act required states to expand their Medicaid programs as a condition of continued participation in the state-federal Medicaid program, but the U.S. Supreme Court found that provision of the act did not pass constitutional muster.[46] Hence, Medicaid expansion was a state by state decision.

Georgia House Bill 990 in the 2014 Session of the General Assembly prohibited the Department of Community Health, the Board of Community Health or any other representative of the state from expanding Georgia Medicaid eligibility by increasing the income threshold without prior legislative approval.[47] Similarly, state agencies were prohibited from operating an insurance "exchange" or providing navigator programs in furtherance of the Affordable Care Act.[48] In 2014, Georgia Medicaid was only available to non-disabled, non-pregnant adults if they were caring for a minor child and had a household income that did not exceed 35% of the federal poverty level. Non-disabled adults without dependent children were ineligible for Georgia Medicaid irrespective of their income level. The decision not to take advantage of Medicaid expansion under the Affordable Care Act left an estimated 500,000 low-income, working poor citizens uninsured.

In 2019, the General Assembly enacted and Governor Brian Kemp signed legislation that permitted the state to seek a federal government waiver to expand Medicaid to individuals earning up to 100% of the federal poverty level.[49] In October 2020, the Centers for Medicare and Medicaid Services approved Georgia's waiver plan.[50] Under the approved plan, some poor Georgians, those at 100% of the Federal Poverty Level (FPL), who meet a work, job training, volunteering or education requirement, would be eligible for Medicaid. However, other poor Georgians, those falling between 100% and 138% of the FPL, would remain ineligible for Medicaid. Georgians would no longer be able to buy individual health insurance on the federal website, *healthcare.gov*. Instead, they would be encouraged to purchase insurance through private companies, which are likely to offer coverage at lower premium prices, but coverage that also is likely to be less comprehensive than coverage

---

[46] *National Federation of Independent Business,* et al. *v. Kathleen Sebelius* et al., 567 U.S. 519, 132 S. Ct. 2566, 183 L. Ed. 2d 450, (2012).

[47] Georgia Laws, 2014: 293–294. HB 990 was approved April 15, 2014. Official Code of Georgia Annotated (O.C.G.A.), 49-4-142.2

[48] Georgia Laws, 2014: 243–247. HB 943 was approved April 15, 2014. Official Code of Georgia Annotated (O.C.G.A.), 31-1-40.

[49] Georgia Laws, 2019: 2–4. SB 106 was approved March 27, 2019. Official Code of Georgia Annotated (O.C.G.A), 49-4-142.3.

[50] State of Georgia, Office of the Governor, "Governor Kemp, CMS Administrator Verma Announce Approval of Georgia Healthcare Reform Package," Press Release, October 15, 2020; Ariel Hart, "Health Care Waivers Win Federal OK," *Atlanta Journal-Constitution*, October 16, 2020: A1; Jeff Amy, "Feds Approve Governor Kemp's Health Care Changes," *Athens Banner-Herald*, October 17, 2020: 1.

required under the Patient Protection and Affordable Care Act.[51] In February 2021, the federal Centers for Medicare and Medicaid Services, under a new administration, changed the status of Georgia's waiver plan from "approved" to "pending," holding that the work, volunteering or education requirement would be too difficult to meet, especially during the COVID-19 pandemic.[52] The federal COVID-19 pandemic and recession relief bill, the American Rescue Plan Act of 2021, offers states that have not expanded Medicaid another incentive to do so. In addition to the federal government paying 90% of the cost of individuals enrolled in expanded coverage (under the Affordable Care Act), states now electing to expand Medicaid would receive a 5 percentage-point increase in their traditional Medicaid assistance percentage for a period of 2 years.[53] For Georgia, one option would be to eliminate the work, volunteering or education requirement from its Medicaid waiver program. Another option would be to take advantage of the new federal funding incentive and fully expand Medicaid. As of this writing, these matters are unresolved.

Corrections

Corrections is a state government responsibility for protecting the public by operating safe and secure facilities for convicted offenders and for operating programs aimed at reducing recidivism, funded primarily from state revenue sources. Funding for the Department of Corrections, formerly the Department of Offender Rehabilitation, has increased from 1–2% of the state budget in the 1960s and 1970s to 5–7% since the 1980s. Among the relatively large state agencies, the Department of Corrections experienced the greatest spending growth with a budget that was nearly 300 times larger in 2015 than it was in 1965, increasing at an average annual rate of 12.1%.

Governor George Busbee had to deal with a crisis in the Georgia prison system as he was coming into office in 1975. The state's prison facilities were old, in poor repair and overcrowded, in part due to the state's mandatory sentencing policies. Based upon a law suit filed on behalf of Black inmates in 1972, U.S. District Court Judge for the Southern District of Georgia, Anthony Alaimo, in 1974 ordered desegregation of the Georgia prison system.[54] In addition to condemning the segregation, Judge Alaimo held that prison conditions and prisoner treatment in the prison

---

[51] Pub. L. 111–148.

[52] Greg Bluestein, "Medicaid Plan Now Up in the Air; Kemp's Proposal for Partial Expansion Runs into Sudden Federal Resistance," *Atlanta Journal-Constitution*, February 16, 2021: A-1. "Government Puts Georgia Medicaid Overhaul on Hold," *Athens Banner-Herald*, February 17, 2021.

[53] HR 1319, American Rescue Plan Act of 2021, 117th Congress, 1st Session (2021–22).

[54] *Guthrie v. Evans*, 93 F.R.D. 390 (S.D. Ga. 1998). The case had various titles, *Guthrie v. MacDougall*, *Guthrie v. Caldwell*, and *Guthrie v. Ault*.

system constituted cruel and unusual punishment.[55] In order to address the problem of prison conditions, Governor Busbee proposed additional state appropriations for facility improvements, to relieve overcrowding and to focus on prisoner rehabilitation. Between FY 1976 and FY 1983, the Department of Offender Rehabilitation appropriation increased by 167.1% from $52,576,281 to $140,454,676, at an average annual rate of 15.1%. During the same period, total state appropriations increased by only 93.1%, at an average annual rate of 9.9%. When prisoner altercations erupted into full-scale rioting at the Reidsville facility in 1978, the desegregation order was temporarily suspended before being reinstated in 1979. Governor Busbee was quoted in the *Atlanta Constitution* as saying, "I've done all that I can as governor of this state to improve the amount of money that is being spent, the amount of space for beds, the amount of training for these people. Everything they (the inmates) have complaints on that's legitimate, I've tried to improve on. The legislature is cooperating."[56] Throughout the life of the litigation, the District Court appointed a Special Master to try complaints (1976), a Special Monitor to survey compliance (1979) and in 1985, Judge Alaimo ended the litigation with a final injunctive order. In 1988, Governor Busbee wrote, "Despite the fact that prison overcrowding was the first problem I faced as governor, and despite the fact that we worked on a solution every year, the problem seemed to intensify instead of getting better. … It remains one of the thorniest of problems for our state."[57]

Criminal justice reform was one of Governor Zell Miller's budget priorities, emphasizing the need for tougher sentencing for repeat offenders. The centerpiece of Governor Miller's criminal justice policy was the "two strikes" constitutional amendment passed in 1994,[58] as he was running for election to a second term, that mandated that anyone convicted twice for one of seven crimes, murder, armed robbery, kidnapping, aggravated child molestation, rape, aggravated sodomy or aggravated sexual battery must be sentenced to life imprisonment without parole. Governor Miller subsequently achieved an increase in the mandatory minimum sentence for first time convictions for one of these seven crimes. After leaving office, Governor Miller wrote:

> We opened a record number of prison beds, more than 20,000, almost doubling the capacity when I took office. The additional bed capacity enabled me to end the practice in Georgia

---

[55] Bradley S. Chilton, *Prisons Under the Gavel: The Federal Court Takeover of Georgia Prisons*. Columbus, Ohio: Ohio State University Press, 1991. Bradley S. Chilton, "Guthrie v. Evans: Civil Rights, Prison Reform, and Institutional Reform Litigation." Doctoral Dissertation, The University of Georgia, (1988).

[56] Henry Eason, "Busbee: Integration Fuels Prison Violence," *The Atlanta Constitution*, April 7, 1978. p. 57.

[57] George D. Busbee, "Building a New Economic Order," Harold P. Henderson and Gary L. Roberts, *Georgia Governors in an Age of Change: From Ellis Arnall to Georgie Busbee*. Athens, Georgia: The University of Georgia Press, 1988. p. 284

[58] The vote on the "two strikes" amendment on November 8, 1994 was: Yes – 81% and No – 19%. Richard Whitt, "Two Strikes Now for Violent Felons," *Atlanta Journal*, November 9, 1994: C-11.

that had gone on for years of managing inmate population through the early release of the criminals, and it also allowed me to implement my "two strikes" law for violent felons.[59]

Increasing the number of prison beds was one of the policy objectives to be achieved by Governor Miller's budget redirection initiative.[60] The Department of Corrections budget increased by 43.3% during the Miller administration, below the 58.6% rate of increase for the government as a whole, but at a rate indicative of Governor Miller's tough criminal justice policy.[61] The "Get Tough on Crime" policies and the "Truth in Sentencing"[62] movement of the 1980s and 1990s increased Georgia's prison population and increased state spending for Corrections.

In 2012, during the administration of Governor Nathan Deal, the General Assembly enacted justice reinvestment reforms,[63] including reforms to reduce the imprisonment of nonviolent offenders, increase the referral of offenders to accountability courts, and to reinvest potential savings in other criminal justice reform programs. According to the Georgia Department of Audits and Accounts, Performance Audit Division, "Accountability courts are state-funded alternatives to incarceration for qualified offenders based upon their offense and characteristics such as drug addiction, mental health concerns, or history as a military veteran. Accountability courts provide supervision, community service options, and treatment to these offenders."[64] In his *Governor's Budget Report, Fiscal Year 2019*, Governor Deal wrote:

> In FY 2011, we had 53,341 offenders residing in our state's prisons. We projected that we would have more than 60,000 in prison by today. Instead of growing our population, today that number is less than 53,000, meaning we are paying for 7,000 fewer inmates than we would otherwise be housing, avoiding more than $156 million in annual costs to imprison these offenders. Sentencing reform has kept low-level, non-violent offenders out of our prison system, and accountability courts have diverted offenders to rehabilitative services within their communities.[65]

The Department of Corrections budget between FY 2012 and FY 2019 increased by 14.8% but probably grew at a lower rate than might have been expected had it not been for cost savings achieved through the accountability court program. A study conducted by the Carl Vinson Institute of Government at the University of Georgia in 2015 in Forsyth County, GA and Hall County, GA showed significant recidivism

---

[59] Senator Zell Miller, *A National Party No More: The Conscience of a Conservative Democrat.* Atlanta, Georgia: Stroud & Hall, Publishing, 2003. p. 58.

[60] Henry M. Huckaby and Thomas P. Lauth, "Budget Redirection in Georgia State Government," *Public Budgeting & Finance*, Vol. 18, No. 4 (Winter 1998): 36–44.

[61] No doubt driving the total state government budget increase was the Department of Education increase of 65.9% and University System of Georgia, Board of Regents increase of 54.9%, reflecting Governor Miller's even higher priority for education spending.

[62] Laws requiring that offenders serve all or most of a sentence imposed by a court and decreasing the possibility of early release.

[63] Georgia Laws, 2012: 899–949. HB 1176 was approved May 2, 2012.

[64] Georgia Department of Audits and Accounts, Performance Division, *Georgia Department of Correction*, Special Examination Report 18–12, December 2018.

[65] *Governor's Budget Report, Fiscal Year 2019*, Governor's Letter: 2.

reduction for graduates of accountability court programs. An economic impact study conducted by the Vinson Institute in 2017 showed the program saved the state millions of dollars. Accountability court programs were found to be both effective and economically beneficial.[66]

During the past 50 years, spending for corrections was characterized by reacting to prisoner protests and complying with federal court orders for prison reform, getting tough with violent felons, and making an effort to keep non-violent offenders out of the prison system.

Transportation

The Georgia Department of Transportation, established in 1972, began as the State Highway Department in 1916. The department plans, constructs and maintains Georgia's state and federal highways, funded with a combination of federal, 55%, and state, 45%, revenue. Early in the twentieth century it provided hard surface roads to enable Georgia's farmers to transport their products to market. In the 1960s and 1970s it partnered with the federal government for the construction of the interstate system[67] which linked Georgia with the rest of the nation.[68] Today, in addition to constructing and maintaining the state's highways and bridges, the Department of Transportation also has responsibility for planning and financial support for airports and mass transit. Funding for transportation, while still a significant share of the state budget, has declined as a proportion of total expenditures from 19.3% in FY 1965 and 15.3% in FY 1975 to 4.0% in FY 2005 and 4.3% in FY 2015. While the amounts of state spending for transportation continued to increase, the share of spending for transportation declined due to a growing complexity of the budget with several more purposes and higher rates of growth in other sectors such as health care and corrections. The motor fuel excise tax of 2015,[69] changed that pattern of decline.

---

[66] Scott Michaux, "Held Accountable: Nonviolent Offenders Get Second Chance—and the State Saves Money—Through Accountability Court Programs," *University of Georgia Research*, Vol. 49, No. 1 (Spring 2019): 32–35.

[67] Federal-Aid Highway Act of 1956, Public Law 84–627, provides that the federal government is responsible for 90% of project construction costs. In 1990, the interstate system became the Dwight D. Eisenhower System of Interstate and Defense Highways.

[68] I-95, along Georgia's east coast, links the northeast corridor of the United States with Florida. I-85 enters Georgia's northeast corner at the South Carolina border and exits the state to the southwest at the Alabama border. I-75 enters Georgia's northwest corner at the Tennessee border and exits the state to southeast at the Florida border. I-85 and I-75 are connected for several miles as they pass through Atlanta. I-20 is an east-west route through the middle of the state from the South Carolina border in the east to the Alabama border in the west, also passing through Atlanta. I-16 is a route through the state from Savannah in the east to I-75 in Macon, GA in the west. I-285 is a circumferential route around Atlanta.

[69] Georgia Laws, 2015: 236–264. HB 170, "Transportation Funding Act of 2015," approved May 4, 2015.

Table 4.3 Department of transportation and Georgia appropriations, FY 2012 – FY 2019

Fiscal year	State appropriation	Percent growth	DOT	Percent growth	DOT percent of state
2012	$18,162,513,870		$710,951,152		3.9%
2013	$19,224,524,133	5.8%	$783,848,668	10.3%	4.1%
2014	$19,864,261,481	3.3%	$810,062,823	3.3%	4.1%
2015	$20,836,744,620	4.9%	$856,106,198	5.7%	4.1%
2016	$21,782,964,314	4.5%	$876,295,966	2.4%	4.0%
2017	$23,739,409,078	9.0%	$1,714,541,590	95.7%	7.2%
2018	$24,997,351,235	5.3%	$1,900,033,551	10.8%	7.6%
2019	$26,226,914,974	4.9%	$1,916,080,040	0.8%	7.3%
2012–19		44.4%		169.5%	
Average annual growth		5.4%		15.2%	

Source: Governor's Budget Report, FY 2012 – FY 2019

The motor fuel excise tax of 2015, discussed in Chapter 3, enabled the state to increase spending for roads and bridges. As can be seen in Table 4.3, appropriations to the Department of Transportation for FY 2017 increased by 95.7% over FY 2016 appropriations, and the department's share of total state appropriations increased from 4% in FY 2016 to more than 7% in FY 2017. Governor Deal's FY 2017 budget proposed $815,522,064 in additional funding for bridges and roads.[70] His amended FY 2016 budget increased funding for bridges and roads by $758,713,485.[71] His FY 2017 budget also included $8,560,000 for debt service on $100 million in bond projects for bridge repair, replacement and renovation.[72] As can also be seen in Table 4.3, appropriations to the Department of Transportation for FY 2018 and FY 2019 continued at the higher level established in FY 2017.

State Spending Over 50 Years

The Georgia budget for FY 2015 ($20,836,744,620) was 42 times larger than the budget for FY 1965 ($488,741,353). It increased at an average annual rate of 8.0% over the 50 years.[73] The state agency with the largest share of the state budget in 2015, the Department of Education, was 32 times larger than it was in 1965, increasing at an average annual rate of 7.4%. Among the other large agencies, the University

---

[70] *Governor's Budget Report, Fiscal Year 2017*: 391–394. Eight items were identified as, "Increased funds to recognize additional revenue from HB 170 (2015 Session) for: capital projects, construction administration, departmental administration, Airport Aid, Local Maintenance and Improvement grants, planning, routine maintenance, and traffic management/engineering/signals."

[71] *Governor's Budget Report, Amended Fiscal Year 2016.* pp. 200–203.

[72] *Governor's Budget Report, Fiscal Year 2017.* p. 421.

[73] The real (June CPI-U, 1982-84 = 100) average annual growth rate was 3.6%.

System of Georgia Board of Regents had a budget that was 43 times larger in 2015 than it was in 1965. It grew at an average annual rate of 8.0%. The Department of Transportation budget was 8.5 times larger in 2015 than it was in 1965, growing at an average annual rate of 4.7%. Spending for human resources (including mental health, welfare and vocational rehabilitation) was 19 times larger in 2015 than it was in 1965, increasing at an average annual rate of 6.3%. Spending for health care was 74 times larger in 2015 than it was in 1965, increasing at an average annual rate of 9.2%.[74] The greatest spending growth among the large state agencies was for corrections with a budget that was nearly 300 times larger in 2015 than it was in 1965, increasing at an annual average annual rate of 12.3%. Table 4.4 and Figure 4.1 show the spending for these agencies between 1965 and 2015.

Since the time Georgia transitioned from a line-item budget format to a program budget format in 2005, the *Governor's Budget Report* has included summaries of appropriations by departments as well as policy areas. The FY 2015 appropriation for education policy was 54.5% of the budget, health policy was 22.3%, public safety was 8.4%, debt management was 5.5%, transportation was 4.0%, general government was 3.7% and economic development was 1.3%.[75]

Between 1965 and 2015 the population of Georgia increased from 4,332,000 to 10,214,860, an increase of 136%, increasing at an average annual rate of 1.8%. Taking into account the effects of population growth, the Department of Education budget per capita was 13 times larger in 2015 than it was in 1965, increasing at an average annual rate of 5.5%. Among the other large agencies, the University System of Georgia Board of Regents budget per capita was almost 18 times larger in 2015 than it was in 1965. It grew at an average annual rate of 6.2%. The transportation budget per capita was 3 times larger in 2015 than it was in 1965, growing at an average annual rate of 2.9%. Spending for human resources (including mental health, welfare and vocational rehabilitation) was more than 7 times larger per capita in 2015 than it was in 1965, increasing at an average annual rate of 4.5%. Spending for health care per capita was almost 31 times larger in 2015 than it was in 1965, increasing at an average annual rate of 7.3%. The greatest spending growth among the large state agencies was for corrections with a budget that was 126 times larger per capita in 2015 than it was in 1965, increasing at an annual average annual rate

---

[74] The Department of Public Health was a stand-alone unit until it was incorporated into the Department of Human Resources in 1972 as the Division of Public Health. In 1999, a new Department of Community Health was established with responsibility for administering the state's Medicaid program and managing health insurance acquisition for state employees, retirees and their dependents. In 2011, the Division of Public Health was transferred from the Department of Human Resources to a newly created Department of Public Health, with responsibility for diagnosing and monitoring diseases, and providing health safety and protective services for Georgia citizens. Community Health is the larger of the two departments. In FY 2015, it was 14.7% of the state budget and Public Health was 1.1%.

[75] These policy areas appear in the *Governor's Budget Report, FY 2016* as, Educated Georgia, Healthy Georgia, Safe Georgia, Debt Management, Mobile Georgia, Responsible and Efficient Government, and Growing Georgia.

Table 4.4 Selected state agency spending, FY 1965 – FY 2015

	FY 1965	FY 1975	FY 1985	FY 1995	FY 2005	FY 2015
Corrections	$3,830,000	$36,643,102	$196,593,359	$669,799,264	$882,663,975	$1,148,527,802
Education	$239,866,325	$602,798,584	$1,656,136,009	$3,531,338,321	$5,933,991,990	$7,944,481,675
Human resources	$25,907,000	$340,481,390	$592,344,802	$1,126,827,006	$1,372,493,286	$523,873,307
Health	$41,020,000		$230,300,935	$1,293,425,783	$2,147,704,748	$3,068,589,491
Board of Regents	$43,950,000	$259,959,207	$628,357,297	$1,180,303,526	$1,658,443,732	$1,939,087,764
Transportation	$94,499,990	$261,812,454	$412,217,504	$450,915,497	$646,858,968	$894,106,198
GO debt sinking fund			$121,834,641	$404,008,338	$923,167,993	$1,116,960,788
Other						
Total	$488,741,353					$20,836,744,620

Source: Governor's Budget Report, FY 1965, FY 1975, FY 1985, FY 1995, FY 2005 and FY 2015

Table 4.5 Selected state agency spending: Per capita, FY 1965 – FY 2015

	FY 1965	FY 1975	FY 1985	FY 1995	FY 2005	FY 2015
Corrections	$0.88	$7.24	$32.97	$92.92	$98.89	$112.40
Education	$55.37	$119.03	$277.75	$489.87	$664.80	$777.74
Human resources	$5.98	$67.23	$99.34	$156.32	$153.76	$51.29
Health	$9.47		$38.62	$179.43	$240.61	$300.40
Board of Regents	$10.15	$51.33	$105.38	$163.73	$185.80	$189.83
Transportation	$21.81	$51.70	$69.13	$62.55	$72.47	$87.53
GO debt sinking fund			$20.43	$56.04	$103.43	$109.35

Table 4.6 Selected state agency spending: Inflation adjusted per capita, FY 1965 – FY 2015

	FY 1965	FY 1975	FY 1985	FY 1995	FY 2005	FY 2015
Corrections	$2.80	$13.50	$30.64	$60.93	$50.84	$47.12
Education	$175.22	$222.08	$258.13	$321.23	$341.80	$325.96
Human resources	$18.93	$125.44	$92.33	$102.50	$79.06	$21.49
Health	$29.97		$35.90	$117.66	$123.71	$125.90
Board of Regents	$32.11	$95.77	$97.94	$107.37	$95.53	$79.56
Transportation	$69.03	$96.46	$64.25	$41.02	$37.26	$36.68
GO debt sinking fund			$18.99	$36.75	$53.18	$45.83

of 10.4%. Table 4.5 shows the per capita spending for these agencies in each of the decennials.

The Consumer Price Index (CPI) is a measure of the average change over time in the prices paid by urban consumers for a market basket of consumer goods and services. It is a widely used measure of inflation used to adjust other series for price change. Taking into account the effects of both inflation[76] and population growth, the Department of Education budget was 0.9 times larger in 2015 than it was in 1965, increasing at an average annual rate of 1.3%. Among the other large agencies University System of Georgia Board of Regents budget was 1.5 times larger in 2015 than it was in 1965. It grew at an average annual rate of 1.9%. The Department of Transportation budget was 0.5 times smaller in 2015 than it was in 1965, decreasing at an average annual rate of 1.3%. Spending for human resources (including mental health, welfare and vocational rehabilitation) was 0.1 time larger in 2015 that it was in 1965, increasing at an average annual rate of .3%. Spending for health care was more than 3 times larger in 2015 than it was in 1965, increasing at an average annual rate of 3.0%. The greatest spending growth among the large state agencies was for corrections with a budget that was nearly16 times larger in 2015 than it was in 1965, increasing at an annual average annual rate of 5.9%. Table 4.6 shows the inflation-adjusted per capita spending for these agencies. When population growth and the

---

[76] CPI-U, 1982-84 = 100

effects of inflation are taken into account, the state's spending growth across the six decennials has been relatively modest.

The purposes of state spending have remained fairly consistent throughout the six decennials, dominated by education (including elementary, secondary, higher and technical). The Department of Technical and Adult Education was added in 1995. More recently, state spending has been impacted by health care needs, especially for lower income individuals and children. The number of agencies receiving state appropriations increased slightly from the low thirties in 1965 to the high thirties in 2015.

Beginning with the administration of Governor Zell Miller, Georgia began to more aggressively and creatively use General Obligation (GO) Debt instead of cash to fund capital projects, freeing up cash for other purposes. The General Obligation Debt Service Sinking Fund appeared as an objective of expenditure in the FY 1985 budget at $121,834,641, 2.8% of the budget. It increased at the mid-point of the Miller administration in FY 1995 to $404,008,338, 4.1% of the budget and was $1,116,960,788 in FY 2015, 5.4% of the budget.

State Grants to Local Governments

Most of the state's spending is for goods and services provided directly by state agencies, but some state spending occurs in the form of grants to local governments that provide services through local agencies. The best example, of course, is spending for elementary and secondary education discussed earlier in this chapter. Other examples are grants from the Department Community Affairs, the Department of Natural Resources and the Department of Transportation.

The Department of Community Affairs, with a mission of local government assistance, safe and affordable housing, and community and economic development, has several grant programs to local governments to promote economic development; to expand the supply of affordable housing through rehabilitation and construction financing and to promote homeownership through mortgage and down payment assistance programs for low and moderate income home buyers; to assist Georgia cities and small towns in the development of core commercial areas and to champion development opportunities for rural Georgia; and to provide grants and loans to local governments and businesses to leverage private investment to promote economic development and job creation. The Department of Natural Resources funds a Solid Waste Trust Fund to assist local governments with the development of solid waste management plans and to promote statewide recycling and waste reduction programs. The Department of Transportation funds Local Maintenance and Improvement Grants to local governments for road and bridge resurfacing projects. The Georgia budget includes appropriations to state agencies for direct spending, as well as appropriations for grants to local governments for spending by local agencies.

A Low Spending State

As was seen in the previous chapter, Georgia is a low taxing state. It also is a low spending state. Based upon data published by the National Association of State Budget Officers, among the 50 states in fiscal year 2018, Georgia ranked 43rd in total expenditures, 26th in elementary and secondary education expenditures, 19th in higher education expenditures, 48th in public assistance expenditures, 49th in Medicaid expenditures, 24th in correction expenditures, 42nd in transportation expenditures and 41st in all other state expenditures.[77] Based upon the U.S. Census Bureau's *2018 Annual Survey of State Government Finances,* Georgia ranked 39th in education expenditures, 30th in health expenditures, 49th in welfare expenditures, 37th in corrections expenditures and 48th in highway expenditures.[78] In 2020, the Fiscal Research Center at Georgia State University ranked Georgia 42nd in per capita total state expenditures, 48th in per capita Medicaid expenditures and 35th in per capita correction expenditures.[79]

Georgia state government spending has been consistent with its economic capacity. Gross Domestic Product (GDP) is a widely used measure of the size of a state's economy. The state budget as a percent of GDP is a measure of the size of state government.[80] The Georgia state budget as a percent of the state GDP, between 1964 and 2018 was an average of 4.65%, with a range of 3.91% and 5.76%, and one standard deviation of ± .38%. The size of Georgia state government has been very stable over the past six decades (Table 4.7), and has been relatively small compared with all other states.[81]

The array of purposes for which the state spends its money and the amounts of current spending for specific functions and programs are no doubt the result of decisions—agreements, bargains and compromises—forged over many years by numerous past participants in the budget process. The purposes and amounts of state spending have evolved over many years, with relatively few changes in direction, to produce the current patterns of state spending.

---

[77] National Association of State Budget Officers, *State 2018 Expenditure Report,* Washington DC: 2019. Using the NASBO report of state spending and the U.S. Bureau of Census state population data, I calculated state spending per capita and ranked the states on that basis.

[78] U.S. Census Bureau, *2018 Annual Survey of State Government Finances,* Table 1, December 2018. Using the Annual Survey expenditure by function data and the U.S. Bureau of Census state population data, I calculated state spending per capita and ranked the states on that basis.

[79] Robert Buschman and Katherine Townsend, *Georgia's Rankings Among the States: Budget, Taxes and Other Indicators.* Atlanta, Georgia: Fiscal Research Center, Andrew Young School, Georgia State University, (January 2020).

[80] The state budget in this calculation is defined as the appropriation of state funds, which in a typical year is slightly more than 50% of the total budget which includes state appropriations, federal grants and other funds such as state agency earnings for provided services.

[81] The website *usgovernmentspending.com,* using data from the U.S. Census of Governments, State and Local Government Finances, annually ranks the 50 states according to spending as a percent of GDP. During the period 1980–2018, Georgia ranked between 39th and 50th among the states on this measure and consistently ranked below the measure of "all states combined".

Table 4.7 Georgia GDP and state budget, 1964–2018

Year	Georgia GDP	Georgia budget	Budget % GDP
1964	$11,253,000,000	$464,946,093	4.13%
1965	$12,519,000,000	$488,979,253	3.91%
1966	$13,808,000,000	$583,049,722	4.22%
1967	$14,711,000,000	$627,916,243	4.27%
1968	$16,424,000,000	$800,643,226	4.87%
1969	$18,082,000,000	$875,695,888	4.84%
1970	$19,365,000,000	$1,115,575,798	5.76%
1971	$21,570,000,000	$1,161,936,639	5.39%
1972	$24,610,000,000	$1,175,191,782	4.78%
1973	$28,226,000,000	$1,313,681,615	4.65%
1974	$30,378,000,000	$1,570,189,409	5.17%
1975	$31,995,000,000	$1,619,685,802	5.06%
1976	$36,425,000,000	$1,955,576,269	5.37%
1977	$40,785,000,000	$1,922,000,000	4.71%
1978	$46,154,000,000	$2,129,144,627	4.61%
1979	$51,550,000,000	$2,419,953,332	4.69%
1980	$56,229,000,000	$2,766,878,000	4.92%
1981	$63,751,000,000	$3,048,202,779	4.78%
1982	$68,451,000,000	$3,419,011,890	4.99%
1983	$76,738,000,000	$3,777,000,000	4.92%
1984	$88,466,000,000	$4,018,000,000	4.54%
1985	$98,223,000,000	$4,279,000,000	4.36%
1986	$108,089,000,000	$4,838,000,000	4.48%
1987	$117,033,000,000	$5,316,000,000	4.54%
1988	$126,565,000,000	$5,772,000,000	4.56%
1998	$133,794,000,000	$6,254,000,000	4.67%
1990	$140,646,000,000	$7,071,000,000	5.03%
1991	$147,760,000,000	$7,785,000,000	5.27%
1992	$160,062,000,000	$7,900,000,000	4.94%
1993	$171,659,000,000	$8,134,000,000	4.74%
1994	$187,996,000,000	$8,948,692,764	4.76%
1995	$203,397,000,000	$9,775,460,431	4.81%
1996	$219,989,000,000	$10,700,856,569	4.86%
1997	$242,153,000,000	$11,324,027,653	4.68%
1998	$263,950,000,000	$11,777,578,880	4.46%
1999	$287,725,000,000	$12,528,603,880	4.35%
2000	$306,528,000,000	$13,291,103,880	4.34%
2001	$318,226,000,000	$14,421,828,880	4.53%
2002	$325,863,000,000	$15,446,828,905	4.74%
2003	$340,627,000,000	$16,177,689,408	4.75%
2004	$364,062,000,000	$16,281,651,592	4.47%
2005	$388,342,000,000	$16,125,208,162	4.15%

(continued)

Table 4.7 (continued)

Year	Georgia GDP	Georgia budget	Budget % GDP
2006	$404,206,000,000	$17,415,249,819	4.31%
2007	$417,700,000,000	$18,654,564,058	4.47%
2008	$411,866,000,000	$20,230,620,936	4.91%
2009	$404,575,000,000	$21,425,140,103	5.30%
2010	$412,485,000,000	$20,193,974,890	4.90%
2011	$424,126,000,000	$18,156,435,820	4.28%
2012	$439,058,000,000	$18,162,513,870	4.14%
2013	$454,238,000,000	$19,224,524,133	4.23%
2014	$479,138,000,000	$19,864,261,481	4.15%
2015	$505,693,000,000	$20,836,744,620	4.12%
2016	$532,657,000,000	$21,782,964,314	4.09%
2017	$554,269,000,000	$23,739,409,078	4.28%
2018	$592,134,000,000	$24,997,351,235	4.22%
Average			4.65%
SD			0.38%

Chapter 5
The Executive Budget in Georgia

This chapter begins with the history of the budget "idea" in the United States, recounts efforts to adopt it in Georgia during the first half of the twentieth century, and identifies the Budget Act of 1962 as achievement of the budget idea in Georgia and the beginning of the modern era of Georgia state budgeting.

The Budget Idea[1]

The Progressive Era in the United States, from roughly the 1890s to the 1920s, was a period of political activism, modernization and reform which sought, among other objectives, the elimination of corruption, waste and inefficiency at all levels of government. The idea of a budget first emerged as a feature of the municipal reform movement early in the twentieth century. Although the budget idea emerged at a somewhat later date in the states, it spread more rapidly among the states than it had among municipalities.[2] The executive budget was in part a reaction to irresponsible government,[3] and was intended to reduce waste and inefficiency. During the first two decades of the twentieth century the task of improving state and local government was seen as having both moral and administrative/technical dimensions, and the executive budget was an important element of the good government movement.

---

[1] An earlier version of this chapter was published in Glenn Abney and Thomas P. Lauth, "The Executive Budget in the States: Normative Idea and Empirical Observation," *Policy Studies Journal*, Vol. 17, No. 4 (Summer 1989): 829–840 at 830–832.

[2] William F. Willoughby, *The Movement for Budget Reform in the States*, New York: J. Appleton and Company, 1918. p. 11.

[3] Frederick A. Cleveland, "Evolution of the Budget Idea in the U.S." *Annals of the American Academy of Political and Social Sciences*, Vol. 62, No. 1 (November 1915): 15–35, at 32 and 35.

Prior to the executive budget movement, it was common practice for executive branch agencies to submit their spending estimates for the next fiscal period directly to the legislature. Neither the governor nor any other executive branch agency had authority to coordinate or revise those estimates, consider them in relationship to each other, or balance them against an estimate of available revenue. Further, agency estimates were submitted at different times, in a variety of forms, and adhered to no common classification schemes. Many advocates of good government considered such practices as insufficient, likely to lead to excessive spending or abuse in the handling of public funds. These problems were exacerbated in state government by the large number of agency heads which were either directly elected, or appointed by independent boards or commissions.[4]

As an antidote to these problems, the executive budget movement advocated an integrated administrative system with the governor as chief administrator.[5] At the structural or institutional level this was expressed as the principle that agency heads should be directly appointed by the governor rather than by boards or commissions, and that gubernatorial appointment was preferable to popular election.[6] At the functional level, it called for a budget system in which agency requests were to be submitted to the legislature only after being coordinated and reviewed by the governor. The governor's budget recommendation to the legislature was to be a comprehensive document which not only verified the accuracy of agency estimates and the soundness of agency requests, but also weighed their importance in relationship to each other, and assessed their compatibility with the policy goals and program objectives of the governor. Reformers argued that as the governor's budget preparation responsibilities increased, his or her ability to direct and control executive branch agencies would be improved. This would serve the democratic values of responsiveness and responsibility.[7]

It was also believed by those associated with the executive budget movement that if governors' budget responsibilities were to amount to more than a routine transmission of agency requests to the legislature, it would be necessary to have a central budget agency under the immediate control of the governor to facilitate these review and coordination functions.[8] Central budget agencies would be empowered to install a system of accounts and reports, to devise common forms and classifications for estimates and requests, and authorized to obtain from agencies the data needed to

---

[4] William F. Willoughby, *The Movement for Budget Reform in the States*, New York: J. Appleton and Company, 1918, p. 8.

[5] William F. Willoughby, *The Movement for Budget Reform in the States*, New York: J. Appleton and Company, 1918, p. 207.

[6] William F. Willoughby, *The Movement for Budget Reform in the States*, New York: J. Appleton and Company, 1918, p. 13.

[7] Frederick A. Cleveland, "Evolution of the Budget Idea in the U.S." *Annals of the American Academy of Political and Social Sciences,* Vol. 62, No. 1 (November 1915): 15–35, at 18–19.

[8] William F. Willoughby, *The Movement for Budget Reform in the States*, New York: J. Appleton and Company, 1918. p. 208.

frame a budget.[9] The budget office would be staffed by a permanent service which represents the government as a whole when reviewing the estimates of spending agencies.[10] It would have the function of balancing the demands of the several spending agencies and protecting the treasury from demands being made upon it by those agencies. It would also function as an agent of the governor charged with responsibility for controlling agency spending and formulating a consolidated spending plan for the coming fiscal period.

On balance, the budget idea was advocated as both an instrument of democracy[11] and a method to improve public administration. The executive budget was intended to help popularly elected chief executives direct and control agencies of the executive branch, and it was expected to improve accountability and efficiency in the performance of executive branch agencies.

The Executive Budget in Georgia

The budget process in Georgia was dominated by the legislative branch until 1931. The executive budget did not fully emerge in Georgia until 1962, following a series of actions between 1931 and 1961 in which some, but not all, of the executive budget principles were incorporated into the financial practices of state government.

Legislative Dominance: During the first three decades of the twentieth century, legislative commissions received agency expenditure estimates and made appropriation recommendations to the General Assembly. The first effort to relate proposed spending to available revenue came in 1918 when the General Assembly created an Examining Commission of State Government consisting of the Chairman of the House of Representatives Appropriations Committee, the Chairman of the Senate Appropriations Committee, the Governor, the Attorney General and the Superintendent of Schools. It was charged with examining the financial needs of all state agencies and making an annual recommendation to the General Assembly whether to increase, decrease or continue existing appropriations.[12]

In 1922, the General Assembly created the Investigating and Budget Commission consisting of the Chairmen of the House of Representatives and Senate Appropriations Committees, the Governor, the Attorney General and the Comptroller. It had responsibility for collating department expenditure estimates and preparing a budget recommendation to the General Assembly.[13] The 1922

---

[9] William F. Willoughby, *The Movement for Budget Reform in the States*, New York: J. Appleton and Company, 1918. p. 187.
[10] William F. Willoughby, *The Movement for Budget Reform in the States*, New York: J. Appleton and Company, 1918. p. 187.
[11] Frederick A. Cleveland, "Evolution of the Budget Idea in the U.S." *Annals of the American Academy of Political and Social Sciences* (November 1915): 15–35, at 35.
[12] Georgia Laws, 1918: 155–158. Approved August 12, 1918.
[13] Georgia Laws, 1922: 128–132. Approved July 26, 1922.

legislation did not abolish the 1918 Examining Commission; both operated from 1922 until 1931. The state budget process during this period was dominated by the General Assembly with the governor's role limited to membership on the two commissions.

According to Barney Reeves,[14] the budget commissions failed to promote good budgeting practices for several reasons. First, the budget presented by the commission did not represent an executive plan. Even though the governor was chairman of the commission, other commission members did not owe allegiance to him because they were either elected executives or legislators. Second, the commission budget was primarily an attempt to confine spending within the total of available revenue, not a proactive financial plan. Third, the legislature enacted permanent appropriations for specific purposes, for example highways, thus reducing the availability of general-purpose funds and limiting the opportunity to consider activities and programs in relationship to each other. Fourth, many state agencies collected taxes and fees, and did so in an uncoordinated manner. Fifth, the legislature often failed to honor the commission's recommendations and instead, according to Reeves, tended to be more responsive to lobbying interests.

Executive Dominance: The three decades between 1931 and 1961 were characterized by a shift of budgetary control away from the legislature to the executive.[15] In 1931, the General Assembly initiated the state's first executive budget system by establishing a Bureau of the Budget in the State Auditor's office with the governor as the ex officio Director of the Budget and the State Auditor as Assistant Director of the Budget.[16] The auditor, as chief operating officer, was to assist the governor in collecting and reviewing agency expenditure estimates, preparing a budget document and drafting a biennial appropriations bill. All state agencies, except the legislative and judicial branches, were required to submit to the Bureau of the Budget spending estimates for the ensuing biennium, subject to revision by the Director.[17] Notably, the budget bureau was located in the auditor's office not the governor's office and no technical staff was provided.[18] Routine budget administration was performed by the auditor's office. The objective, as recommended in the Lutz

---

[14] Barney A. Reeves, "The Georgia State Budget System – Its Origins. Development and Current Administration." Unpublished MA Thesis, Emory University, 1948. pp. 20–23.

[15] Augustus B. Turnbull, III, "Politics in the Budgetary Process: The Case of Georgia," Ph.D. Dissertation, University of Virginia, 1967. p. 67.

[16] Georgia Laws 1931, Extraordinary Session: 94–98. The Act of 1918, creating an Examining Commission, and the Act of 1922, creating a State Investigating and Budget Commission were repealed.

[17] Barney A. Reeves, "The Georgia State Budget System – Its Origins, Development and Current Administration." Unpublished MA Thesis, Emory University, 1948. p. 28. Glenn Ramsey, "Governor Takes First Steps to Inaugurate New Budget Law," *Atlanta Constitution*, November 22, 1931: 8C.

[18] Augustus B. Turnbull, III, "Politics in the Budgetary Process: The Case of Georgia," Ph.D. Dissertation, University of Virginia, 1967. p. 60.

Report,[19] was to "set up a more effective budget system, under which expenditures and revenues can be held in balance." However, after 1931 the budget document was eliminated. The governor was required only to submit a draft appropriations bill and a budget message. After 1935, the requirement that agencies submit spending estimates was eliminated. The records of the State Auditor regarding past appropriations and spending replaced the budget document, and the auditor's conference with agencies was thought to make agency spending estimates unnecessary.[20] These changes contributed to shifting budget control from the legislature to the executive branch, especially to the State Auditor.

In 1943, the General Assembly amended the 1931 Budget Act to establish an Income Equalization Account which authorized the governor to appropriate to agencies any funds designated by the State Auditor to be surplus at the end of the fiscal year.[21] During this period, Georgia operated under a system of biennial appropriations which provided that an appropriations act was in force until repealed or the next one was passed. Gus Turnbull reported that only nine general appropriations acts were passed between 1931 and 1961, and that in many years more than one-half of the state's income was expended without legislative or executive examination of feasibility or need.[22] Because appropriations acts often extended beyond 2 years and a growing state economy was producing a robust revenue yield, the governor was also able to allocate substantial amounts of budget authority to agencies without having to obtain the approval of the General Assembly. After 1951, sales tax revenue[23] was generating funds that in the absence of biennial appropriations were disbursed on behalf of the governor by the State Auditor. In 1960, the state constitution was amended to repeal the automatic appropriation of automobile registration revenue to the Highway Department,[24] providing additional revenue for discretionary appropriation. Although the legislature attempted from time to time during the 1943–1961 period to limit the governor's distribution of surplus funds, the combination of infrequent appropriations acts and the delegation of appropriation authority to the

---

[19] A report to Governor Lamartine Hardman from Harley L. Lutz, Professor of Public Finance, Princeton University, "The Georgia System of Revenues – Its Problems and Their Remedies, A Plan of Revision and Reorganization," 1930.

[20] Barney A. Reeves, "The Georgia State Budget System – Its Origins. Development and Current Administration." Unpublished MA Thesis, Emory University, 1948. p. 29.

[21] Georgia Laws, 1943: 84–96 at 91. Approved January 29, 1943.

[22] Augustus B. Turnbull, III, "Politics in the Budgetary Process: The Case of Georgia," Ph.D. Dissertation, University of Virginia, 1967. p. 61. Augustus B. Turnbull, III, "Georgia Budgeting Comes of Age," *Georgia Government Review*, Vol. 1, No. 3 (September 1968): 1. See also Cullen B. Gosnell and C. David Anderson, *The Government and Administration of Georgia*, New York: Thomas Y. Crowell Company, 1956. pp. 125–126.

[23] In 1951, the General Assembly passed a general sales tax act at the rate of 3% on retail transactions. The tax went into effect on April 1, 1951 and quickly became the largest single source of state revenue.

[24] *Constitution of the State of Georgia*, 1945, Article VII, Section IX, Paragraph IV, as amended 1960.

governor resulted in a shift of budgetary power from the General Assembly to the governor.[25] A contemporary account summarized the situation in the following way:

> In periods of expanding revenues, the total amount of the appropriation act in force may be considerably less than the actual amount of annual receipts, and ... the distribution of the surplus is left to the discretion of the Budget Bureau, in the final analysis, the governor. The lack of a general appropriation act at each session of the legislature surrenders the power of appropriation over large sums of revenue by the legislature to the Budget Bureau.[26]

In 1961, a major political struggle between Governor Ernest Vandiver and the General Assembly over appropriations resulted in actions to limit the nearly total power of the governor in budgetary matters.[27] Funding for the state Highway Department and teacher pay raises were the proximate issues, but the real cause was growing legislative interest in curtailing the budget power of the governor and State Auditor and re-establishing its own budget prerogatives.[28] From the General Assembly's perspective the fight had two opponents, the governor and the State Auditor. The State Auditor, B. E. Thrasher, was perceived to be an honest and dedicated public servant,[29] but he was wearing three hats as deputy budget director, advisor to the legislature and State Auditor. The emerging opinion in the legislature was that he should perform the *post-audit* function only, and that the state needed a budget analyst to perform the *pre-audit* function.[30] The governor was thought to have access to excessively large surpluses, accruing from sales tax revenue as well as from unspent funds that agencies were carrying over from year to year. It was also thought that there should be a budget analyst to consult with agencies and help prepare the executive budget.[31]

Initially, there was enthusiasm for a legislative budget board comprised of members of the General Assembly, the governor, lieutenant governor, treasurer, comptroller and secretary of state, but dominated by the legislature, to make budget recommendations to the General Assembly.[32]

Two unforeseen events impacted the 1961 budget battle. In 1960, Governor Vandiver suffered a heart attack and was unable to participate in drafting the

---

[25] Augustus B. Turnbull, III, "Politics in the Budgetary Process: The Case of Georgia," Ph.D. Dissertation, University of Virginia, 1967. p. 73.

[26] Cullen B. Gosnell and C. David Anderson, *The Government and Administration of Georgia*. New York: Thomas Y. Crowell Company, 1956. pp. 129–130.

[27] Augustus B. Turnbull, III, "Politics in the Budgetary Process: The Case of Georgia," Ph.D. Dissertation, University of Virginia, 1967. pp. 81–118.

[28] Editorial, "We Suggest that Everybody Simmer Down and Get on With the State's Business," *Atlanta Constitution*, February 22, 1961: 4 and Editorial, "Budget Fight Has Run Its Course," *Atlanta Constitution*, February 28, 1961: 4

[29] Eugene Patterson, "B.E. Thrasher Can Lift the Bull," *Atlanta Constitution*, February 14, 1961: 4.

[30] "Relieve Thrasher of Duties on Budget, Rep. Ray Asks," *Atlanta Constitution*, January 25, 1961: 8 and "New Budget Officer Passes House, 121–0," *Atlanta Constitution*, February 1, 1961: 36.

[31] Editorial, "Let Budget Study Stick to Constructive Note," *Atlanta Constitution*, July 14, 1961: 4

[32] "Legislative Control Panel Pushed," *Atlanta Constitution*, January 12, 1960: 7.

appropriations bill for FY 1961.[33] In the same year, B. E. Thrasher, the State Auditor, became ill and did not participate in the preparation of the FY 1961 budget recommendation.[34]

Governor Vandiver's dispute with the Georgia Education Association over teacher pay raises in the FY 1962 budget resulted in political pressure on the General Assembly to assert its prerogatives in budgetary matters. As part of an agreement with the General Assembly over teacher pay raises, Governor Vandiver also agreed to the establishment of a joint Legislative Budget Study Committee to modernize the state's budget process. The 17-member committee was made up of members of the House of Representatives (n = 7), Senate (n = 5) and appointees from the executive branch (n = 5).[35] During 1961, the *Atlanta Constitution* extensively reported on these actions and editorialized in favor of budget reform initiatives, prodding as appropriate and chiding when thought to be necessary.[36] The Legislative Budget Study Committee recommended that:[37]

- Appropriations should be annual or biennial, but certainly regular and recurring
- Unspent funds should lapse back to the treasury at the end of the fiscal period
- There should be a legislative committee to monitor the budget when the legislature was not in session
- During budget preparation, information should be obtained from agencies[38]
- The legislature should be able to question agencies during their consideration of the governor's budget recommendation
- The governor should hire a professionally qualified budget analyst[39]
- The governor's control of surplus funds should be eliminated
- The governor should retain strong budget authority, but not total dominance in the process[40]

---

[33] Augustus B. Turnbull, III, "Politics in the Budgetary Process: The Case of Georgia," Ph.D. Dissertation, University of Virginia, 1967. p. 83.

[34] Augustus B. Turnbull, III, "Politics in the Budgetary Process: The Case of Georgia," Ph.D. Dissertation, University of Virginia, 1967. p. 85.

[35] "Vandiver's House Budget Foes Selected for Study Panel," *Atlanta Constitution*, April 6, 1961: 21, "Vandiver Confers with Budget Unit," *Atlanta Constitution*, May 16, 1961: 17 and Editorial, "Budget Study Group Challenged to Service," *Atlanta Constitution*, June 9, 1961: 4

[36] Editorial, "Revision of State Budget Procedure Needed Despite Political Prospects," *Atlanta Constitution*, November 8, 1961: 4.

[37] "Vandiver Supports Budget Panel's Plan," *Atlanta Constitution*, November 29, 1961: 32, Editorial, "Governor and Legislature Make Peace and the Taxpayer of Georgia Wins," *Atlanta Constitution*, November 29, 1961: 4 and "Budget Panel's Findings Speaker Smith Hails," *Atlanta Constitution*, December 2, 1961: 20.

[38] B. E. Thrasher testified that in past years legislators told him not to bother with agency information because they did not care about such information; it was a waste of time and money. See: "Permanent Panel for Budget Urged: Thrasher Calls for Committee to Work During Recesses," *Atlanta Constitution*, July 13, 1961: 8.

[39] "Cut Governor's Power on Budget, Byrd Asks," *Atlanta Constitution*, November 7, 1961: 7.

[40] Sam Hopkins, "Lawmakers to Ask for Bigger Budget Role," *Atlanta Constitution*, October 11, 1961: 3.

- There should be an "emergency fund" available to the governor, limited to 1% of the appropriation bill.

The idea of a legislative budget board that would make appropriation recommendations to the General Assembly was blocked by Governor Vandiver and Lieutentant Governor Byrd, the presiding officer of the Senate, and was not part of the Study Committee's recommendation.[41]

In his 1962 State of the State address,[42] Governor Vandiver told the General Assembly that he joined their committee in recommending to them:

> First, a constitutional amendment which would require, with no ifs, ands, or buts, a biennial appropriations bill; which would provide for a split session of the General Assembly in odd numbered years – 15 days to organize and receive the budget and 30 more days for an appropriating session in the spring nearer the beginning of the ensuing fiscal year; an amendment which would limit appropriations to income and surplus; which would limit authority debt obligation to 15% of the total budget and which would otherwise provide a system of appropriations control by the General Assembly.
>
> Second, an act to establish a modern-day and universally-accepted, functioning Budget Bureau for Georgia with a qualified staff, evolving a continuing financial plan for capital and recurring expenditures, this plan and related data to be available at all times to the General Assembly, the press, the public and to the governor.

He added, "By the re-assertion of your sovereign prerogatives over the public purse, you will bring responsibility, and accountability to state fiscal administration."

The Budget Act of 1962[43] reduced the fiscal powers of the governor and State Auditor, but it also provided the framework for Georgia's modern executive budget process.[44] It continued the governor as ex officio Director of the Budget but discontinued the State Auditor as Assistant Director of the Budget. Further, the budget office was relocated from the State Auditor's office to the governor's office, the position of State Budget Officer[45] was created and technical staff was authorized.[46] The Bureau of Budget was empowered to establish a system of accounts, classifications and forms and to obtain from agencies the data needed to frame a budget. The governor would set a spending ceiling based upon an estimate of anticipated revenues.[47] Constitutional amendments in 1962 required the governor to present a budget message, budget report and a draft appropriations bill to the General Assembly within 5 days of convening the 1963 legislative session and each subsequent biennial

---

[41] Reg Murphy, "Everyone Gained in Budget Battle," *Atlanta Constitution*, November 29, 1961: 5.

[42] Text of Governor Ernest Vandiver's State of the State address delivered before a joint session of the General Assembly, January 10, 1962, *Atlanta Constitution*, January 11, 1962: 20.

[43] Georgia Laws, 1962: 17–37. HB 742 approved February 12, 1962.

[44] "Budget Reforms Amended, Passed." *Atlanta Constitution*, February 1, 1962: 12.

[45] "Ernest Davis Named State Budget Officer," *Atlanta Constitution*, April 17, 1962: 5.

[46] Georgia Laws, 1962: 20–21. HB 742 approved February 12, 1962.

[47] "Governor Will Set Up Ceiling on Budgets, Conferees Agree," *Atlanta Constitution*, February 7, 1962: 6.

session.[48] The amendments also provided that general appropriations would continue in force for two fiscal years and expire at the end of that fiscal period.[49] This provision effectively ended the nearly unchecked powers of the governor and State Auditor to appropriate surplus funds without legislative approval.

Reflecting on these events many years later, Governor Vandiver recalled:[50]

> Prior to my administration, as I served as lieutenant governor, I observed that the traditional power of appropriating state funds had been abandoned by the General Assembly. The state auditor, working with the governor during that era, prepared an executive budget, presented it to the legislature for adoption, and usually within a thirty or forty-five minute period it was passed just as the governor had presented it. The traditional checks and balances of the three branches of government had gradually been meshed into two branches, and I was determined to leave, as one of my legacies, a stronger legislative branch.
>
> I recommended to the legislature that the budgetary laws be amended to provide for a biennial budget. This recommendation also provided that after the budget was submitted by the governor it be received and studied by the House Committee on Appropriations and by the Senate Finance Committee. The rest of the legislature was to adjourn while the fiscal committees studied the budget request.
>
> I also set up a bureau of the budget in the Executive Department and solicited every department to submit a timely and orderly request to this bureau for appropriations for the next fiscal year. In the off years, amendments would be submitted. This would give the executive branch and the legislative branch ample time to study the requests of the various departments. It would make it less likely that a mistake could be made, or a meritorious request overlooked. I also suggested that we abandon the fiction that the state could not incur debt.

The history of Georgia budgeting in the twentieth century was characterized by periods of legislative domination, prior to 1931, and executive domination, 1931–1961. After 1962, gubernatorial power was curtailed by the requirement that surplus funds lapse at the end of a defined fiscal period, while at the same time it was strengthened by the establishment of a modern executive budget office with professional staff and regular procedures. Since 1962, Georgia governors have set the annual budget agenda, not only because they prepare the *Governor's Budget Report* and the draft appropriations bill, but also because the governor's revenue estimate establishes a spending ceiling for legislative appropriations.[51] In order for legislative leaders to insert their budget priorities into the appropriations bill they must substitute them for the gubernatorial priorities already announced in the *Governor's Budget Report* and draft legislation. Legislative leaders cannot simply increase the

---

[48] *Constitution of the State of Georgia*, 1945, Article VII, Section IX, Paragraph I(a), as amended 1962.

[49] *Constitution of the State of Georgia*, 1945, Article VII, Section IX, Paragraph II(a), as amended 1962.

[50] S. Ernest Vandiver, "Vandiver Takes the Middle Road," in Harold P. Henderson and Gary L. Roberts, eds., *Georgia Governors in an Age of Change: From Ellis Arnall to George Busbee*. Athens, GA: The University of Georgia Press, 1988. p. 165.

[51] The revenue estimate is initiated by a contract employee of the budget office, usually a Ph.D. economist, who estimates a probable range of revenue collections. The specific revenue estimate is a policy decision by the governor.

revenue estimate to fund their priorities.[52] They must negotiate substitution of their priorities for those of the governor within the boundary set by the executive revenue estimate. In most years, some degree of substitution occurs but for the most part gubernatorial priorities tend to define the state's budget.[53] The Budget Act of 1962[54] established a system consistent with the 1961 Legislative Budget Study Committee recommendations, in which the governor retained strong budget authority, but not total dominance in the process. Today, the governor sets the agenda and gets most of his priorities, but the legislature is not without considerable influence.

Conclusion

Separation of powers, with checks and balance, is the most important governing principle in the America political system for protecting citizens against the budgetary abuses of excessive taxation and imprudent spending. The power to claim some portion of the citizenry's wealth for collective or public purposes is one of the most imposing powers governments possess. For this reason, the power to levy taxes and appropriate tax proceeds for government functions has been vested in the most representative branch of government, the legislature.

However, legislatures, especially part-time state legislatures, tend to be ill-suited for carrying out the day to day implementation of state spending. For this reason, they usually have relied upon their governors to coordinate and evaluate state agency spending requests and to present to the legislature a comprehensive annual spending plan. Legislatures also have relied upon their governors to control and direct the financial activities of agencies within the exertive branch.

A workable state budgeting and appropriation system that satisfies the principles of legislative oversight and executive control and direction, does not emerge all at once. Georgia's journey to a modern executive budget system oscillated between a system of legislative dominance in the early decades of the twentieth century and executive dominance in three middle decades of the century before arriving at a modern executive budget system in the last half of the century. The bottom line, so to speak, is that gubernatorial budget priorities tend to prevail most of the time but that legislative priorities are still achievable within the separation of powers system.

---

[52] In the 1979 Session of the General Assembly, the state Senate passed a version of the appropriations bill that was not only higher than the House of Representatives version, but also increased the revenue estimate. Governor George Busbee threatened to veto the appropriations bill if the Senate did not desist, citing an Opinion of the State Attorney General that setting the revenue estimate is an executive branch power not a legislative branch power. Beau Cutts, "Governor to Veto Senate Budget," *Atlanta Constitution*, March 17, 1979: 1 and 4.

[53] Interview with John M. Hackney, Legislative Budget Analyst, Atlanta, Georgia, June 6, 1989.

[54] Official Code of Georgia Annotated (O.C.G.A.), Title 45, Chapter 12.

Chapter 6
The Annual Budget Process

This chapter is about the institutions and process of enacting the annual budget. More specifically, it is about the interaction among state agencies, the governor and the legislature in formulating and enacting an appropriations bill, which, when signed by the governor, becomes the state's annual budget.

The Budget Process in the Constitution

The *Constitution of the State of Georgia* contains several explicit requirements regarding the state's budget. First, "No money shall be drawn from the treasury except by appropriation made by law."[1] Second, "Bills for raising revenue, or appropriating money, shall originate in the House of Representatives."[2] Third, "The Governor shall submit to the General Assembly within five days after its convening in regular session each year a budget message and a budget report, accompanied by a draft general appropriation bill …"[3] Fourth, "The General Assembly shall annually appropriate those state and federal funds necessary to operate all the various departments and agencies."[4] Fifth, "The fiscal year of the state shall commence on the first day of July of each year and terminate on the thirtieth of June following."[5] Sixth, "The general appropriations bill shall embrace nothing except appropriations fixed by previous laws; the ordinary expenses of the executive, legislative and judicial departments of the government; payment of the public debt and interest thereon;

---

[1] Article III, Section IX, Paragraph 1.
[2] Article III, Section V, Paragraph II.
[3] Article III, Section IX, Paragraph II (a).
[4] Article III, Section IX, Paragraph II (b).
[5] Article III, Section IX, Paragraph II (b).

and for support of the public institutional and educational interests of the state."[6] Seventh, "Each general Appropriations Act... shall continue in force and effect for the next fiscal year after adoption and it shall then expire..."[7] Eighth, "The General Assembly shall not appropriate funds for any given fiscal year which, in aggregate, exceed a sum equal to the amount of unappropriated surplus expected to have accrued in the state treasury at the beginning of the fiscal year together with an amount not greater than the total treasury receipts from existing revenue sources anticipated to be collected in the fiscal year, less refunds, as estimated in the budget report ..."[8] Ninth, "The Governor may approve any appropriation and veto any other appropriation in the same bill, and any appropriation vetoed shall not become law unless such veto is overridden ..."[9] Tenth, "All appropriated state funds ... remaining unexpended and not contractually obligated at the expiration of such general appropriations Act shall lapse."[10] In summary, all state spending must be authorized by an appropriation; appropriations are annual; the fiscal year begins in July and ends in June; the legislature must pass an annual appropriations bill; the appropriations bill must be about appropriations only, and not include other legislation; appropriations bills must originate in the House of Representatives, the most populous chamber; the governor must submit a budget proposal and draft appropriation bill to the legislature, and the estimated revenue and spending must be in balance; the governor has the line-item veto; at the end of the fiscal year, appropriations expire and unspent appropriations lapse to the treasury. There are other conventions and rules for the appropriations process, but these requirements are embedded in the Constitution.

The Budget Cycle

The annual budget process[11] begins when state government agencies submit spending requests for their assigned programs to the Governor's Office of Planning and Budget (OPB)[12] in accord with OPB instructions and based upon supporting information about program needs and accomplishments. The submission date is on or

---

[6] Article III, Section IX, Paragraph III.
[7] Article III, Section IX, Paragraph IV (a).
[8] Article III, Section IX, Paragraph IV (b).
[9] Article III, Section V, Paragraph XIII (e).
[10] Article, III, Section IX, Paragraph IV (c).
[11] Georgia is one of 30 states using an annual budget cycle. The other 20 states use a biennial budget cycle. *Budget Processes in the States,* Washington, DC: National Association of State Budget Officers, 2015. p. 5.
[12] Georgia is one of 10 states where the executive budget agency is located in the Governor's Office. In the other states, the executive budget agency is a freestanding agency, located within a finance department or located within a management/administration department. *Budget Processes in the States,* Washington, DC: National Association of State Budget Officers, 2015. p. 28.

about September 1. The OPB reviews agency requests for accuracy, necessity, record of past performance and compatibility with the governor's policy priorities. OPB then recommends a coordinated spending plan to the governor.

The relationship between state agencies and OPB has a natural tension emanating from their different roles in the budget process. Agency officials, as advocates for their programs, usually expect their current level of funding to continue and they have a tendency to ask for funding increases beyond what they may expect to receive. The job of OPB is to manage agency expectations about what they can expect based upon available revenue, the priorities of the governor and the needs of other agencies and programs. In performing this management role, the OPB director relies upon budget analysts assigned to individual agencies to provide accurate and timely information about agency performance and actual needs. In some years, OPB on behalf of the governor instructs state agencies to limit their requests to a maximum percent increase or to submit requests based on a fixed percent reduction.

OPB has seven divisions, each led by a division director. Five divisions, Education, Health and Human Services, Physical and Economic Development, General Government, and Public Safety, have responsibility for budget analysis and program planning in their respective policy areas. Two divisions, Administration and Information Technology, have responsibility for providing fiscal, personnel and technology support for OPB. The agency has approximately 20 professional budget analysts distributed across its divisions.

The process continues when the governor, with assistance from the budget office, makes decisions about agency funding requests, considers them in relationship to each other and in the context of his policy goals for the state, and formulates a comprehensive budget recommendation to the legislature, the *Governor's Budget Report*, taking into account his estimate of the amount of revenue expected to be available to cover the costs of the budget recommendations. The proposed budget must be in balance, with estimated revenue being equal to estimated spending.

The process then moves to the General Assembly where the governor's budget recommendation, submitted within 5 days of the legislature's convening, is reviewed by the Appropriations committees in both the House of Representatives and the Senate, considered in the context of the policy priorities of legislative leaders and eventually enacted by the General Assembly, most likely in somewhat modified form from the governor's original recommendation. Any related tax legislation would have been considered by the Ways and Means Committee in the House of Representatives and the Finance Committee in the Senate.

Both the House and Senate appropriations committees use subcommittees to review selected parts of the *Governor's Budget Report* and to develop corresponding parts of the appropriations bill. The House of Representatives subcommittees are for Economic Development, Education, General Government, Health, Higher Education, Human Resources, Public Safety and Transportation. The Senate subcommittees are for Agriculture and Natural Resources, Community Health, Criminal Justice and Public Safety, Economic Development, Education and Higher Education, Government Operations, Human Development and Public Health, Judicial and Transportation. Each subcommittee has a chairperson and usually a vice chairperson. The House Budget and Research Office and the Senate Budget and Evaluation Office provide analysis to the House and Senate appropriations committees and assist those committees in the preparation of their appropriations bills.

In some years, the appropriations committees meet with agency heads prior to the beginning of the legislative session. This part of the process varies from year to year. For example, in September 2019, legislative leaders invited agency heads to meet with them prior to the opening of the legislative session to discuss their plans for complying with Governor Brian Kemp's directive to reduce their budgets by 4% during the current fiscal year and by 6% for the coming fiscal year. However, Governor Kemp instructed agency heads to decline the invitations, asserting that the budget preparation process is an executive branch matter to be conducted without legislative interference.

The final appropriations bill must be passed in identical form in the House and Senate. Usually, the House and Senate versions of the appropriations act are not initially in identical form, in which case a joint House and Senate conference committee is convened to negotiate inter-chamber differences. The conference committee report then is adopted by each chamber and becomes the final appropriations act.[13] As the appropriations bill moves along during the legislative session, its progress is recorded in a "tracking sheet" showing the governor's recommendation for each agency and/or program, the House recommendation, the Senate recommendation and the conference committee recommendation.[14] Changes made at each stage of the process are thus transparent to other participants in the process.

The process returns to the executive branch where the governor has 40 days to review the enacted budget and sign it into law. When signing the appropriations bill, the governor has the option to sign it as presented to him, veto it in its entirety (highly unlikely) or veto individual items of expenditure, which occurs from time to time. The governor's power to veto individual appropriations does not include the power to reduce an appropriation.[15] However, beginning with the 2005 fiscal year, Georgia transitioned from a line-item, objective-of-expenditure, budget format to a program budget format.[16] The new program budget format makes it more difficult for governors to use the line-item veto to protect their budgets. An item veto, instead of eliminating only a specific item of expenditure, would now eliminate an entire program (both the legislative addition or change, as well as the base budget for the program). Of course, the line-item veto can still be used on bond projects where a single project can be vetoed. This option is discussed in greater detail in Chapter 8.

Budget execution is the next stage in the process, occurring between legislative enactment of spending decisions and the accounting for those decisions during the post-audit phase. State agencies are the primary actors during this stage of the

---

[13] Thomas P. Lauth, "The Governor and the Conference Committee in Georgia," *Legislative Studies Quarterly*, Vol. XV, Number 3 (August 1990): 441–453.

[14] The official title of the document is Comparative Summary of HB 000, Fiscal Year 20XX General Appropriations Bill (or Amended General Appropriations Bill).

[15] 2000 Opinion of the Attorney General, U2000-2, February 11, 2000.

[16] In the *Governor's Budget Report FY 2005*, each agency's proposed appropriation included both program information and objective-of-expenditure information.

process. After the budget is approved, state agencies receive their approved funding at periodic intervals throughout the year, based upon proposed work plans. Funds are not immediately available at the beginning of the fiscal year on July 1. Appropriated funds are allotted on a quarterly basis, and they are not available until an agency has filed a periodic work program with the OPB and that work program has been approved by OPB.[17] The purpose of this procedure is to ensure, at periodic internals through the year, that agency spending comports with the purposes for which funds were appropriated. Further, if the governor and OPB determine that state revenue collections may be falling short of the estimated revenue upon which appropriations were based, the governor is authorized to withhold a percentage of agency allotment requests, and agencies may be requested to reserve already allotted funds, in order to ensure that state spending remains in balance with actual revenue collections.[18]

At the end of the fiscal year, the Department of Audits and Accounts audits state agency spending by object-of-expenditure and by program, noting exceptions if any, and on or before December 31st issues a Budgetary Compliance Report and the Comprehensive Annual Financial Report (CAFR). The purpose of these audit reports is to provide an objective accounting of financial resources and an independent assessment of financial management practices to state government leaders and the citizens of Georgia.

The enacted budget is for a period of one fiscal year, which begins on July 1 and ends on June 30.[19] The state budget is amended once during the fiscal year, by essentially the same process, approximately two-thirds of the way through the fiscal year. A budget cycle is approximately 30 months. The process of agency requests, governor's review and recommendation, and legislative approval lasts slightly less than one year; the fiscal year is one year; and the audit phase is approximately six months. The following is a typical budget cycle.

Georgia Fiscal Year 2020 Budget Cycle

<u>July 1, 2018</u>

- "Budget Call" issued by the Office of Planning and Budget to agencies, and *Budget Preparation Procedures Manual* distributed

<u>July–August 2018</u>

- Agencies review preliminary policy positions and cost estimates. Agency heads and governing boards had been developing policy positions and agency personnel had been developing cost estimates since the spring

---

[17] Official Code of Georgia Annotated (O.C.G.A.), 45–12-82.
[18] Official Code of Georgia Annotated (O.C.G.A.), 45-12-86.
[19] Forty-six states have a fiscal year beginning July 1. One state has a fiscal year beginning October 1, the same as the federal fiscal year, one state begins April 1 and two states begin their fiscal year on September 1.

September 1, 2018

- Agencies submit budget requests to the Office of Planning and Budget

September-December

- Office of Planning and Budget reviews agency budget requests; updated information or additional justifications may be requested
- Office of Planning and Budget makes funding level recommendations to the Governor
- Office of Planning and Budget Director and Professional Staff Economist develop the revenue estimate; Governor specifies the official revenue estimate
- Concurrent with Office of Planning and Budget review of agency requests, House Budget Office and Senate Budget Office review agency requests to develop an estimate of "continuation"
- In some years, Appropriations Committees meet with agency heads prior to the legislative session

January 2019

- The General Assembly convenes on the second Monday in January each year and may meet for not more than 40 days each year, excluding days in recess
- Within 5 days of the convening of the General Assembly, Governor delivers Budget Message to the General Assembly
- Governor presents *Budget Report(s)* to the General Assembly (Fiscal Year 2019 Amended Budget and Fiscal Year 2020 Budget)
- Governor announces Revenue Estimate
- Appropriations Bills introduced in the House of Representatives

January-March

- House and Senate Appropriations Committees hold joint budget hearings
- Appropriations Committees "markup" appropriations bills and report to the House and Senate
- House Budget and Research Office and Senate Budget and Evaluation Office provide analysis to Appropriations Committees
- House adopts Appropriations Bill and transmits it to the Senate; Senate adopts substitute to House Bill and returns it to the House; House rejects Senate substitute; Conference Committee is appointed; Conference Committee Report is adopted by House and Senate with no amendments permitted

February 2019

- House and Senate adopt Amended FY 2019 Appropriations Act
- For each fiscal year, the General Assembly may appropriate from the Revenue Shortfall Reserve an amount up to 1% of the net revenue collections of the preceding fiscal year for funding increased K-12 needs. This occurs in most years.

March 2019

- House and Senate adopt FY 2020 Appropriations Act
- The Governor may release for appropriation by the General Assembly a stated amount from funds in the Revenue Shortfall Reserve that are in excess of 4% of the net revenue of the preceding fiscal year. This does not occur in most years.

April-May 2019

- Governor signs Appropriations Acts within 40 days after legislative adjournment
- Governor may line-item veto selected amounts of money or narrative passages in the Appropriations Bill

June 30, 2019

- 2019 Fiscal Year Ends (FY 2019 begins July 1, 2018 and ends June 30, 2019)

June 2019

- Agencies prepare and submit to the Office of Planning and Budget an Annual Operating Budget in conformity with the Appropriations Act

July 1, 2019

- 2020 Fiscal Year Begins (FY 2020 begins July 1, 2019 and ends June 30, 2020)

July 1, 2019 to June 30, 2020

- Budget Execution
- Agencies receive a Quarterly Allotment of funds based upon a Proposed Work Plan
- Agencies submit a Quarterly Report of Expenditures

July 1, 2020 to December 31, 2020

- As of the end of each fiscal year, an amount shall be released from the Revenue Shortfall Reserve to the general fund to cover any deficit by which total expenditures and contractual obligations exceed net revenue and other amounts in state funds.
- The amount of all surplus in state funds as of the end of each fiscal year shall be reserved and added to the Revenue Shortfall Reserve. Funds in the Revenue Shortfall Reserve shall carry forward from fiscal year to fiscal year, without reverting to the general fund at the end of a fiscal year. The Revenue Shortfall Reserve shall not exceed 15% of the previous fiscal year's net revenue for any given fiscal year.
- State Auditor issues on or before December 31, 2020 final Reports on state agency spending of FY 2020 appropriated funds.

Midyear Appropriations Amendment

One of the more unique features of the Georgia budget process is the midyear appropriations amendment.[20] The General Assembly which meets for 40 legislative days in January, February and March, enacts two budget laws each session, an amendment to the appropriations act passed in the previous legislative session, and an appropriations act for the fiscal year that will begin on the ensuing July 1. The amendment to the appropriations act, approximately 8 months into the fiscal year, redirects previously appropriated funds, increasing some program budgets and reducing others, and adjusts the state's spending plan for the remainder of the fiscal year to conditions of revenue shortfall or surplus.[21] A single omnibus appropriations act sets the annual budget. The governor has authority to transfer appropriations between programs within a department. However, fund transfers between departments, fund transfers between object classes within a department, or increases in the appropriations act total require legislative amendment to the appropriations, accomplished through an omnibus midyear appropriations amendment.[22] All states have procedures for amending their initial appropriations acts. However, the Georgia procedure by which a single initial omnibus appropriations act is amended by a later omnibus appropriations act is unique.

Funding for the midyear appropriations amendment comes from several sources. Surplus funds come from revenue collections that exceed revenue estimates and from unspent appropriations that lapse back to the state treasury and are available for re-appropriation. Lapses are appropriations that were never allotted by the Office of Planning and Budget to agencies for expenditure or that were allotted for expenditure but remained unspent. Revenue collections that exceed the revenue estimate may be the result of a robust economy; they may also be the result of a conservative revenue estimate.

The governor is assisted in making the revenue estimate by a professional economic advisor[23] who estimates a range of likely revenue yields, but the specific

---

[20] The next several paragraphs draw extensively on Thomas P. Lauth, "The Midyear Appropriation in Georgia: A Threat to Comprehensiveness?" *State and Local Government Review*, Vol. 34 (Fall 2002): 198–202.

[21] For a discussion of the many factors that necessitate mid-year appropriation adjustments, see: Ronald Byron Hoskins, "Within-Year Appropriation Changes in Georgia State Government: The Implications for Budget Theory," Doctoral Dissertation, The University of Georgia, (1983): 105–106.

[22] The state constitution provides that in addition to the general appropriations act and its amendments, the General Assembly may pass a "supplementary" appropriation act to change the appropriation for a particular agency. Relatively few supplementary appropriations acts have been passed in recent years, in part because of increased reliance on the amended general appropriations act. See, *Constitution of the State of Georgia 1983*, Art. III, Sec. IX, Par. V.

[23] The economic advisor is a contract employee of the Governor's Office of Planning and Budget. In the 2020 Session of the General Assembly, a bill was passed in the House of Representatives (HB 1112) that would have created a State Council of Economic Advisors, consisting of five members. Three members would be appointed by the Governor, including the governor's economic

revenue estimate is a policy decision of the governor.[24] Revenue estimates traditionally have been conservative, which often has led to an underestimation of actual revenue collections. An advantage of conservative revenue estimates is that they reduce the risk of revenue shortfalls. An "incorrect" estimate that underestimates the actual revenue yield is also politically preferable to one that overestimates collections. Of course, if revenue estimates are too conservative, gubernatorial recommendations and legislative appropriations for state services are restricted. Nevertheless, in most years the practice of underestimating revenue collections has contributed to the presence of a surplus for funding the midyear appropriations amendment. In addition, the governor may recommend that the General Assembly appropriate funds from the Revenue Shortfall Reserve, an amount up to 1% of the net revenue collections of the preceding fiscal year, for funding unmet K-12 education needs. Georgia continues to experience annual population growth that makes it difficult for the state Board of Education to fully and accurately project local school district enrollment. In a typical year, additional funds are required in midyear to provide the state's share of funding for the Quality Basic Education (QBE) program.

Georgia converted in fiscal year 1973 from a biennial to an annual budget.[25] The current practice of a midyear appropriations amendment is a carryover from the previous practice of amending the appropriations act in the second year of the biennium.[26] For nearly a half century, the midyear amendment has been an integral part of the state budgetary process.

---

advisor who would serve as chairperson, one member would be appointed by the Speaker of the House of Representatives and one would be appointed by the President of the Senate. The purpose of the Council would be to estimate the amount of treasury receipts from existing revenue sources anticipated to be collected in the next fiscal year and the amount of unappropriated surplus expected to have accrued in the state treasury at the beginning of the next fiscal year. The Council's revenue estimates would be made available to the Governor, the Speaker of the House of Representatives, the President of the Senate and the chairpersons of the House Appropriations Committee and the Senate Appropriations Committee. The Governor would be required to use the Council's estimates in preparing the *Governor's Budget Report* and draft appropriations acts. The bill did not come up for a vote in the state Senate. If a State Council of Economic Advisors were to be created in the future, it would rebalance the relationship between the governor and the legislature in budget matters, likely in the direction of the legislature.

[24] Conversations with Henry Thomassen, Economic Advisor to several governors, March 2, 1990, May 18, 1993, May 17, 1994, April 30, 1996, May 13, 1997 and April 13, 1999.

[25] Georgia Laws, 1972: 1550–1551. SR 322 approved April 5, 1972. On November 7, 1972, Amendment No. 22, was approved by the voters 394,429 (60.5%) – 257,068 (39.5%).

[26] Interview with John M. Hackney, Legislative Budget Analyst, May 5, 1982.

Dimensions of the Midyear Appropriations Amendment

During the period FY 1991 to FY 2019, that includes the full terms of four governors, Democrats Zell Miller and Roy Barnes and Republicans Sonny Perdue and Nathan Deal, the midyear appropriation amendment increased the state budget in most years. As seen in Table 6.1, the midyear appropriations amendment increased the total state appropriation in 23 of 29 years by an annual average of 1.3%. The fiscally conservative practice of underestimating revenue collections contributed to the presence of a surplus in those years, which permitted funding the amended appropriations bill at midyear, as well as increasing the Revenue Shortfall Reserve

Table 6.1 Midyear change in Georgia Appropriation Acts, FY 1991 – FY 2019

Fiscal year	Original appropriation	Amended appropriation	Percent change
1991	$7,785,427,500	$7,645,067,946	−1.8%
1992	$7,955,482,500	$7,552,871,790	−5.1%
1993	$8,174,000,000	$8,252,216,454	1.0%
1994	$8,958,192,764	$9,201,886,925	2.7%
1995	$9,785,260,431	$10,236,138,444	4.6%
1996	$10,700,856,569	$10,980,393,127	2.6%
1997	$11,341,527,653	$11,793,346,344	4.0%
1998	$11,781,453,880	$12,380,991,546	5.1%
1999	$12,528,603,880	$13,064,694,760	4.3%
2000	$13,291,103,880	$13,939,922,701	4.9%
2001	$14,471,828,880	$15,273,099,418	5.5%
2002	$15,454,610,013	$15,773,307,509	2.1%
2003	$16,105,985,466	$16,142,774,526	0.2%
2004	$16,174,683,712	$16,079,533,973	−0.6%
2005	$16,376,321,131	$16,567,537,539	1.2%
2006	$17,415,249,819	$17,850,546,801	2.5%
2007	$18,654,564,058	$19,317,036,464	3.6%
2008	$20,230,620,936	$20,545,196,148	1.6%
2009	$21,180,140,103	$18,903,699,531	−10.7%
2010	$18,569,866,489	$17,074,653,179	−8.1%
2011	$17,890,512,513	$18,063,622,184	1.0%
2012	$18,299,477,557	$18,503,799,022	1.1%
2013	$19,342,059,819	$19,325,217,673	−0.1%
2014	$19,920,261,481	$20,234,238,575	1.6%
2015	$20,836,744,620	$21,112,906,096	1.3%
2016	$21,828,789,407	$23,065,473,796	5.7%
2017	$23,739,409,078	$24,345,494,024	2.6%
2018	$24,997,351,235	$25,413,015,092	1.7%
2019	$26,226,914,974	$26,933,425,042	2.7%
Average			1.3%

Source: Georgia Laws, 1990–2019 Sessions

at the end of the year. As seen in Table 6.2, between FY 1991 and FY 2019, state revenue was greater than the original state appropriation in 20 of 29 years. The recession years of 1991–1992, 2002–2004 and 2008–2011 are exceptions to these patterns.

As seen in Table 6.3, during the period FY 2011 to FY 2018 that includes the 8 years of Nathan Deal's governorship, the midyear amended appropriation for 40 state agencies increased by an average of 1.8%. However, the range of differences among agencies was substantial, from less than 1% for several agencies to 57.6% for the Department of Community Affairs. Twenty-four agencies increased by an average of 6.3%, 15 agencies decreased by an average of 1.2% and one agency had exactly no change. As seen in Table 6.4, during FY 2016, a not atypical year, 51.5% of midyear amendment increases went to education policy, the Department of

Table 6.2 Appropriations and total state revenues, FY 1991 – FY 2019

Fiscal year	Original appropriation	Total revenues	Revenue less appropriation
1991	$7,785,427,500	$7,295,200,000	−$490,227,500
1992	$7,955,482,500	$7,452,600,000	−$502,882,500
1993	$8,174,000,000	$8,346,376,907	$172,376,907
1994	$8,958,192,764	$9,409,376,943	$451,184,179
1995	$9,785,260,431	$10,303,573,061	$518,312,630
1996	$10,700,856,569	$11,166,835,592	$465,979,023
1997	$11,341,527,653	$11,905,829,999	$564,302,346
1998	$11,781,453,880	$12,478,602,944	$697,149,064
1999	$12,528,603,880	$13,539,916,503	$1,011,312,623
2000	$13,291,103,880	$14,959,980,702	$1,668,876,822
2001	$14,471,828,880	$15,768,578,047	$1,296,749,167
2002	$15,454,610,013	$15,126,479,334	−$328,130,679
2003	$16,105,985,466	$14,737,541,220	−$1,368,444,246
2004	$16,174,683,712	$15,668,810,288	−$505,873,424
2005	$16,376,321,131	$16,789,925,631	$413,604,500
2006	$17,415,249,819	$18,343,186,033	$927,936,214
2007	$18,654,564,058	$19,895,976,559	$1,241,412,501
2008	$20,230,620,936	$19,789,803,318	−$440,817,618
2009	$21,180,140,103	$17,832,365,614	−$3,347,774,489
2010	$18,569,866,489	$16,251,244,424	−$2,318,622,065
2011	$17,890,512,513	$17,546,376,094	−$344,136,419
2012	$18,299,477,557	$18,316,797,048	$17,319,491
2013	$19,342,059,819	$19,539,691,059	$197,631,240
2014	$19,920,261,481	$20,256,765,495	$336,504,014
2015	$20,836,744,620	$21,557,498,541	$720,753,921
2016	$21,828,789,407	$23,476,964,889	$1,648,175,482
2017	$23,739,409,078	$24,519,402,190	$779,993,112
2018	$24,997,351,235	$25,649,499,261	$652,148,026
2019	$26,226,914,974	$26,933,425,042	$706,510,068

Sources: Georgia Laws, 1990–2019 Sessions and *Governor's Budget Report*, FY 1996 – FY 2020

Table 6.3 State agency amended appropriations: average percent change FY 2011 change to FY 2018

Branches of Georgia Government	Percent of Total
Legislative Branch	−0.2%
Judicial Branch	0.4%
Executive Branch	
Accounting Office	7.2%
Administrative Services	17.8%
Agriculture	−0.9%
Banking and Finance	−0.7%
Behavioral Health and Developmental Disabilities	−0.1%
Community Affairs	57.6%
Community Health	3.7%
Community Supervision	1.0%
Corrections	0.7%
Defense	1.9%
Driver Services	0.8%
Early Care and Learning	0.0%
Economic Development	−0.9%
Education	1.6%
Employees' Retirement System	12.1%
Forestry Commission	3.9%
Governor's Office	5.1%
Human Services	3.6%
Insurance Commissioner	−0.6%
Georgia Bureau of Investigation	0.4%
Juvenile Justice	−0.6%
Labor	−1.4%
Law	−0.2%
Natural Resources	2.1%
Pardon and Paroles Board	0.2%
Public Defender Standards Council	3.5%
Public Health	0.9%
Public Safety	2.7%
Public Service Commission	−1.5%
Board of Regents of University System of Georgia	−1.4%
Revenue	7.7%
Secretary of State	2.0%
Soil and Water Conservation Commission	−1.2%
Student Finance Commission	1.4%
Teachers' Retirement System	−3.1%
Technical College System of Georgia	−0.9%
Transportation	13.5%
Veterans Service	−0.7%
Works' Compensation Board	0.5%
General Obligation Debt Sinking Fund	−3.2%
Total	1.8%

Source: *Governor's Amended Budget Report, FY 2011 – FY 2018*

Table 6.4 State agency amended appropriations: percent of total FY 2016 change

	Percent of Total
Legislative Branch	0.3%
Judicial Branch	0.8%
Executive Branch	
Accounting Office	0.0%
Administrative Services	0.0%
Agriculture	0.2%
Banking and Finance	0.1%
Behavioral Health and Developmental Disabilities	4.3%
Community Affairs	0.4%
Community Health	13.7%
Community Supervision	0.2%
Corrections	5.1%
Defense	0.1%
Driver Services	0.3%
Early Care and Learning	1.6%
Economic Development	0.1%
Education	37.5%
Employees' Retirement System	0.1%
Forestry Commission	0.2%
Governor's Office	0.3%
Human Services	2.8%
Insurance Commissioner	0.1%
Georgia Bureau of Investigation	0.5%
Juvenile Justice	1.4%
Labor	0.1%
Law	0.1%
Natural Resources	0.5%
Pardon and Paroles Board	0.2%
Public Defender Standards Council	0.2%
Public Health	1.0%
Public Safety	0.6%
Public Service Commission	0.0%
Board of Regents of University System of Georgia	8.8%
Revenue	0.9%
Secretary of State	0.1%
Soil and Water Conservation Commission	0.0%
Student Finance Commission	3.3%
Teachers' Retirement System	0.0%
Technical College System of Georgia	1.5%
Transportation	7.2%
Veterans Service	0.1%
Works' Compensation Board	0.1%
General Obligation Debt Sinking Fund	5.3%
Total	100.0%

Source: *Governor's Budget Report, Amended FY 2016*

Education (37.5%), the Board of Regents of the University System of Georgia (8.8%), the State Scholarship Commission (3.3%) and the Technical College System of Georgia (1.5%). An additional 31.3% went to four other agencies, the Department of Community Health (13.7%), the Department of Corrections (5.1%), the Department of Transportation (7.2%) and General Obligation Debt Service (5.3%).

Legislator and Agency Expectations

The midyear appropriations amendment is prepared and recommended by the governor in response to changing spending needs and revenue availability. However, legislators also view the midyear appropriations amendment as an opportunity to fund local projects that may not have competed very well with statewide projects when the original appropriations act was being considered and adopted. Local projects funded through the midyear appropriations amendment are also appealing because they tend to be one-time expenditures without recurring costs. For many years, such projects were found in appropriations for the Department of Community Affairs as "local assistance grants" for such items as outdoor lights for athletic facilities, band uniforms, computers, emergency medical service equipment, fire trucks, greenspace acquisition, historic building renovation, historical markers, parking lot pavement, playground equipment, roof repairs or security systems. Most of these projects were funded at between $5,000 and $50,000. From an electoral perspective, they probably were worth more to individual members than their actual dollar value. They were also seen by the governor and legislative leaders as investments in legislative support for their important initiatives. Gradually over the years, local projects shifted from being relatively small cash "local assistance grants" to larger construction projects financed through state multi-year bonds, still with the intent of providing benefits for legislators and their constituencies. The transition from "local assistance grants" to bond projects coincided with the Great Recession, when there was very little money for either kind of special project. Although they have much the same benefit for individual legislators as "local assistance grants," bond projects for economic development or university facilities probably have better optics and better serve state-wide purposes.

Another discernible trend in recent years is use of the midyear appropriations amendment to fund projects for rural economic development, again through the Department of Community Affairs. The Department of Community Affairs appropriation which typically is less than 1% of the total midyear appropriations amendment, increased by an average annual amount of 57.6% during the eight-year period FY 2011 to FY 2018. Of course, the large percentage increase is partially a result of the department's relatively small size among all state agencies. Nevertheless, the department's appropriation was regularly increased by the midyear amendment. Much of the midyear appropriations amendment to the Department of Community Affairs budget was for economic development for rural Georgia. In FY 2011, $19 million of the $22 million increase was for rural economic development. In FY 2012,

$10 million of the $15 million increase was for rural economic development through the OneGeorgia Authority, a unit within the Department of Community Affairs.

The OneGeorgia Authority, in pursuit of economic vitality in rural Georgia, provides grants and loans for land acquisition, infrastructure development, machinery purchases, business relocation assistance and entrepreneurial support.[27] In FY 2014, the Department of Community Affairs again was able to provide $40 million midyear amendment funding through OneGeorgia for broadband internet connectivity for teachers and students in local school systems. In FY 2015, another $55 million was provided through OneGeorgia for broadband internet connectivity for local school systems, and $20 million was provided for grants to local governments and businesses to leverage private investment to promote economic development and job growth. In FY 2016, the Department of Community Affairs, through the OneGeorgia Authority, provided $18 million to local school districts for internet connectivity. In FY 2017, $110 million was provided to create the Georgia Cyber Range, a secure environment for cyber security education, training and testing; for regional economic business grants; for busses for the Georgia Regional Transportation Authority; and for other economic development projects. In FY 2018, $10 million was provided through OneGeorgia for coastal development projects. Most of the Department of Community Affairs midyear amendment funding was for one-time projects, without recurring costs to the state, but with the intention of long-term benefit for economic development for rural Georgia. Legislators from the rural areas of Georgia may be somewhat less influential today than they once were, but midyear amendment funding for the OneGeorgia Authority indicates that they still retain considerable influence in the General Assembly. OneGeorgia was created to distribute a portion of Tobacco Master Settlement Agreement funds to rural Georgia to help that area of the state to recover from the loss of tobacco as a crop.

Like legislators, executive branch agencies have also come to regard the midyear appropriations amendment as a regular part of the state's budget process. Because annual agency budget requests are submitted approximately 10 months prior to the beginning of the fiscal year and at least 16 months prior to consideration of the midyear amendment by the General Assembly, agency program costs and clientele needs are likely to have changed, often increased, between the date of initial estimation and the time of the midyear adjustment. The midyear amendment is their opportunity for funding adjustments. Further, items not recommended for funding in the original appropriation may be deferred for partial-year funding in the midyear amendment. Also, some projects may be initiated through partial-year funding in the midyear amendment with the expectation of full funding in the next year's general appropriation act. In short, agency behavior is influenced by the expectation that two appropriations will be enacted in each legislative session. Aware of agency and legislative perspectives, Governor Sonny Perdue in 2005 instructed state agencies to restrict their midyear appropriation requests to low estimates of student enrollment and true emergencies, not for legislative pork-barrel projects.

---

[27] *Official Code of Georgia Annotated* (O.C.G.A), 50-34-2.

Appropriations Committee Staff

In 1969, the General Assembly established the Legislative Budget Office (LBO) consisting of the legislative budget analyst and approximately ten other professional budget analysts. This agency provided the legislature with alternative expertise to the governor's Office of Planning and Budget. The Legislative Budget Office was intended to serve as a staff agency for both the House and Senate appropriations committees, but in practice had a closer association with the House committee. The Senate appropriations committee relied more extensively on the governor's Office of Planning and Budget for staff assistance. When Republicans won the governorship and gained control of the state Senate in November 2002, divided party control of the House (Democrats) and Senate (Republicans) exacerbated decades of dissatisfaction with the relationship between the Senate and the Legislative Budget Office. In July 2003, a Senate Budget Office (SBO) was established to provide staff support for the Senate appropriations committee. The Legislative Budget Office continued to provide staff support for the House appropriations committee, and eventually became the House Budget Office (HBO). Today these offices are known as the Senate Budget and Evaluation Office and the House Budget and Research Office.

Although the General Assembly has a House Budget and Research Office and a Senate Budget and Evaluation Office, it does not have the institutional capacity to challenge the governor's revenue estimate in anything like the manner in which the Congressional Budget Office (CBO) is able to challenge the U.S. president's revenue estimates based upon different economic assumptions about program costs, revenue, inflation or employment.[28] Nevertheless, any bill introduced in the General Assembly that would have a significant impact on anticipated state revenues or expenditures requires a fiscal note from the State Auditor and the Office of Planning and Budget (OPB) to estimate the anticipated change in revenues or expenditures under the bill.[29]

Fiscal Affairs Subcommittees

During budget execution, legislative control is manifest in the requirement that agency funds cannot be transferred from one object of expenditure classification to another without approval of the legislature's Fiscal Affairs Subcommittee.[30] Even with the transition to performance-based budgeting and a heightened focus on pro-

---

[28] Philip G. Joyce, *The Congressional Budget Office: Honest Numbers, Power and Policy.* Washington, DC: Georgetown University Press, 2011.

[29] Official Code of Georgia Annotated (O.C.G.A.), 28-5-42.

[30] Georgia Laws, 1967: 722–725. SB 107 approved April 18, 1967. Official Code of Georgia Annotated (O.C.G.A.), 28-5-25.

grams, the Office of the Governor and the General Assembly retained spending control by retaining control of agency fund transfers at the object-of-expenditure level. (Reprogramming of funds within the same object class requires only the approval of the Office of Planning and Budget). The Fiscal Affairs Subcommittee[31] is composed of four members of the House of Representatives Appropriations Committee appointed by the Speaker of the House, four members of the Senate Appropriations Committee appointed by the president of the Senate (the Lieutenant Governor), five members of each house selected by the governor, as well as the Speaker of the House and the Lieutenant Governor. State law requires this subcommittee to meet at least once each quarter, or at the call of the governor, for the purpose of reviewing and approving budget unit object class transfers recommended by the governor. However, in recent years it has met only once a year, usually in June, just before the end of the fiscal year and the beginning of the next fiscal year. The midyear amendment to the appropriations act has made additional meetings of the Fiscal Affairs Subcommittee unnecessary.[32] Although Fiscal Affairs is an instrument of legislative control over the transfer of funds, its agenda is set by gubernatorial recommendations. It is, therefore, a reactive rather than a proactive form of legislative influence.

Budget Reduction Behavior

At the end of Chapter 3, it was noted that fiscal Year 2020 was one of only six fiscal years between 1960 and 2020 in which revenue collections were less than in the previous fiscal year. When revenue shortfalls occur, the governor usually reduces his revenue estimate, state agencies are instructed to reduce their spending and funds may be drawn from the Revenue Shortfall Reserve in order to balance the budget.

State agency budgeters in most years seek to protect their agency's budget base (defined as funding for the current level of services), to increase funding for existing programs and to expand funding for new programs. In short, they exhibit *acquisitive* behavior.[33] However, when recessions occur, agency budgeters have to pivot from seeking to protect and expand their budgets to finding ways to reduce their budgets. How do they behave in such situations?

The 1991–1992 Recession: In August of 1991, during a national recession, the General Assembly was called into Special Session by Governor Zell Miller, only one month into the fiscal year, to reduce the state's FY 1992 budget by approximately

---

[31] The Fiscal Affairs Subcommittee is actually the House Fiscal Affairs Subcommittee and the Senate Fiscal Affairs Subcommittee meeting jointly. It is also not a subcommittee of any committee, but a joint committee that reports to the General Assembly.

[32] Interview with John M. Hackney, Legislative Budget Analyst, May 5, 1982.

[33] Ira Sharkansky, *The Politics of Taxing and Spending*. Indianapolis, IN: The Bobbs-Merill Publishing Co., 1969.

$415 million.[34] State agencies had already been instructed to reduce their agency budgets. In a July 12, 1991 memorandum, Governor Miller instructed agencies to assume a reduction of 10%. Agencies were also instructed to identify the programs and service delivery activities that would be eliminated or scaled back, and were told that the identified programs and activities should represent the lowest priorities for their agency. Thirty executive branch agencies made budget reductions, ranging from 0.7% to 15.1%, with the average agency reduction being 6.2% and three agencies exceeding 10%. During the fall of 1991, Katherine G. Willoughby and I interviewed 29 agency principal budget officers, asking them how they reduced their budgets.[35] Several state-wide steps were recommended by the Office of Planning and Budget including furloughs, hiring and purchasing freezes and the curtailment of travel. Most state agencies are personnel-intensive, so we were not surprised to learn that budget reduction focused on personnel. Budget officers reported imposing hiring freezes (96% of the agencies), requiring furloughs (86% of the agencies) and relinquishing vacant positions (71% of the agencies). They imposed deferral of purchases for such items as office supplies and equipment, equipment maintenance, telecommunications, motor vehicles, computer hardware and software, per diem fees and contracts and real estate rentals (86% of the agencies). They also eliminated activities, services or programs (50% of the agencies). Personnel intensive agencies cut personnel positions. Program intensive agencies, protected their core mission programs, but cut or reduced more discretionary programs. Generally, cuts were across the board, but agency decisions about cuts were also guided by agency perceptions of what was available to them. Some agencies sought to emphasize the uniqueness of their agency as a reason for not having to cut as much as was required of them, but most Georgia agencies did not resist, recognizing the state's fiscal condition, even as they sought to minimize the adverse effect on their agency.

The Great Recession: During the Great Recession of 2008–2009, state revenue collections declined compared with the previous fiscal year by 1.1% in FY 2008, 10.5% in FY 2009 and 9.1% in FY 2010. With tax increases politically unacceptable and borrowing for operating expenses prohibited, the only available options were spending reductions and tapping the Revenue Shortfall Reserve.

At the end of FY 2008, Governor Sonny Perdue instructed state agencies to begin thinking about budget reductions on the order of 3–4%; in August state agencies were instructed to reduce their budgets by 6% through the end of FY 2009. The Medicaid program would be subject to a 5% reduction and K-12 education would be subject to a 2% reduction. In January 2009, Governor Perdue presented an

---

[34] HB 285, the FY 1992 appropriation of $7,955,482,500 was approved April 24, 1991. HB-1EX, the amended FY 1992 appropriation of $7,540,744,797 was approved September 5, 1991. The reduction was $414,737,703, or −5.2%.

[35] Katherine G. Willoughby and Thomas P. Lauth, "Cutback Management in Georgia: State Agency Responses to Fiscal Year 1992 Budget Reductions," in Aman Khan and W. Bartley Hildreth, eds., *Case Studies in Public Budgeting and Financial Management*, New York: Marcel Dekker, Inc., 2003. pp. 377–391.

amended FY 2009 budget that reduced state spending by nearly $2 billion, and increased agency budget reductions to 8%.

State agencies restricted hiring, travel and equipment purchases and some implemented furloughs for employees. At the University of Georgia, where I was employed at the time, vacant faculty and staff positions were relinquished, travel was cut, construction projects were delayed, library subscriptions were reduced and campus police activities were curtailed.[36]

Sometimes, agency spending reductions are sufficient to maintain a balance between declining treasury receipts and authorized agency spending. Sometimes, in addition to reduced agency spending, it is necessary to draw upon state reserves to achieve balance at the end of the fiscal year. On yet other occasions, it is also necessary for the governor to reduce his revenue estimate. During the Great Recession, with revenue collections plummeting in FY 2009, the governor reduced his revenue estimate several times, agency spending reductions were required and funds had to be drawn from the Revenue Shortfall Reserve.[37]

The COVID-19 Recession: On March 13, 2020, President Donald Trump declared the outbreak of COVID-19 a national emergency. Governor Brian Kemp the next day declared a Public Health State of Emergency in Georgia. The National Bureau of Economic Research (NBER) on June 8th declared that the U.S. had been in recession since February. State revenues declined in April by 35.9% compared with April 2019, May collections declined by 10.1%, and June collections declined by 8.8%, finishing the year at −4.4% compared with FY 2019. On May 1, state agencies were instructed to revise their FY 2021 budgets, reducing them by 14% from their original FY 2020 base budget. On June 3, agencies were informed they would have to reduce their budgets by only 11%, not 14%.

On June 22, Governor Kemp issued a revised revenue estimate of $25.9 billion, $2.2 billon (7.8%) lower than the original estimate of $28.1 billion, and the General Assembly enacted the FY 2021 budget at the revised level.[38] The governor recommended appropriating $250 million from the Revenue Shortfall Reserve. He previously had included $100 million from the Revenue Shortfall Reserve in the amended FY 2020 budget. The enacted budget was based upon agency operating budget reductions of 10%.

Agency budget reduction plans included hiring freezes and staff furloughs. In the amended FY 2020 budget, 1,200 vacant personnel positions were eliminated. In the FY 2021 budget, an estimated 1,000 filled position were to be eliminated. Programs, as well personnel, were reduced. In the Department of Education, K-12 program funding was reduced, based upon the expectation that local school systems had reserves sufficient to offset a loss of state funds. In the Department of Transportation, funding for construction and maintenance was reduced. In the Department of

---

[36] Thomas P. Lauth, "Budget Deficits in the States: Georgia," *Public Budgeting & Finance*, Vol. 30, No. 1 (Spring 2010): 15–32 at 20.

[37] The state also had the benefit of federal stimulus dollars.

[38] HB 793, FY 2021 Appropriations Bill, June 25, 2020.

Behavioral Health and Developmental Disabilities, funding for mental health and addictive diseases was reduced. The University System of Georgia sustained budget reductions, while at the same time agreeing not to offset its losses by increasing student tuition.

The General Assembly's appropriations committees objected to several of Governor Kemp's proposed agency and program reductions. They expressed concern that areas that have been priorities for the legislature in recent years, such as agricultural research, mental health and substance abuse and programs diverting non-violent offenders from prison, were taking the brunt of budget reductions. In the final appropriations act, budget reductions were rearranged to better reflect legislative priorities,[39] and proposed agency furloughs were eliminated. The state's budget reduction approach to the COVID-19 recession was consistent with its past approaches to responding to revenue shortfalls: reduced state spending, use of reserve funds but no tax increases.

Georgia and Federal Budget Processes: A Comparison

The Georgia budget process is similar to the federal budget process in many ways, but distinctly different in other ways.

The *fiscal period* for both Georgia and the federal government is annual. In Georgia, appropriations are annual and they expire at the end of the fiscal year. Federal government appropriations may be annual, for a single fiscal year, multi-year, for a period in excess of one year, or no-year. Appropriated funds remain available for an indefinite period and do not lapse if they are not obligated by the end of the fiscal year.

The *fiscal year* for Georgia begins July 1 and ends on June 30 of the next calendar year. The fiscal years of 46 states begin on July 1. One state begins on April 1, one begins on September 1 and two begin on October 1. The Georgia fiscal year has been annual since 1973. The federal fiscal year begins on October 1 and ends on September 30 of the next calendar year. Prior to 1977, the federal fiscal year was July 1 through June 30. The mismatch between the Georgia and federal fiscal years is a source of uncertainty in some years because Georgia agencies relying on federal grants-in-aid for a portion of their funding often incur obligations before they have accurate information about federal funding decisions.

The *budget type* for both Georgia and the federal government is executive leadership, which means that in a separation of powers system of government, the legislative branch exercises its authority over government spending by assigning responsibility to the chief executive, governor or president, for preparing and presenting the budget agenda and for directing and controlling the spending activities

---

[39] Jeff Alm, "House Plan Shifts Money to Lawmakers' Priorities," *Athens Banner-Herald*, February 19, 2020: A6.

of executive branch agencies. The chief executive is accountable to the legislature for executive branch spending decisions.

Appropriations bills, when enacted into law, authorize the spending of government funds. Georgia, during its annual 40 legislative-day session, enacts one all-inclusive appropriations bill for the fiscal year. It also enacts an amendment to the appropriations bill passed in the previous legislative session, which makes fund allocation adjustments based upon changing program needs and/or changes in fund availability. The federal government during periods of "regular order"[40] expects to enact 12 appropriations bills. The subjects of these bills correspond to the jurisdictional responsibility and subject expertise of sub-committees of the House of Representative Appropriations Committee and the Senate Appropriations Committee. If the Congress is unable to complete is work on appropriations bills prior to the beginning of the federal fiscal year, it may bundle two or more appropriations bills into an omnibus bill. In recent years, a highly polarized Congress that has largely abandoned "regular order," has resorted more frequently to omnibus appropriation bills.

The *executive budget office* is a unit within the office of the chief executive intended to assist in the dual responsibilities of presenting the governor's, or president's, budget agenda to the legislature and for directing and controlling the spending activities of executive branch agencies. In Georgia that unit is called the Office of Planning and Budget (OPB). In the federal government it is called the Office of Management and Budget (OMB). These units were originally known as the Bureau of the Budget or the Budget Bureau. The Georgia OPB was the result of the state's reorganization in 1972 during the administration of Governor Jimmy Carter and sought to emphasize the role of planning in budget preparation. The federal OMB was the result of a recommendation by the Ash Council on Executive Organization in 1970 during the administration of President Richard Nixon. It was intended to emphasize the importance of the effective management of government programs.

Georgia has two *legislative budget offices*, the House Budget and Research Office and the Senate Budget and Evaluation Office. Although the governor's budget office was established in 1962, it was not until 1969 that the Legislative Budget Office (LBO) was established to provide the legislature with alternative expertise to the governor's budget office. The Legislative Budget Office served as a staff agency for both the House and Senate appropriations committees until Republicans gained control of the Senate in November 2002 and decided that with Democrats still in control of the House of Representatives, the Senate needed its own budget office. In 2003, a Senate budget office was established. The Legislative Budget Office continued to provide staff support for the House appropriations committee and later was renamed the House budget office. The federal government has one legislative budget office, the Congressional Budget Office (CBO) established by the Congressional

---

[40] Regular order refers to a process in which sub-committees review and recommend legislation to full committees, in which there is bi-partisan commitment to the integrity of that process, and in which decision-making is characterized by compromise and accommodation rather that strict partisanship.

Budget and Impound Control Act of 1974.[41] It serves both the House of Representatives and the Senate. From its beginning it has functioned in a bipartisan manner, providing "honest numbers" to Congress.[42] There has been little interest in having a legislative budget office for each house.

Georgia has a *balanced budget requirement* and the federal government does not. The Constitution of the State of Georgia requires a balanced budget, but the words "balanced budget" appear nowhere in that document. However, the language, "The General Assembly shall not appropriate funds for any given fiscal year which, in aggregate, exceed a sum equal to the amount of unappropriated surplus expected to have accrued in the state treasury at the beginning of the fiscal year together with an amount not greater than the total treasury receipts from existing revenue sources anticipated to be collected in the fiscal year, less refunds, as estimated in the budget report …"[43] have long been understood to require a balanced budget. This constitutional requirement is reinforced by Georgia's culture of fiscal conservatism that motivates governors and legislators to adhere to both the letter and the spirit of the law. The tendency of governors to conservatively estimate likely revenue collections, and the presence of a rainy day fund with specific rules governing its use, further promote the goal of a balanced budget. From time to time, there have been movements and proposals for a federal balanced budget requirement, especially during periods of growing deficits and debt, but it seems unlikely that it will ever occur. One of the principal reasons not to have such a requirement is that it would virtually eliminate the federal government's ability to use deficit spending as a counter-cyclical tool to fight a national recession. In addition to this fiscal policy argument, there also is concern that if such a requirement existed, governments of the day would seek to circumvent it, resulting in public cynicism and diminished trust in government.

Georgia and the federal government both incur *debt,* although the purposes of their debt are considerably different. Georgia debt funds capital projects and federal debt funds operating deficits. The Georgia budget must be balanced and the state does not have operating deficits. In 1972, the Constitution of the State of Georgia was amended to authorize the state to incur general obligation debt and to guarantee revenue bonds. The constitution limits the state's debt to 10% of revenue collections in the previous fiscal year. By general agreement and actual practice, state debt is approximately 5–6%, well below the legal capacity, consistently earning for the state AAA status from bond rating agencies. Georgia debt instruments are long-term and debt service appears in the *Governor's Budget Report* as the General Obligation Bond Sinking Fund. The federal government's debt is mostly short-term borrowing to cover the difference between annual receipts and outlays. The national debt is the

---

[41] Pub. L. 93–344, 88 Stat. 297.

[42] Philip G. Joyce, *The Congressional Budget Office: Honest Numbers, Power, and Policy.* Washington, DC: Georgetown University Press, 2011.

[43] Article, III, Section IX, Paragraph IV (b).

accumulation of annual deficits.[44] The majority of the federal debt is "held by the public," that is by financial institutions, individuals and foreign governments, with the remainder held by the government itself. In the first two decades of this century, the proportion of debt held by the public has increased from less than two-thirds to approximately three-quarters.

The governor of Georgia has the *line-item veto* but the president of the United States does not. The line-item veto is a special form of the executive veto available to most governors to defend their budgets against legislative additions or changes that governors deem unnecessary or unwise. It emerged because the executive veto had become ineffective in dealing with riders and pork barrel spending in appropriations bills and was intended to restore the governor's ability to protect the executive budget. It is often thought to be a device for reducing the budget total, but in practice it is mostly an instrument for governors to defend their budgets against legislative attempts to substitute legislative policy priorities for gubernatorial policy priorities. Georgia was the first state to adopt the line-item veto, in 1865, and since that time 43 other states have adopted it. In Georgia, "The Governor may approve any appropriation and veto any other appropriation in the same bill, and any appropriation vetoed shall not become law unless such veto is overridden in the manner herein provided."[45] Georgia governors have used the line-item veto infrequently compared with the use by governors in other states.[46]

The U. S. president was given the functional equivalent of the line-item veto in 1996, when Congress passed the Line-Item Veto Act,[47] but it was declared unconstitutional by the U.S. Supreme Court in 1998. The new authority temporarily ended the requirement that the president must approve or reject a spending bill in its entirety. Proponents of the presidential item veto cited state experiences with the line-item veto, such as controlling pork barrel spending, among the reasons for granting this device to the president. The Line-Item Veto Act gave the president an enhanced version of the rescission authority already granted in the Congressional Budget and Impound Control Act of 1974. Within 5 days of signing a spending bill or tax bill, the president could transmit to Congress a message listing items to be rescinded. Rescissions took effect unless Congress passed a disapproval bill within a period of 30 days in which both houses were in session. The line-item veto act gave the president authority to make substantive changes in a law after it had been enacted and signed, whereas state governors typically are required to veto items as part of the process of signing appropriations bills into law. President Bill Clinton exercised the new power in 1997, vetoing 79 items in nine of the FY 1998 appropriations acts. In 1998, the U.S. Supreme Court declared the Line-Item Veto Act of

---

[44] The last time the federal government had a budget surplus was in fiscal year 2001.

[45] A two-thirds vote in each house of the General Assembly is necessary to override a gubernatorial veto. *Constitution of the State of Georgia*, Article III, Section V, Paragraph III (e), and Article, V, Section II, Paragraph IV.

[46] Thomas P. Lauth and Catherine C. Reese, "The Line-Item Veto in Georgia: Fiscal Restraint or Inter-Branch Politics?" *Public Budgeting & Finance*, Vol. 26, No. 2 (September 2006): 1–19.

[47] Pub. L. 104–130.

1996 unconstitutional. The court ruled that the presentment clause of the Constitution, Article I, Section 7, Clause 2, prohibits the president from amending legislation passed by Congress, by after signing it into law rescinding (vetoing) single items of spending.[48] The U.S. president had a functional equivalent of the line-item veto for little more than a year, but does not now have the line-item veto.[49] To have given the president a line-item veto like the one possessed by governors, it would have been necessary to amend the U.S. Constitution. Congress had a sufficient majority to pass the Line-Item Veto Act of 1996 but did not have the two-thirds majority in each house required to propose a constitutional amendment.

Georgia and the federal government both rely upon the individual income tax as their *primary tax revenue source*, but differ from each other in their second most important tax revenue source. Georgia has a graduated income tax with six tax brackets, with a top rate of 5.75%. In recent years, the income tax has constituted slightly less than 50% of annual tax revenues. It also has a state sales tax of 4% that in recent years has constituted approximately 25% of annual tax revenues. Other state tax revenue sources are the corporate income tax and the motor fuel excise tax. The federal government has a graduated individual income tax with seven tax brackets ranging from 10% to 37%. In recent years it has constituted approximately 50% of annual tax collections. It also has a payroll or social insurance tax that in recent years has constituted approximately 33% of tax receipts. The payroll tax consists of the Old Age, Security and Disability Insurance (OASDI) tax at a rate of 12.4% paid equally by employers and employees, 6.2% each, and the Medicare Hospital Insurance (HI) tax at a rate of 2.9% paid equally by employers and employees, 1.45% each. Other federal government tax revenue sources are the corporate income tax and excise taxes.

GEORGIA AND FEDERAL BUDGET AND APPROPRIATIONS

Federal	Georgia
1.*Fiscal Period*: Annual	*Fiscal Period*: Annual
2.*Fiscal Year*: Oct. 1 – Sept. 30	*Fiscal Year*: July 1 – June 30
3.*Budget Type*: Executive	*Budget Type*: Executive
4.*Appropriations Bills*: 12 or Omnibus	*Appropriations Bills*: 1 and A1 Amended Appropriation Act FY-1 Appropriations Act FY
5. *Executive Budget Office*: Office of Management and Budget (OMB)	*Executive Budget Office*: Office of Planning and Budget (OPB)

---

[48] *Clinton, President of the United States, et al. v. City of New York,* et al., 524 U.S. 417 (1998).
[49] Thomas P. Lauth, "The Separation of Powers Principle and Budget Decision Making," in Aman Kahn and W. Bartley Hildreth, *Budget Theory in the Public Sector*. Westport, CT: Quorum Books, 2002. pp. 42–76.

6. *Legislative Budget Office*
   Congressional Budget Office (CBO)

   Legislative Budget Office:
   Legislative Budget Office (LBO) (1969)
   Senate Budget and Evaluation Office (2003)
   LBO → House Budget and Research Office

7. *Balanced Budget Required*:
   No

   Balanced Budget Required:
   Yes, Constitutional
   Governor's revenue estimate
   Revenue Shortfall Reserve

8. *Debt:* Accumulated annual deficits; Short-term

   Debt: Limited to 10% of FY-1 revenue collections; usually 5–6%; Long-term

9. *Line-Item Veto*: 1997
   Enhanced Rescission
   Unconstitutional (1998)

   Line-Item Veto: 1865

10. *Primary Revenue Sources*:
    Income Tax
    Payroll Tax

    Primary Revenue Sources:
    Income tax (top rate 5.75%)
    Sales tax (4%)

Conclusion

Process matters. It provides rules of the road for participants, manages expectations about possible outcomes and legitimizes chosen outcomes. Participants in the decision-making process are likely to accept decision outcomes, even though they may have preferred different ones, if they perceive the process to be open to their voice, to have transparent procedures, and to be fair for all. The Georgia budget process generally meets these criteria. Participants disagree over policies, but not much about process. The Budget Act of 1962 provides structure for the process, and the absence of divided political party control of the branches of government or the chambers of the legislature has moderated inter-branch and inter-chamber relationships. This stands in contrast to the federal budget process which in recent decades, due primarily to hyper-partisanship and polarization, has abandoned the "regular order" of the budget process that served it well in past decades.

Chapter 7
From Line-Item to Performance Budgeting

Public budgets tend to be organized according to the activities and purposes governments want to identify and control. They may be organized according to agencies and divisions within agencies, by government programs, or by a combination of both. They may emphasize goods and services purchased (objects-of-expenditure), volume of work performed (workload), the efficiency with which work is conducted (productivity) or the impact and effectiveness of the work (performance). Sometimes concepts like inputs, outputs and outcomes are used to describe objects-of-expenditure, productivity and performance.

During the past half century, there has been a growing interest in measuring government performance.[1] Simply put, performance budgeting is about bringing information on program performance to the same decision-making table where financial information is being considered, so as to better inform resource allocation decisions. Lu and Willoughby have summarized this trend, "The objective of performance budgeting is to introduce valid and reliable cost and performance data into the budget process and integrate them throughout the budget cycle, which consists of budget development, appropriations, implementation and audit and evaluation."[2] Performance information does not determine resource allocation decisions, nor should it. Resource allocation in state budgeting is essentially a political process, as it should be in a democratic society. However, those allocation decisions are likely to be better for everyone concerned when the political process is informed by performance information.[3]

---

[1] Elaine Yi Lu and Katherine Willoughby, *Public Performance Budgeting: Principles and Practice*. New York: Routledge, 2019.

[2] Elaine Yi Lu and Katherine Willoughby, *Public Performance Budgeting: Principles and Practice*. New York: Routledge, 2019. p. 3.

[3] Allen Schick, *Budget Innovation in the States*. Washington, DC: The Brookings Institution, 1971. S. Kenneth Howard, *Changing State Budgeting*. Lexington, KY: Council of State Governments,

The Georgia budget process has evolved in the modern era, since 1962, from a system focusing primarily on controlling objects of expenditure, to a system that in succeeding stages has incorporated other kinds of management and performance information such as the costs and accomplishments of programs. This chapter explores those developments.

Line-Item Budgeting

In the period following the 1962 Budget Act, the *Governor's Budget Report* contained two standard object-of-expenditure categories for each agency, personal services and operating expenditures, and one or two others for some agencies, capital outlay and authority lease rental,[4] with lump-sum appropriations for those categories. Some agency budgets also included a category called expenditure by activity. For example, the Department of Revenue listed expenditures by: Administration, Enforcement, Individual Income Tax Unit, Motor Fuel Tax Unit, Motor Vehicle Tax Unit and Sales Tax Unit, and the Department of Public Safety listed expenditures by activity as: Georgia State Patrol, Georgia Bureau of Investigation, Crime Laboratory and Driver's License Division. Other state agencies included institutions in the expenditure by activity category. For example, the Board of Corrections listed state prisons, the Board of Regents of the University System listed colleges and universities and the Department of Parks listed state parks. However, it was not until fiscal year 1976 that the *Governor's Budget Report* began to include a list of standard objects of expenditure for each state agency such as, personal services, regular operating expenses, travel, printing and publications, equipment purchases, per diem and fees and computer charges, as well as several agency specific object categories.[5]

Betty Glad reported that in the 1974 session of the General Assembly, that body line-itemized the FY 1975 appropriations bill in retaliation for the state Department of Human Resources moving blocks of funds for disputed and controversial policy purposes. Governor Jimmy Carter initially responded with a number of line-item vetoes.[6] However, when the dust settled from this skirmish both the governor and the legislature came to appreciate that additional line-items provided greater defini-

---

1973. Janet M. Kelly and William C. Rivenbark, *Performance Budgeting for State and Local Government.* Armonk, NY: M.E. Sharpe, 2003.

[4] As noted in Chapter 3, before 1972 the State of Georgia was constitutionally prohibited from incurring debt. During the 1950s and 1960s this constitutional limitation was circumvented by the creation of public corporations, usually called authorities, with the power to issue bonds to obtain funds for the construction of public facilities, which were then leased to state government agencies. Rental payments by state agencies, under lease contracts, were used to retire the authority's bonds. When the bonds were fully retired, the facility became the property of state government. Rental payments appeared in the budget as, "authority lease rental."

[5] State of Georgia, *Governor's Budget Report, Fiscal Year 1976.*

[6] Seven line-item vetoes for a total of $72,856,254 or 4.2% of total appropriations in that year. See: Thomas P. Lauth and Catherine C. Reese, "The Line-Item Veto in Georgia: Fiscal Restraint or

tion to the budget, enabling both of them to exert better control of state agency spending.[7]

It is interesting to note that in the period following the 1931 Budget Act, the governor's budget report to the General Assembly for 1932–1933 contained several standard object-of-expenditure classifications, such as Personal Services, Travel Expenses, Supplies and Materials, Communication Services, Heat, Light, Power and Water Services, Stamping, Printing, Binding Publication Services, Hired and Contractual Services, Rents and Equipment Purchases. The object of expenditure categories enumerated in the fiscal year 1976 *Governor's Budget Report*, are quite similar to those used in the early 1930s.[8] Over the years between 1931 and 1962 this array of standard object-of-expenditure categories was collapsed into the categories of personal services, operating expenses and capital outlays.

Zero-Base Budgeting

Zero-base budgeting was initiated in Georgia in 1973 by Governor Jimmy Carter. Georgia was the first state in the United States to adopt Zero-Base Budgeting (ZBB) as its official budgeting system.[9] It was a budgeting procedure pioneered at Texas Instruments.[10] As installed in the 1970s, zero-base budgeting was applied to all state government agencies and each agency was expected to use it every year to assess all of its programs and activities. It sought to focus budget deliberations on the whole budget not just on proposed increases, and required state agencies to defend their entire budget each year with no assurance that their prior year budget would be retained.

Agencies developed requests at different funding and service levels for each activity or program and requests were presented in order of decreasing benefit to the agency. It was intended to improve efficiency in allocating available resources. The core techniques were decision packages and a ranking process. Agencies began the zero-base process by identifying cost-centers (agency subunits or programs) for which it was feasible and appropriate to assign costs for activities or services.

Inter-Branch Politics?" *Public Budgeting & Finance*, Vol. 26, No. 2 (Summer 2006): 1–19 at 5 and 7.

[7] Betty Glad, *Jimmy Carter: In Search of the Great White House*. New York: W. W. Norton & Company, 1980. p. 195.

[8] *State of Georgia, Budget for the Years 1932–33*.

[9] Thomas P. Lauth, "Zero-Base Budgeting in Georgia State Government: Myth and Reality," *Public Administration Review*, Vol. 38 (September/October 1978): 420–430.

[10] Peter A. Pyhrr, "Zero-Base Budgeting," *Harvard Business Review*, 49 (November/December 1970): 111–121. Peter A. Pyhrr, *Zero-Base Budgeting: A Practical Management Tool for Evaluating Expenses*. New York: John Wiley and Sons, Inc. 1973. Peter A. Pyhrr, "The Zero-Base Approach to Government Budgeting," *Public Administration Review*, Vol. 37 (January/February 1977): 1–8.

Decision packages were prepared for each cost center. They included a statement of goals, a description of the work program by which goals were to be achieved, a statement of benefits expected from activities or services in relationship to costs, an assessment of alternative methods of achieving goals, alternative levels of funding for the decision packages, and a statement of the consequences of not funding a decision package.

Decision packages typically contained at least three funding levels: *minimum*, a level below which it would no longer be feasible to perform an activity; *continuation*, the cost of providing the same level of activity and service as in the previous year, with salary and price increases reflected in the calculation and non-recurring costs eliminated; and *improvement*, higher levels of spending for ongoing programs and funding for new activities and programs (more than one improvement level of funding could be included in a decision package). Each decision package was ranked in order of decreasing benefit. Minimum level requests were placed ahead of current level requests, and current level requests for most cost centers tended to be ranked ahead of improvement level requests. Each funding level for a decision package was identified by a priority number for that package, such as 1 of 3, 2 of 3 and 3 of 3, for a decision package containing three funding levels. Consolidation of rankings stopped at the department level and was not attempted government-wide. The cumulative total for each decision package entered into the rank order, expressed as a percentage of the previous year, was presented in a summary schedule. Before the first decision package was entered into the ranking, the cumulative total was zero, hence the designation – zero-base budgeting. Decision-makers were able to observe the consequences of each additional package entered into the ranking. Rankings depicted incremental levels of funding effort. A cut-off line identified where available revenue supported funding decision packages above the line but not funding packages below the line. Ranking rules were intended to prevent agencies from gaming the system by ranking improvement packages ahead of minimum or continuation packages in the hope that they would also be funded when the more essential packages behind them were funded.[11] In the Table 7.1 example, at the cut-off line the proposed fiscal year (FY) budget would increase over the previous fiscal year (FY-1) budget by 9% (109%).

In the extreme depiction of zero-base budgeting, no agency was able to assume continued funding for programs, each program was challenged to justify its existence during each budget cycle, and every item included in a proposed budget needed to be justified. The label, zero-base budgeting, implied *tabula rasa* budgeting; taken literally, a zero-base budget would mean no base at all. Zero-base budgeting was promoted as a comprehensive decision-making alternative to incrementalism, an approach to budgeting that tends to focus mostly on proposals for new or additional spending, not the entire budget. In practice, ZBB operated as a refined form of incrementalism. Agencies continued to pursue strategies to protect, increase and

---

[11] Thomas P. Lauth and Steven C. Reick, "Modifications in Georgia Zero-Base Budgeting Procedures: 1973–1980," *Midwest Review of Public Administration*, Vol. 13 (December 1979): 225–258.

Zero-Base Budgeting

Table 7.1 Zero-base budgeting: Department of Public Services

Decision packages	Objects of expenditure	FY -1 amount	FY amount	Percent of FY -1	Cumulative percent FY -1
				0.00	0%
1 of 3	Personal Services		7,551,993	0.69	69%
1 of 3	Regular Operating Expenses		466,380	0.04	73%
1 of 3	Travel		399,855	0.04	77%
1 of 3	Motor Vehicle Purchases		78,955	0.01	78%
1 of 3	Equipment		6,800	0.00	78%
1 of 3	Computer Charges		312,033	0.03	81%
1 of 3	Real Estate Rental		327,850	0.03	84%
1 of 3	Telecommunications		78,912	0.01	85%
1 of 3	Per Diem, Fees and Contracts		15,000	0.00	85%
2 of 3	Personal Services		962,879	0.09	94%
2 of 3	Regular Operating Expenses		233,165	0.02	96%
2 of 3	Travel		199,928	0.02	98%
2 of 3	Motor Vehicle Purchases		39,478	0.00	98%
2 of 3	Equipment		3,400	0.00	98%
2 of 3	Computer Charges		156,017	0.01	99%
2 of 3	Real Estate Rental		163,925	0.01	100%
2 of 3	Telecommunications		39,456	0.00	100%
2 of 3	Per Diem, Fees and Contracts		7,500	0.00	100%
3 of 3	Personal Services		<u>962,879</u>	<u>0.09</u>	<u>109%</u>
3 of 3	Regular Operating Expenses		116,583	0.01	110%
3 of 3	Travel		250,500	0.02	112%
3 of 3	Motor Vehicle Purchases		75,500	0.01	113%
3 of 3	Equipment		2,500	0.00	113%
3 of 3	Computer Charges		15,000	0.00	113%
3 of 3	Real Estate Rental		175,050	0.02	115%
3 of 3	Telecommunications		40,000	0.00	115%
3 of 3	Per Diem, Fees and Contracts		10,000	0.00	115%
	Total	$10,944,918	$12,691,538		

Ranking Decision Packages
   Minimum level – 1
   Continuation level – 2
   Improvement level – 3

expand the base. Managers tended to use the minimum package as an opportunity to argue against reductions in the base, citing negative consequences of operating with only minimal level funding. Managers tended to use the current level package to argue for protection of the base and to use improvement level funding requests to argue for increases in program funding. Ironically, when decision packages were arrayed in rank order, incremental decision-making was facilitated, not discouraged.

It may have been unrealistic to expect major cost savings from zero-base budgeting or even major reallocations within budgets. Budget decisions, in addition to the management tools used to frame them, are also the products of political pressures and constraints exerted by actors and events outside of state agencies. The ability of zero-base budgeting to achieve budget reductions or reallocations tended to be constrained by several factors: constitutional or statutory requirements for programs; public expectations that service levels would not be reduced from one year to the next; interest group demands for the funding of new programs and the protection of existing ones; legislative support for programs which benefitted the districts and constituencies of individual members; cost-matching requirements of intergovernmental grant-in-aid programs and some uncontrollable spending in entitlement programs. Nevertheless, zero-base budgeting was able to improve the quantity and quality of information available to managers about agency operations. As a bottom-up approach, it presented to managers at each organizational level, information through the ranking process that better informed them of projected costs and expected benefits at each funding level.

Zero-base budgeting had a much-publicized beginning in Georgia, but on balance was only moderately successful. The formal documents and procedures including decision packages, multiple funding levels, and ranking processes were in place in the 1970s. However, the existing budget process had difficulty assimilating the program focus and decision package techniques of ZBB into its routine practices and procedures. The architects and advocates of zero-base budgeting underestimated the volume of information that would be generated, which turned out to defy the ability of decision makers to digest and use that information during the annual budget cycle. The result was that state agencies came to believe that the executive budget office was overwhelmed by the information they produced and that the legislative budget office, as well as legislators, disregarded the information in making their appropriation decisions. Agencies soon began to take the process less seriously. When management shortcomings were combined with political constraints, the process eventually broke down and gradually fell into disuse.[12]

---

[12] Thomas P. Lauth, "Zero-Base Budgeting in Georgia State Government: Myth and Reality," *Public Administration Review*, Vol. 38 (September/October 1978): 420–430. Henry M. Huckaby and Thomas P. Lauth, "Budget Redirection in Georgia State Government," *Public Budgeting & Finance*, Vol. 18 (Winter 1998): 36–44.

Performance Evaluation Measures

Performance evaluation measures made their way into the state budget process in conjunction with zero-base budgeting. Prior to the advent of zero-base budgeting, performance data were almost entirely workload data. As examples: in the Department of Education, cost per student in average daily attendance (ADA) across such organization functions as administration, instruction, transportation, and plant operation and maintenance; in the University System of Georgia, Board of Regents, hours of instruction by degree and type of institution, number of equivalent full time (EFT) faculty, average salaries by type of institution, degrees conferred by type of degree and type of institution; for the Public Service Commission, number of complaints investigated by type of utility; and in the Department of Public Health, number of patients treated by institution, number of air and water quality studies conducted, and number of sanitation and occupational safety inspections performed.[13]

Following the reorganization of state government in 1972,[14] executive branch departments were divided for budgetary purposes into activities, and following the initiation of ZBB in 1973, budget requests were formulated in decision packages. Each decision package contained financial information presented in line-item format with approximately 10 or 12 object classifications and several sub-object classifications. In addition to financial information, program information was presented for each activity and decision package. Such information as the purpose or goal of an activity, its legal and administrative mandates, the major objectives to be undertaken in order to achieve goals, and evaluation measures keyed to levels of performance were provided. Although the zero-base budget system required agencies to state their goals and objectives in narrative form, it was not in any generally accepted sense a program budget system. The budget assembly format was line-item, object-of-expenditure, and information was grouped according to organizational unit rather than by programs. Although agencies had been required since 1973, the first year of zero-base budgeting, to submit quantitative measures regarding workload, efficiency and effectiveness associated with their programs and activities, those measures eventually came to be regarded by the Office of Planning and Budget as inadequate. Agencies were put on notice in 1977 that a renewed effort at reporting performance measures would be "of vital importance to you in the fall budget hearing with the Governor and during the legislative session."[15] Two types of measures were utilized for several years following the 1977 admonition: program effectiveness measures, that is, indicators of the degree to which program objectives were or would be achieved, and workload efficiency measures, that is, indicators of the degree to which the program economically managed the workload associated with

---

[13] State of Georgia, *Budget FY 1972 and FY 1973*.

[14] Betty Glad, *Jimmy Carter: In Search of the Great White House*. New York: W.W. Norton & Company, 1980. pp. 161–178.

[15] State of Georgia, Office of Planning and Budget, *General Budget Preparation Procedures: Fiscal Year 1977 Budget Development* (June 1975). p. 2.

meeting its objectives. These performance evaluation measures were intended to inform the zero-base budgeting decision-making process.

In a 1985 study of performance evaluation in Georgia, I reported that agency and central budget office personnel did not take evaluation measures seriously during budget preparation and review because they believed state policy makers did not use such information in budget decision-making. The state budget director and legislative budget analyst confirmed the accuracy of those perceptions.[16] This did not mean that program performance was not evaluated in Georgia; it meant that performance information had not yet been systematically integrated into the annual budget process.

Budget Redirection

"Redirection" was added to the budget process by Governor Zell Miller beginning with the FY 1997 *Governor's Budget Report,* as an innovation designed to achieve both managerial and policy objectives within a constricted fiscal environment. Lessons learned from previous state experience with ZBB were used to design a reform that was compatible with both the administrative system and the political system.[17]

State agencies were directed to eliminate or downsize those activities that were no longer needed or had a low priority compared to higher priority services. Funds realized through this process became available for redirection to activities or programs that had a high priority for the agency, or to other sectors of state government that had a high priority for the governor. Agencies were required to identify a minimum of 5% of their adjusted base budget that then became the primary means for funding new programs and services in the coming fiscal year. The adjusted base was determined by deducting non-recurring expenditures and adding annualized expenses. A limit, based upon revenue projections, was set by the Office of Planning and Budget on the amount an agency might request above the current year's budget. The limit was 6.5% for fiscal year 1997 and 4.5% in fiscal years 1998 and 1999. This feature was intended to force agencies to recognize that revenues were limited and the governor's priorities, in addition to those of agencies, had to be accommodated within revenue limitations.

The three stated purposes of redirection were to: fund ongoing services or enhancements within an agency using the current level of resources, fund growth in formula and entitlement-related services in a way that minimized the amount of new resources required for those services, and increase fund availability for priority areas within state government as a whole.

---

[16] Thomas P. Lauth, "Performance Evaluation in the Georgia Budget Process," *Public Budgeting & Finance,* Vol. 5 (Spring 1985): 67–82 at 74.

[17] Henry M. Huckaby and Thomas P. Lauth, "Budget Redirection in Georgia," *Public Budgeting & Finance,* Vol. 18 (Winter 1998): 36–44.

Governor Miller's policy priorities included increasing teachers' salaries, removing the sales tax from food purchased for at-home consumption, funding the operating cost of new prisons, providing the state's share of funding for kindergarten through high school education, and meeting the state's Medicaid obligations. Fiscal constraints on these policy priorities included loss of revenue from the removal of the sales tax on food, federal government deficit reduction plans that were likely to result in reduced federal funds for state governments and the belief that new state taxes or increased tax rates were politically out of the question.

What were the results of budget redirection? In fiscal year 1997, $627,316,414 was identified for redirection, $412,252,237 was retained by agencies (66%), and $215,064,177 was allocated outside agencies (34%) to other parts of state government. In fiscal 1998, $349,001,410 was identified for redirection and $308,355,077 was retained by agencies (88%) but for different purposes. In fiscal year 1999, 88% was retained by agencies.[18] During the period of budget redirection, the Miller administration removed the 4 cent sales tax on food in three phases,[19] increased the salary of public school teachers and university system personnel by an average of 6% each year for four consecutive years, FY 1996 through FY 1999, and increased prison beds between 1996 and 1998 by 6,583. Even agencies that sustained a net reduction in their budget benefited from redirection by having greater flexibility to internally redirect funds. They were able to redirect funds away from activities or programs that otherwise might have been politically difficult to accomplish, and able to redirect funds to activities or programs that otherwise might not have been able to compete successfully outside the agency for new funding. Budget redirection continued through FY 2001, but by FY 2002 under a new administration it was discontinued. A study by James W. Douglas concluded that budget redirection resulted in the shifting of resources within agency base budgets, the reallocation of resources from low to higher priorities and the reduction of acquisitive behavior by state agencies seeking to expand their budgets.[20]

Results-Based Budgeting

Results-Based Budgeting (RBB) was implemented in Georgia in the 1998 fiscal year,[21] as required by the state's Budget Accountability and Planning Act of 1993 which established an outcome-based budget system.[22] Initially, all government

---

[18] Henry M. Huckaby and Thomas P. Lauth, "Budget Redirection in Georgia," *Public Budgeting & Finance*, Vol. 18 (Winter 1998): 36–44 at 42.

[19] From 4¢ to 2¢ in FY 1997, to 1¢ in FY 1998 and 0¢ thereafter.

[20] James W. Douglas, "Redirection in Georgia: A New Type of Budget Reform," Doctoral Dissertation, The University of Georgia, (1997).

[21] *Governor's Budget Report FY 1998*. pp. 18–19.

[22] Georgia Laws, 1993: 1914–1941. SB 335, Budget and Accountability and Planning Act of 1993, was approved April 28, 1993. Official Code of Georgia Annotated (O.C.G.A.), Title 45, Chapter

activities were divided into programs. RBB required that a purpose, goal, and desired result that could be accomplished during the fiscal year be developed for each program. Progress toward achieving the desired result for each program was to be measured at the end of each funding period. The future funding level of programs would be determined by how well they met the performance measures established for them. The objectives of RBB were to enable the governor and legislature, agency managers, and program customers to identify successful and unsuccessful programs, to aid policy makers in determining if expended funds were worth it in terms of achieving intended results, and to make government more accountable to Georgia citizens. The governor stated RBB was a method to achieve accountability for tax dollars, with documentation of whether or not expenditures are achieving their intended results.[23] The Budget Accountability and Planning Act created the Budget Responsibility Oversight Committee (BROC), composed of five members of the House of Representatives and five members of the Senate, to review and evaluate program evaluation reports provided to it by the Governor's Office of Planning and Budget and the Department of Audits, and to share its findings with the entire General Assembly prior to adoption of the annual appropriations act. All programs were to be evaluated at least every 10 years.[24]

The 1998 fiscal year was set as the benchmark year for most programs. The FY 1998 *Governor's Budget Report* provided information on each program by name, purpose and goals. The FY 1999 *Governor's Budget Report* identified the results expected from each program during that year. The FY 2000 *Governor's Budget Report* identified benchmarks against which programs were to be measured.

Some programs had difficulty in identifying measurable program outcomes. The FY 2000 *Governor's Budget Report* noted that because RBB was a new process, many agencies and programs were slow in collecting information on program results, and some programs had difficulty identifying measurable program outcomes. Commenting on progress with the new process, the *Budget Report* stated that while approximately 49% of the FY 1999 performance measures addressed actual results, at least 70% of FY 2000 agency budget submissions included quantified measures of actual and desired results. Program managers were encouraged to improve their data collection systems and to identify more valid and reliable measures for program results. The FY 2004 *Governor's Budget Report* included comparisons of desired results with actual performance. RBB trend data were expected to be used as a "report card" on government program performance.

The objective of RBB was to change budget conversations by shifting the focus from inputs to outcomes. However, that was easier said than done. It was easier to obtain executive agency participation than to obtain legislative participation. The

---

12, Article 4, Part 1.

[23] *Governor's Budget Report, FY 1998.* p. 19.

[24] Georgia Laws, 1993: 1914–1940. SB 335, Budget and Accountability and Planning Act of 1993, Sections 16 (d) and (e), 18 (a), (d) and (f).

General Assembly preferred to use what they knew best, inputs, and to control the budget by controlling line items.

Initially, RBB and Budget Redirection co-existed, but because Governor Miller was more interested in the ability of Budget Redirection to generate funds for his program priorities (elimination of the sales tax on food, increasing teacher salaries and increasing prison capacity), RBB as a management approach was of less interest to him. In the absence of either legislative support or strong gubernatorial support, RBB rapidly diminished in importance as either a management or budget tool. Results-Based Budgeting information was no longer included in the FY 2005 *Governor's Budget Report*. This development illustrates the importance of support from top policy makers if budget innovation techniques are to be successful.

In a study conducted in the middle 1990s, after the passage of the 1993 Budget Accountability and Planning Act, but before the implementation of Results-Based Budgeting in 1998, Chilik Yu reported that evaluation results were not extensively used by Georgia budgeters in their funding deliberations, that legislative budgeters had the lowest inclination of all budgeters to use program evaluation in budget deliberations, and that executive office budgeters made somewhat greater use of program evaluation information than did agency budgeters. He reported that in most cases, "evaluation results are used to verify or legitimate funding level decisions which have been made by other considerations."[25] On the positive side, he reported, "Utilization is higher when program evaluation contains valid, reliable, clearly-presented, widely disseminated, relevant and reasonable findings, produced by objective and capable evaluators."[26]

Prioritized Program Budgeting

Prioritized Program Budgeting (PPB) was introduced in 2004 as Georgia's new budgeting system. The state began the process of converting its budget from a line-item, object-of-expenditure format to a program format in 2003, as part of a larger effort by newly elected Governor Sonny Perdue to implement performance-based budgeting. Transition to the new budgeting system was initiated by the governor's Office of Planning and Budget (OPB) in its 2004 budget preparation instructions. Agencies were required to prepare a strategic plan, develop performance measures/ indicators, and submit a budget based on programs. PPB emphasizes programs, rather than agencies, as the primary budgetary units, and requires that measures of demand for the program, program efficiency, program output, and program results be delineated for each program. According to the then-Director of OPB, if agencies receive lump sum appropriations for programs and greater flexibility in the use of

---

[25] Chilik Yu, "The Use of Program Evaluation in Public Budgeting: Evidence from the 1993 Georgia Budget Reform," Doctoral Dissertation, The University of Georgia, (1996): 147.

[26] Chilik Yu, "The Use of Program Evaluation in Public Budgeting: Evidence from the 1993 Georgia Budget Reform," Doctoral Dissertation, The University of Georgia, (1996): 147.

those funds, some mechanism must be put in place to achieve accountability.[27] Performance measures are intended to be mechanisms assuring citizens that public managers and political decision makers are attempting to provide services efficiently and effectively.

In the FY 2005 *Governor's Budget Report*, agencies reported programs and performance measures, as well as object-of-expenditure information.[28] The relatively small Department of Banking and Finance, that enforces and administers all state laws, rules, and regulations governing the operation of state-chartered financial institutions, provides a simple example of presenting information by both object classes and programs. Traditionally, Georgia state agencies used ten standard object-of-expenditure classifications, as well as several other agency-specific object classes. The standard object classifications were: Personal Services, Regular Operating Expenses, Travel, Motor Vehicle Purchases, Equipment, Computer Charges, Real Estate Rentals, Telecommunications, Per Diem and Fees and Contracts. In the FY 2005 *Governor's Budget Report*, the programs for the Department of Banking and Finance were: Financial Institution Supervision, Mortgage Supervision, Chartering, Licensing and Applications, and Consumer Protection and Assistance. The Department of Banking and Finance also reported data on seven performance measures, for example, the percentage of troubled or problematic financial institutions visited, the percentage of certain reports examined, and the percentage of customer satisfaction with the department's services.

As part of the prioritizing initiative, agencies were initially required to propose program budgets at three levels: a 5% reduction of the base budget; *redistribution* of an amount equal to 3% of the base budget; and enhancement limited to 2% of the base budget. In the FY 2006 *Governor's Budget Report*, agencies were required to "submit three budget scenarios: one reprioritizing their current funding level, one reflecting a 3% reduction, and one representing a 5% growth in funding."[29] Redistribution was seen as a way to shift existing funds from low priority programs or sub-programs to higher priority programs or sub-programs. *Redistribution* seems conceptually indistinguishable from budget *redirection* used in the 1990s, and the requirement that program results be measured is very similar to Results-Based Budgeting (RBB) of the 1990s. Nevertheless, a new governor and administration sought to promote its own brand of program budgeting.

In an informative and insightful article, Carolyn Bourdeaux described Georgia's transition to performance-based budgeting.[30] She described an implementation pro-

---

[27] Conversation with Timothy A. Connell, Director, Office of Planning and Budget, May 9, 2005.

[28] *Governor's Budget Report, Fiscal Year 2005.* pp. 55–57.

[29] *Governor's Budget Report, FY 2006.* Governor Sonny Perdue Message to Members of the General Assembly. p. 1.

[30] Carolyn Bourdeaux, "The Problem with Programs: Multiple Perspectives on Program Structure in Program-Based, Performance-Oriented Budgets," *Public Budgeting & Finance*, Vol. 28, No.2 (Summer 2008): 20–47. See also Carolyn Bourdeaux, *An Analysis of the Implementation of Program Budgeting in Georgia.* Atlanta, GA: Fiscal Research Center, Andrew Young School of Policy Studies, Georgia State University, (March 2007).

cess in which the perspectives and expectations of agencies, the governor's budget office and the legislature were not entirely in alignment with each other. According to Bourdeaux, agency managers expected that if they were going to be held accountable for results, they should have program structures that gave them discretion and flexibility to deploy their resources so as to achieve their intended results. The Office of the Governor, where program budgeting was initiated, expected that it would help align agency activities with broad state-wide goals, identify "waste, fraud and abuse," and improve agency operations in general, but not necessarily increase managerial flexibility. From the legislative perspective, the linking of funds to programs rather than to objects-of-expenditure and increasing managerial discretion and flexibility in deploying funds tended to make legislative control over its policy priorities more difficult, especially so for controlling the movement of funds during budget execution. However, according to Bourdeaux, even with the transition to performance-based budgeting and a heightened focus on programs, the Office of the Governor and the legislature retained spending control by retaining control of agency fund transfers at the object-of-expenditure level. The Office of Planning and Budget continued to require agencies to receive formal approval of fund transfers across both programs and traditional object classes, and the legislature acting directly when it is in session and through its Fiscal Affairs Committees when it is out of session, maintained control of the transfer of funds by object class.

The extent to which budget innovations have been able to penetrate existing budget routines has been a perennial problem for innovators seeking to improve government performance and accountability.[31] In studies of Georgia performance budgeting reported in 2005 and 2006, Yi Lu concluded that the use of performance information in Georgia had increased compared with the extent of its use 20 years earlier, state agencies were more extensive users of performance information compared with past years when performance information was used mostly by the central budget office, and performance information continued to be used by agencies mostly to inform program management decisions and only moderately to inform budget decisions.[32]

Further indicating the perceived success of program budgeting in state government was the repeal of the Budget Responsibility Oversight Committee (BROC) in 2008. With the emergence of program budgeting in the state's budget system during the Sonny Perdue administration, the General Assembly decided there was no longer a need for a separate legislative entity to evaluate programs.[33]

---

[31] Allen Schick, *Budget Innovation in the States*. Washington, DC: The Brookings Institution, 1971.

[32] Yi Lu, "Performance Budgeting: The Perspective of State Agencies," *Public Budgeting & Finance*, Vol. 27, No. 4 (Winter 2007): 1–17. Yi Lu, "Individual Engagement to Collective Participation: The Dynamics of Participation Pattern in Performance Budgeting," *Public Budgeting & Finance*, Vol. 31, No. 2 (Summer 2011): 79–98.

[33] Georgia Laws 2008: v01-v16. HB 529 became effective January 28, 2008. This legislation also abolished the Legislative Budget Office and established a Senate Budget Office and a House Budget Office. Thank you to David Tanner and Brenda Purcell for helping me to identify these legislative actions.

Zero-Base Budgeting Redux

Zero-base budgeting (ZBB) reentered the Georgia budgetary process in 2012 after a hiatus of approximately three decades. In the 1970s, Governor Jimmy Carter was the principal advocate of zero-base budgeting in Georgia. It was an executive branch initiative intended to improve managerial efficiency and effectiveness in the operations of the executive branch of state government.[34] The legislative branch largely rejected zero-base budgeting, preferring instead continuation or incremental budgeting with its presumption that resource allocation commitments of previous years would, for the most part, be continued and that the current year budget process would focus mostly on reviewing proposals for new resource commitments.[35] In contrast, in the 2000s members of the Georgia General Assembly were the principal advocates of ZBB with the governor initially rejecting it. In 2010, the General Assembly passed a zero-base budgeting bill, but Governor Sonny Perdue vetoed it saying that it was unnecessary because his staff already examined all facets of each agency's budget each year.[36] The Senate voted to over-ride the governor's veto, but the House did not. In 2011, the House of Representatives passed a zero-base budgeting bill, but the Senate did not. In those years, the House and Senate versions differed on such matters as how frequently agencies would be subject to zero-base budgeting review (every 5, 8, or 10 years), and who would select the agencies or programs for annual review, the executive branch Office of Planning and Budget or the legislative branch Fiscal Affairs Committees. In 2012, the Georgia General Assembly enacted and Governor Nathan Deal signed a bill requiring zero-base budgeting for selected state agencies to begin with the FY 2014 budget.[37] Governor Deal voluntarily implemented zero-base budgeting for selected state agencies beginning with the FY 2013 budget. The zero-base budgeting act passed in 2012 requires that agencies and programs are subject to zero-base budgeting review at least once every 10 years but not more often than once every 8 years, and that agencies and programs are selected for zero-base budgeting review by the House Budget and Research Office and Senate Budget and Evaluation Office in consultation with the Governor's Office of Planning and Budget.

There are generally two explanations for why Governor Sonny Perdue vetoed zero-base budgeting legislation in 2010 and Governor Nathan Deal signed such legislation in 2012. The political explanation is that Governor Perdue's relationship with the General Assembly was more contentious and Governor Deal's relationship

---

[34] Governor Carter's 1972 reorganization initiative generally streamlined the executive branch of state government, eliminated or consolidated agencies, and reconstituted the Bureau of the Budget as the Office of Planning and Budget.

[35] Thomas P. Lauth, "Zero-Base Budgeting in Georgia State Government: Myth and Reality," *Public Administration Review*, Vol. 38 (September/October 1978): 420–430.

[36] Governor's Veto Message, SB 1, June 8, 2010. He also stated that other states that have used zero-base budgeting have abandoned it because of the additional bureaucratic process and overhead while producing few identifiable results.

[37] Georgia Laws, 2012: 987–989. SB 33 was approved May 2, 2012.

was more cooperative.[38] The policy explanation, while not discounting the political explanation, is that the bill presented to Governor Perdue applied zero-base budgeting to every agency every 4 years, but the bill presented to Governor Deal was for a selected number of agencies not more than every 8 years.[39]

The new zero-base budgeting did not have any of the hallmark practices and procedures of the Carter-era zero-base budgeting: decision packages, funding levels (minimum, continuation and improvement), ranking process, cutoff line and rules governing the ranking process. Instead, it relies upon the program categories and performance measurement procedures that have evolved in the state's budget process since the establishment of program budgeting in 2004. The new zero-base budgeting undertakes detailed evaluations of selected agencies and programs each year, "assessing a particular program's activities against its statutory responsibilities, purpose, cost to provide services and desired performance outcomes."[40] Agencies are asked to identify their program's "key activities" and explain why the program and its activities are critical and necessary and if there are alternative ways of delivering the services of the program.[41] Key activities are seen by some observers as the new zero-base budgeting counterpart to the Carter-era decision packages.[42] In addition to the performance evaluation of programs and activities, as to their efficiency and effectiveness, financial analysis of programs examines historical expenditures by object class, with the goal of assessing cost effectiveness and return on investment.

Legislative advocates of the new zero-base budgeting wanted something that would "drill" into the base or continuation budget. The design and implementation of the new zero-base budgeting was left up to the Office of Planning and Budget. OPB viewed the zero-base innovation as a renewed opportunity to identify activities and programs that had become part of the historic budget base through annual appropriation decisions and to require that their continuance be justified. Of course, this could have been done through the existing program budget structure, and likely was being done, but the zero-base budgeting innovation gave such reviews greater impetus and legitimacy.

The other significant difference was that the Carter-era zero-base budgeting required all state agencies to be involved in the process every year. The new zero-base budgeting required the involvement of approximately 10% of agencies each year, with all agencies receiving full zero-base review at least once every 8 years. In FY 2013, the first year of the new zero-base budgeting, 35 programs across 25 state agencies, approximately 10% of the state's approximately 370 programs, were subject to zero-base budgeting review. The number was based mostly on a reasonable

---

[38] Interview with Senator Jack Hill, Chair, Senate Appropriations Committee, March 8, 2013. Also see Thomas P. Lauth, "Budget Deficits in the States: Georgia," *Public Budgeting & Finance*, Vol. 30, (Spring 2010): 15–32 at 25–29.

[39] Interview with John E. Brown, Vice Chancellor for Fiscal Affairs, University System of Georgia, August 10, 2012.

[40] Office of Planning and Budget, *General Budget Preparation Procedures for Prioritized-Based Budgets, Amended Fiscal Year 2012 and Fiscal Year 2013*. July 25, 2011.

[41] Official Code of Georgia Annotated (O.C.G.A.), 45-12-75.1.

[42] Interview with David Tanner, Deputy Director, Office of Planning and Budget, August 1, 2012.

workload for OPB staff. The programs chosen for review were a combination of what programs OPB already had targeted for closer review, a few volunteers, such as the Department of Agriculture,[43] and a reasonable workload based upon size and scope of programs. Recalling that one of the reasons for the failure of the Carter-era zero-base budgeting was that the process became over-burdened by the requirement that all programs of all agencies were reviewed every year, applying zero-base budgeting to only a segment of state agencies and programs each year was thought to be a sensible approach. The Chair of the House Appropriations Committee reported that he had received advice from a veteran budget staff member to avoid the Carter-era zero-base budgeting model because it would "load us down with mounds of paper."[44] In FY 2014, the second year of the new zero-base budgeting, 57 programs across 24 agencies, including most of the programs from the Department of Education,[45] were subject to zero-base budgeting review. In FY 2020, 28 programs across 12 agencies, 13% of state programs, were reviewed.

In FY 2013 the Governor's Office of Planning and Budget reported in the *Zero-Base Budgeting Report* a total reduction amount for the 35 programs.[46] In FY 2014, the governor's office did not report a total reduction amount for 57 programs but did display in the *Zero-Base Budgeting Report* a program's current year funding level and the governor's recommended funding level for the upcoming fiscal year. This presentation revealed which programs were increased, decreased or remained the same following their zero-base budgeting assessment. In FY 2020 and other more recent years, the governor's recommended funding level for the upcoming year has appeared only in the *Governor's Budget Report*, but has not been included in the *Zero-Base Budgeting Report*. One interpretation of these evolving information changes is that in the beginning of the new zero-base budgeting process it was thought to be important to reflect legislative interests in using zero-base budgeting as a tool for reducing the state budget, while in later years the governor and budget office have been more interested using zero-base budgeting as a conventional tool for evaluating the performance of programs.

When the Carter-era version of zero-base budgeting was introduced in the 1970s, the existing Georgia budget process did not have much in the way of performance measurement. Zero-base budgeting introduced a distinct set of performance measurement procedures into the state's budget process. When zero-base budgeting reappeared in 2012, the state budget process already had a well-developed performance measurement system. Consequently, the new zero-base budgeting was able to utilize the existing program format and analytical procedures. See Figure 7.1.

---

[43] The newly elected Commissioner of the Department of Agriculture requested a thorough review of his agency, which under its previous leadership had for decades resisted any use of program or performance budgeting. Interview with Gary Black, Commissioner of Agriculture, January 3, 2013.

[44] Interview with Terry England, Chair, House Appropriations Committee, April 22, 2013.

[45] Twenty-three in FY 2014; two had been included in FY 2013.

[46] Thomas P. Lauth, "Zero-Base Budgeting Redux in Georgia: Efficiency or Ideology?" *Public Budgeting & Finance*, Vol. 34 (Spring 2014): 1–17 at 12–15.

Zero-Base Budgeting Redux

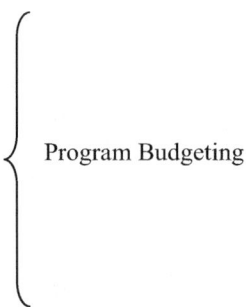

Carter Era Zero-Base Budgeting	New Zero-Base Budgeting
➢ All Programs Every Year	➢ 10% of Programs Each Year
➢ Decision Packages	➢ Key Activities
➢ Funding Levels • Minimum Level • Continuation Level • Improvement Level	} Program Budgeting
➢ Ranking Process	
➢ Cutoff Line	
➢ Rules to Preventing Gaming the System	

Fig. 7.1 Carter era and the new zero-base budgeting: a comparison

Whereas the Carter-era zero-base budgeting purported to build each agency budget anew every year from a base of zero, the new zero-base budgeting sought to drill down into agency programs, looking for duplication waste and obsolescence,[47] to determine which elements must be retained and what elements might be eliminated to either repurpose the existing resources or reduce the program. However, what the Carter-era zero-base budgeting and the new zero-base budgeting have in common is the symbol of "zero," signaling a budget cutting exercise in the service of management efficiency and fiscal conservatism.

Budget reform in the states usually has been initiated by the executive branch and the success of the reform has been affected by the extent to which the state legislature has embraced it. Carolyn Boudreaux found that legislative involvement is crucial in promoting use of performance information throughout the budget process.[48] In Georgia, the new zero-base budgeting was a legislative initiative, supported by the governor and the executive budget office. Senator David Shafer was the principal advocate of zero-base budgeting from the time he arrived in the state Senate in 2003. Senator Shafer expressed how surprised he was to find upon his arrival in the General Assembly that the state budget was not considered as a whole each year but that the focus of review was only on new spending proposals.[49] It probably is not entirely

---

[47] Interview with Senator David Schafer, September 6, 2012.
[48] Carolyn Bourdeaux, "Do Legislatures Matter in Budgetary Reform?" *Public Budgeting & Finance*, Vol. 26, No. 1 (Spring 2006): 120–142.
[49] Interviews with David Shafer, September 6, 2012 and April 17, 2013.

accurate to say that the base or continuation budget was never considered,[50] but that was the senator's perception of how things worked. He also believed zero-base budgeting expressed his Republican conservative philosophy in fiscal matters.[51]

Even though the Georgia legislature embraced zero-base budgeting philosophically, it did not fully integrate it into its budget process. At the beginning of each session of the General Assembly, the Governor and the Office of Planning and Budget present to the legislature the *Governor's Budget Report* for the next fiscal year, and since the adoption of zero-base budgeting, a *Zero-Base Budget Report*. The Georgia General Assembly meets for only 40 legislative days, and finds it difficult during that time to integrate the *Zero-Base Budget Report* into the appropriations process. The Chair of the House Appropriations Committee acknowledges that during the annual session of the General Assembly it is difficult for the Appropriations Committee to focus on the *Zero-Base Budgeting Report*.[52] The Chair of the Senate Appropriations Committee noted that for his committee, zero-base budgeting activity is mostly in the off-season when sub-committees drill into agencies at the activity level, asking questions about program activities or expenditure amounts, not during the session.[53] Selected individuals in the Georgia General Assembly today are much more enthusiastic about zero-base budgeting than were their counterparts in the 1970s.[54] However, even today, zero-base budgeting remains primarily an executive branch budget activity with the legislative branch cheering it on but leaving most of the heavy lifting to the executive agencies and the Governor's Office of Planning and Budget.

Conclusion

During the past 50 years, budgeting reforms in Georgia, as in the other states, have attempted to integrate program and performance information into budget deliberations. The reforms sought to consider program performance in relationship to organizational mission and goals, alternative methods to achieve mission and goals, as well as the costs and benefits associated with various alternatives. The objectives of such reforms were to focus attention on strategic planning, policy analysis, and program performance evaluation, without of course, diminishing the vital importance of financial control.

---

[50] Alan Essig, Director of the Georgia Budget and Policy Institute and former state budget analyst said, "The idea that they never look at existing programs is an old wives' tale. I never believed that." "1st Year of Zero-Based Budgeting Impresses Some," www.times-herald.com, Newnan, Georgia, March 21, 2012.

[51] Interviews with David Shafer, September 6, 2012 and April 17, 2013.

[52] Interview with Terry England, Chair of the House Appropriations Committee, April 22, 2013.

[53] Interview with Jack Hill, Chair of the Senate Appropriations Committee, March 8, 2013.

[54] Thomas P. Lauth, "Zero-Base Budgeting in Georgia State Government: Myth and Reality," *Public Administration Review*, Vol. 38 (September/October 1978): 420–430.

Chapter 8
The Line-Item Veto in Executive-Legislative Relations

Introduction

This chapter examines use of the line-item veto by Georgia governors, focusing on the executive budget era since 1962. Georgia was the first state to adopt the line-item veto, doing so in 1865. The line-item veto first appeared in the United States in 1861 in the *Constitution of the Confederate States of America:*

> The President may approve any appropriation and disapprove any other appropriation in the same bill. In such case he shall, in signing the bill, designate the appropriations disapproved; and shall return a copy of such appropriations, with his objections, to the House in which the bill shall have originated; and the same proceedings shall then be had as in case of other bills disapproved by the President.[1]

Similarly, the *Constitution of the State of Georgia* provides: "The Governor may approve any appropriation and veto any other appropriation in the same bill, and an appropriation vetoed shall not become law unless such veto is overridden in the manner herein provided."[2] Today, 44 governors have some form of the line-item veto.[3]

---

[1] *Constitution of the Confederate States of America*, Article 1, Section 7 (2).
[2] *Constitution of the State of Georgia*, 1983, Article III, Section V, Paragraph XIII (e).
[3] Indiana, Nevada, New Hampshire, North Carolina, Rhode Island and Vermont do not have the line-item veto. Thomas P. Lauth, "The Other Six: Governors Without the Line-Item Veto," *Public Budgeting & Finance*, Vol. 36, Number 4 (Winter 2016): 26–49.

This chapter incorporates segments of my article with Catherine C. Reese, "The Line-Item Veto in Georgia: Fiscal Restraint of Inter-Branch Politics?" *Public Budgeting & Finance*, Volume 26, Number 2 (Summer 2006): 1-19, and segments of my paper with Charles S. Bullock, III, "The Line-Item Veto in Georgia State Government: A Comparison of Governor Sonny Perdue with Democratic Predecessors," Georgia Political Science Association Annual Meeting, Savannah, GA, November 12, 2010. I thank my co-authors for their contributions to this chapter.

The line-item veto is a special form of the executive veto available to governors to defend budget proposals against legislative additions or changes that governors deem unnecessary, unwise or inconsistent with their own policy priorities. It emerged because the executive veto had become ineffective in dealing with riders and pork barrel spending in appropriations bills and was intended to restore the governor's ability to protect the executive budget. Governors frequently encounter appropriations bills containing many spending items they favor, indeed proposed, bundled with some spending items they oppose. The option of vetoing the entire bill usually is unacceptable and without the line-item veto the only feasible alternative is to sign the bill. The line item-veto enables a governor to defend against this dilemma.[4] The line-item veto often is thought to be a device for reducing the budget total and thereby the size of government, but in actual practice it is mostly an instrument for governors to defend their budgets against legislative attempts to substitute legislative policy priorities for gubernatorial policy priorities. In a separation of powers system with co-equal legislative and executive branches, it is not surprising that even though the governor has responsibility for preparing the budget, the legislature will want to insert some of its spending priorities into the budget it enacts.

The Line-Item Veto in Georgia

The governor, in addition to proposing the annual budget, also prepares an estimate of revenue to be collected in the coming fiscal year. The revenue estimate establishes a budget ceiling which the appropriations bill cannot exceed. As a practical matter this means that legislative changes to the governor's proposed budget do not increase the budget total, but occur within the ceiling established by the official revenue estimate, usually by substituting legislative policy preferences for some of the governor's policy preferences. Sometimes, this takes the form of substitution of legislative spending priorities for gubernatorial spending priorities. At other times, it takes the form of designating or restricting the use of appropriated funds. In short, the line-item veto is not an instrument for reducing the size of the budget that the governor himself has proposed, but an instrument for the governor to protect his spending priorities from legislative attempts to substitute or impose their spending priorities. Vetoed amounts revert to the state treasury, where they might be available for appropriation at a future time. However, the governor does not get to repurpose the funds in the same fiscal year. That would be tantamount to the governor having the authority to legislate, which in a separation of powers system is the prerogative of the legislature.

Once cast, Georgia line-item vetoes are not overridden. There is, of course, a constitutional provision for overriding vetoes by extraordinary legislative

---

[4] Glenn Abney and Thomas P. Lauth, "The Line-item Veto and Fiscal Responsibility," *The Journal of Politics*, Vol. 59, Number 3 (August 1997): 882–891.

majorities.[5] However, item vetoes almost always occur after the General Assembly has adjourned its 40-day annual session, and legislative leaders have not been inclined to revisit vetoed items when the body meets again eight or nine months later. There have been no overrides of line-item vetoes in the modern era.

This chapter considers the line-item veto behavior of nine Georgia governors, from Carl Sanders to Nathan Deal, seven Democrats and two Republicans. Examination of how each of these modern era governors used the line-item veto will provide insight into executive-legislative relationships in the Georgia budget process.

Ninety-nine appropriations acts were passed in the 1971 through 2018 sessions of the General Assembly, 48 appropriations acts and 51 amended appropriations acts.[6] As can be seen in Table 8.1, 33 were passed without an item veto. Thirty-two other appropriations acts contained line-item vetoes of legislative language (designations or restrictions), but the vetoes did not eliminate specific amounts of money. Only 34 of the 99 appropriations acts had line-item vetoes that eliminated specific dollar amounts.

Governors Carl Sanders and Lester Maddox did not use the line-item veto. Governor Jimmy Carter used the line-item veto extensively during his last year in office, and used it to eliminate specific appropriations of money. Governors George Busbee, Joe Frank Harris and Zell Miller frequently vetoed legislative language that did not result in the elimination of specific amounts of money. Governors Sonny Perdue and Nathan Deal sought to accomplish much the same thing, not by vetoing legislative language, but by identifying such language as non-binding and to be disregarded by state agencies. Governor Roy Barnes relied on impoundments (denials of fund allocations) to counter legislative attempts to designate or restrict appropriated funds.

Each of Governor Carter's 19 line-item vetoes was directed at specific appropriations of money, a total of $74,047,578 or .66% of total state-fund appropriations enacted in 1971–1974. However, many of Carter's item vetoes eliminated legislative language which designated specific amounts of money for specific purposes, but did not actually reduce the budget by those amounts. They simply negated the legislative attempts to designate how those funds should be spent. Eight of Governor Busbee's 11 line-item vetoes eliminated legislative language; only three vetoes were directed at specific appropriations of money, a reduction of $35,300,000 or .08% of total state-fund appropriations enacted in 1975–1982. Thirty-four of Governor Harris's 36 line-item vetoes eliminated legislative language; only two vetoes were directed at specific

---

[5] A two-thirds vote in each house of the General Assembly is necessary to override a gubernatorial veto. *Constitution of the State of Georgia*, Article III, Section V, Paragraph XIII, and Article V, Section II, Paragraph IV.

[6] The General Assembly enacts two appropriations bills during each legislative session (January through April), an amendment to the appropriations bill for the current fiscal year that will end on June 30, and an appropriation for the next fiscal year that will begin on July 1. This practice is a hold-over from the time when the General Assembly enacted biennial appropriations bills but usually amended them in the second legislative session of the biennium.

8 The Line-Item Veto in Executive-Legislative Relations

Table 8.1 Line-Item Vetoes by Governor, 1971–2019

Legislative Session	Appropriations Act	Total State Appropriations	Number of Item Vetoes	Total of Vetoed Items	Vetoed Items as Percent of Total Appropriations	Non-Binding Language to be Disregarded
Carter						
1971	AFY 1971	$1,081,773,064	0			
1972	FY 1972	$1,224,342,003	0			
	AFY 1972	$1,175,542,951	0			
1973	FY 1973	$1,318,323,996	0			
	AFY 1973	$1,358,729,375	0			
1974	FY 1974	$1,664,168,762	1	$300,000	0.018%	
	AFY 1974	$1,675,135,461	11	$891,324	0.053%	
1975	FY 1975	$1,736,675,803	7	$72,856,254	4.195%	
1971–1974	Total	$11,234,691,415	19	$74,047,578	0.659%	
	Average		2.4			
Bushee						
1975	AFY 1975	$1,702,971,923	1	$5000,000	0.294%	
	FY 1976	$1,965,919,490	0			
EX 1975	AFY 1976 (1)	$1,841,125,220	0			
1976	AFY 1976 (2)	$1,790,000,000	0			
	FY 1977	$1,902,800,000	0			
1977	AFY 1977	$1,918,345,530	1	$30,000,000	1.564%	
	FY 1978	$2,143,976,000	0			
1978	AFY 1978	$2,262,816,271	0			
	FY 1979	$2,379,691,195	0			
1979	AFY 1979	$2,714,211,109	0			
	FY 1980	$2,712,820,751	0			
1980	AFY 1980	$2,850,152,707	2	$300,000	0.011%	
	FY 1981	$3,039,420,957	2	$0	0.000%	

1981	AFY 1981	$3,217,056,705	2	$0	0.000%
	FY 1982	$3,450,000,000	1	$0	0.000%
1982	AFY 1982	$3,498,883,445	0		
	FY 1983	$3,732,000,000	2	$0	0.000%
1975–1982	Total	$43,122,191,303	11	$35,300,000	0.082%
	Average		0.6		
Harris					
1983	AFY 1983	$3,633,184,311	1	$0	0.000%
	FY 1984	$4,018,000,000	1	$0	0.000%
1984	AFY 1984	$3,960,829,559	1	$0	0.000%
	FY 1985	$4,302,000,000	3	$0	0.000%
1985	AFY 1985	$4,352,327,675	1	$0	0.000%
	FY 1986	$4,838,000,000	3	$800,000	0.017%
1986	AFY 1986	$5,225,947,058	2	$0	0.000%
	FY 1987	$5,316,000,000	2	$0	0.000%
1987	AFY 1987	$5,412,225,000	3	$0	0.000%
	FY 1988	$5,782,000,000	2	$0	0.000%
1988	AFY 1988	$5,936,113,339	3	$0	0.000%
	FY 1989	$6,254,000,000	3	$0	0.000%
1989	AFY 1989	$6,399,179,662	2	$0	0.000%
	FY 1990	$7,498,000,000	2	$0	0.000%
1990	AFY 1990	$7,643,807,302	3	$0	0.000%
	FY 1991	$7,785,427,500	4	$70,000	0.001%
1983–1990		$88,357,041,406	36	$870,000	0.001%

(continued)

168 8 The Line-Item Veto in Executive-Legislative Relations

Table 8.1 (continued)

Legislative Session	Appropriations Act	Total State Appropriations	Number of Item Vetoes	Total of Vetoed Items	Vetoed Items as Percent of Total Appropriations	Non-Binding Language to be Disregarded
Miller	Average		2.3			
1991	AFY 1991	$7,645,067,946	3	$0	0.000%	
	FY1992	$7,955,482,500	7	$5000	0.000%	
EX 1991	AFY 1992 (1)	$7,540,744,797	5	$0	0.000%	
1992	AFY 1992 (2)	$7,552,871,790	7	$0	0.000%	
	FY 1993	$8,174,000,000	9	$38,595,089	0.472%	
1993	AFY 1993	$8,252,216,454	5	$0	0.000%	
	FY 1994	$8,958,192,764	5	$0	0.000%	
1994	AFY 1994	$9,201,886,925	6	$9,864,199	0.107%	
	FY 1995	$9,785,260,431	5	$0	0.000%	
1995	AFY 1995	$10,236,138,444	6	$0	0.000%	
	FY 1996	$10,700,856,569	9	$9,545,242	0.089%	
1996	AFY 1996	$10,980,393,127	2	$0	0.000%	
	FY 1997	$11,341,527,653	5	$342,500	0.003%	
1997	AFY 1997	$11,793,346,344	5	$0	0.000%	
	FY 1998	$11,781,453,880	16	$36,377,245	0.309%	
1998	AFY 1998	$12,380,991,546	6	$0	0.000%	
	FY 1999	$12,528,603,880	8	$6,730,520	0.054%	
1991–1998	Total	$166,809,035,050	109	$101,459,795	0.061%	
	Average		6.4			
Barnes						
1999	AFY 1999	$13,064,694,760	10	$3,125,395	0.024%	
	FY 2000	$13,291,103,880	5	$0	0.000%	
2000	AFY 2000	$13,939,922,701	5	$50,000,000	0.359%	

The Line-Item Veto in Georgia 169

2001	FY 2001	$14,471,828,880	5	$3,250,000	0.022%	
	AFY 2001	$15,273,099,418	7	$1,793,350	0.012%	
2002	FY 2002	$15,454,610,013	5	$0	0.000%	
	AFY 20002	$15,773,307,509	8	$2,050,000	0.013%	
	FY 2003	$16,105,985,466	7	$0	0.000%	
1999–2002	Total	$117,374,552,627	52	$60,218,745	0.051%	
	Average		6.5			
Perdue						
2003	AFY 2003	$16,142,774,526	10	$653,804	0.004%	3
	FY 2004	$16,174,683,712	6	$348,000	0.002%	0
2004	AFY 2004	$16,079,533,973	5	$0	0.000%	0
	FY 2005	$16,376,321,131	9	$233,135	0.001%	0
2005	AFY 2005	$16,567,537,539	0			0
	FY 2006	$17,415,249,819	16	$9,343,226	0.054%	0
2006	AFY 2006	$17,850,546,801	0			0
	FY 2007	$18,654,564,058	0			0
2007	AFY 2007	$19,317,036,464	1	$142,412,625	0.737%	0
	FY 2008	$20,230,620,936	31	$18,026,287	0.089%	51
2008	AFY 2008	$20,545,196,148	2	$250,000	0.001%	0
	FY 2009	$21,180,140,103	18	$14,257,587	0.067%	6
2009	AFY 2009	$18,903,699,531	0			2
	FY 2010	$18,569,866,489	3	$192,980	0.001%	12
2010	AFY 2010	$17,074,653,179	0			0
	FY 2011	$17,890,512,513	5	$1,152,252	0.006%	15

(continued)

Table 8.1 (continued)

Legislative Session	Appropriations Act	Total State Appropriations	Number of Item Vetoes	Total of Vetoed Items	Vetoed Items as Percent of Total Appropriations	Non-Binding Language to be Disregarded
2003–2010	Total	$288,972,936,922	106	$186,869,896	0.065%	89
	Average		6.6			5.6
Deal						
2011	AFY 2011	$18,063,622,184	0			0
	FY 2012	$18,299,477,557	11	$3,645,704	0.020%	0
2012	AFY 2012	$18,503,799,022	0			0
	FY 2013	$19,342,059,819	2	$390,276	0.002%	8
2013	AFY 2013	$19,325,217,673	0			0
	FY 2014	$19,920,261,481	0			0
2014	AFY 2014	$20,234,238,575	0			0
	FY 2015	$20,836,744,620	0			3
2015	AFY 2015	$21,112,906,096	0			0
	FY 2016	$21,828,789,407	1	$809,900	0.004%	0
2016	AFY 2016	$23,065,473,796	0			1
	FY 2017	$23,739,409,078	1	$138,840	0.001%	8
2017	AFY 2017	$24,345,494,024	0			0
	FY 2018	$24,997,351,235	0			1
2018	AFY 2018	$25,413,015,092	0			0
	FY 2019	$26,226,914,974	0			0
EX 2018	AFY 2019	$26,497,741,251	0			0
2011–2018	Total	$345,254,774,633	15	$4,984,720	0.001%	21
	Average		0.88			1.3

In the column "Total of Vetoed Items," blank indicates no items were vetoed and $0 indicates the items vetoed did not involve dollar deletions.

appropriations of money, a reduction of $870,000 or .001% of total state-fund appropriations enacted in 1983–1990. Eighty-four of Governor Miller's 109 line-item vetoes eliminated legislative language; only 25 vetoes were directed at specific appropriations of money, a reduction of $101,459,795 or .061% of total state-fund appropriations enacted in 1991–98. Forty-one of Governor Barnes's 52 line-item vetoes eliminated legislative language; only 11 vetoes were directed at specific appropriations of money, a reduction of $60,218,745 or .051% of total state-fund appropriations enacted in 1999–2002. Twenty-three of Governor Perdue's 106 line-item vetoes eliminated legislative language; 83 vetoes directed at specific appropriation of money, a reduction of $186,869,896 or .065% of total state-fund appropriations enacted in 2003–2010. Each of Governor Deal's 15 line-item vetoes was directed at specific appropriations of money, a reduction of $4,984,720 or .001% of total state-funded appropriations enacted in 2011–2018. In summary, only 158 of 348 line-item vetoes (45.4%) were directed at specific appropriations of money, a reduction of $463,750,734 or .04% of total state-fund appropriations for 1971–2018. Georgia governors used the line-item veto infrequently compared with most other states that have it. They often used it to eliminate legislative language that did not include specific amounts of money. The total amounts removed from budgets by the item veto were relatively small. This underscores the idea that the line-item veto is less about controlling the size of the state budget and more about governors protecting their spending priorities.

Governor Carter's item vetoes were expressions of policy disagreements with the legislature as well as an effort to assert executive branch prerogatives in state budgeting.[7] Governor Busbee began the practice of vetoing objectionable legislative language even though that language did not include specific appropriations of money. Governor Harris continued the practice of vetoing objectionable language, most of which did not include specific appropriations of money. Governors Busbee and Harris preferred not to use the line-item veto[8] and often appeared to use it with prior legislative agreement. Governor Miller had celebrated confrontations with leaders of the General Assembly over two of his vetoes that eliminated specific appropriations of money, but many of his vetoes eliminated objectionable language that did not include specific appropriations of money. Governor Miller's veto style fell somewhere between that of Governor Carter and that of Governors Busbee and Harris, using the item veto to prevail in inter-branch conflict. Governor Barnes unsuccessfully attempted to reduce but not entirely eliminate specific appropriations of money, but more than three quarters of his line-item vetoes were legislative language vetoes which did not include specific appropriations of money. Governor Barnes's veto style resembled that of Governor Miller, more activist than that of Governors Busbee and Harris.[9] Most of Governor Perdue's vetoes occurred in his first three legislative sessions. Thereafter, he began dealing with offending legislative designations or restrictions, not by vetoing them, but by declaring them

---

[7] Telephone interview with Jimmy Carter, August 13, 1992.
[8] Telephone interview with George Busbee, August 18, 1992.
[9] Telephone interview with Roy Barnes, November 19, 2003.

non-binding and directing state agencies to disregard them. Governor Deal continued the practice of issuing non-binding/disregard statements. Most of his line-item vetoes occurred in his first term.

Carl Sanders (1963–1967)

Governor Carl Sanders did not use the line-item veto during his administration because, in his words, "I controlled the budget. The executive budget was *the* budget. I did not face the possibility that the legislature was going to mess with the budget."[10] Governor Sanders had handpicked the Speaker of the House of Representatives to replace the sitting Speaker who had backed former-governor Marvin Griffin, Sander's 1962 opponent for governor. The new Speaker was elected by a vote of one, Governor Sanders.[11] Under these conditions, it is not surprising that Sanders found it unnecessary to use the line-item veto.

Lester Maddox (1967–1971)

Lester Maddox also did not use the line-item veto. Governor Maddox did not dominate the General Assembly as did Governor Sanders. Indeed, Lester Maddox regarded himself as an outsider who was usually opposed by Democratic leaders, including leaders of the General Assembly.[12] However, the format of the Georgia budget and appropriations act during the Sanders and Maddox administrations made item vetoes unlikely. During those administrations, agencies received lump-sum appropriations for three object classifications, personal services, operating expenses and, in some cases, capital outlays. A veto of one of these line items would have effectively closed down an agency for the fiscal year.

Jimmy Carter (1971–1975)

Although Georgia governors have had the line-item veto since 1865, it had fallen into disuse for many years[13] until Governor Jimmy Carter reactivated it in 1973, the third year of his governorship. It had been so long since the line-item veto was used,

---

[10] Telephone interview with Carl Sanders, August 3, 1992.

[11] Thomas B. Murphy, "Sophistication Marks Current Generation of State Legislators," *Atlanta Journal and Constitution* (December 15, 1985): C-1.

[12] Telephone interview with Lester Maddox, September 15, 1992.

[13] Frank W. Prescott, "A Footnote on Georgia's Constitutional History: The Line-Item Veto of Governors," *The Georgia Historical Quarterly*, Volume 42 (1958): 1–25.

that when Governor Carter vetoed a $300,000 capital outlay item in the Department of Natural Resources section of the FY 1974 appropriations bill, an opinion of the state Attorney General[14] was sought to determine that it was a proper exercise of the authority vested in the governor by the Georgia Constitution.[15] The item that Carter vetoed, "Provided that of the appropriation relating to Capital Outlay $300,000 is designated and committed for the Crooked River Project," is an example of eliminating legislative language designating funds for a specific purpose. The sponsor of the Crooked River State Park improvement appropriation, House Appropriations Committee Chairman James (Sloppy) Floyd, was reported to be displeased by Governor Carter's veto.[16]

In the 1974 session of the General Assembly, the Amended General Appropriations Act for FY 1974 and the Appropriations Act for FY 1975 contained approximately 10 standard object classifications as well as a number of agency-specific object classifications. Prior to that time, each agency had received lump-sum appropriations for personal services, operating expenses and capital outlays. The new line-item budget was an attempt to protect legislative intent. Governor Carter opposed this move on the part of the legislature as "an encroachment into executive prerogatives," at one time threatening a lawsuit to prevent the action and later threatening to veto the entire appropriations act.[17] In the end, he vetoed a combined total of 18 items in the FY 1974 amended appropriations act and FY 1975 appropriations act. Two of his vetoes, a $50 million ad valorem tax relief measure and a related provision that would have released $22,641,254 from reserve funds if state revenue had fallen short of funding the tax program, represented policy disagreements with the legislature. Governor Carter believed the tax relief plan gave too much relief to industry and the wealthy while providing little relief to average citizens.[18] Fifteen vetoes, amounting to approximately $1.1 million, were aimed at pork barrel items that legislators had included in the newly line-itemed budget. Carter characterized selected items as "not needed," "not appropriate," "in violation of state priorities," and "setting a bad precedent."[19] One veto restored an executive budget

---

[14] Georgia Department of Law, Opinions of the Attorney General, Unofficial Opinion U73-94, (September 19, 1973): 366-377.

[15] *Constitution of the State of Georgia*, (1945) Article V, Section I, Paragraph XV.

[16] Milo Dakin, "River Park Wasn't Worth Aid – Carter," *Atlanta Constitution*, April 21, 1973: 5.

[17] Howell Raines and Jeff Nesmith, "Carter to Speak on Funds," *Atlanta Constitution*, January 17, 1974: 17-A, Prentice Palmer, "Carter Issues Warning on Restrictive Budget," *Atlanta Constitution*, January 27, 1974: 1-A and 16A, Jeff Nesmith, "Rep. Floyd Vows to Defy Carter," *Atlanta Constitution*, January 28, 1974: 1-A, Frederick Allen, "Line-Item Budget Assailed," *Atlanta Constitution*, January 28, 1974: 7A and Jeff Nesmith, "Some Shown Line-Item Budget Plan," *Atlanta Constitution*, January 29, 1974: 7-A.

[18] Rex Granum, "Carter Vetoes Property Tax Relief Plan" *Atlanta Constitution*, March 29, 1974: 1-A.

[19] Rex Granum, "Carter Slashes $73 Million from 1974, 1975 Budgets," *Atlanta Constitution*, April 3, 1974: 2-A.

recommendation and increased the state appropriation by $100,000.[20] The General Assembly's effort to restructure the appropriations bill in order to assert legislative intent was met by Governor Carter's reactivation of the line-item veto to protect executive prerogative and reduce pork barrel spending.

George Busbee (1975–1983)

Governor George Busbee used the line-item veto primarily to eliminate legislative directives from appropriations bills. Some members of the legislature contended that the governor could only veto items that appropriated sums of money, not legislative directives. Indeed, a 1973 opinion of the Georgia Attorney General supported this view.[21] In rebuttal, the executive branch contended that language seeking to prescribe or proscribe state agency activities or programs was of questionable standing in an appropriations act. A separate general act would be required for such purposes. The dilemma for the legislature was that it wished to prevent the governor from using the line-item veto on substantive language included in appropriations bills, yet recognized that its prerogative to include such language was not clearly established.[22]

The line-item veto enables governors to defend their budgets against legislative additions or changes that they deem unnecessary or unwise. Such defensive measures do not necessarily achieve spending reductions, although they may yield long-term cost savings. The most significant item veto in the Busbee years occurred in 1977. The General Assembly in the 1976 session had approved in the FY 1977 appropriations act a $17 million capital outlay item for road repairs. In the 1977 session, the General Assembly amended that item, increasing it to $47 million. Governor Busbee vetoed "so much of the appropriation ... as increases [it] above the amount of $17 million..."[23] The controversy between the governor and one branch of the legislature was a policy issue with fiscal implications, but not strictly speaking a matter of budget reduction. The Georgia House of Representatives

---

[20] The FY 1974 Appropriations Act, passed in the 1973 Session of the General Assembly, appropriated $200,000 for Operating Expenses for the World Congress Center. The Amended FY 1974 Appropriations Act, passed by the General Assembly in its 1974 Session, reduced that amount to $100,000. In his veto message, Governor Carter wrote, "Veto so much of the amendment to the appropriation for the operating expenses of the World Congress Center as reduces the appropriation of $200,000 made in the Appropriation Act approved April 19, 1973." The veto restored the appropriation to the original amount of $200,000.

[21] Georgia Department of Law, Opinions of the Attorney General. Unofficial Opinion U73–94, (September 19, 1973): 366–377.

[22] Interviews with John M. Hackney, Legislative Budget Analyst, May 5, 1982 and September 24, 1992.

[23] The effect of this item veto was to restore the existing appropriation. Georgia does not permit governors to reduce an appropriation. Georgia Department of Law, Opinions of the Attorney General, Unofficial Opinion U74–36, (May 3, 1974): 387.

wanted to pay for road repair by converting $30 million from bonds to capital outlay in the appropriations act, whereas Governor Busbee and the Senate preferred bond financing in this instance. In his veto message, Busbee stated that as governor and as a legislator he usually favored funding "as many projects through capital outlay rather than bonds as we could without sacrificing essential programs." However, Busbee believed bond financing was financially responsible in this case because the alternative of a capital outlay threatened the state's surplus in a time of economic uncertainty.[24] Busbee's veto reclassified the $30 million to surplus, and made it available for appropriation in the FY 1978 appropriations act later in the 1977 legislative session.[25] This veto is an example of the line-item veto being used not for budget reduction but to enforce the governor's policy preferences.

Joe Frank Harris (1983–1991)

Governor Joe Frank Harris also used the line-item veto primarily to remove legislative directives that did not include an appropriation of money; 34 of his 36 item vetoes were of this variety. Governor Harris had an opinion from the state Attorney General which held that such language did not have the force of law,[26] but he "went ahead and vetoed the items anyway to be safe."[27] In the absence of a court test, the Busbee and Harris vetoes prevailed.

This controversy over the definition of an "item" is not unique to Georgia. Many state courts have addressed the question of whether the item veto can be used against directives or restrictions in appropriations bills without also vetoing the appropriations to which they pertain.[28] In such cases the issue is not so much about budget savings but about whose spending priorities will prevail, those of the executive or those of the legislature.

The existence of the line-item veto makes it possible for legislatures to include symbolic items in appropriations bills, knowing that the governor is likely to veto them. Legislators, with narrow local constituencies, take credit for their actions and

---

[24] *House Journal I* (1978): 9–10.

[25] Vetoed funds revert to the state treasury where they may become available for appropriation in a subsequent appropriation bill. They are not immediately available for reallocation by the governor.

[26] The Attorney General wrote, "Consistently, this office has held that appropriations acts cannot constitutionally alter discretionary authority for the expenditure of ... money which the General Assembly has granted an agency by general law." Georgia Department of Law, Opinions of the Attorney General, Official Opinion 84–19, (March 16, 1984): 44. See also Official Opinion 75–4, (January 9, 1975): 7, and Official Opinion 75–71, (July 8, 1975): 137.

[27] Telephone interview with Joe Frank Harris, August 17, 1992.

[28] State courts have not always arrived at the same conclusion when presented with similar fact patterns. Richard Briffault, "The Item Veto in State Courts," *Temple Law Review*, Vol. 66 (1993): 1171–1204; Louis Fisher and Neal Devins, "How Successfully Can the States' Item Veto Be Transferred to the President?" *Georgetown Law Review*, Vol. 75 (1986): 159–197; and Stephen Masciocchi, "The Item Veto in Washington," *Washington Law Review*, Vol. 64 (1989): 891–912.

blame the governor for thwarting their efforts. Governors, with statewide constituencies, suffer few, if any, consequences for such actions. During the 1980s and 1990s two such items regularly appeared in the appropriations bill and the amended appropriations bill.

Georgia Indigent Legal Services (GILS) was created by the General Assembly in 1979 to oversee a state network of public defender offices. In the FY 1981 appropriations act the legislature inserted language that no state funds should be paid to GILS, nor should any state facility including the state's long-distance telephone network be made available for use by GILS. Apparently, according to Justice Charles Weltner, some legislators and locally-based state judges feared that Atlanta lawyers might be appointed to "make trouble" in their counties.[29] The provision was of dubious constitutionality.[30] Governor Busbee vetoed it in 1980 and on three subsequent occasions. Governor Harris vetoed the provision 16 times. According to Harris, "It became an item that was always included by the General Assembly. They knew it would be vetoed."[31]

A second provision involved the requirement of legislative approval before a state agency could spend federal money obtained in excess of federal funds anticipated at the time of the passage of the state appropriations act. Excess federal funds were to supplant state appropriated funds, and state funds thereafter would be unavailable to agencies unless re-appropriated by the General Assembly. Governor Harris vetoed this provision 12 times.[32] He believed it was a legislative intrusion on executive branch authority.[33] Approximately three-fourths of Governor Harris's item vetoes, 28 of 36, were directed at these two provisions that the General Assembly included each year in the appropriations act and the amended appropriations act.[34]

---

[29] Opinion expressed by Charles L. Weltner, Georgia Supreme Court Justice, as reported by Tracy Thompson, "No Money Likely for Indigent Defense Fund," *Atlanta Constitution*, February 16, 1987: 1-E.

[30] The Georgia Department of Administrative Services (DOAS) has authority to contract for use of the Georgia Interactive State Telecommunications Network. In 1979, the Georgia Attorney General offered the opinion that an appropriations act constitutionally may not alter the responsibilities or powers of a state agency (namely, DOAS) that are derived from general law. Georgia Department of Law, Opinions of the Attorney General, Official Opinion 79–46, (August 6, 1979): 91–92

[31] Telephone interview with Joe Frank Harris, August 17, 1992.

[32] The first veto of this provision occurred in 1984. However, in 1977 the Georgia Attorney General had stated his official opinion that a similar provision of the FY 1978 Appropriations Act "clearly does not have the force of law…" because it is in conflict with the *Constitution of the State of Georgia*, Article III, Section X, Paragraph V, which provides that all federal funds received by the state are continuously appropriated in the amount and for the purposes authorized and directed by the federal government in making the grant. Georgia Department of Law, Opinions of the Attorney General, Official Opinion 77–87, (December 1977): 159.

[33] Telephone interview with Joe Frank Harris, August 17, 1992.

[34] See note 6.

Zell Miller (1991–1999)

Governor Zell Miller continued Governor Harris's practice of vetoing the symbolic indigent legal services provision and the excess federal funds provision each time they appeared in appropriations bills. In his veto message, Miller stated that the latter provision "inhibits the state from accepting additional federal funds as they become available throughout the fiscal year."[35]

In 1992, Governor Miller vetoed language that would have permitted the Department of Corrections to use unspecified agency funds to plan three correctional units. Miller and the Office of Planning and Budget believed such expenditures would only be the tip of the iceberg, likely to lead to future financial obligations that the governor should have the opportunity to approve from the outset.[36] He vetoed similar items in subsequent years because of potential out-year costs associated with them. Miller's Executive Secretary wrote, "… often cared about the long-term impact of funding rather than the impact of a single item."[37]

In a separation of powers system, the legislature's power of the purse is intended to protect against an authoritarian executive, and the chief executive, as a representative of all the people, is expected to check the narrow local interests of the legislature in the appropriations process --- pork barrel spending. In one of the most celebrated uses of the item veto in Georgia, Governor Zell Miller vetoed a $479,479 item in the Department of Education section of the FY 1993 appropriations act. Miller vetoed the item following the 1992 session of the General Assembly when neither the governor's staff nor the Office of Planning and Budget could identify its purpose or origin. It was subsequently learned that the item has been added by the House of Representatives to fund special projects for local school districts. House leaders had since 1986 been operating the secret fund. Money from the fund was to be released by the Legislative Budget Office, through the Department of Education, on the approval of the Speaker of the House or Chairman of the House Appropriations Committee. The Lieutenant Governor and Chairman of the Senate Appropriations Committee denied knowledge of the fund, and expressed outrage that it had been hidden in the bill approved by the House-Senate Conference Committee and enacted by the Senate.[38] The state Attorney General ruled that the secret fund was in violation of state law.[39]

Governor Miller's other highly celebrated line-item veto occurred at the end of the 1997 legislative session when he vetoed more than $36 million in local projects

---

[35] *Georgia House Journal II* (1992): 4618.

[36] Telephone conversation with Winford Poitevint, Director, General Government Division, Office of Planning and Budget, September 1, 1992.

[37] Communication from Steve W. Wrigley, May 6, 2000.

[38] Dick Pettys, "Secret Budget Account Used by House Leaders," *Atlanta Constitution*, May 1, 1992: F-5.

[39] Steve Harvey, "Bowers Says House Leaders Violate Laws," *Atlanta Constitution*, July 21, 1992: D-1.

that he believed the General Assembly had funded at the expense of his higher education initiatives. The vetoed item in the Department of Community Affairs section of the appropriations bill enumerated 89 community projects slated to receive funds (sometimes reported as 89 vetoes). Miller recounted the situation: "The General Assembly had reduced my recommended appropriation for the University System, and I looked for a like amount to veto. Legislators understand two things: what you can do for them and what you can do to them."[40] He later restored some of the funds out of the governor's emergency fund. While this veto represents an executive check on pork barrel politics, it also reflects the differing policy preferences of Governor Miller for higher education spending compared with legislative preferences for community project spending.

Roy Barnes (1999–2003)

The issue of institutional prerogatives emerged in a different form during the administration of Governor Barnes. Following the 1999 session of the General Assembly, Governor Barnes reduced two appropriations items but did not veto them in their entirety. However, an opinion from the Attorney General ruled that the governor did not have the authority to reduce items appropriated by the General Assembly. His only options are to sign them into law or to veto them in their entirety.[41]

Following the 2001 and 2002 sessions of the General Assembly, Governor Barnes turned to impoundment to assert gubernatorial prerogatives in the budget and appropriations process. Throughout the appropriations process, the General Assembly keeps track of the development of the appropriations bill through a legislative document called the Comparative Summary, commonly referred to as the tracking document.[42] Often legislative intent is only generally stated in the appropriations bill, but the tracking document contains more specific language earmarking funds for particular projects or purposes. The line-item veto reaches items in the appropriations bill, but it does not reach legislative intent specified in the tracking document because that document does not have the force of law. Governor Barnes directed executive branch department heads not to commit funds that were appropriated but listed only in the tracking document until such funds were discussed with the Office of Planning and Budget (OPB) and a determination was made that such spending was good policy. He advised the Lieutenant Governor and the Speaker of the House of Representatives on April 26, 2001 that in addition to

---

[40] Interview with Zell B. Miller, November 12, 1999.

[41] Georgia Department of Law, Opinions of the Attorney General, Unofficial Opinion U2000–2, (February 11, 2000): www.ganet.org/ago/opinions/html

[42] The Comparative Summary is to the appropriations bill in Georgia as a committee report is to an appropriations bill in the federal budget appropriations process.

line-item vetoing sections of the Amended FY 2001[43] and FY 2002[44] appropriations bills, he was also directing the OPB to implement fund allocation denials for several other appropriation items.[45] There were five such allotment denials in the Amended FY 2001 budget and seven allotment denials in the FY 2002 budget. These impoundments involved disagreements between the governor and appropriators over such items as: changes in the compensation rate for vendors providing transportation services to the Department of Community Health; funding for central office positions in the Department of Education; funding for operating expenses and equipment in the Department of Natural Resources; fund transfers related to the Temporary Assistance for Needy Families (TANF) program in the Department of Human Resources; use of general obligation bonds for Department of Juvenile Justice facilities; a General Assembly repositioning of state and federal funds for the Georgia Early Learning Initiative in the Department Human Resources; program funding in the Department of Labor; the purchase of software for the Department of Labor; and the purchase of an airplane by the Department of Transportation.

On March 25, 2002, Governor Barnes advised the Lieutenant Governor and Speaker of four allotment denials in the Amended FY 2002 budget.[46] One of the 2002 impoundments was a $300,000 appropriation of tobacco settlement funds to the Georgia Institute for Lung Cancer Research, on grounds that such funds should be made available to researchers on a competitive basis rather than be designated to a specific entity. Some of the 2001 and 2002 impounded funds were made available for obligation following OPB review, but these actions amounted to a new assertion of gubernatorial authority in the state's budget and appropriations process. Governor Barnes also vetoed the federal funds provision eight times during his one term in office, following the leads of Governors Harris and Miller.

Political Party Transition

In 2002 Georgia voters elected their first Republican governor since early Reconstruction, Governor Sonny Perdue. Following the 2002 election, four Senators switched political parties giving Republicans control of the state Senate. During the 2003 and 2004 sessions of the General Assembly, Republicans controlled the governor's office and the Senate, and Democrats by a narrow margin retained control of the House of Representatives. In the 2004 election, Republicans also gained control

---

[43] Georgia Laws, 2001: 505–627. HB 174 approved April 22, 2001.

[44] Georgia Laws, 2001: 628–738. HB 175 approved April 26, 2001.

[45] Letter from Governor Roy E. Barnes to Mark Taylor, Lieutenant Governor and Thomas B. Murphy, Speaker of the House of Representatives, April 26, 2001.

[46] Georgia Laws, 2002: 11–140. HB 1101 approved March 25, 2002. Letter from Governor Roy E. Barnes to Mark Taylor, Lieutenant Governor and Thomas B. Murphy, Speaker of the House of Representatives, March 25, 2002.

of the House of Representatives and since that time have controlled both branches of government, as the Democrats had for many decades.

From the time of the reactivation of the line-item veto in 1973 by Governor Jimmy Carter, there were five Democratic Governors. Three exercised the item veto sparingly, Governors Carter, Busbee and Harris, less than three times per appropriations bill presented to them, and two exercised it somewhat more frequently, Governors Miller and Barnes, slightly more than six times per appropriations bill presented to them. Governor Sonny Perdue, a Republican, between 2003 and 2010, exercised the item veto an average of more than six times per appropriations bill presented to him, almost exactly the same rate as Democratic governors Miller and Barnes.[47] Governor Nathan Deal, also a Republican, between 2011 and 2018, exercised it less than once per appropriations bill presented to him, less than all but one of the Democratic governors. Political party does not appear to be a determinant of how often governors use the line-item veto, which is not to say it never has been used in a partisan manner. However, in Georgia the line-item veto is mostly an instrument of inter-branch relations through which governors seek to protect their budget priorities.

A closer inspection of the Perdue and Deal line-item vetoes reveals that a change that occurred in the state budget process during their administrations, the transition to program budgeting with attendant changes in the appropriations bill, shifted the focus of item vetoes almost entirely to bond projects and introduced the practice of identifying legislative language as non-binding, to be disregarded by state agencies. Governor Perdue faced recessions in FY 2002 and FY 2003 and again in FY 2008, FY 2009 and FY 2010.[48] Governor Deal had the benefit of a recovering, post-recession, economy between 2011 and 2018.

Sonny Perdue (2003–2011)

As can be seen in Table 8.1, there were 10 line-item vetoes in the AFY 2003 appropriation bill, including some bond projects. In addition to the vetoed items, Governor Perdue also imposed several "expenditure controls." For example, the General Assembly had increased the funding for the Department of Technical and Adult Education to replace obsolete equipment at its institutions, beyond the annual funding level recommended by the governor. Governor Perdue stated, "I will direct the Georgia State Financing and Investment Commission to withhold from sale that proportion of these bonds that exceed the austerity level of funding … included in

---

[47] For comparison, Governor David Patterson of New York in 2010 year vetoed more than 1000 line items added to the state's budget by the legislature; http://www.northcountrypublicradio.org, July 9, 2010.

[48] Thomas P. Lauth, "Georgia: Shared Power and Fiscal Conservatism," in Edward J. Clynch and Thomas P. Lauth, eds., *Budgeting in the States: Institutions, Processes and Politics*. Westport, Connecticut: Praeger Publishers, Inc., 2006. p. 33.

my budget report."[49] While these actions were not line-item vetoes, they were clear assertions of executive power in opposition to legislative intent. Several were projects located in districts of House Democratic leaders. The governor's office stated that item vetoes were required by the state's deteriorating fiscal condition; that local projects were not fiscally prudent when tax revenues were declining and state agencies and programs were being cut because of the sluggish economy.[50]

House Democrats characterized the decisions as partisan, perhaps payback for the difficulty the governor had getting some of his legislative agenda through the Democratic controlled House.[51] The *Atlanta-Journal Constitution* cited several examples,[52] including a bond project for rural economic development and a technology center at East Georgia College, Swainsboro in the district of a member of the House Conference Committee; a bond project for renovations at Columbus Technical College in the district of the Chairman of the House Appropriations Committee and the Chairman of the House Rules Committee; funding for work on an allied health building at Georgia Technical College, Thomasville and funding for renovations of buildings at Georgia Southwestern State University, Americus, in the districts of prominent Democratic leaders.

There were six line-item vetoes in the FY 2004 appropriation bill. However, Governor Perdue instructed state agencies to defer spending for several other local bond projects until more information was available about the state's economic situation.[53] Item vetoes and deferrals were touted by the governor as a change in the way the state makes fund allocation decisions, especially with regard to bond projects benefiting local areas.[54]

There were five line-item vetoes in the AFY 2004 appropriation bill. All five removed language expressing legislative intent; none of the vetoes eliminated dollar amounts, a pattern reminiscent of the Harris years. The FY 2005 appropriation bill passed by the General Assembly was out of balance by $57 million because the House and Senate could not reach agreement on a bill to raise court filings, fees and fines to pay for the state's indigent defense/public defender program and the session adjourned without this dispute being resolved. That expenditure amount was in the budget as adopted, but without passage of the separate bill to enact funding for the public defender program, HB 869, the budget was out of balance by $57 million. The *Constitution of the State of Georgia* requires the General Assembly to pass a

---

[49] Press Release, Office of the Governor, May 14, 2003.

[50] Press Release, Office of the Governor, May 14, 2003.

[51] James Salzer, "Perdue Cuts Democrats' Pet Projects: Line-Item Veto Spares Millions in GOP Pork," *Atlanta Journal-Constitution*, May 15, 2003: E1.

[52] James Salzer, "Perdue Cuts Democrats' Pet Projects: Line-Item Veto Spares Millions in GOP Pork," *Atlanta Journal-Constitution*, May 15, 2003: E1.

[53] James Salzer, "Governor Signs Budget and Tax Bill," *Atlanta-Journal Constitution*, June 5, 2003: A1.

[54] Press Release, Office of the Governor, June 3, 2003.

balanced budget.[55] Governor Perdue called the General Assembly back into session to repair the budget.

The dispute over the public defender program was primarily between Governor Perdue and the House of Representatives, and the governor and the state judiciary system. It played out within a larger controversy over judicial spending, with each branch asserting its separation of powers prerogatives. Even though the governor submits the judiciary's budget to the legislature as part of the executive budget, the governor does not have the authority to alter the judiciary's budget request.[56] Some observers[57] believed that the judiciary budget has often been padded beyond actual judicial needs, thereby providing the General Assembly an opportunity to reduce the governor's recommendation and redirect some of the requested funds to legislative priorities, with the attendant weakening of gubernatorial control of the executive budget. In 2004, the controversy was resolved when Chief Justice of the Supreme Court Norman Fletcher assured the governor that future judiciary budgets would be sensitive to the fiscal condition of the state. This satisfied the governor, without quite promising not to continue the practice of providing something in the judiciary budget for the General Assembly to redirect. The Speaker of the House of Representatives and Chairman of the Senate Appropriations Committee informed the Chief Justice that if the judicial branch cooperated entirely with the governor, there would be negative consequences for the judiciary the following year.[58]

There were nine line-item vetoes in the FY 2005 appropriations bill. Five item vetoes removed language expressing legislative intent with no dollar amounts eliminated. Of the other four, three were construction projects to be financed by bonds, reducing the budget by approximately $233,000. However, of even greater significance was that the governor again instructed state agencies to defer spending on a number of projects that had been added to the executive budget by the legislature. Nevertheless, *Atlanta Journal-Constitution* reporter James Salzer noted that "… Perdue's spending deferrals on university and technical school funding were less partisan than last year."[59]

There were no line-item vetoes in the AFY 2005 appropriation bill. There were 16 line-item vetoes in the FY 2006 appropriation bill. Thirteen were bond projects

---

[55] Article III, Section IX, Paragraph IV(b).

[56] Official Code of Georgia Annotated (O.C.G.A.), 45–12-78 [c] and [d]: "Budget estimates for the judiciary shall be prepared by the Chief Justice of the Supreme Court and the Chief Justice of the Court of Appeals and such other officials as appropriate and shall be submitted to the director of the budget at the same time as other budget estimates are submitted. All the data relative to the legislative and judicial branches of the government shall be for the information and guidance of the Office of Planning and Budget in estimating the total fiscal needs of the state for the ensuing period, but none of these estimates shall be subject to revision or review by the Office of Planning and Budget and must be included in the budget report as prepared by it."

[57] Conversation with Tim Connell, Director of the Office of Planning and Budget (2003–2005), July 1, 2010.

[58] Conversation with former Chief Justice Norman Fletcher, August 23, 2010.

[59] James Salzer, "Both Sides Take Hit in Budget: Perdue Signs Bill, Delays Pet Projects." *Atlanta Journal-Constitution*, May 18, 2004: B1.

and two were aimed at the judicial branch. Most of the bond projects were vetoed because they were not on a state agency's priority list and contributed excessively to the overall amount of new state debt. The 2005 session was the first one in which both houses of the General Assembly were controlled by Republicans. Governor Perdue was quoted by reporter Dick Pettys as saying that while he was not pleased by the number and amount of special projects inserted into the budget, he did not veto many of them because he was giving a "special dispensation to first-time appropriators."[60] The two items relating to the judicial branch were funding for the Prosecuting Attorney Council Program ($5.5 million) and for the Council of Superior Courts Program ($883,000). Former Chief Justice of the Georgia Supreme Court, Norman Fletcher, thought the governor cannot line-item veto items for the judicial branch, but this matter has not been litigated.[61] There were no line-item vetoes in the AFY 2006 appropriations bill, and there were none in the FY 2007 appropriations bill.

Governor Perdue's First Term in Retrospect

By the end of Governor Sonny Perdue's first term, three patterns had emerged regarding his use of the line-item veto: his focus on bond projects inserted by the General Assembly, his treatment of legislative intent language in the appropriations bill as "non-binding," and his instructions to executive branch agencies to "withhold" from spending certain funds appropriated by the General Assembly.

Governor Perdue believed that one way to stimulate the state's economy was to have robust bond packages. In a particular year, the magnitude of the bond package was determined by the overall debt capacity of the state, the attractiveness of the bond market, how much debt service seemed reasonable compared with other state spending, and in general, what seemed to be a reasonable capital project package at the time.[62] However, control over the state's capital projects was often a source of conflict between the governor and the General Assembly.

Early in his administration Governor Perdue established a capital project priority system intended to make capital project funding somewhat more rational and less political. Based upon his prior experience as a legislator, Perdue believed that capital projects, especially those inserted by legislators, frequently were based more upon politics than systematic analysis. He also was concerned that capital projects sometimes were enacted without consideration of their full costs, such as furnishings, equipment and personnel. The University System of Georgia, Board of Regents and the Department of Technical and Adult Education (DTAE) were the foci of this

---

[60] Dick Pettys, "Perdue Cuts UGA Facility from Budget but Few Vetoes," *Athens Banner Herald*, May 11, 2005.
[61] Conversation with former Chief Justice, Norman Fletcher, August 23, 2010.
[62] Conversation with Tim Connell, Director, Office of Planning and Budget (2003–2005), July 1, 2010.

concern. DTAE had a long history of obtaining funding for projects through legislative politics and the governor's capital project priority system was an attempt to curtail that approach.

The capital project priority system required agencies to establish a capital funding priority list which then was vetted by the Office of Planning and Budget (OPB) and adjusted to reflect the governor's priorities. Capital projects that showed up in the appropriations bill passed by the General Assembly as "differences" from the governor's recommendations were likely candidates for the line-item veto.[63] One of Governor Perdue's early budget directors stated that in his years of service as OPB Director, most of the line-item vetoes were about nullifying efforts by the legislature to circumvent the capital project priority system.[64] Another budgeter who worked in both the executive and legislative branches noted that if the General Assembly appropriated a bond project that was not on the agency list it had no chance of surviving the governor's item veto; if it was on the list but a low priority, maybe it would survive the governor's item veto depending upon circumstances such as the size of the projected bond package and who was supporting the project.[65]

Prioritized Program Based Budgeting (PPB) was initiated in Georgia in FY 2005, and the FY 2006 appropriation act was reformatted to appropriate funds by program and funding source, not to agencies or object classes.[66] However, with the shift to a program budget, it became more difficult for the governor to use the line-item veto. Broad program categories without discrete objects of expenditure provided fewer veto targets and vetoing an entire program usually is not a realistic option. One result of this budgeting innovation was that Governor Perdue came to focus his line-item vetoes on bond projects. The combination of the PPB format and the capital project priority system resulted in bond projects being a much higher proportion of line-item vetoes in the Perdue administration than in previous administrations.

The reformatted appropriations bill that accompanied the Prioritized Program Based Budget, not only reduced the governor's line-item veto options, but also made it more difficult for the General Assembly to indicate legislative intent. The new format identified departmental programs by title, included a brief description of the program, and listed funding by source (state, federal, and other) assigned to the

---

[63] Conversation with Trey Childress, Director of the Office of Planning and Budget (2007–2010), July 14, 2010.

[64] Conversation with Tim Connell, Director of the Office of Planning and Budget (2003–2005), July 1, 2010.

[65] Conversation with John Brown, Director, House Budget Office, September 14, 2010.

[66] One of the side effects of the reformatted appropriations bill was that several provisos that for many years had continuously appeared in the template of the appropriations bill only to be routinely vetoed by governors, were removed, e.g., to control the purchase of communications equipment that was not compatible with an 800-megahertz system, authorizing the Department of Transportation to transfer positions counts between budget functions, and limiting the state's ability to accept additional federal funds as they become available throughout the fiscal year, items routinely vetoed by Governors Busbee, Harris and Miller. Conversation with Kevin Fillion, Director of the Senate Budget Office, May 25, 2006.

program. However, gone were the dozen or so standard object classifications and additional agency-specific object classifications where legislative leaders could embed funding for favored agencies and programs. To counteract this disadvantage the General Assembly began inserting proviso language, such as, "of the total appropriation to the program, a specific amount shall be spent for a designated purpose."

For many years, the General Assembly has used a tracking sheet to provide a running summary throughout the legislative session comparing the governor's recommended appropriation bill, House and Senate revised versions, and the Conference Committee report, which becomes the final version of the bill. Legislative intent is embedded in narrative portions of the tracking sheet. Beginning with the FY 2007 appropriation act, the General Assembly began incorporating narrative from the tracking sheet into the appropriation act, framed in a line box. The appropriation act included the statement, "Text within a box is not an appropriation and is for information only."[67]

To counteract this legislative move, the governor's office obtained advice from the office of the Attorney General[68] to the effect that because such provisos were not appropriations they were not binding upon agencies of the executive branch. Specifically, the advice was, "An appropriation cannot enact general law or instruct an agency's executive discretion given by general law." Based upon this interpretation, Governor Perdue began issuing, along with his line-item vetoes, instructions to state agencies to ignore the legislative provisos and spend appropriated funds in ways consistent with the mission of the agency and in accord with existing state law.[69] A typical statement would be, "The General Assembly seeks to instruct the department to [intent language]. The department is authorized to operate the program in accordance with the purpose of the program and its general law powers of the Department."[70]

Georgia's governor is authorized to require state agencies during the first six months of a fiscal year to reserve specified appropriations for budget reductions to be recommended to the General Assembly at its next regular session for inclusion in the midyear budget amendment,[71] and to withhold a percentage of agency allotments to maintain spending within actual revenues.[72] This provision of the Georgia Code was added in 2005,[73] after Governor Perdue's experience early in his first term dealing with declining revenues and the need for budget reductions. The practice of

---

[67] For example, FY 2007 Appropriations Act, Section 57: 187 or FY 2011 Appropriations Act, Section 54: 164.
[68] Memorandum to Judson H. Turner, Executive Counsel, from John B. Ballard, Jr., Counsel for Fiscal Policy, Department of Law, State of Georgia, May 24, 2007.
[69] Conversation with Trey Childress, Director of the Office of Planning and Budget (2007–2010), July 14, 2010.
[70] Press Release, Office of the Governor, June 8, 2010.
[71] See note 6.
[72] Official Code of Georgia Annotated (O.C.G.A.), 45-12-86.
[73] Georgia Laws, 2005: 976–980. HB 509 was approved May 9, 2005.

requiring agencies not to obligate all of the funds appropriated to them facilitates midyear budget reductions if such reductions become necessary, but when used or perceived to be used to thwart legislative intent, this practice heightens executive-legislative tensions. As noted earlier, Governor Roy Barnes used a variant of this practice following the 2001 and 2002 sessions of the General Assembly.

As can be seen in Table 8.1, there was one line-item veto in the AFY 2007 appropriations bill. On April 19, 2007, Governor Perdue vetoed HB 94, the AFY 2007 budget. House Republicans had loaded it with special projects, as Democrats had done in the past, and the House passed it overwhelmingly. However, the Senate, particularly Lieutenant Governor Casey Cagle, resisted and scolded the House for the inclusion of so many pork barrel projects saying that the midyear appropriation should be used for emergencies not pork. The House regarded the Lieutenant Governor's stance as disingenuous. The House then added an extension of the Homeowners Tax Relief Grant, $142.4 million, and somewhat surprisingly the Senate acquiesced and passed the bill. The governor said there were certain things not in the bill that had to be in it in order for him to sign it, such as funding for PeachCare-for-Kids, a health care program for uninsured children living in Georgia.[74] On the day before the end of the session the governor vetoed the entire appropriation bill and threatened a special session. Before adjourning, the House overrode the governor's veto, but the Senate did not concur. After a period of stalemate, on May 8, 2007, the governor withdrew his veto of the entire bill, signed the AFY 2007 budget, but line-item vetoed the addition to the Homeowners Tax Relief Grant, $142.4 million, with those funds reverting to the state's reserve fund. Lieutenant Governor Cagle voiced his support for the line-item veto, even though he usually favored tax cuts.[75]

There were 31 line-item vetoes in the FY 2008 appropriations bill, the largest number in any of Governor Perdue's 16 opportunities (eight years with two appropriations bills each year). The vetoes amounted to slightly more than $18 million in debt service and cash projects, and approximately $123 million in bonded indebtedness. Several of the vetoes eliminated projects important to House leaders who had crossed the governor on the AFY 2007 budget.[76] Examples provided by the *Atlanta Journal-Constitution* included: a bond project for the Georgia Golf Hall of Fame in the district of the House Appropriations Committee Chairman; a bond project for repairs and improvements on GA 141 in Johns Creek in the district of the House Speaker Pro-Tempore; a bond project for a Charter School operated by Cobb County

---

[74] Conversation with Shelley Nickel, Director, Office of Planning and Budget (2005–2007), July 1, 2010.

[75] James Salzer and Jim Galloway, "Budget Brawl of '07 Ends - Wait for '08: Governor Sonny Perdue Rescinds Veto and Drops Plan for Special Session; GOP Rivals Go to Their Corners but Appear as Divided as Ever," *Atlanta Journal Constitution*, May 9, 2007: A1. James Salzer, "Legislature 2007: '08 Budget Likely Faces Perdue Cuts," *Atlanta Journal Constitution*, May 10, 2007: D1.

[76] Conversation with Shelley Nickel, Director, Office of Planning and Budget (2005–2007), July 1, 2010.

in the district of the House Rules Committee Chairman; and a bond project for improvements to the Buckhead, Midtown, and Peachtree Street areas in Atlanta, supported by the House Speaker Pro-Tempore. The House Rules Committee Chairman was quoted as saying the governor was paying back House members who opposed his veto of the $142.2 million Homeowners Tax Relief Grant program.[77]

In addition to the vetoed items in the FY 2008 appropriations bill, Governor Perdue issued messages instructing 17 different agencies to disregard 51 separate legislative instructions regarding spending that do not constitute appropriations. Such language, he said, is non-binding.[78] Typically, agencies were instructed by the governor to disregard the non-binding language and to expend their funds in accordance with the program's stated purpose and the general powers of the agency.

There were two line-item vetoes in the AFY 2008 appropriation bill, one veto of $250,000 that the governor characterized as "non-critical spending" and a second veto of legislative intent with no specific dollar reduction included. The governor's veto message stated that "The good news is that it is virtually free of special-interest earmarks…".[79]

Perhaps indicating the status of Georgia executive-legislative relations, the General Assembly immediately transmitted the AFY 2008 appropriations to the governor, thereby triggering a constitutional provision[80] requiring the governor to sign or veto the bill within six days, ensuring that it would have time to override any gubernatorial item vetoes.[81] When bills are routinely transmitted to the governor as the legislature adjourns *sine die*, the governor has 40 days to sign or veto them and attempted veto overrides must wait until the next legislative session.

There were 18 line-item vetoes in the FY 2009 appropriation bill. Even though the bill as approved contained many local construction projects, several projects added by the General Assembly were item vetoed, including several projects advocated by House leaders. Examples provided by the *Atlanta Journal-Constitution* included: a bond project for airport improvement at the Paulding County Regional Airport in the district of the Speaker of the House; a bond project for airport improvement in Glynn County in the district of the House Majority Leader; and a

---

[77] James Salzer, "Perdue Slashes Millions in Budget. 41 Bills Killed: Governor Sprinkles in Political Payback While Nixing $130 Million in Spending. But Teachers Get a 3% Raise; 'Go Fish' is Funded," *Atlanta Journal Constitution*, May 31, 2007: A1. James Salzer and Jeremy Redmon, "Perdue Veto Leaves Many Holes to Fill. Metro Atlanta Hit Hard: Elementary School Foreign Language Program to Fold, and Cuts Take Toll on Campus, Library Projects," *Atlanta Journal Constitution*, June 1, 2002: A1.

[78] Press Release, Office of the Governor, May 20, 2007.

[79] Press Release, Office of the Governor, March 21, 2008.

[80] *Constitution of the State of Georgia*, Article III, Section V, Paragraph XIII. Approval, veto and override of bills and resolutions.

[81] James Salzer, "Row Over Spending. Budget Gets an Icy Nod. Governor Reluctantly Signs Plan, Rushing Help to Grady and Schools, but Says Legislators Flunked Frugality Test," *Atlanta Journal Constitution*, March 22, 2008: A1.

bond project for a Charter School in Cobb County in the district of the House Rules Committee Chairman.[82]

In addition to the vetoed items in the FY 2009 appropriations bill, Governor Perdue issued messages instructing the Department of Community Health and two other state agencies to disregard non-binding legislative instructions. For example, with regard to the General Assembly's instructions to provide a rate increase, to adjust reimbursement rates or to pay a contractor the department was to allocate its funds in accordance with the purposes of the program and the department's general law powers.[83]

There were no line-item vetoes in the AFY 2009 appropriation bill. However, Governor Perdue issued two messages instructing the Department of Community Health and the Department of Education to ignore non-binding directions from the General Assembly. For example, when the General Assembly sought to earmark funds for a specific vendor, the governor authorized the department to utilize "appropriate procurement and vendor management procedures to ensure that program services intended by the General Assembly are provided in a fair, equitable, efficient and effective manner."[84]

There were three line-item vetoes in the FY 2010 appropriation bill. The FY 2010 budget was less than the FY 2009 budget. The chairmen of the House and Senate Appropriations Committees were quoted in the *Atlanta Constitution* as saying that because of the lean budget there were few local projects to attract the governor's attention.[85] In addition to the vetoed items in the FY 2010 appropriations bill, Governor Perdue issued messages instructing five different agencies to ignore 12 separate legislative instructions included in the budget and to utilize funds in accordance with the overall purpose of appropriation and within the agency's general law authority.[86]

There were no line-item vetoes in the AFY 2010 appropriation bill. There were five line-item vetoes in the FY 2011 appropriation bill, all authorizing debt service to finance capital projects. Consistent with his capital project priority system, Governor Perdue stated that these projects were not identified as a priority and were not requested by the agency.[87] In addition to the vetoed items in the FY 2011 appropriations bill, Governor Perdue issued messages instructing five different agencies to disregard 15 separate legislative instructions regarding spending that do not constitute appropriations. For example, the General Assembly issued directives to reduce or eliminate funds for various programs, to provide a rate increase for certain

---

[82] James Salzer, "Guns Legal in More Places. Perdue Signs Bill Allowing Concealed Weapons in Public Venues and OKs State Budget, Auto Insurance Measure," *Atlanta Journal-Constitution*, May 15, 2008: A1.

[83] Press Release, Office of the Governor, May 14, 2008.

[84] Press Release, Office of the Governor, March 13, 2009.

[85] Aaron Gould Sheinin, "Governor Perdue OKs Budget, Vetoes Only 3 Line Items," *Atlanta Journal-Constitution*, May 14, 2009:A1.

[86] Press Release, Office of the Governor, May 13, 2009.

[87] Press Release, Office of the Governor, June 8, 2010.

hospital reimbursements, and to restore funding to a state hospital facility. In all cases, Governor Perdue instructed agencies to ignore the legislative directives and utilize their funds in accordance with their mission and general state law.[88]

Governor Perdue's Second Term in Retrospect

At the end of Governor Sonny Perdue's second term, the three use patterns observed during his first term persisted: the focus on bond projects inserted in the appropriations bill by the General Assembly, the treatment of legislative intent language in the appropriations bill as "non-binding," and instructions to executive branch agencies to "withhold" from spending certain funds appropriated by the General Assembly. However, during the second term an additional pattern became evident, intensified inter-branch conflict with items favored by members of the House leadership becoming the target of Governor Perdue's line-item vetoes. This was especially evident following the 2007 session, AFY 2007 and FY 2008 appropriations, and the 2008 session, FY 2009 appropriation. Relationships between the governor and leaders in the General Assembly, all of the same political party, were generally uncooperative during this period.[89] Governor Perdue appears to have used the item veto more contentiously with legislators of his own party than did his Democratic predecessors. During the last quarter of the twentieth century Democratic governors competed and occasionally collided with the Democratic Speaker of the House of Representatives, but they avoided political disasters. In contrast, Governor Perdue and the Republican Speaker of the House of Representatives seemed not to have been able to avoid major collisions. These differences were not about political party; the governor and the speaker were of the same party. They were inter-branch differences, likely exacerbated by the personalities and dispositions of the participants.

Nathan Deal (2011–2019)

Nathan Deal became governor in 2011 as the state was recovering from the Great Recession. Although over the span of his eight years in office his General Obligation debt spending was similar to that of his predecessors at 5–6%, in his first budget he sought to curtail state borrowing and used the line-item veto of legislative add-ons to send his message to the General Assembly.

---

[88] Press Release, Office of the Governor, June 8, 2010.
[89] Thomas P. Lauth, "Budget Deficits in the States: Georgia," *Public Budgeting & Finance*, Vol. 30 (Spring 2010): 25–29.

As can be seen in Table 8.1, there were no line-item vetoes in the AFY 2011 appropriations bill, but there were 11 line-item vetoes in the FY 2012 appropriations bill. All of the vetoed items in HB 78, Section 51,[90] pertaining to the General Obligation Debt Sinking Fund were projects for the University System of Georgia, Board of Regents. The governor's reason for four of the vetoes was that the authorized funding was insufficient to complete the planned construction. The rational for the other seven vetoes was that the authorized funding was for design only and that design should not be funded with 20-year bonds. Design is a short-term, limited-life asset, he said, and does not result in a physical asset. The State's priority should be to fund construction for which the design phase has already been funded.

When a line-item veto is of a bond project, the amount vetoed is the debt service for the fiscal year of the veto. The total amount of the project to be funded with 20-year borrowing is a much larger amount, and often is the amount reported in the media. However, that amount is not the amount by which the budget is reduced. For example, Governor Deal used the line-item veto 11 times before signing the FY 2012 appropriations bill to remove proposed construction projects on several campuses of the University System of Georgia. The total amount of the vetoes was $3,645,704. However, the media reported the total as approximately $42 million.[91] The total amount of the 11 proposed bond projects was $42,590,000 to be paid off with interest over 20 years, but the principal and interest payments on that debt in FY 2012 would have been only $3.6 million.

There were no line-item vetoes in the AFY 2012 appropriations bill, but there were two line-item vetoes in the FY 2013 appropriations bill. One of the vetoed items in HB 742, Section 51,[92] pertaining to the General Obligation Debt Sinking Fund authorized $256,800 in debt service[93] for a University System of Georgia, Board of Regents project at a branch campus of the University of Georgia. The governor's reason for vetoing this project was that it had not been requested by the Board of Regents and was not identified as a priority in the Board of Regents capital plan. The second item vetoed authorized $133,476 in debt service[94] for Department of Transportation projects upgrading railway bridges and grade crossings. The governor's reason for vetoing this project was his belief that the Department had sufficient funding within its existing authorized general obligation debt for these projects.

In addition to the two vetoed items in the FY 2013 appropriations bill, Governor Deal issued messages instructing five different agencies to disregard eight legislative instructions regarding appropriations. The legislative intent language was considered non-binding by the governor for several reasons, including: the initiative

---

[90] Georgia Laws, 2011: Appendix. HB 78 was approved May 12, 2011.

[91] James Salzer, "Governor Vetoes College Project; $42 Million Nixed in State Budget," *Atlanta Journal-Constitution*, May 18, 2011: B3, and *Athens Banner-Herald*, May 19, 2011, onlineathens.com/051911/uga_831601807.shtml

[92] Georgia Laws, 2012: Appendix. HB 742 was approved May 7, 2012.

[93] The project would have issued $3,000,000 in 20-year bonds.

[94] The project would have issued $1,470,000 in 20-year bonds.

would have been outside the scope of the purpose of the program; not operationally feasible; would have limited the Department's ability to effectively manage its program and control its expenses; would have circumvented the Department's process for reimbursing vendors; the initiative should be prioritized state-wide rather than regionally focused; the appropriation recipient has sufficient resources for the initiative without an additional appropriation; and grant funding for such projects should be awarded on a competitive basis. Unlike the effect of line-item vetoes, the appropriation amount of non-binding intent language is not deleted from the bill. Instead, agencies are authorized to utilize the funds in accordance with the purpose of their program and the general law powers of the Department.

There were no line-item vetoes in the AFY 2013 appropriations bill or the FY 2014 appropriations bill. There were no line-item vetoes in the AFY 2014 or the FY 2015 appropriations, but there were three Intent Language Considered Non-Binding statements attached to HB 744, the FY 2015 Appropriations Bill, Sections 15, 17 and 27.[95] In two instances, the General Assembly sought to have agencies redirect funds between agencies. The governor judged such actions premature in the absence of a detailed plan for doing so. In the third instance, the General Assembly sought to have an agency provide a service for which the governor believed no funds had been appropriated. Agencies were instructed to disregard the legislative intent language, and to utilize their funds in accordance with the purpose of the program and the general law powers of the Department.

There were no line-item vetoes in the AFY 2015 appropriations bill, but there was one line-item veto in the FY 2016 appropriations bill. The vetoed item in HB 76, Section 50,[96] pertaining to the General Obligation Debt Sinking Fund authorized $809,900 in debt service[97] for the Department of Community Affairs for construction of a seawall on an island in Savannah. The governor's veto stated that "the state does not have ownership of the land identified for the seawall, and thus is prohibited from using general obligation debt to finance this project."

There were no line-item vetoes in the AFY 2016 appropriations bill, but there was one line-item veto in the FY 2017 appropriations bill. The vetoed item in HB 751, Section 50,[98] pertaining to the General Obligation Debt Sinking Fund authorized $138,840 in debt service[99] for the Department of Community Affairs for construction of a seawall on an island in Savannah. The governor's veto again stated that "the state does not have ownership of the land identified for the seawall, and thus is prohibited from using general obligation debt to finance this project."

In addition to the vetoed item in the FY 2017 appropriations bill, Governor Deal issued messages instructing six different agencies to disregard eight legislative instructions regarding appropriations in the FY 2017 appropriations bill, and one of

---

[95] Georgia Laws, 2014: Appendix. HB 744 was approved April 28, 2014.
[96] Georgia Laws, 2015: Appendix. HB 76 was approved May 12, 2015.
[97] The project would have issued $3,500,000 in five-year taxable bonds.
[98] Georgia Laws, 2016: Appendix. HB 751 was approved May 2, 2016.
[99] The project would have issued $600,000 in five-year taxable bonds.

those agencies to disregard a legislative instruction in the AFY 2016 appropriations bill. Appropriations in the Department of Economic Development budget specifically for the National Infantry Museum and the Georgia Historical Society were thought to be better used to promote tourism in accordance with the highest priorities of the state. Appropriations in the Employee's Retirement System budget for benefits to appellate court judges and the judicial retirement system were considered non-binding because legislation providing these benefits failed to pass during the 2016 legislative session. An appropriation in the University System of Georgia, Board of Regents budget to assist in the operations of a county charter review commission was considered non-binding because local legislation to this effect failed to pass during the 2016 legislative session. Appropriations in the General Obligation Debt Sinking Fund to change the replacement cycle for motor vehicles operated by three agencies was considered non-binding because the governor believed the change would adversely impact the safety and operations of the vehicles. Agencies were instructed to disregard the legislative intent language, and to utilize their funds in accordance with the purpose of the program and the general law powers of the Department.

There were no line-item vetoes in the AFY 2017 or the FY 2018 appropriations, but there was one Intent Language Considered Non-Binding statement attached to HB 44, the FY 2018 Appropriations Bill, Section 28,[100] pertaining to the Department of Human Services. The General Assembly sought to appropriate funds to the Georgia Vocational Rehabilitation Agency for a designated provider to assist veterans in transitioning to private employment. The governor concurred with the purpose of the appropriation but stated that the Vocational Rehabilitation Agency should have the authority to select the provider that best served this statewide population. The agency was instructed to disregard the legislative intent language, and to utilize the funds in accordance with the purpose of the program and the general law powers of the Department.

There were no line-item vetoes in the AFY 2018 appropriations bill, the FY 2019 appropriations bill or the AFY 2019 appropriations bill.

Governors Perdue and Deal

Governor Deal had a more cooperative relationship with the General Assembly on budget matters than did his Republican predecessor, Sonny Perdue. One indicator of their legislative relationships is the number of times each used the line-item veto. Between 2003 and 2010, Governor Perdue used the line-item veto 106 times in eight years across 16 appropriations and amended appropriations bills, or an average of 6.6 times per appropriations bill. Between 2011 and 2018, Governor Deal used it 15 times in eight years across 17 appropriations and amended appropriations

---

[100] Georgia Laws, 2017: Appendix. HB 44 was approved May 1, 2017.

bills,[101] or an average of less than one time per appropriations bill. Eleven of those 15 came following his first legislative session in 2011 when he was seeking to send a message to the legislature about add-ons to his bond proposals. Although Governor Perdue faced a Democratic legislative majority during his first two years in office and a Republican majority thereafter, and Governor Deal had only Republican legislative majorities, partisanship alone does not account for the difference in use of the item veto. Governor Perdue and Republican legislative leaders had an uncooperative relationship.[102] The relationship between Nathan Deal and the House of Representatives and Senate was more cooperative.

A governor's motives for using the line-item veto vary from time to time but often include some combination of fiscal necessity, personal philosophy of government, inter-branch competition and political payback. Sometimes items are eliminated because they are thought to be imprudent and unaffordable especially during difficult economic times. Sometimes items are eliminated because they are incompatible with the governor's philosophy of the kinds and scope of activities which the government should be undertaking. Sometimes eliminated projects are marginally important state-wide, but of great importance to individual legislators and their constituencies. Whenever these kinds of projects are item vetoed, legislators are likely to perceive the veto as politically motivated, intended to punish them and to be an assertion of executive power. Motivation is difficult to attribute with certainty. Often, there are multiple motives at work. Sometimes, however, the motivation is mostly political.

Governor Sonny Perdue faced the effects of national recessions at both the beginning, 2001–02, and the end, 2008–09, of his eight years, 2003–10, which necessitated use of the state's rainy day funds in five of his eight budgets, FY 2004, FY 2005, FY 2009, FY 2010 and FY 2011. Surely, fiscal restraint was a motive for use of the line-item veto during these times. The capital project priority system reflected Governor Perdue's philosophy of the kinds of activities which the government should be undertaking, and was another motive for using the line-item veto.

Governor Perdue also served during a time of political transition in Georgia. In the 2003 and 2004 Sessions of the General Assembly, Perdue faced a Democratic controlled House of Representatives. Beginning in 2005 he had a Republican Speaker of the House, but the Lieutenant Governor, the presiding officer of the state Senate, was a Democrat. After the 2006 election, Republicans controlled both the executive and legislative branches. The new Republican Speaker of the House, Representative Glenn Richardson and Governor Perdue each sought to assert the power of their respective institutions. This inter-branch competition, compounded by the personalities of the principals, often led to a lack of cooperation in the budget process. There seems to be little doubt that in certain years some of Governor Perdue's line-item vetoes were directed at projects of legislators who had not

---

[101] See note 6.
[102] Thomas P. Lauth, "Budget Deficits in the States: Georgia," *Public Budgeting & Finance*, Vol. 30 (Spring 2010): 15–32, at 25–29.

cooperated with him on budgetary or other policy matters. This seems to have been true following the 2003 session, AFY 2003 appropriations, when the victims were Democrats, and following the 2007 session, AFY 2007 and FY 2008 appropriations, and the 2008 session, FY 2009 appropriations, when the victims were fellow Republicans. Legislators and journalists think Governor Perdue by both personality and political circumstances engaged at times in political payback.[103]

A former Director of the Office Planning and Budget acknowledged that when executive - legislative relations were harmonious and legislative bond projects were inconsistent with the governor's capital project priority system, the governor's office had on occasion been willing to "look the other way." However, he did acknowledge that the governor's office might not have been willing to "look the other way" when legislative bond projects were inconsistent with the governor's capital project priority system AND legislative leaders had been uncooperative on other matters.[104]

Following Governor Deal's first legislative session in 2011, he met with legislative leaders to inquire about what had worked well during the session, what had not worked so well, and what could be improved in the next legislative session. Legislative leaders were reported to have been "floored by such treatment," in contrast with their previous experience with Governor Sonny Perdue. An outcome of the meeting was a plan for informal meetings during subsequent legislative sessions between legislative leaders and members of the governor's staff to get to know each other and talk about things that were important to each other. The Chairman of the House Appropriations thinks this process worked well.[105]

Governor Deal also included in his annual budget proposals undesignated funding for capital projects to meet the needs of legislators.[106] These funds which were part of the General Obligation Debt Sinking Fund recommendation enabled legislative leaders to accommodate projects of local importance for their members, and thereby to achieve support for the governor's budget. As described by the Chair of the House Appropriations Committee, the governor agreed that his bond package would include the large, state-wide projects that are needed but of little political benefit to individual members. The General Assembly would get $100 million, $150 million in 2018, shared 50–50 between the House and Senate to be used for projects of benefit to individual members. Through this arrangement, the governor achieved respect for his bond projects as well as support for other program initiatives during the legislative session, and the General Assembly received bond money to distribute

---

[103] Conversations with Representatives Mark Burkhalter and Earl Ehrhart and *Atlanta Journal-Constitution* journalist James Salzer, August 11, 2010.

[104] Conversation with Trey Childress, Director, Office of Planning and Budget (2007–2010), July 1, 2010.

[105] Conversation with Terry England, Chair, Appropriations Committee, Georgia House of Representatives, August 13, 2018.

[106] Conversation with David Shafer, President Pro Tempore, Georgia Senate, Athens, Georgia, June 13, 2017. See also: James Salzer, "Deal Horse-Trades Bond Money to Move His Budget," *Atlanta Journal-Constitution*, March 23, 2013.

to it members. Knowledge that there will be only $50 million, later $75 million, undesignated each year also helped the House and Senate appropriations committee chairs manage member expectations about the availability of bond project money.[107]

Frequency of Use of the Line-item Veto

Georgia governors use the line-item veto, but not very often. Governors Carl Sanders and Lester Maddox never used it. Governor Jimmy Carter used it an average of 2.4 times per appropriations bill per legislative session during his administration (1971–1974). Governor George Busbee used it an average of 0.6 times per appropriations bill per legislative session during his administration (1975–1982). Governor Joe Frank Harris used it an average of 2.3 times per bill per legislative session (1983–1990). Governor Zell Miller used it an average of 6.4 times per bill per legislative session (1991–1998). Governor Roy Barnes used it an average of 6.5 times per bill per legislative session (1992–2002). Governor Sonny Perdue used it an average of 6.6 times per bill per legislative session during his administration (2003–2010). Governor Nathan Dean used it an average of 0.9 times per bill per legislative session (2011–2018).[108]

In 2011, I surveyed the budget directors of the 44 states where the governor has line-item veto authority. Of the 41 states responding to the survey question, "How frequently is the line-item veto used each year in your state?" 24 (59%) reported "not very often, less than 10 times," 13 (32%) reported "somewhat, between 10 and 49 times," three (7%) reported "often, between 50 and 99 times," and one (2%) reported "very often, between 100 and 500 times." Using these survey responses as a measurement standard, all seven Georgia governors fall into the "not very often" category, with about 60% of the line-item veto states.

Conclusion

Although the line-item veto has been used for fiscal restraint in specific years, for example by Governor Perdue who had to cope with declining state revenues in FY 2008, FY 2009 and FY 2010, over all it has not been an instrument to reduce the size of the budget. The governor's authority to set the revenue estimate,[109] which establishes an upper limit on spending that the legislature may not increase, has been

---

[107] Conversation with Terry England, Chair, Appropriations Committee, Georgia House of Representatives, August 13, 2018.

[108] See note 6.

[109] It is not a consensus estimate, not a competitive estimate with the legislature having its version, and not an estimate provided by an independent or third-party. It is the governor's estimate based upon information provided by his professional economist.

more useful than the line-item veto for controlling the size of the state budget. The line-item veto has been useful for governors to protect their spending proposals from legislative attempts to substitute their spending priorities for those of the governor. From time to time it has also been used as payback for perceived legislative political transgressions.

The reformatted appropriations bill that accompanied the Prioritized Program Based Budget (PPB), not only reduced the line-item veto options for Governors Perdue and Deal, but also made it more difficult for the General Assembly to indicate legislative intent. To counteract this disadvantage, the General Assembly began inserting designation language. To counteract this legislative move, Governors Perdue and Deal began issuing, along with line-item vetoes, instructions to state agencies to ignore the legislative designations and spend appropriated funds in ways consistent with the mission of the agency and in accord with existing state law. This was a major budget process innovation that in recent years has strengthened the governor's position vis-à-vis the General Assembly.

Chapter 9
Budget Priorities and Achievements of Georgia Governors, 1963–2019

Georgia governors set the annual budget agenda through the preparation of the *Governor's Budget Report,* a draft appropriations bill and a budget message. The governor's revenue estimate determines the amount of state funding available for spending and also establishes a spending ceiling for legislative appropriations. The executive budget, by delineating resource commitments, communicates the governor's policy priorities.[1] This chapter describes the budget priorities and achievements of governors from Carl Sanders to Nathan Deal.[2] Carl Sanders was the first governor to serve following the enactment of the Budget Act of 1962[3] which established Georgia's modern executive budget system. Nathan Deal was the last governor to have completed a full term at the time of this writing. Table 9.1 shows the annual budgets for each of these governors.

Carl E. Sanders

Carl E. Sanders was elected governor in 1962 and served from 1963 through 1966. He was the first governor since the early twentieth century to be elected strictly by popular vote. Before then, statewide elections were determined by the county unit

---

[1] For an insightful study of how governors in 14 states in the 1970s and 1980s used the executive budget to advance their policy agendas, see: James J. Gosling, "Patterns of Stability and Change in Gubernatorial Policy Agendas," *State and Local Government Review*, Vol. 23 (Winter 1991): 3–12.

[2] An excellent source for information about the priorities and achievements generally of Georgia governors is the *New Georgia Encyclopedia*. Athens, Georgia: University of Georgia Press, 2013. Budget figures for each administration were obtained from the more than fifty *Governor's Budget Reports* submitted to the General Assembly between 1963 and 2018. All percentages were calculated by the author.

[3] Georgia Laws, 1962: 17–37. HB 742 approved February 16, 1962. O.C.G.A, Title 45, Chapter 12.

Table 9.1 Budgets by Governors and State Funds

Governor	Fiscal Year	Total State Funds	Percent Change
Carl Sanders	1964	$464,946,093	
	1965	$488,979,253	5.2%
	1966	$583,049,722	19.2%
	1967	$627,916,243	7.7%
	1964–67		35.1%
	Average Annual Growth		10.5%
Lester Maddox	1968	$800,643,226	
	1969	$875,695,888	9.4%
	1970	$1,115,575,798	27.4%
	1971	$1,161,936,639	4.2%
	1968–71		45.1%
	Average Annual Growth		13.2%
Jimmy Carter	1972	$1,175,191,782	
	1973	$1,313,681,615	11.8%
	1974	$1,570,189,409	19.5%
	1975	$1,619,685,802	3.2%
	1972–75		37.8%
	Average Annual Growth		11.3%
George Busbee	1976	$1,955,576,269	
	1977	$1,922,000,000	−1.7%
	1978	$2,129,144,627	10.8%
	1979	$2,419,953,332	13.7%
	1980	$2,766,878,000	14.3%
	1981	$3,048,202,779	10.2%
	1982	$3,419,011,890	12.2%
	1983	$3,777,000,000	10.5%
	1976–83		93.1%
	Average Annual Growth		9.9%
Joe Frank Harris	1984	$4,018,000,000	
	1985	$4,297,000,000	6.9%
	1986	$4,838,000,000	12.6%
	1987	$5,316,000,000	9.9%
	1988	$5,772,000,000	8.6%
	1989	$6,254,000,000	8.4%
	1990	$7,071,000,000	13.1%
	1991	$7,785,000,000	10.1%
	1984–91		93.8%
	Average Annual Growth		9.9%
Zell Miller	1992	$7,900,000,000	
	1993	$8,134,000,000	3.0%
	1994	$8,948,692,764	10.0%
	1995	$9,775,460,431	9.2%

(continued)

Table 9.1 (continued)

Governor	Fiscal Year	Total State Funds	Percent Change
	1996	$10,700,856,569	9.5%
	1997	$11,324,027,653	5.8%
	1998	$11,777,578,880	4.0%
	1999	$12,528,603,880	6.4%
	1992–99		58.6%
	Average Annual Growth		6.8%
Roy Barnes	2000	$13,291,103,880	
	2001	$14,421,828,880	8.5%
	2002	$15,446,828,905	7.1%
	2003	$16,177,689,408	4.7%
	2000–03		21.7%
	Average Annual Growth		6.8%
Sonny Perdue	2004	$16,281,651,592	
	2005	$16,125,208,162	−1.0%
	2006	$17,415,249,819	8.0%
	2007	$18,654,564,058	7.1%
	2008	$20,230,620,936	8.4%
	2009	$21,425,140,103	5.9%
	2010	$20,193,974,890	−5.7%
	2011	$18,156,435,820	−10.1%
	2004–11		11.5%
	Average Annual Growth		1.6%
Nathan Deal	2012	$18,162,513,870	
	2013	$19,224,524,133	5.8%
	2014	$19,864,261,481	3.3%
	2015	$20,836,744,620	4.9%
	2016	$21,782,964,314	4.5%
	2017	$23,739,409,078	9.0%
	2018	$24,997,351,235	5.3%
	2019	$26,226,914,974	4.9%
	2012–19		44.4%
	Average Annual Growth		5.4%

Source: Governor's Budget, FY 1964 – FY 2019

system. This system gave more weight to smaller, rural, more numerous counties, over larger, urban but fewer counties.[4] Sanders was elected to the Georgia House of Representatives in 1954 and the Georgia Senate in 1956, where he served for two years as the president pro tempore of the Senate. In 1962, he defeated former Governor Marvin Griffin in the Democratic primary for governor, which at that time was tantamount to election. Marvin Griffin favored the county unit system.[5]

Funding for both public and higher education were Governor Sanders top budget priorities. Over his four years, the Georgia budget increased by 35% from $464,946,093 in FY 1964 to $627,916,243 in FY 1967, at an average annual rate of 10.5%. The Department of Education budget increased by 38% from $184,412,500 in FY 1964 to $254,096,300 in FY 1967, slightly more than the state budget as a whole, and the budget of the University System of Georgia Board of Regents increased by 69% from $35,700,000 in FY 1964 to $60,350,000 in FY 1967, a substantially greater increase than for the state budget. In 1964, Governor Sanders convinced the General Assembly to increase taxes on cigarettes, beer and spirits to raise additional revenue for education. In addition to operating funds for the Department of Education and the Board of Regents, Sanders recommended bond funds to build public schools and for university campus construction in each of his four budgets: $21.2 million in FY 1964, $23.2 million in FY 1965, $31.9 million in FY 1966 and $31.8 million in FY 1967.[6] During the Sanders years, between 52 and 55% of the state budget was allocated to the Department of Education, the University System of Georgia Board of Regents and bonds for public and higher education facility construction. By the time of the Sanders administration, Georgia had decided to keep its public schools open, eschewing the massive resistance to the *Brown v. Board of Education* decision[7] that had plagued other southern states. The work of the Sibley Commission[8] and Governor Ernest Vandiver's recognition of the inevitability of school desegregation contributed to this decision. Carl Sanders enjoyed budgetary success with the Georgia General Assembly because, as was the

---

[4] The Georgia county unit system was a method of nominating candidates for state-wide office in primary elections. Winning the primary election was tantamount to election. The candidate who received the most popular votes in a county was entitled to all the county's unit votes. The eight most populous of Georgia's 159 counties each had six county unit votes, the next 30 in size had four county unit votes and the remaining 121 counties had two county unit votes each. The 121 counties with a minority of the state's population had approximately 60% (242/410) of the county unit votes. The county unit system was struck down by the U.S. District Court in *Sanders v. Gray*, 203 F. Supp. 158 (N.D. Ga. 1962). The U.S. Supreme Court affirmed that decision in *Gray v. Sanders*, 372 U.S. 378 (1963) because it violated the principle of one person, one vote. James H. Gray was Chair, Executive Committee, Democratic Party of Georgia and James O'Hear Sanders was a voter in Georgia's most populous county.

[5] Numan V. Bartley, *The Creation of Modern Georgia*, Athens, Georgia: The University of Georgia Press, 1990. p. 223.

[6] *Governor's Budget Report, FY 1963–1965 and FY 1965–1967.*

[7] *Brown et al. v. Board of Education of Topeka, Kansas, et al.* 347 U.S. 483 (1954).

[8] The report of the Sibley Commission, the General Assembly Committee on Schools, became the basis for averting massive resistance to desegregation.

practice at that time, he picked the successful candidate for Speaker of the House of Representatives and designated the chair of the most influential legislative committees.[9]

Lester G. Maddox

Lester G. Maddox, an outspoken segregationist, was elected governor in 1966 and served from 1967 through 1970. Maddox was an unsuccessful candidate for mayor of Atlanta in 1957 and again in 1961. He also was unsuccessful in a bid to become Georgia Lieutenant Governor in 1962. In 1966, Maddox defeated former Governor Ellis Arnall in the Democratic primary and faced former Republican Congressman Howard "Bo" Callaway in the general election. Callaway won the popular vote but because of write-in votes for Arnall, neither candidate received the required majority of the vote. Under the prevailing election rules at that time, the Democratic controlled Georgia House of Representatives selected Maddox as governor.

In contrast with Governor Sanders's one-sided budgetary relationship with the General Assembly, two events occurred in the Maddox administration that somewhat improved the legislature's influence in the budgetary process. First, when the House of Representatives convened on January 10, 1967, there was not yet a governor to pick the Speaker. When the House elected its officers without suggestions from the executive branch, a new era of legislative independence began. Further, in return for selecting Maddox as governor, the House obtained his agreement to greater legislative independence in the budget process. This allowed the House to have greater input into the appropriations bill they returned to the governor for his signature.[10] Second, in 1969 the General Assembly established the position of Legislative Budget Analyst[11] to provide the legislature with counterpart advice and expertise to the governor's Bureau of the Budget.

Over Governor Maddox's four years, the Georgia budget increased by 45% from $800,643,226 in FY 1968 to $1,161,936,639 in FY 1971, at an average annual rate of 13.2%. To the surprise of some, perhaps many, Governor Maddox significantly increased funding for the University System of Georgia. The Department of Education budget increased during that period by 22%, but the budget of the University System of Georgia Board of Regents increased by 66%. Governor Maddox's first University System budget increased by 65% over the last budget of his predecessor Carl Sanders, who also had been a strong supporter of higher education in Georgia. Consistent with Governor Maddox's priority of prison reform the Department of Corrections budget increased by 55% during his four years.

---

[9] Thomas B. Murphy, "Sophistication Marks Current Generation of State Legislators," *Atlanta Journal and Constitution* (December 15, 1985): C-1. Bill Shipp, "Carl Sanders: The Man, the Legend, the Era," *Georgia Trend*, Vol. 7 (1992): 20.

[10] Steve Anthony, Memorandum re: "The Executive Budget in Georgia," February, 2018.

[11] Official Code of Georgia Annotated, (O.C.G.A.), 28–4–6.

Jimmy Carter

Jimmy Carter was elected governor in 1970 and served from 1971 through 1974. Carter was a progressive who promoted economic and industrial expansion, and advocated modern government administration and planning.[12] Among his budget priorities were education, government reorganization and reform of the judicial system. Prior to being elected to the state Senate, Carter was Chairman of his local Board of Education and during his time in the Senate he served on the Education Committee.[13] During the Carter administration, the Adequate Program for Education in Georgia (APEG) was introduced and funding for vocational education increased. Judicial reform meant rationalizing the court system (Supreme Court, Appellate Court and Superior Courts). Jimmy Carter was strongly committed to greater efficiency and economy in the provision of government programs, planning (he had been President of the Georgia Planning Association),[14] and rational-comprehensive decision making. These commitments were manifest through a major reorganization of state government in 1972 in which numerous agencies that were no longer being funded but still in existence were eliminated, and many small and free-standing agencies were consolidated within the framework of a few larger state agencies. The *Governor's Budget Report, FY 1972–1973*[15] lists 70 agencies being funded; the *Budget Report, FY 1975* list 30 agencies being funded.

The other manifestation of Carter's commitment to rational-comprehensive decision making was Zero-Base Budgeting (ZBB). ZBB sought to focus budget deliberations on the whole budget not just proposed increases, and required state agencies to defend their entire budget each year with no assurance that their prior year budget would be retained. It included a precise set of forms, procedures and rules. Each agency was expected to use it every year to assess all of its programs and activities.[16]

Over Governor Carter's four years, the Georgia budget increased by 38% from $1,175,191,782 in FY 1972 to $1,619,685,802 in FY 1975, at an average annual rate of 11.3%. Reflecting Governor Carter's judicial reform priority, the budget for the Judiciary increased by 60% over the four-year period. The *Governor's Budget Report, FY 1973* is a dizzying display of data purported to demonstrate how the combination of state government reorganization and ZBB achieved economy and efficiency in Georgia state government.

---

[12] Numan V. Bartley, *The Creation of Modern Georgia*, Athens, Georgia: The University of Georgia Press, 1990. p. 221.

[13] Jimmy Carter, *Turning Point: A Candidate, A State and a Nation Come of Age*. New York: Times Books, a Division of Random House, 1992. pp. 42, 176 and 178.

[14] Jimmy Carter, *Turning Point: A Candidate, A State and a Nation Come of Age*. New York: Times Books, a Division of Random House, 1992. p. 49.

[15] The FY 1972–73 budget was the last biennial Georgia budget. Beginning with FY 1973, state budgeting became an annual process.

[16] Thomas P. Lauth, "Zero-Base Budgeting in Georgia: Myth and Reality," *Public Administration Review*, Vol. 38, No. 5 (September–October 1978): 420–430.

George D. Busbee

Georgia D. Busbee served as governor from 1975 through 1983. Among his budget priorities were education, establishing a state-wide kindergarten program and increasing salaries for University System of Georgia faculty; economic development, including the attraction of international investment to Georgia; prison reform and early completion of the interstate highway system through Georgia. As a fiscal conservative, he also supported local property tax relief. Upon entering office in January 1975 Busbee was confronted with a recession. Although he had proposed funding for the kindergarten program, state employee and teacher pay raises[17] and property tax relief in his first budget, he was forced to eliminate funding for those programs during a Special Session of the General Assembly in the summer of 1975 in which the state budget was reduced by $125 million.[18]

Based upon his experience of having to reduce the budget three times in 1975, Governor Busbee proposed and the General Assembly established in early 1976 a rainy day fund, the Revenue Shortfall Reserve.[19] The law required that an amount equal to three% of revenue collections of the previous fiscal year be set aside to enable an end-of-year balanced budget in the event annual revenue collections fell short of revenue estimates.[20] In 1982, the General Assembly established the Midyear Adjustment Reserve,[21] intended to be the primary source of additional midyear funds for public education. Georgia was experiencing population growth that made it difficult for the State Board of Education to accurately project local district enrollments. Additional funds were usually required midway through the fiscal year to provide the state's share of the education funding formula.

Over Governor Busbee's eight years, the Georgia budget increased by 94%[22] from $1,955,576,269 in FY1976 to $3,777,000,000 in FY 1983, at an average annual rate of 9.9%. Including funding for the new kindergarten program, the Department of Education budget increased by 95%, about the same rate as the budget as a whole. After the setback in the 1975 Special Session, kindergarten was partially funded in the FY 1977 budget and was receiving full funding by the beginning of Busbee's second term. Reflecting Governor Busbee's court-mandated prison

---

[17] The pay raise for University System of Georgia faculty was reinstated following a Supreme Court of Georgia decision. *Busbee et al. v. Georgia Conference, American Association of University Professors et al.*, 235 Ga. 752 (1975). 221 S.E.2d 437.

[18] *Rome News Tribune*, January 12, 1976: A1.

[19] Georgia Laws, 1976: 420–421. SB 466 approved March 5, 1976.

[20] Jim Merrimer, "Busbee Keeps Tight Budget Despite Gains in Economy," *Atlanta Constitution*, January 16, 1976: 8A, and John Martin, "Budget Reserve Bill Signed," *Atlanta Constitution*, March 6, 1976: 9A

[21] Georgia Laws, 1982: 1288–1289. SB 663 approved April 14, 1982.

[22] This high rate of increase is at least partially attributable to a period of high inflation. The average annual inflation rate during the 1970s exceeded 7% and was higher than for any other post-Depression decade. The annual inflation rate is the change in the Consumer Price Index (1982–84 = 100) from the previous year.

reform initiatives, the budget of the Department of Offender Rehabilitation increased by 167% over the eight-year period. Reflecting another of Busbee's priorities, economic development through the attraction of international investment to Georgia, a new Department of Industry and Trade was funded beginning in 1979 at approximately $8 million annually. Property tax relief for local school systems finally received funding in the amount of $75 million in both the FY 1980 and FY 1981 budgets. Despite the recessions of 1974–75 and 1981–82 that bookended the Busbee years, they were generally characterized by economic progress and fiscal stability.

During the Busbee years, the appropriations process of the House of Representatives became the focus of controversy over its "green door" committee. The committee's name derived from a popular song of 1956 describing a private club with music, smoke and laughter, with a green door that excluded the singer.[23] The green door committee was a group of six members of the House of Representatives that essentially wrote the state budget out of view from the press, the public, members of the General Assembly, even the other approximately 40 members of the Appropriations Committee,[24] and sometimes the governor.[25] The committee's recommendations were usually adopted by the General Assembly without change.[26] Members included the Speaker of the House, Tom Murphy, Chair of the Appropriations Committee, Joe Frank Harris, Democratic Majority Leader, Clarence Vaughn, Chair of the House Ways and Means Committee, Marcus Collins, Speaker *Pro Tempore*, Jack Connell and Representative Joe Mac Wilson, joined by the Legislative Budget Analyst, Pete Hackney.[27]

The green door committee may have been slightly more democratic than when the governor and State Auditor dictated the budget between 1931 and 1961, but groups such as Common Cause and the American Civil Liberties Union thought it was not open enough.[28] Following a rebellion in the 1979 session of the General Assembly when members of the House approved higher pay raises for state teachers than the amount recommended by the green door committee, Joe Frank Harris, Chair of the House Appropriations Committee announced the establishment of a subcommittee system that included a Budget Subcommittee pledged to holding open meetings. Representative Harris sought to avoid the embarrassment of being

---

[23] https://www.songfacts.com/lyrics/jim-lowe/the-green-door

[24] Beau Cutts, "'Inside' Panel Sees Budget Cut," *Atlanta Constitution*, January 11, 1977: 11A.

[25] Claudia Townsend and Rex Granum, "What Gives Behind the Green Door," *Atlanta Constitution*, March 7, 1975: 1-A.

[26] Editorial, "Green Door Panel," *Atlanta Constitution*, November 19, 1979: 4A.

[27] A cartoon depicting the committee members behind the green door was published in the *Atlanta Constitution*, February 7, 1978: 4.

[28] Editorial, "Open the Green Door," *Atlanta Constitution*, February 7, 1978: 4A; Beau Cutts, "Green Door Deals Called 'A Disgrace'," *Atlanta Constitution*, February 4, 1978: 1-A.

in violation of the state's open meetings policy[29] and was likely looking toward 1982 when he would be a candidate for governor.[30]

Joe Frank Harris

Joe Frank Harris was elected governor in 1982 and served from 1983 through 1990. Before being elected governor, he served nine terms in the Georgia House of Representatives, 1964–1982, and was chair of the Appropriations Committee, 1974–1982. His most notable budget priority was the improvement of public education as reflected in his financial support for the state's new Quality Basic Education (QBE) program and increases in teacher salaries.

Over Governor Harris's eight years, the Georgia budget increased by 94%[31] from $4,018,000,000 in FY 1984 to $7,785,000,000 in FY 1991, at an average annual rate of 9.9%. The Department of Education budget, approximately 36% of the state budget, increased by 93%, about the same rate as the budget as a whole. Various elements of the QBE program were phased into the budget over several years. During the first term of the Harris administration, employee compensation adjustments, including both salary and the state's contribution to employee and teacher retirements systems, increased between 3 and 7%; during the second term those compensation adjustments were 2.5% each year. In 1985 classroom teacher compensation was increased by an additional 7%, for a total of 10%.

Zell B. Miller

Zell Miller was elected governor in 1990 and served from 1991 through 1998. Among Miller's budget priorities were education and criminal justice reform emphasizing the need for tougher sentencing for repeat offenders. His signature education accomplishment was the Lottery for Education Act that dedicated lottery proceeds to fund pre-kindergarten programs, the HOPE[32] Scholarship program providing college and university tuition to any state resident graduating from high school with a B average, and technology enhancement for Georgia schools. The Georgia lottery was approved by the voters in 1992 and began in 1993, with the first

---

[29] Interview with John M. Hackney, Legislative Budget Analyst, Atlanta, GA, May 5, 1982.
[30] Charles Hayslett, "'Green Door' to Open for More Members of House," *Atlanta Constitution*, April 1, 1979:1-B; Associated Press, "Assembly Closes Its Green Door," *Atlanta Constitution*, November 15, 1979: 24-C; Beau Cutts, "The Door Ajar; Open Politics for the '80s," *Atlanta Constitution*, January 21, 1980: E-18.
[31] The 1980s were also characterized by high annual inflation rates, only slightly lower than during the Busbee years. The average annual inflation rate during the 1980s was almost 6%.
[32] HOPE is the acronym for Helping Outstanding Pupils Educationally.

proceeds becoming available in 1994. However, early in his administration Governor Miller had to deal with a recession that delayed the implementation of his other priorities.

Georgia experienced a revenue shortfall early in the 1991 fiscal year, necessitating state agency budget reductions. Declining revenue collections had required the state to totally deplete its $194 million Revenue Shortfall Reserve, the state's rainy day fund, in order to balance the budget at the close of the 1990 fiscal year. Shortly after the beginning of FY 1991, state agencies were ordered to cut their operating budgets by 3–4%, and funds were sequestered for the remainder of the fiscal year. With the Revenue Shortfall Reserve depleted, the state was forced to borrow $95 million from its Medicaid trust fund in order to balance the budget at the close of the 1991 fiscal year. Because those borrowed funds had to be restored for FY 1992, the state entered the 1992 fiscal year with an imbalance in its operating budget, estimated at between $400 and $500 million. When revenue collections for May and June 1991 were substantially behind the required rate of growth, Governor Miller in July 1991, less than two weeks into FY 1992, ordered a one day per month furlough for all state employees,[33] and imposed a freeze on travel and new equipment purchases. Governor Miller also called the General Assembly into special session, August 19–September 5, 1991, to amend the FY 1992 appropriations act. Only two months after the beginning of the 1992 fiscal year, the Georgia General Assembly amended the state's FY 1992 appropriations act, reducing it by approximately $415 million.[34]

In the regular session of the General Assembly which convened in January of 1992, the midyear amendment was used to make additional reductions in the FY 1992 appropriations act. In January and February, Governor Miller reduced the official revenue estimate by $125 million but reduced appropriations by only $85 million.[35] This was made possible because of post-audit lapses and anticipated payments to the Treasury. Compared with the budget reductions of $415 million made in the August special session, the February midyear amendment reductions were modest. Whereas budget cutting in the August special session largely consisted of agency budget reductions, budget balancing in the February regular session took the form of "forward borrowing" against the 1993 fiscal year.

Over Governor Miller's eight years, the Georgia budget increased by 59% from $7,900,000,000 in FY 1992 to $12,528,603,880 in FY 1999, at an average annual rate of 6.8%. The Department of Medical Assistance budget increased by 72%, reflecting the growth in eligibility for the Medicaid and PeachCare-for-Kids programs. The Department of Corrections budget increased by 43%, below the rate of increase for the government as a whole, but at a rate indicative of Governor Miller's get-tough-on-crime policy. The Department of Education budget increased by 66%

---

[33] The furlough plan was subsequently disallowed by a state Superior Court.

[34] Thomas P. Lauth, "Reductions in the FY 1992 Georgia Budget: Responses to a Revenue Shortfall," in Aman Kahn and W. Bartley Hildreth, eds. *Case Studies in Public Budgeting and Financial Management.* Dubuque, Iowa: Kendall/Hunt Publishing Company, 1994. pp. 221–248.

[35] The proposed Amended FY 1992 Appropriations Act compared with HB 1-EX (August 1991).

and the University System of Georgia Board of Regents budget increased by 55%, slightly above and below respectively the average for the state budget as a whole. However, when lottery proceeds are considered, which increased steadily from $125,000,000 in FY 1994 to $530,000,000 in FY 1999, state support for education[36] was substantial, reaching 55% of the state budget in his second term. In addition, during Miller's second term funding was allocated for public school teachers and university system faculty that permitted average salary increases of 6% during four consecutive years, FY 1996 through FY 1999.

The other budget innovation during Zell Miller's administration was budget redirection.[37] Redirection was an approach to budgeting that sought to fund ongoing agency services and enhancements using the current level of resources, to fund formula and entitlement-related services in a way that minimized the need for additional resources and to increase fund availability for priority areas within state government as a whole. Governor Miller's state-wide policy priorities included increasing teachers' salaries, removing the sales tax from food purchased for at home consumption,[38] providing the operating costs of new prisons, funding the K-12 education formula and funding the state's share of the Medicaid program, all within the financial constraint of revenue collections that were increasing at a decreasing rate and the belief that new taxes or increased tax rates were politically unacceptable.

Roy E. Barnes

Roy E. Barnes was elected governor in 1998 and served from 1999 through 2002. Educational reform was one of Governor Barnes top priorities. With the goal of improving public education in Georgia and improving the state's position on educational rankings, the A Plus Reform Act of 2000[39] abolished tenure for new teachers entering the state's system, established rewards for schools based upon student achievement, sought to reduce pupil-teacher ratios, provided help for failing schools, provided teacher training and development, established an independent Office of Accountability, and sought to end the practice of social promotion by requiring students to pass state tests as a condition of promotion. Although his education reform proposals were well intentioned, Governor Barnes encountered opposition

---

[36] The total for education includes funding for the Department of Education, the Department of Technical and Adult Education, the University System of Georgia Board of Regents and the Student Finance Commission (lottery proceeds).

[37] Henry M. Huckaby and Thomas P Lauth, "Budget Redirection in Georgia State Government," *Public Budgeting & Finance*, Vol. 18, Number 4 (Winter 1998): 36–44.

[38] In an action intended to improve vertical equity, the sales tax was removed from food over a three-year period beginning, October 1, 1996. During FY 1997 the sales tax was reduced from 4% to 2%; it was reduced by an additional 1% in each of the following two years.

[39] Georgia Laws, 2000: 618–754. HB 1187 was approved April 25, 2000.

from teachers which contributed to his defeat in 2002 after one term in office. Many teachers did not support his proposal for ending tenure for new teachers and some thought he was blaming teachers for poor student performance. His initiative to change the state flag no doubt also contributed to his defeat.

Over Governor Barnes's four years, the Georgia budget increased by 22% from $13,291,103,880 in FY 2000 to $16,177,689,408 in FY 2003, at an average annual rate of 6.8%. The Department of Education budget increased by 16% and the University System of Georgia Board of Regents budget increased by 6%, both below the average for the state budget as a whole. However, when lottery proceeds are considered which increased steadily from $543,000,000 in FY 2000 to $625,000,000 in FY 2003, state support for education appears to have been more favorable. In addition to education reform, Governor Barnes initiated a grant plan for local property tax relief, Homeowners Tax Relief Grant, which if implemented over an eight-year period would have increased the state homestead exemption from $2,000 to a projected $20,000. It was funded in FY 2000 at $83,000,000 and in FY 2003 at $329,000,000, an increase of just under 300%, at an average annual rate of 58%.

Like a couple of his predecessors, Governor Barnes had to deal with the effects of a national recession. The 2002 fiscal year was the first year in more than a half century that Georgia revenue collections were significantly less than those of the previous year. Early in FY 2002, Governor Barnes imposed a 2.5% spending reduction on state agencies for FY 2002 with an additional 2.5% reduction estimated for FY 2003. When revenue collections remained weak, the governor imposed additional agency budget reductions totaling 5% for FY 2003. Combined with the reduction made in FY 2002, state agency budgets were reduced by 7.5% through FY 2003. The governor's budget for FY 2003 allocated substantial amounts for salary increases for state public school teachers and University System of Georgia personnel and slightly smaller amounts for other state employees, as well as continuation of state funding of the local government property tax relief program. Governor Barnes also proposed the issuance of approximately $1.3 billion in state bonds in the midyear amendment to the FY 2002 budget (ultimately approved by the General Assembly at $700 million), substituting bond proceeds for tax revenue to initiate several capital construction projects. This initiative was intended to free up additional resources for his policy initiatives, take advantage of low borrowing rates, and have a stimulus effect on the state economy. Governor Barnes used state budget reductions, 2.5% in FY 2002 and an additional 5% in FY 2003, to ensure fund availability for his FY 2003 policy of teacher salary increases and continued state funding of local government property tax cuts, while keeping the state budget in balance.

George E. "Sonny" Perdue

Governor Sonny Perdue was elected in 2002 and served from 2003 through 2010. He defeated incumbent Democrat Governor Roy Barnes, capitalizing on opposition to Barnes from teachers who disliked his education reform program and other Georgians who disliked his initiative to change the state flag. Perdue was reelected in 2006, defeating Democrat Lieutenant Governor Mark Taylor.

Sonny Perdue was a fiscal conservative whose administration was characterized less by signature policy achievements but more by his approach to balancing the state budget through spending reductions during the Great Recession. He entered office as the state was recovering from the FY 2002–03 recession, had the benefit of several strong economic years and left office with the state struggling with the effects of the FY 2008–09 recession. In 2003, Governor Perdue signed a modest tax increase in the state's tobacco excise tax from 12 to 37 cents per package of cigarettes. Later attempts to further increase the cigarette tax were not supported by his successor, Governor Nathan Deal.

Over Governor Perdue's eight years, the Georgia budget increased by only 12% from $16,281,651,592 in FY 2004 to $18,156,435,820 in FY 2011, at an average annual rate of 1.6%. It decreased, year-over-year in FY 2010 by 5.7% and in FY 2011 by 10.1%. The Department of Education budget increased by 14%, decreasing year-over-year in both FY 2010 and FY 2011, and the University System of Georgia Board of Regents budget increased by 15%, also decreasing year-over-year in both FY 2010 and FY 2011. However, when lottery proceeds are considered which increased steadily from $691,795,656 in FY 2004 to $1,127,652,261 in FY 2011, state funding for education was approximately 55% of the state budget. The Department of Community Health budget increased by almost 14% during Governor Perdue's eight years, despite a year-over-year decrease in FY 2011 of 18%.

In December 2008, the National Bureau of Economic Research declared that the U.S. was in an economic recession and had been for a year. The first sign of the recession for Georgia was when the 2008 fiscal year ended with revenue collections 1.1% lower than collections in FY 2007. Governor Sonny Perdue drew down $600 million from the Revenue Shortfall Reserve to offset the revenue shortfall. In August 2008, little more than a month into FY 2009, state agencies were instructed to reduce their budgets by 6% through the end of FY 2009. Reductions for the Medicaid program, 5%, and K-12 education, 2%, were slightly lower, and approved but not yet implemented state employee salary increases were put on hold. State agencies restricted hiring, travel and equipment purchases and some implemented furloughs for employees. Education and law enforcement agencies were exempted from furloughs. The University System of Georgia sought to offset state funding losses by imposing a temporary fee on students during the 2009 spring semester[40] and reduced employer contributions to health insurance plans from 75 to 70%.

---

[40] The FY 2009 temporary fee imposed to soften the impact of the Great Recession remains in place, generating more than $200 million annually for the 26 institutions of the University System

As the General Assembly was coming into session in January 2009, revenue collections for the first six months of FY 2009 had decreased by 2.7% compared with the same period in FY 2008; revenue collections for the entire fiscal year would be down by 10.5% compared with FY 2008. At the beginning of the session Governor Perdue revised downward his revenue estimate, presented an amended budget that reduced state spending by nearly $2 billion based upon state agency budget reductions of 8%. At the end of the 2009 session the General Assembly appropriated an additional $200 million from the Revenue Shortfall Reserve to balance the budget at the end of the fiscal year and adopted a FY 2010 appropriations act that further reduced projected state spending. The Homeowners Tax Relief Grant program begun by Governor Barnes in FY 2000 and continued by Governor Perdue through FY 2009 was discontinued in the FY 2010 budget.

Governor Perdue responded to the FY 2008–09 fiscal crisis by reducing the revenue estimate, cutting agency spending, tapping rainy day funds, reducing reserves in the health insurance programs, incorporating federal stimulus dollars, and enacting a few minor revenue enhancements such as increasing employee health insurance contributions and imposing temporary fees for university system students.

During the Perdue administration the budget process reform, Prioritized Program Budgeting (PPB) was introduced. It restructured the *Governor's Budget Report* from an agency and object-of-expenditure classification format to a program and fund source structure.

Nathan Deal

Nathan Deal was elected governor in 2010, defeating former Governor Roy Barnes. He was re-elected in 2014, defeating state Senator Jason Carter. Prior to being elected governor, he served for eighteen years in the U.S. House of Representatives.

The major areas of accomplishment during his administration were: policies to make the state more attractive for economic development and to improve the climate for business, criminal justice reform, promoting accountability courts with less emphasis on maximum sentencing and less spending on prison beds, and support for education, with the full funding of the QBE formula for financing public schools, focus on educating a workforce for future jobs and stabilizing the HOPE scholarship program. The state economy was good to Nathan Deal as he came into office during an economic recovery following the Great Recession. His economic development policies were also good for the growth and development of the state economy. He was able to build up the Revenue Shortfall Reserve to $2.3 billion.

Over Governor Deal's eight years, the Georgia budget increased by 44% from $18,162,513,870 in FY 2012 to $26,226,914,974 in FY 2019, at an average annual rate of 5.4%. The Department of Education budget increased by 42%, at an average

---

of Georgia.

annual rate of 5.2% and the University System of Georgia Board of Regents budget increased by 39%, at an average annual rate of 4.9%. Both education increases were slightly below the growth rate of the state budget as a whole. When the Technical College System budget, the Student Finance Commission budget and lottery proceeds are considered, state funding for education was approximately 56 of the entire state budget during the Deal years. It was even a larger percentage of the budget when the proportion of bond projects dedicated to education is taken into account. The Great Recession caused the state to reduce the K-12 budget by imposing teacher furlough days, increasing class sizes, reducing the number of days in the school year and providing little or no cost-of-living salary increases for teachers. Governor Deal with more robust revenue collections in his years sought to gradually restore these budget reductions.

The budget of the Department of Community Health increased by 25%, at an average annual rate of 3.3% despite the state's decision not to expand the Medicaid program under conditions offered by the Patient Protection and Affordable Care Act.[41] The Department of Corrections budget increased by only 15%, at an average annual rate of 2.0%, in part attributable to cost savings achieved through the accountability court program. The Department of Transportation's budget increased by a whopping 169%, at an average annual rate of 15%, due in large part to the increased revenue generated from a change in the motor fuel tax.

The Georgia General Assembly in 2015 enacted the motor fuel excise tax, a levy of 26 cents per gallon[42] which is constitutionally earmarked for the construction and maintenance of the state's roads and bridges.[43] Prior to the effective date of the levy, July 1, 2015, the motor fuel tax was 7½ cents per gallon plus a 4% sales tax on total motor fuel sale, 3% of which went to the transportation fund and 1% of which went to the state general fund. Now all of the motor fuel tax goes to the Department of Transportation. One of the consequences of the 2015 change in the motor fuel tax rate was a substantial increase in motor fuel tax revenue in FY 2016 ($1,655,027,765) over FY 2015 ($1,025,819,044), an increase of 61.3% compared with an increase in state general fund receipts of 8.8%. This enabled a substantial state funds appropriation increase to the Department of Transportation for FY 2017 ($1,714,541,590) over FY 2016 ($876,295,966), an increase of 95.7% compared with an increase in state appropriations as a whole of 9.0%.[44] The new funds enabled much needed attention to highway and bridge repair and some new construction.

Governor Deal signed some tax legislation. In 2013 and 2017 he signed bills requiring hospitals in the state to pay a 1.45% tax on their net revenue which the state uses to obtain federal matching funds which in turn permit larger Medicaid

---

[41] The General Assembly in 2014 enacted and the governor signed legislation transferring power to expand Medicaid from the governor to the General Assembly, an action that virtually ensured that even if a Democrat were elected governor the executive could not expand Medicaid without legislative approval.

[42] The motor fuel excise tax is adjusted each year based upon the Consumer Price Index.

[43] *Constitution of the State of Georgia*, Article III, Section IX, Paragraph VI(b).

[44] *Governor's Budget Report, FY 2016, FY 2017* and *FY 2018*.

reimbursements to hospitals.[45] Despite the health care benefits of these transactions, they drew criticism from anti-tax groups.

The Georgia General Assembly in 2012 enacted and Governor Deal signed a package of tax reforms that among other things increased the personal exemption for a married couple filing a joint income tax return so as to eliminate a "marriage penalty" in the tax code; removed the state sales tax on energy used in manufacturing intended to increase the state's competitiveness; and eliminated the annual *ad valorem* tax on motor vehicles, replacing it with a one-time title fee of 7% on the purchase price of new and used vehicles. Governor Deal supported these and other one-off tax benefits, but was not encouraging of efforts in the General Assembly to reduce or eliminate the state income tax, apparently recognizing the benefit to the state's economy of a diverse revenue base.

Zero-base budgeting reappeared during the Deal administration. In 2012, the General Assembly enacted and Governor Deal signed a bill requiring zero-base budgeting for selected state agencies beginning with the FY 2014 budget. Governor Deal voluntary implemented zero-base budgeting for 10% of state agencies beginning with the FY 2013 budget. The new ZBB shares with the Carter-era ZBB the powerful symbol, "zero," which signifies fiscal conservatism. However, in practice the new ZBB and the Carter-era ZBB are considerably different.[46]

Another priority for Governor Deal was building back the Revenue Shortfall Reserve. The state may draw funds from its Revenue Shortfall Reserve to achieve budget balance at the end of the fiscal year and the governor may recommend the appropriation of reserve funds in excess of 4% of net revenue of the preceding fiscal year. Governor Sonny Perdue faced the effects of national recessions at both the beginning and the end of his eight years which necessitated use of the state's rainy day funds. He drew down funds in his FY 2004 and FY 2005 budgets, built back funds in his FY 2006, FY 2007 and FY 2008 budgets, but needed to again draw down funds for his FY 2009, FY 2010 and FY 2011 budgets. Governor Deal began building back the Revenue Shortfall Reserve and in his last six budgets, FY 2014 through FY 2019, had exceeded the important threshold of 4% of the previous year's revenue collections.

The Nine Governors

All of these nine governors were fiscal conservatives,[47] committed to balanced budgets, low taxes, limited debt and limited government spending. Everyone except Lester Maddox had served in the General Assembly and most held leadership posi-

---

[45] Nathan Deal, State of the State Address, January 11, 2017.

[46] Thomas P. Lauth, "Zero-Base Budgeting Redux in Georgia: Efficiency of Ideology?" *Public Budgeting & Finance,* Vol. 34, Number 1 (Spring 2014): 1–17.

[47] Thomas P. Lauth, "Budget Deficits in the States: Georgia," *Public Budgeting & Finance*, Volume 30, Number 1 (Spring 2010): 15–32.

tions there. In most cases, this experience facilitated their relationship with the legislature when they were governor.

Education has been the largest component of state budgets for each of the nine governors. In recent years, when public education (K-12), post-secondary education (including both the University and Technical College systems) and lottery for education funds are combined, the budget for education has exceeded 50% of the state budget as a whole. The most rapidly growing proportion of the state budget is for healthcare, including the state's share of the Medicaid program and the state's own PeachCare-for-Kids program. This is especially so during periods of recession when the number of eligible recipients increases.

Governors Maddox and Miller prioritized prison reform that emphasized incarceration and led to increased spending for the Department of Corrections. Governor Busbee also emphasized prison reform but in response to court orders that required improvement in prison conditions. Governor Deal took an approach to prison reform that emphasized less incarceration for low-risk offenders, decreasing the rate of increase in spending for Corrections.

As was noted in Chapter 3, a constitutional amendment in 1972 authorized the state to incur both general obligation debt and guaranteed revenue debt. Debt service is limited by the state constitution to 10% of net Treasury receipts of the preceding fiscal year. In recent years, the state's debt management plan has set the limit at 7%, and actual use has been in the range of 5–6%. General Obligation Debt Sinking Fund appeared as an object of expenditure in the *Governor's Budget Report* for the first time in 1978, in the administration of Governor Busbee. Beginning with Governor Harris, governors more actively and creatively used General Obligation (GO) Debt instead of cash to fund capital projects, freeing up cash for other purposes. Table 9.2 shows appropriations for the GO Bond Sinking Fund as a percent of total state appropriations for the fiscal years 1978–2019.[48] Governor Harris increased the use of GO Debt during his administration, more than doubling the total of debt service from FY 1984 to FY 1991. Governors Miller and Barnes used GO Debt to an extent similar to Governor Harris, an eight-year average of 4.2% of the budget for Harris and Miller and a four-year average of 3.8% for Barnes. Governor Perdue increased the use of GO Debt during his administration, in part as a recession fighting tool, increasing it by more than half from FY 2004 to FY 2011. Governors Perdue and Deal had somewhat larger bond packages than their predecessors, with eight-year averages of 5.3% and 5.4% of the budget respectively.

In most years, budget growth for each of the nine governors was the result of increasing student enrollments, increasing healthcare costs,[49] retirement system obligations, cost-of-living salary increases for employees and only then, new

---

[48] The constitutional debt limit is defined as debt service as a percent of net treasury receipts for the previous fiscal year. It is a measure of adherence to the debt limit. The data shown here are debt service as a percent of appropriations in the same fiscal year. They are intended as a measure of gubernatorial use of debt.

[49] Healthcare costs continue to increase despite the fact that Georgia is one of the very lowest states in Medicaid spending.

Table 9.2 GO Debt Sinking Fund: Governors Busbee, Harris, Miller, Barnes, Perdue and Deal

Year	Total State Funds	GO Bonds	Percent Change Year Over Year	GO Bonds as Percent of Total
Busbee				
1976	$1,955,576,269	–		
1977	$1,922,000,000	–		
1978	$2,129,144,627	$43,105,052		2.0%
1979	$2,419,953,332	$37,988,616	−11.9%	1.6%
1980	$2,766,878,000	$37,572,828	−1.1%	1.4%
1981	$3,048,202,779	$39,385,751	4.8%	1.3%
1982	$3,419,011,890	$39,947,850	1.4%	1.2%
1983	$3,777,000,000	$85,036,602	112.9%	2.3%
1976–83				1.6%
Harris				
1984	$4,018,000,000	$143,090,933	68.3%	3.6%
1985	$4,297,000,000	$145,447,166	1.6%	3.4%
1986	$4,838,000,000	$203,952,448	40.2%	4.2%
1987	$5,316,000,000	$222,279,489	9.0%	4.2%
1988	$5,772,000,000	$273,901,462	23.2%	4.7%
1989	$6,254,000,000	$275,433,628	0.6%	4.4%
1990	$7,071,000,000	$325,965,892	18.3%	4.6%
1991	$7,785,000,000	$341,049,249	4.6%	4.4%
1984–91			138.3%	4.2%
Miller				
1992	$7,900,000,000	$347,675,623	1.9%	4.4%
1993	$8,134,000,000	$427,711,741	23.0%	5.3%
1994	$8,948,692,764	$447,486,238	4.6%	5.0%
1995	$9,775,460,431	$419,457,463	−6.3%	4.3%
1996	$10,700,856,569	$429,914,625	2.5%	4.0%
1997	$11,324,027,653	$415,033,101	−3.5%	3.7%
1998	$11,777,578,880	$390,622,155	−5.9%	3.3%
1999	$12,528,603,880	$418,346,710	7.1%	3.3%
1992–99			20.3%	4.2%
Barnes				
2000	$13,291,103,880	$501,747,662	19.9%	3.8%
2001	$14,421,828,880	$532,461,866	6.1%	3.7%
2002	$15,446,828,905	$580,920,721	9.1%	3.8%
2003	$16,177,689,408	$621,114,074	6.9%	3.8%
2000–03			23.8%	3.8%
Perdue				
2004	$16,281,651,592	$781,495,609	25.8%	4.8%
2005	$16,125,208,162	$886,972,623	13.5%	5.5%
2006	$17,415,249,819	$955,851,159	7.8%	5.5%
2007	$18,654,564,058	$866,354,612	−9.4%	4.6%

(continued)

Table 9.2 (continued)

Year	Total State Funds	GO Bonds	Percent Change Year Over Year	GO Bonds as Percent of Total
2008	$20,230,620,936	$954,125,401	10.1%	4.7%
2009	$21,425,140,103	$1,036,224,934	8.6%	4.8%
2010	$20,193,974,890	$1,138,833,815	9.9%	5.6%
2011	$18,156,435,820	$1,189,663,128	4.5%	6.6%
2004–11			52.2%	5.3%
Deal				
2012	$18,162,513,870	$1,083,263,065	−8.9%	6.0%
2013	$19,224,524,133	$1,129,800,503	4.3%	5.9%
2014	$19,864,261,481	$1,199,853,710	6.2%	6.0%
2015	$20,836,744,620	$1,118,666,821	−6.8%	5.4%
2016	$21,782,964,314	$1,189,909,310	6.4%	5.5%
2017	$23,739,409,078	$1,209,918,231	1.7%	5.1%
2018	$24,997,351,235	$1,213,323,164	0.3%	4.9%
2019	$26,226,914,974	$1,267,392,608	4.5%	4.8%
2012–19			17.0%	5.4%

Source: Governor's Budget Report, FY 1978 – FY 2019

spending for the governor's policy priorities. Gubernatorial budget priorities have been a combination of short-term individual initiatives and responses to long-term financial requirements.

Chapter 10
Milestones and Comparative Perspective

The previous chapters have examined the purpose of budgeting, fiscal conservatism and fiscal conservatives, patterns and trends in revenue and spending, the executive budget model, the annual budget process, performance budgeting, the line-item veto in executive-legislative relations, and the budget priorities and accomplishments of nine modern-era governors. This concluding chapter identifies several milestones in the evolution of the state's budget process and in the patterns and trends of its taxing and spending. It concludes by placing Georgia's budget process and its patterns and trends in revenue and spending in comparative perspective.

Georgia appropriations grew over 56 years and nine administrations from $464,946,093 in FY 1964 to $26,226,914,974 in FY 2019, an increase of 5,541%, at an annual rate of 7.6%. Controlling for the effects of inflation, state appropriations grew at an average annual rate of approximately 4%.[1] Annual appropriations, which enact the state's budget, *routinely* provide funding for elementary and secondary education as well as for higher and technical education; for health, welfare, and medical assistance; corrections and offender rehabilitation; criminal investigations and public safety; economic development and community assistance; transportation and various other state services. However, from time to time over the years, there have been milestone events marking changes in the state's budget process and/or its patterns of taxing and spending.

---

[1] Calculated using the Consumer Price Index (CPI: 1982–84 = 100), the average annual growth rate is 3.9%. Calculated using the Gross Domestic Product (GDP Chained Index: FY 2012 = 100), the average annual growth rate is 4.0%.

© The Author(s), under exclusive license to Springer Nature Switzerland AG 2021
T. P. Lauth, *Public Budgeting in Georgia*, Studies in Public Budgeting, https://doi.org/10.1007/978-3-030-76023-6_10

Milestones

Income Tax and Sales and Use Tax

Adoption of the individual income and corporate income taxes in 1929, and adoption of the sales and use tax in 1951, were major milestones for the state's fisc. In 1929, the state had a deficit and debt which were the result of appropriations exceeding revenues. In 1951, there were demands for expanding such vital state services as schools and roads, and simply increasing existing taxes was thought to be insufficient.

The property tax was once the principal source of state revenue. It was an *ad valorem* levy on the market value of real property. The tax rate was 5 mills from 1904 until to 1952 when the rate was reduced to .25 mills. Beginning in tax year 2011, the state-level property tax was gradually phased out. Under the *ad valorem* tax, all property was taxed at the same millage rate. However, as Georgia transitioned from agricultural use of land to commercial use, the advantages of taxing income rather than property became more apparent. The income tax was thought to be a method of reaching the salaries and incomes of taxpayers who had the capacity to pay taxes but who paid relatively little through the *ad valorem* tax. A graduated income tax structure for Georgia was established in 1931. The sales tax was established at 3% and was increased to 4% in 1989.

In the 2019 fiscal year, the individual income tax was 51.3% of state revenues and the sales and use tax was 26.3%, a combined total of more than three-fourths of state own-source revenue.

The Budget Act of 1962

The executive budget fully emerged in Georgia with the enactment of the Budget Act of 1962. An executive budget is one in which agency requests are submitted to the legislature only after being reviewed and coordinated by the chief executive and balanced against an estimate of available revenue. A central budget unit, usually located in the office of the chief executive, reviews agency requests for program needs, accomplishments and compatibility with the chief executive's policy priorities.

The Georgia budget process was dominated by the legislative branch until 1931. Between 1931 and 1961, several actions were taken that incorporated some of the executive budget principles into the fiscal practices of state government. The Budget Act of 1931 established a Bureau of the Budget with the governor as the ex officio Director of the Budget and the State Auditor as Assistant Director of the Budget. However, the act did not establish a professional budget staff. Budget administration was conducted by staff in State Auditor's office. Initially, all state agencies, except the legislative and judicial branches, were required to submit spending estimates to the Bureau of the Budget. The governor was required to submit a budget for the biennium, a budget message and a draft appropriation bill. Eventually, the budget document and agency estimates were discontinued.

In 1943, the Budget Act of 1931 was amended to establish an Income Equalization Account which authorized the governor to appropriate to agencies any funds deemed to be surplus at the end of the fiscal year. At this time, Georgia operated under a system of biennial appropriations in which an appropriations act remained in force until it was repealed or the next one was passed. With a growing state economy and robust revenue collections, the governor and the State Auditor were able to allocate substantial amounts of budget authority to agencies without having to obtain the approval of the General Assembly. Despite its shortcomings, the Budget Act of 1931 began the executive budget movement in Georgia.

The Budget Act of 1962 reduced the fiscal powers of the governor and auditor, but it also provided the framework for Georgia's modern executive budget process. The governor was continued as Director of the Budget, but the State Auditor was discontinued as Assistant Director of the Budget. Administration of the state budget was relocated from the Auditor's office to the governor's office. A position of State Budget Officer was created and a technical budget staff was authorized. Constitutional Amendments in 1962 required the governor to present a budget message, budget report and a draft appropriations bill to the General Assembly within five days of convening the legislative session. The amendments also provided that general appropriations would continue in force for two years (one year after 1973 when the state adopted an annual appropriations process) and expire at the end of that fiscal period. This provision ended the nearly unchecked powers of the governor and State Auditor to appropriate surplus funds without legislative approval. The governor was also empowered to set an estimate of anticipated revenues which established a spending ceiling for legislative appropriations.

The Budget Act of 1962 curtailed gubernatorial power by requiring surplus funds to lapse at a defined fiscal period, while at the same time it strengthened gubernatorial power with the revenue estimating prerogative and the establishment of an executive budget office with professional staff and specific financial procedures.

General Obligation Debt Authority

In 1972, the state constitution was amended to authorize the state to incur general obligation debt and to guarantee revenue bonds, effective January 1, 1973. Prior to that time, the state used public authorities with the power to issue bonds to obtain funds for the construction of public facilities, which were then leased to state government agencies. Rental payments by state agencies were used to retire the authority's bonds. When the bonds were fully retired, the facility became the property of state government.

General obligation (GO) bonds are sold to investors to raise revenue to fund capital projects,[2] and are backed by the full faith, credit and taxing power of the state.[3] Revenue bonds can only be issued for specific purposes as outlined in the state constitution, and are retired from the earnings of a public enterprise.[4]

The state's debt service limit is 10% of prior year net Treasury receipts.[5] Even though the constitutional limit is 10%, the state Debt Management Plan has since FY 2006 utilized a debt limit cap of 7%.[6] In FY 2019, state debt service as a percentage of prior year treasury receipts was 5.1%.[7] The GO Debt Sinking Fund in FY 2019 was 4.8% of state appropriations.[8] The State of Georgia enjoys AAA bond ratings from all three rating firms.[9]

Executive Branch Reorganization, 1972 and Zero-Base Budgeting, 1973

Governor Jimmy Carter was strongly committed to greater efficiency and economy in the provision of government programs, long-range planning, and rational-comprehensive decision making. These commitments were manifest through a major reorganization of the executive branch of state government in 1972, in which numerous agencies that were no longer funded but still in existence were eliminated, and many small and free-standing agencies were consolidated within the framework of a few larger state agencies. The centerpiece of the reorganization was a new Department of Human Resources (DHR), a health and human services umbrella agency that incorporated two of the state's largest social service agencies, Health (mental and physical) and Welfare, along with such smaller agencies as Vocational Rehabilitation. A new Department of Administrative Services (DOAS) took over functions previously performed by 18 other agencies, including purchasing, data processing, printing, personnel management and space allocation.[10] Although the Carter administration claimed to have abolished 278 of 300 state agencies,[11] a more accurate accounting is that 65 funded agencies were reduced to

---

[2] *Constitution of the State of Georgia*, Section IV, Paragraph I (c).
[3] *Constitution of the State of Georgia*, Section IV, Paragraph VI.
[4] *Constitution of the State of Georgia*, Section IV, Paragraph I (f).
[5] *Constitution of the State of Georgia*, Section IV, Paragraph II (b).
[6] State of Georgia, *Debt Management Plan, Fiscal Year 2019 – Fiscal Year 2023*. p. 18.
[7] *Governor's Budget Report Amended, FY 2020 and FY 2021*. p. 30.
[8] *Governor's Budget Report FY 2019*. p. 26.
[9] Moody's, Standard and Poor's and Fitch.
[10] Betty Glad, *Jimmy Carter: In Search of the Great White House*. New York: W.W. Norton & Company, 1980. p. 176.
[11] Betty Glad, *Jimmy Carter: In Search of the Great White House*. New York: W.W. Norton & Company, 1980. p. 168.

22.[12] The FY 1972–73 *Governor's Budget Report*[13] listed 70 agencies being funded and the FY 1975 *Budget Report* listed 30 agencies being funded, which would seem to corroborate the latter accounting. Nevertheless, reorganization of the executive branch was a major milestone in Georgia budgeting and financial management because it streamlined and updated state government.

The other manifestation of Governor Carter's commitment to rational-comprehensive decision making was Zero-Base Budgeting (ZBB), which aimed to focus budget deliberations on the entire budget not just proposed increases, and required state agencies to defend their entire budget each year. Each agency was expected to use it to assess all of its programs and activities.[14] It was intended to improve efficiency in allocating available resources. The Carter-era ZBB fell into disuse in the 1980s and was considerably different from the new ZBB adopted in 2012.

Revenue Shortfall Reserve

The Revenue Shortfall Reserve is Georgia's rainy day fund. It was established in 1976, during the administration of Governor George Busbee, "in lieu of the Working Reserve."[15] The law required that an amount equal to 3% of revenue collections of the previous fiscal year be set aside to enable an end-of-year balanced budget in the event annual revenue collections fall short of revenue estimates.[16] The set-aside amount was increased to 4% in 2000[17] and to 5% in 2001.[18]

In 1982, the General Assembly established the Midyear Adjustment Reserve,[19] intended to be the primary source of additional midyear funds for the state Board of Education. In a typical year, additional funds are required midway through the fiscal year to provide the state's share of the education funding formula.

In 2005, the Revenue Shortfall Reserve and Midyear Adjustment Reserve were merged into a revised Revenue Shortfall Reserve.[20] In 2010, the General Assembly

---

[12] Betty Glad, *Jimmy Carter: In Search of the Great White House*. New York: W.W. Norton & Company, 1980. p. 177. Thomas P. Lauth, "Zero-Base Budgeting in Georgia: Myth and Reality," *Public Administration Review*, Vol. 38, No. 5 (September–October 1978): 420–430 at 426.

[13] The FY 1972–73 budget was the last biennial Georgia budget. Beginning with FY 1973, state budgeting became an annual process.

[14] See Thomas P. Lauth, "Zero-Base Budgeting in Georgia: Myth and Reality," *Public Administration Review*, Vol. 38, No. 5 (September–October 1978): 420–430.

[15] In FY 1976 the Working Reserve was $30,000,000. In FY 1977 the Revenue Shortall Reserve was $57,773,254.

[16] Georgia Laws, 1976: 420–421. SB 466 was approved March 5, 1976.

[17] Georgia Laws, 2000: 1505. HB 1671 was approved May 1, 2000.

[18] Georgia Laws, 2001: 333. HB 601 was approved April 19, 2001.

[19] Georgia Laws, 1982: 1288–1289. SB 663 was approved April 14, 1982.

[20] Georgia Laws 2005: 976–980. HB 509 was approved May 9, 2005.

increased the Revenue Shortfall Reserve cap from 10% to 15% of the previous fiscal year's net revenue.[21]

Lottery for Education

The Georgia lottery for education began in 1993 and lottery proceeds were part of the state budget in FY 1994, after voters approved a constitutional amendment in November 1992 to establish the lottery.[22] Georgia lottery proceeds were initially earmarked for education programs in three areas: voluntary pre-kindergarten for four-year-olds, HOPE scholarships[23] and student loans, and capital improvements for education, especially the development and maintenance of instructional technology. After FY 2002, lottery proceeds were appropriated only for pre-K and HOPE. Governor Zell Miller conceived of the lottery for education as a way to increase higher education accessibility, and to improve school readiness for Georgians. Availability of the HOPE Scholarship program has also had the effect of retaining many of the state's best and brightest students in Georgia for their higher education. When demand for the HOPE Scholarship program threatened to outstrip available resources, the program was modified in 2003 and again in 2011 to maintain its financial viability. Between FY 1994 and FY 2019, a total of $19.4 billion was appropriated to the Lottery for Education Account. Annual appropriations to the account, on average, have been 4.2% of total state appropriations.

Criminal Justice Reform

Criminal justice reform was a subject addressed by Governors George Busbee, Zell Miller and Nathan Deal during their administrations, although the nature of reform was quite different for each of them. Governor Busbee had to address a crisis in the state's prison system when he came into office in 1975. A federal court order required the state to desegregate its prison system, to address problems of overcrowding and poor physical conditions, and to focus on prisoner rehabilitation.

One of Governor Miller's policy priorities was tougher sentencing for repeat offenders and life imprisonment without parole for anyone convicted a second time for one of seven major crimes, his "two strikes" policy. Miller's tough-on-crime

---

[21] Georgia Laws 2010: 166–167. SB 421 was approved May 20, 2010.
[22] The lottery was approved on November 4, 1992, with 1,131,168 (52%) in favor and 1,031,675 (48%) opposed.
[23] HOPE is the acronym for Helping Outstanding Pupils Educationally.

policy necessitated increasing the number of prison beds in order to end the practice of managing the inmate population through early release of criminals.[24]

Governor Nathan Deal proposed and the General Assembly enacted justice reinvestment reforms,[25] to reduce the imprisonment of nonviolent offenders, increase the referral of offenders to accountability courts, and to reinvest potential savings in other criminal justice reform program. Each of these criminal justice reforms had a financial impact on the state's budget; increased spending in the Busbee and Miller administrations, and likely cost savings in the Deal administration.

Program Budget Format

Program budgeting was introduced in Georgia in 2004. The state began the process of converting its budget from a line-item, object-of-expenditure format to a program format in 2003, as part of the effort to implement performance-based budgeting. Agencies were required to prepare a strategic plan, develop performance measures/indicators, and submit a budget based on programs. Prioritized Program Budgeting (PPB), as the system is known, emphasizes programs rather than agencies as the primary budgetary units, and requires that measures of demand for the program, program efficiency, program output, and program results be delineated for each program. The PPB system was integrated with Zero-Base Budgeting in 2012.

During the past fifty years, budgeting reforms in Georgia, as in the other states, have attempted to integrate program and performance information into budget deliberations, so as to better inform resource allocation decisions. Among the milestone markers were Zero-Base Budgeting in 1973, Budget Redirection in 1997, Results-Based Budgeting in 1998, Prioritized Program Budgeting in 2005 and the new Zero-Base Budgeting in 2012. All of these reforms sought to consider program performance in relationship to organizational mission and goals, alternative methods to achieve mission and goals, as well as the costs and benefits associated with various alternatives. The objectives of such reforms were to focus attention on strategic planning, policy analysis, and program performance evaluation without, of course, diminishing the vital importance of financial control.

Great Recession

The Great Recession, according to the National Bureau of Economic Research, lasted from December 2007 through June 2009, a period of 19 months. The first sign of the recession for Georgia was when FY 2008 revenue collections were 1.1%

---

[24] Senator Zell Miller, *A National Party No More: The Conscience of a Conservative Democrat.* Atlanta, Georgia: Stroud & Hall, Publishing, 2003. p. 58
[25] Georgia Laws, 2012: 899–949. HB 1176 was approved May 2, 2012.

lower than collections for FY 2007. Revenue collections for FY 2009 were 10.5% lower than collections for FY 2008 and FY 2010 collections were 9.1% lower than for FY 2009. Recovery began in FY 2011 with revenue collections increasing by 7.8%, year-over-year, compared with FY 2010.

Governor Sonny Perdue had the misfortune to have recessions bookending his eight years in office. He entered office as Georgia was recovering from the 2002–2003 recession and left office in January 2011 as the state was struggling with the effects of the 2008–2009 recession. He responded to the Great Recession's impact on Georgia by reducing his revenue estimate, cutting agency spending, tapping the Revenue Shortfall Reserve, reducing reserves in the health insurance programs, incorporating federal stimulus dollars, and enacting a few minor revenue enhancements such as increasing health insurance contributions by employees and imposing temporary fees for university system students. Beginning in FY 2008, he increased annual funding for GO bonds as an economic stimulus measure. Although Governor Perdue in 2003 had signed a modest increase in the state's cigarette (tobacco excise) tax from 12 to 37 cents per pack, he eschewed a tax increase in 2008 or 2009 as a recession fighting option. The response to the Great Recession created a "reduced normal" level of state spending for most of the next decade.

Department of Behavioral Health and Developmental Disabilities (DBHDD)

The Department of Behavioral Health and Developmental Disabilities (DBHDD) was established in 2009[26] to provide treatment and support services for individuals with mental illnesses and addictive diseases. Concern about patient treatment in the mental health division of the Department of Human Resources provided the incentive for the new department. Georgia entered into an agreement with the U.S. Department of Justice in 2009 in which the state did not admit to violating patients' constitutional rights by compromising their safety, but agreed to a five-year plan of improvements in state psychiatric hospitals.[27] The settlement agreement established targets from FY 2011 to FY 2015 for developmental disabilities, mental health and quality management, with state compliance with the targets established in the agreement to be verified by an independent reviewer.

Medicaid Expansion

Sometimes the important policy decision is about *not* spending. The Patient Protection and Affordable Care Act (2010) enabled states to expand their Medicaid programs to cover uninsured adults at or below 138% of the federal poverty level,

---

[26] Georgia Laws, 2009: 453–610. HB 228 was approved May 4, 2009.
[27] Alan Judd and Andy Miller, "State, Feds Agree to Plan to Fix Mental Care," *Atlanta Journal-Constitution*, January 16, 2009: A1.

with the federal government paying 100% of expanded coverage for the first three years, 2014, 2015 and 2016, and 90% of the cost thereafter.[28] Georgia not only declined to expand its Medicaid program, but also placed restrictions on its ability to so. In 2014, the General Assembly enacted legislation requiring its approval before the state could expand its Medicaid program. Prior to this action, Medicaid expansion could have been an executive decision. The General Assembly also prohibited any state agency from expanding Georgia Medicaid eligibility by increasing the income threshold without prior legislative approval.[29] In 2016, Governor Deal said the state could not afford to expand Medicaid services to potential new enrollees.[30] As of 2020, only 12 states had not expanded their Medicaid programs.

Despite partial Medicaid expansion under a waiver approved in 2020,[31] the decision not to take advantage of full Medicaid expansion under the Affordable Care Act left an estimated 500,000–600,000 low-income, working poor citizens uninsured. State minority-party Representative Mary Margaret Oliver wrote, "Failure to take advantage of the federal ACA Medicaid dollars is the single biggest public policy mistake the state's leadership has made during my time at the Capitol." … "Since enactment of the ACA 10 years ago this month, Georgia has forfeited some $21 billion federal dollars and will forfeit billions more over the next 10 years by not expanding Medicaid to the state's approximately 600,000 uninsured, low-income and working poor citizens."[32] The legislative majority in favor of the decision not to expand Medicaid supports the basic Medicaid program for children and disabled adults, but not an expanded program that would include the able-to-work poor.

A poll conducted for the *Atlanta Journal-Constitution* by the University of Georgia, School of Public and International Affairs, Survey Research Center found that 71% of registered Georgia voters favored Medicaid expansion. Democrats favored Medicaid expansion (97%), Independents favored expansion (73%), and a significant minority of Republicans favored expansion (40%).[33]

---

[28] Pub. L. 111–148 (2010).

[29] Georgia Laws, 2014: 293–294. HB 990 was approved April 15, 2014. Official Code of Georgia Annotated (O.C.G.A.) 49-4-142.2

[30] State of the State Address, January 13, 2016.

[31] The waiver granted by the Centers for Medicare and Medicaid Services (CMS) in 2020 in the administration of President Donald J. Trump was shifted by CMS from "approved' to "pending" in 2021 in the administration of President Joseph R. Biden.

[32] Mary Margaret Oliver, "Pandemic Shows Need to Improve Health Care," Guest Column, *Atlanta Journal-Constitution*, April 19, 2020: A23. Ms. Oliver has served a combined 29 years in the Georgia House of Representatives and Senate.

[33] Mark Niesse, "AJC Poll: Georgians Support Paper Ballots and Oppose Voter Purges," *Atlanta Journal-Constitution*, January 21, 2019: A1.

Motor Fuel Excise Tax

The motor fuel excise tax,[34] effective July 1, 2015, was probably the largest tax increase since the initial income and sales taxes. It was an excise tax of 26 cents per gallon which is constitutionally earmarked[35] for the construction and maintenance of the state's roads and bridges. Prior to July 1, 2015 the motor fuel tax was 7½ cents per gallon plus a 4% sales tax on total fuel sales, 3% of which went to the transportation fund and 1% of which went to the state general fund. Now, all of the motor fuel tax goes to the Department of Transportation. The new excise tax of 26 cents per gallon was a tax increase thought to be needed to improved roads, highways and bridges in order to facilitate commerce in the state. The tax increase on motor fuel was probably more acceptable to consumers because it was dedicated entirely to road and highway improvement and more palatable for legislators because of the local economic benefits of construction projects.[36]

The COVID-19 Recession

On March 13, 2020, President Donald Trump declared the outbreak of COVID-19 a national emergency. Governor Brian Kemp the next day declared a Public Health State of Emergency in Georgia.[37] The General Assembly concurred with Governor Kemp's Executive Order giving the governor broad emergency powers.[38] The 2020 Session of the General Assembly was suspended on March 14th. The amended FY 2020 appropriation had been passed and was soon to be signed by the governor. The House of Representatives had passed its version of the FY 2021 appropriation but the Senate had not yet passed its version of the bill. The amended 2020 budget included $100 million appropriation from the Revenue Shortfall Reserve to the Governor's Emergency Fund to finance the state's initial response to the pandemic.

While the General Assembly was in recess, state revenues declined in April by 35.9% compared with April 2019, year-to-date −3.4%, and May collections declined by 10.1%, year-to-date −4.0%. Later, June collections would decline by 8.8%, finishing the fiscal year at −4.4% compared with FY 2019. Year-over-year, the state collected a total of $1 billion less than expected in taxes. The National Bureau of Economic Research (NBER) declared on June 8th that the U.S. had been in recession since February.

---

[34] Georgia Laws, 2015: 236–264. H.B. No. 170, "Transportation Funding Act of 2015," Approved May 4, 2015.

[35] Georgia Constitution Article III, Section IX, Paragraph VI (b).

[36] Conversation with Terry England, Chair, Appropriations Committee, House of Representatives, August 13, 2018.

[37] State of Georgia, Executive Order No. 03.14.20.01.

[38] Georgia Laws, 2020 Extraordinary Session: ES3-ES4. H. Res. 4EX approved, March 16, 2020.

The General assembly reconvened on June 15, 2020. Governor Kemp issued a revised revenue estimate of $25.9 billion, $2.2 billon lower than the original estimate of $28.1 billion. He recommended appropriating $250 million from the Revenue Shortfall Reserve. He also increased state funding for debt service, with the intent of using capital spending for economic stimulus.[39]

One of Governor Nathan Deal's top priorities during his administration was building back the Revenue Shortfall Reserve following the Great Recession. He began rebuilding it early in his administration and was able to steadily increase it from $116 million in FY 2010 to $2.5 billion in FY 2018. By FY 2019, it had increased to $2.8 billion.[40] The robust rainy day fund built by Governor Deal provided a safety net for Governor Kemp to help offset the sharp drop in revenues caused by the COVID-19 pandemic.

On June 25, the House of Representatives and Senate agreed to an FY 2021 appropriation/budget of $25.9 billion,[41] a reduction of $2.2 billion from the budget of $28.1 billion passed by the House before the recess, based upon the governor's original proposal. State agency spending was reduced by approximately 10%. The state's budgeting approach in responding to the COVID-19 recession was consistent with its past approaches to responding to revenue shortfalls. First, it reduced state spending. Second, it utilized funds from the rainy day fund. Finally, it rejected legislative recommendations to increase taxes.[42]

Milestones Impact

Adoption of the income tax in 1929 and the sales tax in 1951 provided the necessary revenue for modern Georgia government. In the 2019 fiscal year, the individual and corporate income taxes and the sales and uses taxes amounted to 83% of net tax receipt.[43] The authorization of general obligation debt authority in 1972 enabled transparency in state borrowing for public purposes. The Revenue Shortfall Reserve in 1976, as revised in 2005, provided anti-recession security for the state which was successfully used on several occasions, especially during the Great Recession in 2008–2010 and the COVID-19 recession beginning in 2020. The lottery for education in 1993 provided revenue for early childhood and post-secondary education opportunities for generations of Georgians. The Motor Fuel Excise Tax in 2015, the

---

[39] Letter from Governor Brian P. Kemp to Terry England, Chairman, House of Representatives Appropriations Committee and Blake Tillery, Chairman, Senate Appropriations Committee, June 22, 2020.

[40] *Governor's Budget Report, Fiscal Year 2020 and Fiscal Year 2021*: 29.

[41] HB 793, FY 2021 Appropriations Bill, June 25, 2020.

[42] Danny Kanso and Thomas P. Lauth, "Recession Readiness in Georgia: From the Great Recession to the COVID-19 Recession," *Municipal Finance Journal*, Vol. 41 (Summer 2020): 37–48.

[43] They amounted to 77% of general revenue receipts. *Governor's Budget Report, Amended FY 2020 and FY 2021*. p. 12.

largest tax increase since the initial income and sales taxes, enabled Georgia to improve the state's roads, highways and bridges which had become operationally inadequate and structurally deficient.

The Budget Act of 1962 provided a modern decision-making process for allocating state resources to public programs and human purposes. The reorganization act in 1972 streamlined state government. The evolution to performance budgeting culminating in 2004, with its many variations along the way, enabled the state to better assess the relationship between the dollars it spends on activities and programs and their operational efficiency and program effectiveness.

Criminal justice reform over four decades, between 1975 and 2018, and mental health reform in 2009 addressed serious deficiencies in state programs and policies. The decision in 2014 to restrict expansion of the state's Medicaid program remains questionable.

Georgia in Comparative Perspective

Process and Politics

Georgia has an executive budget system. The state's budget office is located in the office of the governor, not as in some states in a line Department of Administration or a Department of Finance.[44] The governor has responsibility for presenting to the legislature a proposed budget and a draft appropriations bill, which sets the state's spending agenda. The General Assembly does not independently prepare an alternate spending plan, as happens in some states. It reviews the spending plan prepared by the governor, makes some modifications or substitutions, but usually approves most of the governor's spending plan as presented. State agency spending requests are reviewed by the central budget office, checked for financial accuracy, program accomplishment and consistency with the spending priorities of the governor. State agency heads appear before the House and Senate Appropriations Committees, and while they may appeal to legislators for funding that the governor was not willing to recommend, they generally are singing from the song sheet composed by the governor.

The governor has sole responsibility for estimating revenue collections to fund his proposed budget, unlike other states where the governor is only one member of a legislative-executive consensus revenue estimating panel or where an independent blue-ribbon panel of economists provides the revenue estimate.[45] This is the

---

[44] *Budget Processes in the States,* Washington, DC: National Association of State Budget Officers, 2015. p. 28.

[45] John L. Mikesell and Justin M. Ross, "State Revenue Forecasts and Political Acceptance: The Value of Consensus Forecasting in the Budget Process," *Public Administration Review*, Vol. 74 (2014): 188–203.

linchpin of the governor's budget authority and one of the most important overall prerogatives of the Georgia governorship. The legislature may not increase the revenue estimate, which means that efforts to substitute the spending priorities of legislative leaders for those of the governor must take place within the constraints of the revenue estimate established by the governor. Budget controversies between the governor and the legislature, and within the legislature between the House of Representatives and the Senate, are not complicated by party differences as they are in some states; they are strictly between the branches or the chambers.

The Republican party has controlled the governorship and the state Senate since 2002 and the House of Representatives since 2004. Prior to 2002, the Democratic party controlled the governorship and both chambers of the legislature since the end of Reconstruction. While executive-legislative disagreements and House-Senate differences are not uncommon, as disagreements between Governor Sonny Perdue and House Speaker Glenn Richardson or between House Speaker Tom Murphy and Lieutenant Governor Zell Miller illustrate, the absence of party differences that might have hardened positions even further has enabled budget controversies to usually be resolved through compromise and comity. From time to time, governors have used their line-item veto authority to protect their budget priorities, but the change from an object-of-expenditure budget format to a program budget format has made use of the item veto less feasible for governors. Also, because the legislature may not increase the governor's revenue estimate, Georgia governors, unlike governors in some states, have not been confronted with legislative spending increases to be rolled back, only legislative substitutions which are easier to accommodate. Georgia budgets are delivered on time and they are balanced, as the constitution requires, not late and unbalanced as in some states.[46]

Low Taxes and Low Spending

Georgia has low taxes and is vigilant for opportunities to reduce them rather than increase them, low levels of spending and low debt limits with low use of debt. According to a policy brief by researchers at Georgia State University, Georgia real per capita own-source revenue ranked 50th and real per capita direct expenditures ranked 48th among all states and the District of Columbia in the 2013 fiscal year.[47]

---

[46] Elaine Yi Lu and Gang Chen, "A Day Late and A Dollar Short? A Study of Budget Passage in New York State," *Public Budgeting & Finance*, Vol. 36, No. 3 (Fall 2016): 3–21. Dall W. Forsythe and Donald J. Boyd, "New York: The Growth, Waning, and Resurgence of Executive Power," in Edward J. Clynch and Thomas P. Lauth, eds., *Budgeting in the States: Institutions, Processes and Politics*. Westport, Connecticut: Praeger Publishers, 2006. pp. 60–62.

[47] Mels de Zeeuw, Lindsey Kuhn and Carolyn Bourdeaux, "Georgia's Revenue and Expenditure Portfolio in Brief: FY 2013 Data," Fiscal Research Center and Center for State & Local Finance, Andrew Young School, Georgia State University, August 16, 2016. See also: Elton Davis, Xixi Lin and Carolyn Bourdeaux, "Georgia's Revenue and Expenditure Portfolio in Brief, FY 1995-FY 2012, Center for State and Local Finance, April 2015, and Carolyn Bourdeaux, Nicholas Warner,

According to the Tax Foundation, among the 50 states in FY 2018 Georgia ranks 42nd in state tax collections per capita, 24th in individual income tax collections per capita, 36th in corporate income tax collections per capita, 43rd in sales tax collections per capita, 48th in a cigarette excise tax rate per package, 47th in state debt per capita and 50th in state revenue per capita.[48] What's not to like about this pattern of low taxes and low debt?

The evidence of low spending presented in Chapter 4 bears repeating. Georgia, among the 50 states, in fiscal year 2018 ranked 43rd in per capita total expenditures, 26th in per capita elementary and secondary education expenditures, 19th in per capita higher education expenditures, 48th in per capita public assistance expenditures, 49th in per capita Medicaid expenditures, 24th in per capita correction expenditures, 42nd in per capita transportation expenditures and 41st in all other per capita state expenditures.[49]

What are the consequences of low spending? In FY 2020, education and health care constituted nearly three quarters of the state's budget at 73%. Spending for education through the Department of Education (K-12), the Department of Early Childhood Learning (Pre-K), the University System of Georgia, the Student Finance Commission and the Technical College System was more than half of the state budget at 54.5%, and spending for health care through the Department of Behavioral Health and Developmental Disabilities, the Department of Community Health and the Department of Public Health was almost one-fifth of the budget at 18.5%.

How does Georgia's performance in education compare with that of other states? The most recent assessment by *U.S. News & World Report*[50] ranks Georgia 30th among the states and the District of Columbia, 31st in Pre-K-12 and 25th in higher education. The Pre-K-12 ranking was based upon the percentages of children enrolled in pre-school, test scores of eighth-grade students in mathematics and reading, graduation rates from high school and college readiness based upon SAT and ACT scores. The higher education ranking was based upon the percentage of adults with associate or higher degrees, the rates of students completing public four-year and two-year college programs within 150% of the normal time, the average of tuition and fees for in-state students at public institutions and the average debt load of graduates from public and private colleges.

How about health care? *The Commonwealth Fund* 2020 scorecard on state health system performance[51] ranked Georgia 46th among the states and the District of Columbia. The ranking was based upon several health system performance indica-

---

Sandy Zook and Sungman Jun, "Georgia's Revenue and Expenditure Portfolio in Brief, 1989–2010," Fiscal Research Center, January 2013.

[48] Tax Foundation, *Facts & Figures*, Washington, DC: 2019.

[49] National Association of State Budget Officers, *State 2018 Expenditure Report*, Washington DC: 2019. Using the NASBO report of state spending and the U.S. Bureau of Census for state population data, I calculated state spending per capita and ranked the states on that basis.

[50] *U.S. News & World Report*, "Education Rankings," 2020.

[51] David C. Radley, Sara R. Collins and Jesse C. Baumgartner, "2020 Scorecard on State Health System Performance," The Commonwealth Fund, 2020.

tors: (1) access and affordability, that is, uninsured children and adults, individuals without health care because of cost, out-of-pocket medical costs relative to annual household income and employee insurance costs as a share of median income; (2) prevention and treatment, that is, age and gender appropriate tests, screening, preventive care and vaccines; (3) avoidable hospital use and costs, that is, emergency department visits, hospital readmissions, and Medicare spending per beneficiary; (4) healthy living, that is, death rates for cancer, alcohol and drug use, infant death rates and smoking and obesity rates; and (5) income and race disparity rates. Georgia's relatively low ranking on the health scorecard was no doubt influenced by the percentage of adults without health insurance and the percentage of adults who went without medical care because of its cost. As noted earlier, Georgia is one of 12 states that opted not to expand its Medicaid program under provisions of the Patient Protection and Affordable Care Act.

Because of the state's balanced budget requirement, low taxes and low debt result in relatively low levels of spending for public services. These patterns have persisted no matter which political party controls state government. Low levels of spending for services means lower levels of citizen benefits compared with many other states. Georgia's culture of fiscal conservatism favoring low taxation, low debt, and limited government spending is a manifestation of the state's cultural of conservatism favoring individualism, limited government, and trusting the private sector and the market economy to address the state's economic and social problems -- the state's balance of payment relationship with the federal government notwithstanding.

As the demographics of Georgia change and political realignment occurs in the coming years, there will likely be greater demand and greater support for social benefit programs such as health care, mental health, child care and criminal justice reform --- in addition to the continuing demand for education spending. Extension of the sales tax to online transactions and transactions in the service sector will likely contribute to growth in sales and use tax revenue. However, with a growing demand for social benefit programs, it may have been fortunate that the economic downturn caused by the COVID-19 pandemic in 2020 prevented further reduction in the state's top income tax rate,[52] potentially weakening the state's most productive revenue source.

---

[52] The House of Representatives passed a bill early in the 2020 Session to reduce the top income tax rate from 5.75% to a flat rate of 5.375%, eliminating the current graduated rate system. Following the suspension of the Session (March 14th) and the reconvening of the Session (June 15th), that bill was not enacted.

Articles on Public Budgeting in Georgia by the Author

Thomas P. Lauth, "Zero-Base Budgeting in Georgia State Government: Myth and Reality," *Public Administration Review*, Vol. 38, No. 5 (September-October 1978): 420–430.

Thomas P. Lauth and Stephen C. Rieck, "Modifications in Georgia Zero-Base Budgeting Procedures: 1973–1980," *Midwest Review of Public Administration*, Vol. 13, No. 4 (December 1979): 225–235.

Thomas P. Lauth, "Methods of Agency Head Selection and Gubernatorial Influence Over Agency Appropriations," *Public Administration Quarterly*, Vol. 7, No. 4 (Winter 1984): 396–409.

Thomas P. Lauth, "Performance Evaluation in the Georgia Budgetary Process," *Public Budgeting & Finance*, Vol. 5, No. 1 (Spring 1985): 67–82.

Thomas P. Lauth, "The Executive Budget in Georgia," *State and Local Government Review*, Vol. 18, No. 2, (Spring 1986): 56–64.

Thomas P. Lauth, "Exploring the Budgetary Base in Georgia," *Public Budgeting & Finance*, Vol. 7, No. 4 (Winter 1987): 72–82.

Thomas P. Lauth, "Mid-Year Appropriations in Georgia: Allocating the Surplus," *International Journal of Public Administration*, Vol. 11, No. 5 (1988): 531–550.

Thomas P. Lauth, "The Governor and the Conference Committee in Georgia," *Legislative Studies Quarterly*, Vol. 15, No. 3 (August 1990): 441–453.

Thomas P. Lauth, "Georgia: Shared Power and Fiscal Conservatives," in Edward J. Clynch and Thomas P. Lauth, eds., *Governors, Legislatures, and Budgets: Diversity Across the American States*. Westport, Connecticut: Greenwood Press, 1991. pp. 53–62.

Thomas P. Lauth, "Reductions in the FY 1992 Georgia Budget: Responses to a Revenue Shortfall," in Aman Kahn and W. Bartley Hildreth, eds., *Case Studies in Public Budgeting and Financial Management*. Dubuque, Iowa: Kendall/Hunt Publishing Company, 1994. pp. 221–248.

Henry M. Huckaby and Thomas P. Lauth, "Budget *Redirection* in Georgia," *Public Budgeting & Finance*, Vol. 18, No. 4 (Winter 1998): 36–44.

Thomas P. Lauth and Mark D. Robbins, "The Georgia Lottery and State Appropriations for Education: Substitution or Additional Funding?" *Public Budgeting & Finance*, Vol. 22, No. 3 (Fall 2002): 89–100.

Thomas P. Lauth, "The Midyear Appropriation in Georgia: A Threat to Comprehensiveness?" *State and Local Government Review,* Vol. 34, No. 3 (Fall 2002): 198–204.

Katherine G. Willoughby and Thomas P. Lauth, "Cutback Management in Georgia: State Agency Responses to Fiscal Year 1992 Budget Reductions," in Aman Khan and W. Bartley Hildreth, eds., *Case Studies in Public Budgeting and Financial Management*. Second Edition. New York: Marcel Dekker, Inc., 2003. pp. 377–391.

Thomas P. Lauth, "Budgeting During a Recession Phase of the Business Cycle: The Georgia Experience," *Public Budgeting & Finance*, Vol. 23, No. 2 (Summer 2003): 26–38.

Thomas P. Lauth and Catherine C. Reese, "The Line-Item Veto in Georgia: Fiscal Restraint or Inter-Branch Politics?" *Public Budgeting & Finance*, Vol. 26, No. 2 (Summer 2006): 1–19.

Thomas P. Lauth, "Georgia: Shared Power and Fiscal Conservatism," in Edward J. Clynch and Thomas P. Lauth, eds., *Budgeting in the States: Institutions, Processes, and Politics*. Westport, Connecticut: Praeger Publishers, 2006. pp. 33–53.

Thomas P. Lauth, "Budget Deficits in the States: Georgia," *Public Budgeting & Finance*, Vol. 30, No. 1 (Spring 2010): 15–32.

Thomas P. Lauth, "Zero-Base Budgeting Redux in Georgia: Efficiency or Ideology?" *Public Budgeting & Finance*, Vol. 34, No. 1 (Spring 2014): 1–17.

Danny Kanso and Thomas P. Lauth, "Recession Readiness in Georgia: From the Great Recession to the COVID-19 Recession," *Municipal Finance Journal,* Vol. 41, Nos. 2 and 3 (Summer and Fall 2020): 37–48.

Index

A
AAA, 11, 37–40, 62, 140, 220
Abney, G., 109, 164
Accountability courts, 38, 99, 100, 210, 211, 223
Adequate Program for Education in Georgia (APEG), 85, 202
Ad valorem tax, 59, 60, 85, 173, 212, 218
Alaimo, A.A., 97, 98
Allen, I. Jr., 27
Allotment, 2, 4, 5, 123, 125, 179, 185
Amended Appropriations Act, 165, 173, 176
American Independent Party, 8, 29
American Recovery Act of 2009, 4
American Rescue Plan Act of 2021, 97
Anderson, W., 11, 14, 15
Annual Operating Budget, 125
Annual Survey of State Government Finances, 106
Anthony, S., 201
A Plus Reform Act of 2000, 207
Appropriations Act, 19, 24, 31, 61, 89, 113, 120, 122, 124–127, 132, 135, 138, 141, 142, 154, 165, 172–177, 206, 210, 219
Appropriations subcommittees, 93, 121
Arnall, E., 11, 13, 14, 17–19, 21, 25–27, 29, 33, 41, 98, 117, 201
Atlanta, 5–7, 15, 27, 30, 67, 116, 118, 176, 186, 187, 190, 201
  Atlanta Constitution, 33, 50, 52, 53, 80, 89, 98, 114, 115, 118, 188
Atlanta Journal, 33, 51, 52, 68, 98, 172, 181, 186–188, 201
Atlanta-Journal Constitution, 68, 91, 181, 182, 186–188, 194, 225

Augusta, 6
Authority lease rental, 61, 146

B
Balanced budget, 3, 4, 9–11, 13, 32, 33, 39, 40, 58, 74, 75, 140, 143, 182, 203, 221, 231
Barnes, R.E., 29, 35–36, 38, 41, 52, 93, 128, 165, 171, 178–180, 186, 195, 207–210, 213
Bartley, N.V., 11, 13, 16, 18, 20, 30, 31, 200, 202
Biden, J.R., 8, 225
Biennial budget, 27, 117
Board of Corrections, 146
Bond proceeds, 43, 61–62, 208
Bourdeaux, C., 156, 157, 229
Bowdoin Commission, 25
Brasstown Bald, 6
Brown v. Board of Education, 85, 200
Buchanan, S.E., 19, 22
Budget Accountability and Planning Act of 1993, 153
Budget Act of 1931, 13, 41, 218, 219
Budget Act of 1962, 26, 41, 43, 109, 116, 118, 143, 197, 218–219, 228
Budget Compliance Report, 123
Budget cycle, 29, 120–129, 132–142, 145, 148, 150
Budget idea, 109–111
Budget Preparation Procedures Manual, 123
Budget Redirection, 35, 99, 152, 153, 155, 156, 207, 223

Budget Responsibility Oversight Committee (BROC), 154, 157
Bullock, C.S. III, 8, 19
Bureau of the Budget, 112, 117, 139, 201, 218
Burkhead, J., 1
Busbee, G.D., 11, 19, 21, 25, 26, 29, 31–33, 97, 98, 117, 118, 165, 171, 174–176, 180, 184, 195, 203–205, 213, 221–223
Bush, G.H.W., 8
Bush, G.W., 8
Byrd, G., 115, 116

C

Cagle, C., 68, 186
Callaway, H. "Bo", 27, 201
Carl Vinson Institute of Government, 99
Carter, J., 8, 27–31, 41, 51, 85, 93, 139, 146, 147, 151, 158, 165, 171–174, 180, 195, 202, 220, 221
Centers for Medicare and Medicaid Services (CMS), 96, 97, 225
Checks and balances, 26, 117, 118
Childress, T., 184, 185, 194
Chilton, B.S., 98
Cigarette tax, 22, 58–59, 72, 74, 75, 209
Classical liberalism, 9
Cleveland, F.A., 109–111
Clinton, B., 8, 141, 142
Cobb, J.C., 36, 186, 188
Coleman, T., 52
Collins, M., 204
Columbus, 6, 181
Comprehensive Annual Financial Report (CAFR), 123
Conference committee, 32, 122, 124, 177, 181, 185
Congressional Budget and Impoundment Control Act of 1974, 134, 139–141
Congressional Budget Office (CBO), 134, 139, 140, 143
Connell, J., 204
Connell, T., 156, 182–184
Constitution of the State of Georgia, 2, 3, 10, 56, 113, 117, 119, 126, 140, 141, 163, 176, 181, 187
Consumer Price Index (CPI), 104, 211
Continuation, 124, 148, 158, 159, 162, 208
Cook, J.F., 25, 26
Cooper, S.A., 66
Coronavirus Aid, Relief and Economic Security (CARES) Act of 2020, 4
Corporate income tax, 5, 25, 43, 44, 49, 60, 68, 72, 84, 142, 218, 227, 230
Cost-centers, 147, 148
Council on Aging, 94
County unit system, 197–200
COVID-19 recession, 3, 81, 86, 137, 138, 226–227
Crooked River State Park, 173
Cut-off line, 29, 148

D

Deal, N., 38–41, 68, 69, 91, 95, 99, 101, 128, 129, 158, 159, 165, 171, 172, 180, 189–194, 196, 197, 209–213, 222, 223, 225, 227
Debt service, 61, 62, 101, 105, 132, 140, 183, 186, 188, 190, 191, 213, 220, 227
Decision packages, 29, 147, 148, 150, 151, 159
Delta Airlines, 5
Department of Administrative Services (DOAS), 176, 220
Department of Adult and Technical Education, 217
Department of Agriculture, 160
Department of Audits and Accounts, 6, 66, 67, 99, 123
Department of Behavioral Health and Development Disabilities (DBHDD), 94, 95, 224
Department of Community Affairs (DCA), 69, 94, 105, 129, 132, 133, 178, 191
Department of Community Health (DCH), 65, 69, 72, 93–96, 132, 179, 188, 209, 211, 230
Department of Corrections, 83, 97, 99, 132, 177, 201, 206, 211, 213
Department of Defense (DOD), 69
Department of Early Care and Learning, 71, 86
Department of Economic Development, 5, 67, 192
Department of Education (DOE), 25, 83, 84, 91, 101, 102, 104, 132, 137, 151, 160, 177, 179, 188, 200, 201, 203, 205, 206, 208–210, 230
Department of Human Resources (DHR), 31, 32, 83, 93–95, 146, 179, 220, 224
Department of Human Services (DHS), 71, 94, 95, 192
Department of Industry and Trade, 28, 204
Department of Juvenile Justice, 179
Department of Labor (DOL), 69, 179
Department of Medical Assistance (DMA), 32, 206

Index 237

Department of Natural Resources (DNR), 105, 173, 179
Department of Offender Rehabilitation (DOR), 204
Department of Parks, 146
Department of Public Health (DPH), 93, 95, 151, 230
Department of Public Safety, 146
Department of Revenue, 55, 67, 68, 146
Department of Transportation (DOT), 51–53, 57, 71, 83, 100–102, 104, 105, 132, 137, 179, 184, 190, 211, 226
Division of Aging Services, 94
Division of Child Support Services, 94
Division of Family and Children Services, 94
Division of Residential Child Care, 94
Division of Vocational Rehabilitation, 93
Douglas, J.W., 153

E
Elementary and Secondary Education Act of 1965, 86
Emergency Economic Stabilization Act of 2008, 4
Employment, 4, 66, 71, 75, 77, 80, 134, 192
Employment Act of 1946, 4
England, T., 57, 72, 162, 194, 195, 226, 227
Examining Commission of State Government, 111
Exclusion, 48
Executive branch reorganization, 220–221
Executive budget, 6, 23, 24, 41, 43, 109–118, 139, 141, 142, 150, 161, 163, 164, 172, 173, 182, 197, 217–219, 228
Exemptions, 22, 35, 36, 47, 48, 50, 52–54, 66–68, 74, 208, 212

F
Federal funds, 65, 69, 71, 119, 153, 176, 177, 179
Federal poverty rate, 7
Fink, G.M., 29, 30
Fiscal Affairs Subcommittees, 6, 134–135
Fiscal conservatism, 6, 9–41, 73, 140, 161, 212, 217, 231
Fiscal year (FY), 2, 3, 6, 9, 10, 16, 18, 28, 31, 35–40, 44, 51, 53, 58, 59, 61, 62, 64, 65, 69, 71, 72, 80, 81, 83, 86, 87, 91, 94, 95, 98–102, 105, 106, 113, 115–117, 119, 120, 122–129, 132–142, 146, 147, 152–156, 158–160, 162, 164, 172–177, 179–195, 200–213, 217–224, 226, 227, 229, 230

Fite, G.C., 12, 13
Fletcher, N., 182, 183
Floyd, J. (Sloppy), 173
Food for at home consumption, 54, 74
Fortson v. Morris, 27
Full Employment and Balanced Growth Act of 1978, 4

G
Geer, P.Z., 27
General Assembly, 2, 3, 5–6, 8, 10, 12, 13, 15, 19–22, 24–28, 31, 32, 34–40, 46, 48, 50–53, 55, 56, 58, 60, 62, 64, 65, 67, 68, 74, 85, 89–91, 93–96, 99, 111–117, 119–121, 124–127, 133–135, 137, 138, 140, 146, 147, 154, 155, 157, 158, 161, 162, 165, 171–174, 176–189, 191–194, 196, 200, 201, 203, 204, 206, 208, 210–212, 219, 221, 223, 225–228
Georgia Budget Policy Institute (GBPI), 6, 23, 30, 67, 69, 101, 105, 113, 117, 126, 138, 140, 143, 146, 147, 152, 155, 158, 160, 165, 172, 200–203, 205, 206, 208–210, 218, 221, 229
Georgia Indigent Legal Services (GILS), 176
Georgia State Financing and Investment Commission (GSFIC), 62, 180
Georgia Student Finance Commission, 89, 90
Glad, B., 29, 31, 146
GO Bonds, 62, 224
Goldwater, B.M., 8, 9
Governor's Budget Report, 2, 6, 35–40, 61, 99, 102, 117, 121, 140, 152, 154–156, 160, 162, 197, 210, 213, 227
Great Recession, 3, 4, 7, 40, 44, 77, 80, 87, 132, 136, 137, 189, 209–211, 223–224, 227
Green door committee, 204
Griffin, M.E., 21–23, 40, 51, 172, 200
Gross domestic product (GDP), 62, 75, 77, 80, 106
Guthrie v. Evans, 97, 98

H
Hackney, J.M. "Pete", 118, 127, 135, 174, 204, 205
Handel, K., 38
Hardman, L.G., 12, 46, 113
Harris, J.F., 33–34, 40, 51–53, 85, 165, 171, 175–177, 179–181, 184, 195, 204, 205, 213
Hartsfield-Jackson International Airport, 7, 67

Hartsfield, W.B., 27
Hayek, F.A., 9
Henderson, H.P., 11, 13, 17–20, 23, 24, 29, 30, 32, 98, 117
Hepburn, V.A., 65
Highway Department, 14, 17, 25, 55, 56, 100, 113, 114
Hill, J., 159
Homeowners Tax Relief Grant, 36, 186, 187, 208, 210
Hooks, G., 11
HOPE Scholarships, 34, 43, 64, 86, 87, 89–91, 210, 222
Hoskins, R.B., 126
Hospital Provider Fee, 65
House Appropriations Committee, 33, 52, 93, 134, 139, 160, 162, 173, 177, 181, 186, 194, 204
House Budget and Research Office, 122, 124, 134, 139, 158
House Ways and Means Committee, 51, 52, 204
Huckaby, H.M., 10, 99, 150, 152, 207

I
Impoundment, 165, 178, 179
Improvement, 25, 28, 38, 57, 64, 85, 86, 89, 90, 94, 98, 105, 148, 150, 159, 173, 186, 187, 205, 213, 222, 224, 226
Income Equalization Account, 113, 219
Individual income tax, 10, 40, 43, 44, 46–49, 72, 74, 75, 84, 142, 146, 218, 230
Intent Language Non-Binding, 183, 189–192
Intra-State Government Transfers, 72
Investigating and Budget Commission, 111

J
Joyce, P.G., 134, 140

K
Kemp, B.P., 96, 97, 122, 137, 138, 226, 227
Kennedy, J.F., 8
Key activities, 159
Keynes, J.M., 9
Key, V.O. Jr., 13

L
Lapse factor, 2, 115, 117, 120, 126, 219
Lauth, T.P., 11, 30, 31, 36, 72, 90, 99, 109, 122, 126, 136, 141, 146, 147, 150, 152, 158, 162, 163, 180, 189, 193, 202, 206, 212, 221, 227, 229
Lease-rental, 61, 146
Legislative Budget Study Committee, 115, 118
Liberalism, 9
Line-item veto, 6, 31, 120, 122, 125, 141–143, 163–196, 217, 229
Line-Item Veto Act of 1996, 141–142
Local assistance grants, 132
Local option sales tax (LOST), 17, 34, 54
Lottery for education, 64, 86, 87, 89–91, 205, 213, 222, 227
Lottery proceeds, 43, 64, 72, 86, 89, 90, 205, 207–209, 211, 222
Low spending, 106, 229–231
Low taxes, 9–11, 13, 21, 40, 212, 229–231
Lu, E.Y., 145, 157, 229
Lutz Report, 112–113

M
Macon, 6
Maddox, L.G., 18, 27–29, 34, 165, 172, 195, 201, 212, 213
Marketplace facilitators, 55, 74
McCain, J.S., 8
McDonald, L. "Bubba", 29, 52
Medicaid, 5, 28, 32, 65, 71, 93, 95–97, 106, 136, 153, 206, 207, 209, 211, 213, 224, 225, 228, 230, 231
Medicaid expansion, 95, 96, 224–225
Medicare Hospital Insurance (HI) tax, 142
Midyear Adjustment Reserve, 203, 221
Midyear appropriation, 126–133, 186
Milestones, 6, 217–231
Miller, Z.B., 16, 17, 29, 34–35, 40, 41, 52, 53, 64, 86, 89–91, 98, 99, 105, 128, 135, 152, 153, 155, 165, 171, 177–180, 184, 195, 205–207, 213, 222, 223, 229
Minimum, 13, 14, 16, 85, 90, 98, 148, 150, 152, 159
Minimum Foundation Program for Education (MFPE), 20, 50, 85
Motor fuel tax, 17, 20, 22, 43, 44, 49, 51–53, 55–57, 60, 72, 74, 146, 211, 226
Motor vehicle tax, 60–61, 72, 146
Murphy, T.B., 51, 53, 172, 179, 201, 204, 229

N
National Bureau of Economic Research (NBER), 80, 137, 209, 223, 226
National Rifle Association (NRA), 68
Nixon, R.M., 8, 139

Norman, R.C., 46, 47
Nursing Home Provider Fees, 43, 65–66

O
Objective-of-expenditure, 105, 122
Office of Management and Budget (OMB), 139, 142
Office of Planning and Budget (OPB), 3, 5, 6, 10, 39, 120, 121, 123–126, 134–136, 139, 142, 151, 152, 154, 155, 157–160, 162, 177–179, 184, 194
Old Age, Security and Disability Insurance (OASDI) tax, 142
OneGeorgia Authority, 133
Other funds, 69–72, 106

P
Pajari, R.N., 20, 21
Patient Protection and Affordable Care Act of 2010, 97, 211, 224, 231
Payroll tax, 142, 143
PeachCare for Kids, 65, 93, 186, 206, 213
Per capita personal income, 7, 44, 75, 77, 80
Perdue, G.E. "Sonny", 36–38, 40, 58, 94, 128, 133, 136, 155–158, 165, 171, 179–189, 192–196, 209, 210, 212, 213, 224, 229
Performance, 1, 2, 5, 6, 35, 99, 111, 121, 145–162, 208, 217, 223, 228, 230
Pork barrel spending, 30, 31, 141, 164, 174, 177
Post-audit, 5, 114, 122, 206
Pre-K, 64, 86, 222, 230
Prioritized Program Budgeting (PPB), 155–157, 184, 196, 210, 223
Productivity, 145
Progressive Era, 109
Public Service Commission, 151
Pyhrr, P.A., 147

Q
Quality Basic Education (QBE), 33, 85, 86, 127, 205, 210

R
Ranking process, 29, 147, 150, 159
Rational-comprehensive decision making, 202, 220, 221
Reagan, R., 8
Reese, C.C., 31, 141, 146

Reeves, B., 112, 113
Regular order, 53, 139, 143
Reorganization Act of 1931, 12
Results-Based Budgeting (RBB), 153–156
Revenue forecast, 37, 228
Revenue Shortfall Reserve, 10, 11, 37–41, 72, 124, 125, 127, 128, 135–137, 203, 206, 209, 210, 212, 221–222, 224, 226, 227
Richardson, G., 193, 229
Rivers, E.D., 16–17, 41, 47
Rockefeller Institute of Government, 71
Romney, M., 8
Roosevelt, F.D., 8, 13
Russell, R.B., 7, 12–13, 29

S
Sales and use tax, 43, 44, 49, 51, 56, 60, 72, 218, 231
Salzer, J., 58, 59, 80, 90, 181, 182, 187, 188, 190, 194
Sanders, C.E., 25–29, 41, 165, 172, 195, 197, 200, 201
Savannah, 6, 7, 67, 191
Schick, A., 145, 157
Schlesinger, A.M. Jr., 9
Second motor fuel tax, 52, 56, 57
Senate Appropriations Committee, 11, 80, 111, 121, 122, 124, 127, 134, 135, 139, 159, 162, 177, 182, 188, 195, 227, 228
Senate Budget and Evaluation Office, 122, 124, 134, 139, 143, 158
Senate Finance Committee, 117
Separation of powers, 26, 118, 138, 142, 164, 177, 182
Shafer, D., 161, 194
Sharkansky, I., 135
Short, B., 27–29
Sibley Commission, 200
Sjoquist, D.L., 44, 59
Smith, G.T., 23
South Dakota v. Wayfair, Inc., 54, 55
Special Council on Tax Reform and Fairness, 74, 75
Special purpose local option sales tax (SPLOST), 54
Standard deductions, 48, 66, 68
State Auditor, 6, 18, 23, 112–117, 125, 134, 204, 218, 219
State Board of Education, 84, 127, 203, 221
State Health Benefit Plan (SHBP), 72, 93
State Program Study Commission, 21

State School Building Authority, 85
Stevenson, A.E., 8

T
Talmadge, E., 11, 14, 15
Talmadge, H.E., 13–21, 34, 40, 49, 85
Tax and expenditure limitation (TEL), 75
Tax credits, 5, 66, 67, 69, 74
Tax Foundation, 230
Taylor, M., 36, 179, 209
Technical College System, 91, 132, 211, 230
Temporary Assistance for Needy Families (TANF), 71, 179
Thompson, M.E., 18–19, 176
Thrasher, B.E., 114, 115
Three governors, 19
Title ad valorem tax (TAVT), 60
Tobacco settlement funds, 43, 64, 179
Tracking sheet, 122, 185
Truman, H.S., 8
Trump, D.J., 8, 137, 225, 226
Turnbull, A.B. III, 23, 112–115
Two strikes, 98, 99, 222
Tybee Island Lighthouse, 6

U
Unemployment, 4, 12, 69, 75, 77, 80

University System of Georgia Board of Regents (USG), 12, 32, 83, 87, 91, 102, 104, 200, 201, 207–209, 211

V
Vandiver, S.E., 20, 23–24, 114–117, 200
Vaughn, C., 204

W
Wallace, G.C., 8, 29
Wheeler, L., 66
Willoughby, K.G., 44, 136, 145
Willoughby, W.F., 109, 110
Wilson, J.M., 204
Working reserve, 221
Workload, 39, 145, 151, 160

Y
Young, A., 29, 59, 66, 106, 156, 229
Yu, C., 155

Z
Zero-base budgeting (ZBB), 29, 30, 147–152, 158–162, 202, 212, 220–221, 223
Zero-Base Budgeting Report, 160, 162

Printed by Printforce, the Netherlands